HOLY LAND PILGRIMAGE
IN THE LATER
ROMAN EMPIRE
AD 312–460

Holy Land Pilgrimage
in the
Later Roman Empire
AD 312–460

E.D. HUNT

CLARENDON PRESS • OXFORD

*This book has been printed digitally and produced in a standard specification
in order to ensure its continuing availability*

OXFORD
UNIVERSITY PRESS

Great Clarendon Street, Oxford OX2 6DP

Oxford University Press is a department of the University of Oxford.
It furthers the University's objective of excellence in research, scholarship,
and education by publishing worldwide in

Oxford New York

Auckland Bangkok Buenos Aires Cape Town Chennai
Dar es Salaam Delhi Hong Kong Istanbul Karachi Kolkata
Kuala Lumpur Madrid Melbourne Mexico City Mumbai Nairobi
São Paulo Shanghai Singapore Taipei Tokyo Toronto

with an associated company in Berlin

Oxford is a registered trade mark of Oxford University Press
in the UK and in certain other countries

Published in the United States
by Oxford University Press Inc., New York

© E. D. Hunt 1982

The moral rights of the author have been asserted
Database right Oxford University Press (maker)

Reprinted 2002

ISBN 0-19-826449-6

Preface

It is more than ten years ago that I was first prompted to consider the subject of Christian pilgrimage in late antiquity, while reading for the B.Phil. in Ancient History at Oxford. The subject has since grown into a D.Phil. thesis, and now into a book; meanwhile I have moved on to posts at Swansea and Durham, where this volume · received its finishing touches, appropriately enough, only a stone's throw from the shrine of St. Cuthbert—a great focus of pilgrimage in a different age. The book remains, though, substantially a product of Oxford, and my debt to that university (and especially to St. John's College, which nurtured me 'man and boy' for nine years and elected me to its Woodhouse Junior Research Fellowship) is a profound one. The regular seminars in late Roman studies, where some of these chapters had their first airing, were a friendly meeting-point and a constant stimulus; while over the years I have come to appreciate more keenly the unrivalled facilities and congenial atmosphere of the Bodleian Library, where in the Lower Reading Room much of late antiquity can still be comprehensively studied under one roof.

It was John Matthews who first guided my steps in late Roman history and supervised my work throughout; I am conscious that this book would never have been written but for his unfailingly helpful advice and genial encouragement. My D.Phil. examiners, Dr Henry Chadwick and Professor Alan Cameron, made judicious recommendations about the conversion of the thesis into a book; Joan Booth read the thesis and gave me a literary scholar's valuable impressions of my text; Claudine Dauphin, with her first-hand knowledge of the Byzantine Holy Land, has meticulously perused the whole manuscript and rescued me from points of error and obscurity. To these, and to many other friends in Oxford, Swansea and Durham, I am grateful. The faults that remain, needless to say, are my own.

Durham   E.D.H.
January 1981

Contents

Abbreviations

Acta Conc. Oec.	*Acta Conciliorum Oecumenicorum* (ed. E. Schwartz, Berlin 1914–74)
Acta SS.	*Acta Sanctorum*
Amer. Journ. Arch.	*American Journal of Archaeology*
Amer. Journ. Phil.	*American Journal of Philology*
Anal. Boll.	*Analecta Bollandiana*
BCH	*Bulletin de Correspondence Hellénique*
Bibl. Sanct.	*Bibliotheca Sanctorum*
Bull. Lit. Eccl.	*Bulletin de Littérature Ecclésiastique*
Byz. Zeitschr.	*Byzantinische Zeitschrift*
CC	*Corpus Christianorum Series Latina* (Turnholt 1954–)
CIL	*Corpus Inscriptionum Latinarum*
CJ	*Codex Justinianus*
CSEL	*Corpus Scriptorum Ecclesiasticorum Latinorum* (Vienna 1866–)
CTh	*Codex Theodosianus*
Chron. Min.	*Chronica Minora* (ed. T. Mommsen, 1892–8)
Class. Rev.	*Classical Review*
Frag. Hist. Graec.	*Fragmenta Historicorum Graecorum* (ed. C. Müller, Paris 1848–70)
GCS	*Die griechischen christlichen Schriftsteller der ersten drei Jahrhunderte* (Leipzig/Berlin 1897–)
GRBS	*Greek, Roman and Byzantine Studies*
ICUR	*Inscriptiones Christianae Urbis Romae* (ed. De Rossi, Rome 1861–88)
IEJ	*Israel Exploration Journal*
ILCV	*Inscriptiones Latinae Christianae Veteres* (ed. E. Diehl, Berlin 1925–31)
ILS	*Inscriptiones Latinae Selectae* (ed. H. Dessau, Berlin 1892–1916)

JbAC	*Jahrbuch für Antike und Christentum*
JEH	*Journal of Ecclesiastical History*
JRS	*Journal of Roman Studies*
JTS	*Journal of Theological Studies*
Journ. Pal. Or. Soc.	*Journal of the Palestine Oriental Society*
MEFR	*Ecole Française de Rome, Mélanges d'archéologie et d'histoire*
Or. Christ. Period.	*Orientalia Christiana Periodica*
PBSR	*Papers of the British School at Rome*
PEFQS	*Palestine Exploration Fund Quarterly Statement*
PEQ	*Palestine Exploration Quarterly*
PG	*Patrologia Graeca* (ed. J.–P. Migne, Paris 1857–1912)
PL	*Patrologia Latina* (ed. J.–P. Migne, Paris 1844–64)
PLRE	*The Prosopography of the Later Roman Empire* (Cambridge 1971–)
PO	*Patrologia Orientalis* (Paris 1903–)
RAC	*Reallexikon für Antike und Christentum*
RE	*Real-Encyclopädie der classischen Altertumswissenschaft* (Pauly/Wissowa)
Rev. Bénédict.	*Revue Bénédictine*
Rev. Bibl.	*Revue Biblique*
Rev. Et. Anc.	*Revue des Etudes Anciennes*
Rev. Et. August.	*Revue des Etudes Augustiniennes*
Rev. Et. Byz.	*Revue des Etudes Byzantines*
Rev. Et. Lat.	*Revue des Etudes Latines*
Rhein. Mus.	*Rheinisches Museum für Philologie*
SChr	*Sources Chrétiennes* (Paris 1942–)
Subs. Hag.	*Subsidia Hagiographica* (Société des Bollandistes, Brussels 1886–)
TU	*Texte und Untersuchungen zur Geschichte der altchristlichen Literatur* (Leipzig/Berlin 1882–)
Vig. Christ.	*Vigiliae Christianae*
ZDPV	*Zeitschrift des deutschen Palästina-Vereins*
ZKG	*Zeitschrift für Kirchengeschichte*
ZNTW	*Zeitschrift für die neutestamentliche Wissenschaft*

Introduction

When Constantine defeated his rival Maxentius at the Milvian Bridge outside Rome on 28 October 312, he attributed this victory to the intervention of the God of the Christians. The momentous consequences of this event are familiar to all. Yet the entry into Rome of an emperor who professed Christianity might seem a matter of little consequence for Christians in the biblical land where the new faith had originated. They were only now emerging from a period of violent persecution by a pagan Roman government which had sent many of them to torture and hard labour in the mines, and had claimed the lives of a procession of martyrs: the last to be recorded in Palestine had gone to their deaths in March 310.[1] Such action was only the culmination of centuries of Roman indifference—and antagonism—to the exceptional status of Palestine in the eyes of Christian believers. Long ago the government had sought to deny this province any religious identification other than the universally applied label of official Roman paganism. Two Jewish wars had resulted in the destruction of the Temple in Jerusalem and the expulsion of the Jewish population; Hadrian had refounded the holy city as the Roman colony of Aelia Capitolina, whose presiding deities—as its official name emphasizes—were to be the Roman Jupiter Capitolinus and the emperor himself (Hadrian's family name was 'Aelius').[2] Statues of Jerusalem's new gods now dominated the site of the ruined Temple and, as far as the Roman regime was concerned, the

[1] Eus. *Mart. Pal.* 11, 30.
[2] On the foundation of Aelia, see Cassius Dio, lxix. 12, with E. Schürer (1973), 553ff.

memory of the God of the Jews and Christians was
obliterated.[3]

The adherents of this God, however, would less easily ac-
quiesce in the 'secularizing' of their holy city. In Christian
eyes, Jerusalem was not only the scene of the historical origins of their faith as recorded in the New Testament; for
many of them, besides, it exercised a no less binding attraction as the location of the expected Second Coming—the
place of Christ's last moments on earth would also witness
his ultimate return (the Montanists, in seeking to shift the
Second Coming to Phrygia, were careful to name the spot
'Jerusalem').[4] To maintain the tradition of this Christian
Jerusalem, and to foster apocalyptic hopes, a congregation
continued to assemble there despite the imposition of Roman
paganism by Hadrian. The church where they met on
Mount Sion had escaped destruction, and now lay outside
the new perimeter of Aelia Capitolina, to the south.[5] As evident proof of its continuity with Christian origins this church
would display (certainly by the beginning of the fourth century) an episcopal throne said to be that of James, the Lord's
brother and first bishop of Jerusalem.[6] But it was the recollection of Christ himself which must have been the main-
spring of this community. Here tradition centred on an area
alongside the Forum in the midst of Hadrian's colony, where
the Roman builders had raised a temple to Venus—to the
Christians of Jerusalem this pagan shrine was none other
than the site of the Sepulchre from which Christ had been
raised from the dead;[7] while close at hand lay Golgotha, the

---

[3] According to Dio, l.c., Hadrian founded a 'temple' to Jupiter on the site, but
Christian writers saw only statues of Jupiter and Hadrian: Jer. *Comm. in Esai.* i,
2.9 (*CC* 73, 33), and *Comm. in Matt.* iv, 24.15 (*CC* 77, 226—an equestrian statue of
Hadrian). The Bordeaux pilgrim thought they were both statues of Hadrian: *It.
Burd.* 591, 4. On the confused identification of these statues, cf. J. Wilkinson (1976),
77–8.

[4] Eus. *Hist. Eccl.* v. 18.2. On the Christian significance of Jerusalem, cf. H.
Chadwick (1959); G. Kretschmar (1971), 167ff.

[5] See Epiphanius, *De Mens. et Pond.* 14 (*PG* 43, 261). The Bordeaux pilgrim
went *out* of Jerusalem to ascend Sion: *It. Burd.* 591, 7.

[6] Eus. *Hist. Eccl.* vii. 19, with Pet. Diac. *Liber de locis sanctis*, E (*CC* 175, 95).

[7] Eus. *V. Const.* iii. 26.3 saw a shrine of Venus at the spot; Jerome, *Ep.* 58.3.5,
transferred Venus to the 'rock of the Cross', and had an 'image of Jupiter' over the
Sepulchre (cf. Paul. Nol. *Ep.* 31.3). On the traditional site of the Holy Sepulchre,
see J. Jeremias (1926), 7–22; A. Parrot (1957), 49ff.; C. Coüasnon (1974), 8–11.

place of the Crucifixion.[8] There is some confirmation that the
Christians were looking to this spot as early as the second
century, by the time that Melito of Sardis came to compose
his sermon *On Pascha* (probably in the 160s): there he insists
that Christ was crucified 'in the *middle* of the city', an apparent departure from the New Testament location of Golgotha
which, it has been argued, may be explained by Melito's
knowledge of the local tradition at Jerusalem.[9] Melito in fact
is known to have paid a visit to the Holy Land in an effort to
establish an accurate canon of the books of the Old
Testament.[10] The second century is also the time that we
begin to hear of a cave at Bethlehem assuming the location of
Christ's Nativity;[11] and it may have been at the same period
that another cave near the summit of the Mount of Olives
came to attract New Testament associations—here Christ
was believed to have told the disciples of the forthcoming
mysteries of the end of the world, and from this spot to have
ascended into heaven.[12] As the Bethlehem cave recalled
Christ's first moments on earth, so its counterpart on the
Mount of Olives represented his last, and the expectation of
a second coming. Together with the presumed site of the
Tomb of the Resurrection these holy places were the original
core of the Christian Holy Land in the Roman empire, looking to a biblical past and a future hope.[13]

The presence of Melito of Sardis in the Holy Land in the
middle years of the second century makes him the earliest
known Christian 'pilgrim'. He records how, to establish
accurately the books of the Old Testament, he had travelled to
'the place *where these things were preached and done*'.[14] To the

---

[8] Cf. Eus. *Onomastikon*, 74.

[9] *On Pascha* (ed. S. G. Hall, 1979), 72, 94; cf. A. E. Harvey (1966). O. Perler,
by contrast, in his edition of the text (*SChr* 123, 177) found the expression merely
'une exagération rhétorique'.

[10] Eus. *Hist. Eccl.* iv. 26.14.

[11] The earliest record is the apocryphal *Protevangelium of James*, 18 (ed. de Strycker, *Subs. Hag.* 33 (1961), 146), and Justin Martyr, *Dial. c. Tryph.* 78.

[12] The apocryphal *Acts of John* (late 2nd/early 3rd cent.?), 97, knows of a cave
on the Mount of Olives (= *Acta Apost. Apocr.* (ed. Bonnet) ii. 1, 199); cf. Eus. *Dem.
Evang.* vi. 18.23, with G. Kretschmar (1971), 183ff.

[13] Cf. Eus. *Tricen. Orat.* 9.17 'three places revered for three mystical caves'; *V.
Const.* iii. 41.

[14] Eus. *Hist. Eccl.* iv. 26.14.

Christian bishop from Asia, Roman Palestine was thus essentially the land of the Bible, and his 'pilgrimage' was a journey in search of the biblical past. Melito was the first of a handful of pre-Constantinian Christian travellers to Palestine of whom we happen to hear—there may indeed have been many more whose journeys have gone unrecorded.[15] For all of them it was a combination of biblical tourism and Christian devotion which brought them to the Holy Land: Alexander, for example (a future bishop of Jerusalem), in the reign of Caracalla travelled from Cappadocia to the holy city 'for prayer and investigation of the sites'; and Origen, as a biblical scholar based at Caesarea, was to travel round Palestine seeking out the location of events recorded in the scriptures.[16] We gather, too, that Origen was visited by the Cappadocian bishop Firmilianus who had arrived 'for the sake of the holy places'.[17] Another of these early travellers to the Holy Land was Origen's contemporary, Pionius, who was to be a victim of Roman persecution under the emperor Decius.[18] Such instances reveal Palestine as already a place of Christian pilgrimage long before the advent of Constantine.

It becomes apparent that, for Christians both on the spot and far afield, Roman Palestine and Hadrian's Aelia Capitolina had not swept away the lure of a Holy Land. For the Roman authorities the province of Palestine might have no unusual significance, but to the Christian it harboured the past and the future of his faith. The gulf between them was seemingly unbridgeable. At the provincial headquarters in Caesarea, on 16 February 310, the Roman governor was interrogating his Christian prisoner Pamphilus:

> Firmilianus . . . next asked him what his city was. But the martyr let fall a second expression in harmony with the former one, saying that Jerusalem was his city, meaning, to be sure, that one of which it was said by Paul: 'But the Jerusalem that is above is free, which

---

[15] On these early pilgrims, see H. Windisch (1925), and B. Kötting (1950), 83–9; for the conclusion that 'the volume of devout tourism must have been much greater than these isolated examples suggest', see H. Chadwick (1959), 7.

[16] Alexander: Eus. *Hist. Eccl.* vi. 11.2. On Origen, see below, pp. 92ff.

[17] Jer. *De Vir. Illust.* 54.

[18] See below, p. 101.

is our mother', and 'Ye are come unto Mount Sion, and unto the city of the living God, the heavenly Jerusalem'. This was the one he meant; but the other had his thoughts fixed on this world here below, and enquired closely and carefully as to what city it was, and in what part of the world it was situated; and then he applied tortures as well, to secure a confession of the truth. But our martyr, though his hands were wrenched behind his back, and his feet crushed by certain strange machines, stoutly affirmed that he spoke the truth. The judge next asked him again and again as to what and where situated that city was of which he spoke, and he replied that it was the country of the godly alone. For, said he, none others save they alone had a share in it, and it lay toward the far East and the rising sun . . . . . But the judge, on the other hand, was puzzled and shook with impatience, thinking that the Christians had certainly established a city somewhere at enmity and hostile to the Romans; and he was much occupied in discovering it, and enquiring into the said country in the East.[19]

The Roman magistrate's resolutely earthbound ignorance of the Christian's celestial Jerusalem is a remarkable testament to two worlds unreconciled—sacred and secular, Christian and pagan. Little had changed, it might appear, since the reign of Tiberius, when one of Firmilianus' predecessors had condemned a similarly unyielding defendant to death by crucifixion.

---

[19] Eus. *Mart. Pal.* 11, 9–12 (transl. Lawlor/Oulton (1927), 386).

1. Constantine and the Holy Land
(i) Pilgrim Churches

TWO years and a few months after the martyrdom of Pamphilus and his companions at Caesarea Constantine was victorious at the Milvian Bridge. But the eastern provinces did not see their Christian emperor until he arrived for the reckoning with Licinius in 324: the final battle took place in September at Chrysopolis, on the Asian shore of the Bosphorus. After the victory Constantine announced to his eastern subjects that he had arrived in their lands from distant Britain as the chosen vessel of God's purposes, and gave proof of his mission by putting an end to all the measures of persecution under which Christians had laboured.[1] Later in the year he set off on a journey through his new domains which took him as far as Antioch, and possibly further: writing to the Christian congregation in Alexandria he claimed to have travelled 'most of the way' to their city before being turned back by the news of the dissension over Arius.[2] The Christian emperor may thus have reached Palestine. He had been seen there many years before, as a young prince travelling in the retinue of Diocletian.[3] We cannot, regrettably, know when Constantine conceived his (unfulfilled) intention of being baptized, like Christ himself, in the river Jordan;[4]

[1] See the emperor's letter to eastern provincials quoted by Eus. *V. Const.* ii. 24ff. Britain: ibid. 28.2.

[2] Eus. *V. Const.* ii. 72.2. For an expected imperial arrival in Egypt, cf. *P. Oxy.* x, 1261; xiv, 1626. Antioch: P. Bruun, *The Roman Imperial Coinage*, vii (1966), 70.

[3] Eus. *V. Const.* i. 19—often assumed (as in Winkelmann's edition) to be the expedition against the rebellion of Domitianus in Egypt (297–8), but other occasions are possible: T. D. Barnes, *Phoenix* 30 (1976), 180–2.

[4] Ibid. iv. 62.2.

but we may take it that, as the emperor's awareness of his new faith deepened, he came to know the traditions and expectations with which Christians had invested the land of the Bible.[5]

It was probably at the great council of bishops which the emperor summoned to Nicaea in 325 that he was approached about the holy places. Prominent among the delegation from the province of Palestine was the bishop of Jerusalem, Macarius, whose influence at the council may be estimated from his success in winning from the assembled bishops a declaration of the 'ancient' and 'customary' standing of his see (to rival the metropolitan status of the bishop of the provincial capital, Caesarea).[6] Discussion about the position of the see of Jerusalem must inevitably have introduced mention of the traditional biblical sites which its Christian congregation honoured. Macarius and his parishioners may well have taken encouragement from Constantine's letter to the eastern provincials after the defeat of Licinius, which, in ordering the restoration of the churches' properties, had specifically included the tombs of martyrs, 'the memorials of their glorious deaths'.[7] Under the same terms Macarius might lay claim to the Lord's tomb, the Holy Sepulchre itself, which his congregation had for generations believed to lie beneath the temple of Venus beside the Forum of Aelia Capitolina. The emperor, for his part, the conviction of his personal mission as God's chosen servant confirmed in the vanquishing of Licinius, would need little persuading to order the demolition of the pagan shrine which disfigured what was, potentially, Christianity's most hallowed spot. In writing afterwards to Macarius Constantine was to claim that nothing less than an 'order from God' had induced him to 'relieve' the holy place of the 'burden' of its pagan idol;[8] but, wherever the emperor might ascribe the responsibility, it was on his own authority that the temple was destroyed and the

---

[5] Cf. W. Telfer (1957).

[6] Nicaea Canon 7: cf. Hefele/Leclercq, *Histoire des conciles*, i (1907), 569–76. The bishop of Caesarea, Eusebius, came to the council with the disadvantage of suspicion of heresy: see J. Stevenson (1929), 95ff.; D. S. Wallace-Hadrill (1960), 26–8; H. Chadwick (1960), 173ff.

[7] Eus. *V. Const.* ii. 40.　　[8] Ibid. iii. 30.4.

site excavated.[9] Constantine's sense of his standing with the Almighty, and the Christians' attachment to the traditions of their holy city, combined to make only one outcome conceivable: in the area of tombs, outside the wall of old Jerusalem, which the excavators uncovered, one particular rock-tomb was identified (Eusebius does not say how)[10] as the Holy Sepulchre. Eusebius found the discovery 'contrary to all expectation', while for the emperor himself it 'surpassed all astonishment'[11]—it is tempting to suppose, however, that the surprise would have been all the greater if nothing had been found.

Constantine's response to this latest indication of the divine favour with which his reign was blessed was to write to bishop Macarius and order the building of appropriately fine surroundings for the Sepulchre. There was nothing in itself remarkable in a Roman emperor lavishing splendid new buildings on a favoured city: Rome itself and dozens of other cities in the empire could boast such imperial patronage. But Constantine was not merely setting out to embellish the Roman colony of Aelia Capitolina; as a Christian emperor he was also acknowledging the holy places of a Christian Jerusalem—the city whose existence had been unknown to a Roman magistrate fifteen years earlier. Those two separate worlds of Firmilianus and Pamphilus now stood close to being reconciled: indeed Eusebius, exulting in the new order of things, saw nothing less than the 'new Jerusalem' of the Apocalypse, the celestial city of which Pamphilus had claimed citizenship, now rising in splendour around the rediscovered Tomb.[12]

It is perhaps a discouragement to the historian that a source capable of such flights of imagination is our principal witness of the appearance of Constantine's new buildings in the Holy Land. Eusebius' contemporary description remains the fundamental account, and all the proposed reconstructions (of which there have been an abundance) have had to

---

[9] Ibid. 26.6ff.
[10] There is no mention of the wood of the cross as a clue: cf. below, pp. 38ff.
[11] Eus. *V. Const.* iii. 28, 30.1.
[12] Ibid. 33.

grapple with it.[13] It is true that now, in the light of intensive archaeological investigation, we know much more of the fourth-century buildings on Golgotha (and elsewhere in the Holy Land);[14] but Eusebius is the only author who described in detail the new edifices as he saw them, and can thus give us some idea of how they impressed contemporary observers —of the 'new Jerusalem' as the physical setting of the growth of pilgrimage, and as the focus of the pilgrims' faith and worship.[15]

Concentration on the unique situation which prevailed in Jerusalem as a result of the revelation of the Holy Sepulchre should not blind us to the widespread appearance of new churches throughout the eastern provinces in the age of Constantine.[16] Eusebius exulted in the frequent festivals of dedication occurring in the cities, and the great assemblies of bishops and laity which accompanied them;[17] he had himself, of course, delivered an oration at such an occasion before his friend bishop Paulinus at Tyre, where a new church had arisen on the site of one demolished during the persecutions.[18] The Jerusalem structures will not then have been isolated from a pattern of church building throughout the provinces—their architectural features naturally have much in common with the other churches of the period.[19] To illuminate the nature of the Jerusalem buildings we can thus legitimately invoke common characteristics, extending our

[13] All reconstructions acknowledge their debt to the standard work of H. Vincent & F. M. Abel (1914). Cf. (among others) J. W. Crowfoot (1941), 9–36; A. Grabar (1946), i, ch. 3 'Les martyria fondés par Constantin'; J. Conant (1956); J. G. Davies (1957); R. Krautheimer (1965), 38–41. For the literary evidence, see A. Heisenberg (1908), vol. i; E. Wistrand (1952).

[14] See the reports of Fr. V. Corbo in *Liber Annuus*, 12 (1962), 221–316; ibid. 14 (1964), 293–338; 15 (1965), 318–36; 19 (1969), 65–144. Cf. P. Testini (1964) and, most importantly, C. Coüasnon (1974). There is summary information in A. Ovadiah (1970), 75ff., and a convenient sketch in J. Wilkinson (1971), 36–53.

[15] On Constantinian buildings from this perspective, cf. M. H. Shepherd (1967), 70ff.

[16] Eus. *V. Const.* iii. 47.4, and following chs.; *Tricen. Orat.* 9.14ff.

[17] *Hist. Eccl.* x. 3.1.

[18] Ibid. x. 4 preserves the speech of Eusebius; for the earlier destruction, 4.26, 33.

[19] For the *genre* of Constantinian church building, see R. Krautheimer (1965), ch. 2; id. (1967); J. B. Ward-Perkins (1954); G. Downey (1961); S. S. Alexander (1971) and (1973).

horizons beyond the holy city itself. Eusebius' description of the church at Tyre, for instance, provides welcome evidence.[20]

It is generally agreed that what is preserved as the second half (chs. 11–18) of Eusebius' *Tricennial Oration* is in fact the survivor of the speech which he composed and addressed to the emperor in celebration of the new buildings in Jerusalem.[21] He was a leading participant in the dedication ceremonies in 335, and tells us that his contribution to the occasion included 'prophetic interpretations of the symbols set before us'[22]—suggesting that, as at Tyre, any description of the new buildings served only as a springboard for a sermon on the progress of the faith and the Christian empire. This is certainly borne out by chs. 11–18 of the *Tricennial Oration*, which (as they now stand) do not furnish an account of the new church at all, but indulge in an exploration of the wider theological implications arising from the emperor's building works.[23] We are left only with the bare summary of the new edifices which occurs in the *Tricennial Oration* itself.[24] Eusebius' detailed description of the Golgotha buildings is in fact reserved for the third book of the *Vita Constantini*, and it may reasonably be assumed that this material was originally contained in the speech delivered in 335.[25] It is certainly the first-hand account of one who observed closely the building operations as they progressed, and who knew in detail the completed precinct.

The whole complex of buildings at the centre of the new Christian Jerusalem was designed to focus attention on the newly-discovered Tomb. To accord with this purpose, the 'orientation' of the site was the reverse of the familiar pattern, rising westwards from the main north/south thoroughfare of Aelia[26] past the hill of Golgotha, towards the rocky tomb at the head. The area around the tomb will have been cleared,

---

[20] See below, p. 16.

[21] For this speech, see Eus. *V. Const.* iv. 46, with iv. 33.1. Cf. the discussion of H. A. Drake (1976), 30–45, and T. D. Barnes (1977).

[22] *V. Const.* iv. 45.3.　　　[23] *Tricen. Orat.* 11.2ff.

[24] Ibid. 9. 16–17.　　　[25] *V. Const.* iii. 34ff.; cf. Drake (1976), 44–5.

[26] A street still to be followed in the Old City, running south from the Damascus Gate: K. M. Kenyon (1974), 258. The Bordeaux pilgrim followed it northwards, approaching Constantine's precinct on the left: *It. Burd.* 593, 4.

and the rock cut back in such a way that the sacred spot was isolated to allow both the free access of the faithful and suitable scope for the builders in constructing an appropriate climax to the whole site.[27] Bishop Cyril, who would have been a young man in Jerusalem at the time of Constantine's building, implies that the rock which overhung the tomb had been cut away, so that it was possible to see into it: 'Look into the hard rock, which you have hewn out'.[28] By the second half of the century it is clear that the actual Tomb was completely enclosed by a church of its own, the familiar 'rotunda' of the archaeological reconstructions (and described in detail by the seventh-century Gallic pilgrim, Arculf)[29]—the texts refer to this building as the church of the *Anastasis*.[30]

Since Wistrand's careful examination of the text of Eusebius, however, it has been clear that there was no such building to be seen in his day: the work was either incomplete,[31] or, more probably, was not executed until the next decade.[32] Remains of the open courtyard which surrounded the Tomb before the construction of the rotunda have now come to light.[33] The arrangement observed by Eusebius emphasized the dominant position at the head of the precinct of the Tomb in isolation, by leaving it in the open but suitably beautified with a surround of columns and 'all forms of embellishment'.[34] Something of the nature of the monument's appearance, with the cave partitioned off by a grille, can be ascertained from the pictorial representations on later pilgrims' mementos—*ampullae* from the Tomb, or a stone re-

[27] Cf. J. Wilkinson (1971), 242ff. For comparable tombs in Jerusalem, A. Parrot (1957), 84ff.

[28] *Catech.* xiii. 35 (quoting Isaiah); cf. xiv. 9.

[29] Discussion of the rotunda stems from Vincent/Abel (1914), ch. 6. Cyril's language at *Catech.* xviii. 33 implies that by 350 there was a separate church around the Tomb. Cf. Arculf, *De Locis Sanctis*, i. 2 (= J. Wilkinson (1977), 95–6).

[30] Cyril used the term 'anastasis' sometimes to refer to the whole precinct, e.g. *Catech.* xiv. 6, 14; later the term had settled on the separate church at the Sepulchre—*It. Eg.* 24.1, *et passim*; cf. Jer. *C. Ioh. Hier.* 11, *Apol. c. Ruf.* iii. 33. On the recent archaeology on the site, see Coüasnon (1974), 21–36.

[31] As Coüasnon, 14–17.

[32] Work on the site was certainly continued by Constantine's successors: Cyril, *Catech.* xiv. 14.

[33] Coüasnon, 21ff.   [34] Eus. *V. Const.* iii. 34.

plica at Narbonne.[35] The Sepulchre, thus adorned, was enclosed in its circular church by the next generation of builders.

To approach the Lord's tomb, the pilgrim passed through an extensive courtyard which spread before it to the east.[36] This 'very large space' was exposed to the air, and paved with glittering stones; it preserved, according to Cyril, the remains of the garden in which the Sepulchre had stood.[37] On three sides it had long colonnades; the centrepiece of the fourth side was the Sepulchre itself. The later construction of the *Anastasis* would eventually dominate this courtyard. It had another significant feature, which Eusebius does not mention in his description of the scene: it emerges from the narrative of the pilgrim from Bordeaux, who visited Jerusalem as early as 333, that in the corner of this courtyard lay the 'little hill' of Golgotha, where the Lord had been crucified—separated by 'a stone's throw' from his tomb.[38] Indeed to this visitor the site of the Constantinian buildings *was* Golgotha; it was this which first caught his attention. Cyril, too, in the middle of the century makes the prominence of Golgotha among the Jerusalem buildings quite clear. He seems to have regarded it as dominating the scene, using the term to describe the place where his congregation was assembled;[39] the actual hill 'stood above' the basilica where he was lecturing his catechumens.[40] By the 380s Golgotha was surmounted by a replica of the cross, and 'Ante Crucem' and 'Post Crucem' were frequent 'stations' of the Jerusalem liturgy.[41] Eusebius had registered the position of Golgotha in his topographical guide, the *Onomastikon*, and his failure to mention it in his description of the site is puzzling.[42] He may perhaps have regarded the crude outcrop of rock where the Crucifixion was taken to have occurred as no more than an intrusive element into what he interpreted as a coherent

---

[35] Cf. J. Wilkinson (1971), 246ff., and (1972).   [36] Eus. *V. Const.* iii. 35.

[37] *Catech.* xiv. 5.   [38] *It. Burd.* 593–4.

[39] *Catech.* iv. 10, together with i. 1, iv. 14, xiii. 4, 22ff., xiv. 6, xvi. 4.

[40] Ibid. x. 19, xiii. 39.

[41] *It. Eg.* 24.7, *et passim.* Coüasnon, 50–3, believes there was a separate church in this corner of the courtyard.

[42] The omission was noted long ago by Heisenberg (1908), 41ff. Cf. *Onomastikon*, 74 '..... in Aelia, to the north of Mt. Sion'.

and unified scheme of building, which looked to Christ's triumph over death in the Tomb, rather than to the events which preceded. But the visiting pilgrim, as we shall see, was more concerned with differentiating the biblical sites, and attached no less significance to the place of the Crucifixion than to the Tomb.[43]

In the creation of an appropriate focus of devotion it wâs not enough simply to embellish the Sepulchre and lay out a magnificent courtyard before it; there needed to be a suitable building in which the faithful would congregate for acts of worship. Thus on the side of the courtyard which faced the Tomb there arose Constantine's Golgotha basilica, to be known subsequently as the *Martyrium*.[44] With regard to its building the bishop of Jerusalem received precise instructions from the emperor. In view of the unique distinction of the site, the bishop was to supervise the construction of a building which would surpass not only every other basilica, but indeed every other comparable edifice in the empire. The spot deserved nothing less: 'it is right that the most marvellous place in the world should be fittingly adorned'.[45] As with other church building of the period, the resources of the state were harnessed to the bishop's requirements: the praetorian prefect's vicar, Dracilianus (attested in office in 326), and the provincial governor were to arrange the supply of craftsmen, labourers, and necessary materials.[46] The emperor himself took personal concern over the decoration of the interior: the gilding of the panelled roof, the provision of marble and columns—the spoils, it would seem, of the demolished pagan temple.[47]

The completed building[48] at which Eusebius marvelled was an impressively spacious basilica, of 'boundless' height (the nave was in fact some 22m. high), and appearing as broad as it was long; the inside walls were faced all over with

[43] Cf. below, p. 118.

[44] Confusingly, as it was the actual Tomb which was the true 'witness': see e.g. Eus. *Comm. in Psalm.* 87.13 (*PG* 23, 1064). For 'Martyrium' of the basilica, see Cyril, *Catech.* xiv. 6; *It. Eg. passim*, esp. 30.1 (giving wrong reason for the name).

[45] Eus. *V. Const.* iii. 31.   [46] Dracilianus: *PLRE* i, 271.

[47] *V. Const.* iii. 32; for the spoiling of temples, cf. ibid. iii. 54.

[48] Ibid. iii. 36–9. On the interpretation of these chapters, besides the bibliography at n. 13 above, see Coüasnon (1974), 41–4.

marble, while their smooth and gleaming stone gave the same appearance to the exterior. The roof, covered on the outside with lead, was coffered on the interior and completely gilded, so that its glitter illumined the whole church. The nave was flanked by double aisles on either side, from which it was separated by huge columns.[49] The apse of the basilica (at its western end) was lined with twelve columns, recalling the number of the apostles, surmounted by silver bowls—an offering from the emperor himself.[50]

The congregation entered the church through three doors on the east; before these another colonnaded court was laid out, as the approach to the basilica. Into this the main entrance gates of the whole precinct opened, behind the magnificent *propylaea* which formed part of the colonnaded main street of the city—alongside the forum (the 'market place', as Egeria would see it).[51] It is clear that the façade was not only meant for the basilica, but for the complete complex—basilica, courtyard, and Sepulchre 'at the head'—for Eusebius remarks that it afforded to passers-by in the street a striking glimpse of the edifices within.[52] This suggests that the Constantinian buildings were all enclosed in a single precinct wall, separating them from the world outside, which was allowed only a passing glance into the 'new Jerusalem'.

The Sepulchre was one of the three sites which had been most revered by the Christians of Palestine;[53] the other two, the sacred caves at Bethlehem and on the Mount of Olives, were also honoured with churches in the reign of Constantine (built under the supervision of his mother, Helena).[54] Eusebius does not supply us with a description of the appearance or lay-out of these two churches, but excavation of the sites has been able to furnish enough to indicate the affinity of the buildings with those of Golgotha. The present church in

---

[49] The aisles had upper storeys, '$\dot{\alpha}\nu\alpha\gamma\epsilon\dot{\iota}\omega\nu$ $\tau\epsilon$ $\kappa\alpha\dot{\iota}$ $\kappa\alpha\tau\alpha\gamma\epsilon\dot{\iota}\omega\nu$'.

[50] Eusebius' term for the climax of the basilica is 'hemisphere' (ch. 38), which appeared as an apse to Egeria: *It. Eg.* 46.5 ('retro in absida post altarium ....'). The symbolism of the twelve columns points to the twelve monuments which were to surround Constantine's own tomb in Constantinople (*V. Const.* iv. 60). On the foundations of this apse, see Coüasnon, 41.

[51] *It. Eg.* 43.7: the crowd waits outside the gates 'quae sunt de quintana parte'. For the Roman colonnade, see K. M. Kenyon (1974), 260, and below, p. 18.

[52] *V. Const.* iii. 39.   [53] Cf. above, p. 3.   [54] *V. Const.* iii. 41, 43.

Bethlehem dates back to Justinian's restoration; but underneath can be discerned something of the fourth-century building:[55] a basilica, almost square, with an octagonal focus at its head which enclosed the actual cave of the Nativity; the basilica itself preceded by a huge colonnaded atrium and forecourt, their dimensions exceeding those of the church.[56] The remains identified as those of the 'Eleona' church on the Mount of Olives presented a similar plan: the sacred grotto was marked out as the climax of the basilica, which in turn was approached from an extensive colonnaded courtyard.[57]

With these Constantinian churches in Jerusalem and the vicinity can be compared the emperor's other basilica in the Holy Land, at the shrine of Abraham at Mamre (close by Hebron)—where the patriarch had entertained his three visitors.[58] Alerted by his mother-in-law to the paganism which she had witnessed flourishing at this site, Constantine wrote to Macarius and the other bishops of Palestine ordering the destruction of the idols and the building of an appropriate Christian basilica.[59] Again, as with the Jerusalem buildings, the imperial resources were mobilized, in the person of the *comes* Acacius.[60] Excavation has revealed a Christian basilica incorporated in an existing pagan precinct (of Hadrianic date?).[61] To the west of the basilica the precinct served as the church's atrium, containing within it the principal sacred features of the site: the altar of Abraham, together with well and oak-tree. The precinct wall continued to surround the new, Christian Mamre. The pattern here revealed is strikingly similar to that around the Holy Sepulchre, except in reverse: whereas in Jerusalem the dominant feature of the shrine and the courtyard by which it was

---

[55] See R. Krautheimer (1965), 38–9, with bibliography, 319. There is a useful summary in R. W. Hamilton (1947). For more recent developments, B. Bagatti (1952), ch. 1, and id. (1968b); cf. Ovadiah (1970), 33–5, and Avi-Yonah (ed.), *Encyclopedia*, i, 202ff.

[56] For measurements, see below, pp. 20–1.

[57] See L. H. Vincent (1957); Ovadiah (1970), 82–3.

[58] As recounted in Genesis, ch. 18.

[59] Eus. *V. Const.* iii. 51ff.; Soz. *Hist. Eccl.* ii. 4.

[60] *V. Const.* iii. 53.2; cf. *PLRE* i. 6 'Acacius (4)'.

[61] E. Mader (1957); for the Constantinian building, see esp. 95ff. Cf. R. de Vaux, *Rev. Bibl.* 65 (1958), 594–8; G. Kretschmar (1972); A. Ovadiah (1970), 131-3; Avi-Yonah (ed.), *Encyclopedia*, iii, 776ff.

approached came *beyond* the basilica, at Mamre the corresponding focus for the pilgrim was arrived at *before* entering the church. Yet the scheme of sacred precinct containing a central object of devotion, surrounded by an expanse of open courtyard and accompanied by a basilica for the assemblies of the faithful, is common to Mamre and Golgotha.[62]

Eusebius' oration at the dedication of the new church in Tyre provides, as has been hinted, a valuable comparison with his description of the new buildings in Jerusalem—particularly so if this latter is indeed a survival of the corresponding Jerusalem oration. Eusebius is explicit that it was a totally enclosed precinct at Tyre ('the outside circuit he strengthened with a wall surrounding the whole'), the entrance of which, as in Jerusalem, was behind imposing *propylaea*. Through this the bystanders would catch a glimpse of the buildings within; 'strangers to the faith', struck by the contrast with the desolation of a few years before, would be impelled to take steps towards the entrance.[63] Within lay the courtyard, open to the air, and surrounded on all four sides by colonnades; its centre was adorned with fountains. This atrium, separating the church from the monumental entrance and the outside world, represented for Eusebius more than mere grandeur and embellishment; it was also a place of purification. Unhallowed and unwashed feet would not straightway set foot in the house of God; the pure waters of the fountains would cleanse the unclean; and those who needed instruction in the rudiments of the faith (i.e. candidates for baptism) could be taught in this courtyard before approaching the altar of the Lord. For all entering the basilica this space provided an opportunity for 'refreshment', both physical and spiritual.[64]

The basilica itself seems to have followed the conventional pattern: a nave and side aisles, separated by rows of columns. The magnificence and splendour of the interior, with its cedar-wood ceiling, goes without saying; it led up to an apse lined with seats for the presbyters, and with the altar in

---

[62] For the basilica as a pilgrim church, see Kretschmar (1972), 289ff.

[63] Eus. *Hist. Eccl.* x. 4.37–8.

[64] Ibid. 39–40: 'supplying at once adornment and splendour to the whole, and a place of rest suitable for those still in need of their first instruction'.

the centre, surrounded by a wooden lattice fence, 'so that it would be untrodden by the multitude'. The floor of the church was a marble pavement. Additional buildings, including the baptistery, were attached to the exterior of the basilica.[65]

The idea which underlies Eusebius' account of the church building at Tyre, of a gradual progress from the ignorance of the bystander, through purification and instruction in the faith, before coming face to face with the holy of holies, is reminiscent of that long-standing analogy in Christian thinking between the building of a personal faith and a physical edifice.[66] Christianity had replaced the Temple of the Jews with a spiritual temple; 'the temple of God is holy; and that temple you are.'[67] The worshipper at one of Constantine's Holy Land churches would be meant to find in the surrounding buildings an echo of his own faith, a process of penetrating further into the sacred precinct towards the centre of devotion which it enshrined. Nowhere was this process more accentuated than at the Holy Sepulchre, where the whole lay-out of the buildings, as we have outlined, was designed to emphasize the crowning glory of the Tomb.

But the Golgotha buildings not only mirrored the spiritual temple of each of the faithful; they also represented the consummation of the faith of *all* Christians, the 'new Jerusalem' announced in the Apocalypse. That this was not merely a fancy of Eusebius is confirmed by the famous mosaic in the apse of the Roman church of S. Pudenziana, which, despite the loss of its edges in the later rebuilding of the church, still appears substantially in its original form dating from the end of the fourth century.[68] Here the heavenly Jerusalem is presented in terms of the actual contemporary buildings in the Holy Land. Christ is shown enthroned among the disciples, with the hill of Golgotha, surmounted by a jewelled cross, in the background. Behind is a roofed colonnade, which may well represent that which surrounded the courtyard before the Sepulchre—the courtyard which enclosed the hill of Gol-

---

[65] Ibid. 41ff.

[66] More fully expounded at ibid. x. 4.63ff.; cf. Paul. Nol. on St. Peter's in Rome, *Ep.* 13.13.

[67] I Cor. 3.10ff., Ephes. 2.20–2.   [68] W. Oakeshott (1967), 65–7.

gotha. The buildings portrayed in the rear of the mosaic represent Jerusalem and Bethlehem: on the one hand Constantine's precinct at the Holy Sepulchre, including, by this date,
the *Anastasis* rotunda; on the other, the church of the Nativity, showing the octagon which rose over the actual cave.
The striking realism of these depictions can be contrasted
with the entirely symbolic representations of Jerusalem and
Bethlehem only a few yards away on the triumphal arch of
Sixtus III's S. Maria Maggiore.[69] The S. Pudenziana mosaic
is confirmation both of the actual appearance of the Holy
Land buildings to a fourth-century visitor, and of their significance as the embodiment of a spiritual ideal in earthly surroundings.

The same readiness to place the Jerusalem buildings at the
heart of Christendom emerges from the sixth-century mosaic
map of biblical Palestine which decorates the floor of a
church at Madaba in Transjordan.[70] Jerusalem is represented at the very centre of this map, with Hadrian's *cardo
maximus* clearly visible (in a 'bird's eye' view); at a prominent
central position on the west side of this street the colonnade
is broken by the steps leading up to the entrance of Constantine's basilica;[71] the three doorways mentioned by Eusebius
can be easily distinguished. The Constantinian precinct on
Golgotha is the most obvious group of buildings depicted on
the map, the unquestioned centrepiece of the city, culminating in the rotunda surrounding the Sepulchre. The topography of the Madaba map owes much, it is recognized, to the
work of Eusebius;[72] and, certainly as far as the Jerusalem
buildings are concerned, its simple visual impressiveness
confirms what could be deduced from Eusebius' florid Greek:
a sacred precinct dominating the centre of Jerusalem, meeting the non-Christian world at its imposing entrance on the
main street.

The central position of the Constantinian buildings, deliberately emphasized in the Madaba map, was answering to
a Christian tradition which had already placed Jerusalem at

[69] Ibid. 66.
[70] M. Avi-Yonah (1954); cf. H. G. Thümmel (1973), esp. 76ff.
[71] For these steps, cf. Marc. Diac. *V. Porph.* 5; Coüasnon (1974), 45–6.
[72] Avi-Yonah (1954), 30ff.

the centre of the world. Where the Jews in the past had focused their attention on the Temple, Christians concentrated
on the hill of Golgotha,[73] and even transferred here fundamental traditions like the life and death of Adam.[74] But it
was the appearance of Constantine's new precinct, rising—
as Eusebius exulted—at this heart of the city, which gave the
clearest expression (as in the apse of S. Pudenziana) to the
Christian perspective of Jerusalem.[75] It also pointed strikingly to the contrast with the earlier situation of the Jerusalem
church, confined to its place of worship on Mount Sion outside the walls of Aelia and confronting the pagan deities of
Hadrian's city. Christian worship was now transplanted into
the midst of the Roman colony. Sion itself none the less retained its strong local tradition as the first church of Jerusalem, and hence of all Christendom—'mother of all the
churches' as it came to be known in the liturgy and to
pilgrims.[76] When the pilgrim Egeria visited Jerusalem in the
380s this place had joined the sites adorned by Constantine
as one of the principal locations of worship at the holy
places, and was by then the setting of an impressively large
new church (appearing larger on the Madaba mosaic than
the Golgotha basilica) built in the period of Constantine's
successors.[77]

The news of the discovery of the Holy Sepulchre and the
Christian reclamation of the holy city must have substantial-
ly increased the number of pilgrims visiting the Holy Land.
This influx seems certain to have been a determining factor

---

[73] E.g. Cyril, *Catech.* xiii. 28. Cf. J. Jeremias (1926), esp. 40ff.

[74] Jeremias, 34ff. Origen claimed the story of Adam's burial place on Golgotha
came to him from the 'Jews': *In Matt. Comm. Ser.* 126 (*GCS* 38, 265). Cf. Jer. *Ep.*
46.3.2, with *Comm. in Eph.* iii, 5.14 (*PL* 26, 526) and *Comm. in Matt.* iv, 27.33 (*CC*
77, 270)—rejecting the tradition.

[75] Eus. *Tricen. Orat.* 9.16. Cf. the Jerusalem *Breviarius*, 1 'in medio civitatis est
basilica Constantini', and Pet. Diac. *Liber de locis sanctis*, C1 (*CC* 175, 94). On this
central position of the Christian buildings in Jerusalem, see A. Grabar (1946),
234ff.

[76] In the *Liturgy of St. James* (ed. Mercier, *PO* 26 (1946), 206), echoed by monks
in a letter to the emperor Anastasius: Cyril Scyth. *V. Sabae*, 57. The 6th cent.
pilgrim Theodosius used the same expression: *De situ terrae sanctae*, 7.

[77] The building first appears as the 'upper church of the apostles' in Cyril,
Catech. xvi. 4. Cf. Vincent/Abel (1914); Ovadiah (1970), 89–90. For its size, see
the *Breviarius*, 4 ('basilicam magnam nimis'), and Avi-Yonah (1954), 56 (appearance on Madaba map).

in the planning of the new buildings. Otherwise it is difficult
to explain the regular and dominant appearance of the
atrium, the colonnaded courtyard, as an architectural feature
in the new Holy Land churches, enveloping and emphasizing
the focal points of each shrine.[78] Clearly for any place of pilgrimage open space, accompanied by the shelter of the colonnade, was an essential requirement. It had been as much a
feature of the great shrines of the pagan world as it was to be
of the new Christian sites; it would not indeed be surprising
if these characteristic architectural elements were in fact bor-
rowed from the ruins of Hadrian's temple which had covered
the site of the Holy Sepulchre. A comparable ecclesiastical
precinct has been excavated at Gerasa which again replaced,
and may have incorporated, earlier classical temples on the
site.[79] Its fourth-century buildings bear a remarkable resemblance to those in Jerusalem: a monumental entrance
opening off a colonnaded street, leading to a basilica and a
court beyond containing the miraculous fountain which was
the principal feature of the precinct. Similar features, *propylaea* and atrium, also characterized the churches at Gaza
which were to be described by Choricius in his speeches in
honour of bishop Marcianus.[80]

That the open courtyard was unmistakably the main feature in the architectural scheme of the Holy Land buildings
is emphasized by a consideration of their measurements.
Constantine's Holy Land basilicas were surprisingly short—
smaller than many English village churches.[81] To some extent this was the result of existing features of the site: the
Golgotha church could not extend westwards beyond the hill
of Golgotha, which determined the position of its apse;[82]
while the basilica at Mamre was restricted to a length of
16m. by the need to respect the siting of the altar of Abraham in the centre of the precinct.[33] No such limitation seems
to have been necessary at Bethlehem; yet the basilica was

[78] Cf. J. W. Crowfoot (1941), 39 'the atrium in front of the church is the most
significant feature in its setting'; S. S. Alexander (1973).
[79] Crowfoot, 41ff.
[80] Choricius, *Laud. Marc.* i. 17ff., ii. 28ff. Cf. R. W. Hamilton (1930).
[81] Crowfoot, 34.
[82] C. Coüasnon (1974), 41 'the apse was contiguous to the rock of Calvary'.
[83] See Mader (1957), 106, 108ff.; Ovadiah (1970), 131ff.

only some 28m. square, whereas its approach, through a forecourt and extensive atrium, amounted to twice this distance.[84] The church on the Mount of Olives was a similar length (30m.), preceded by a courtyard covering an area quite as large as the actual basilica.[85] At the Golgotha site the Tomb was separated from the street façade of the precinct by a distance of *c*. 130m., of which the intervening basilica covered a length of only 50m.; the rest was open space, courtyard and colonnades. With the completion of the *Anastasis* church around the Tomb this space was, of course, reduced—but there still remained a substantial area of forecourt separating the basilica and the rotunda.[86] A comparison with the Roman basilicas is sufficient to point the contrast: the nave of the church of St. Paul, as rebuilt in the reign of Theodosius, was itself 97m. long; while the total length of St. Peter's on the Vatican was 112m.—even the distance from the head of the nave to the apse alone (*c*.28m.) was equivalent to the whole length of the basilicas at Bethlehem or the Mount of Olives.[87]

This relative smallness of Constantine's Holy Land churches, and the correspondingly larger areas of open space and surrounding colonnades, clearly is not irrelevant to their role as pilgrims' basilicas. At the very least it provided room to admire the 'wonderful beauty' which so impressed the pilgrim from Bordeaux.[88] But we should recall Eusebius' stress on the opportunity for 'refreshment' at Tyre, for an adjustment to the sanctity of the place before approaching the shrine. This would have to take a practical form in the provision of facilities for visitors;[89] pilgrims who came to worship at the holy places would seek to be accommodated as close by as possible, in the numerous ancillary buildings which would grow up around the edges of the precinct. 'Let the church have a house for entertaining near by, where the chief

---

[84] According to Krautheimer (1965), 38. On the measurements of the church of the Nativity, cf. the (discrepant!) figures in Ovadiah, 34, and Avi-Yonah (ed.), *Encyclopedia*, i, 202ff.

[85] Cf. the plan in Vincent/Abel (1914), 356. Measurements: Ovadiah, 82.

[86] Cf. the plan in C. Coüasnon (1974), pl. viii.

[87] St. Paul's: Krautheimer (1965), 63. St. Peter's: ibid. 35.

[88] *It. Burd.* 594, 3; 599, 6.

[89] On the functions of the atrium, see Ch. Delvoye (1962), esp. 288–9.

deacon shall entertain strangers'—so runs an injunction of
the eastern church order known as the *Testament of our Lord*.[90]
When the younger Melania arrived in Jerusalem (in 417) she
first stayed 'in the *Anastasis*', and such was her attachment to
the spot that at night she never left the cross on Golgotha.[91]
Many other lesser pilgrims must surely have expected to do
the same. The Jerusalem buildings can hardly have coped
with pilgrims and worshippers without some provision of
lodgings and services. Melania may have resided in one of
the dependent buildings around the *Anastasis*, the foundations of which are set out in Coüasnon's plans of the fourth-
century rotunda—perhaps on the upper floor of the monastic
cells to the north.[92] The variety of buildings which could fall
within a sacred precinct such as that in Jerusalem is interestingly shown in a law of 431 governing the extent of the area
in which the sanctuary of the church might be claimed:[93] the
privilege is to reach beyond the church building itself as far
as 'the first doors after the public places'. This clearly
confirms that at Jerusalem, for instance, the precinct should
be regarded as a single complex stretching to the *propylaea* in
the main street. Within that area of sanctuary there is to be
no distinction between the different types of buildings,
'houses, gardens, porticos, baths, or colonnades'—the requirements of the Mediterranean traveller, it seems, were not
to be neglected, even within the church's boundaries. The
demands of hospitality (it will emerge) were a matter to
which the bishop must give his attention, and we may expect
them to have influenced the character of the buildings.[94]

Yet it is as well to recall that the buildings were the work
of an architect who was not only under the supervision of the
bishop of Jerusalem but who was also accompanied by a
clergyman from Constantinople.[95] Their concern with visitors would be more than merely that of food and shelter; it

[90] i. 19 (Eng. transl. of the Syriac by J. Cooper & A. J. Maclean (1902), 64); cf.
i. 34 (ibid. 99).
[91] *V. Mel.* 35 (with Gorce's note), 36.
[92] Coüasnon, pl. xi; for the monastic cells, ibid. 24ff.
[93] *CJ* i. 12.3 (= *Corpus Iuris Civilis*, ii, 65).
[94] For the duties of hospitality, cf. below, pp. 62ff.
[95] Theophanes, *Chron.* (ed. de Boor) 33, 11 (cf. Jer. *Chron.* s.a. 336): 'Eustathius,
presbyter of Constantinople'.

must have extended as well to the demands of faith and worship. All was designed, as we have seen, to emphasize the dominance of the Sepulchre. The worshipping congregation approached the Tomb over the whole length of the precinct, through courtyards and colonnades; crowds could assemble, processions could form—essentially there was room for *movement*. Constantine's buildings were the backcloth for these gatherings of the faithful; it was thus thronged with people that they were seen and marvelled at by the visitors. The pilgrim Egeria would see the gates of the precinct open wide, to admit the whole congregation accompanying the bishop amid hymn-singing;[96] on the afternoon of Good Friday she would observe the 'large and beautiful' courtyard before the Sepulchre so packed by the faithful that it was impossible to enter.[97] It was, indeed, as the context of a distinctive *liturgy* that the buildings came into their own, providing an appropriately spacious framework for worship.[98]

To convey something of the activity which characterized a great shrine like Constantine's Jerusalem it may be instructive to consider some comparable evidence from the rest of the empire. The great assemblies at the martyrs' festivals provide the closest parallel.[99] Whole cities would flock to their memorials; the roads were filled with pilgrims; the sick and destitute came to seek relief.[100] It was to cope with these crowds that the basilicas rose next to the martyrs' tombs,[101] like the church described by Prudentius at Hippolytus' grave on the Via Tiburtina: 'the church when full hardly admits the struggling pilgrims, and there is congestion and turmoil at its packed doorways'.[102] Outside, the poet saw the countryside of the *campagna* thronged with the pilgrims flocking to the scene.[103] Jerome's allusions to the crowded Roman basilicas are well-known. The young Paula is to cling to her mother's side during the festival vigils, to be exposed to no danger

---

[96] *It. Eg.* 43.7.   [97] Ibid. 37.4.
[98] Cf. below, ch. 5 *passim*.   [99] Cf. H. Delehaye (1933), 44ff.
[100] E.g. Asterius of Amasea, *Hom.* (ed. C. Datema, 1970) ix. 2. Id. *Hom.* lx. ('without the martyrs our life would have no festivals').
[101] For the conjunction of *martyria* and basilicas, cf. Krautheimer (1965), 30ff.
[102] Prudent. *Peristeph.* 11, 215ff. (the lines quoted are 227–8).
[103] Ibid. 195ff., esp. 211–12 'vix capiunt patuli populorum gaudia campi/haeret et in magnis densa cohors spatiis'.

from the throng; on such an occasion the younger Melania preferred to stay at home.[104] Jerome, whose own faith had been fashioned in the midst of such gatherings, praised the 'enthusiasm and the throngs' of the Roman congregation.[105]

The Roman basilica of St. Peter's was the scene of an exceptional assembly on the occasion of Pammachius' 'funeral feast' in honour of his deceased wife, Paulina.[106] Paulinus of Nola's account of this gathering furnishes a vivid picture of the whole precinct packed with people pouring into the church to partake of the feast: the whole length of the nave, the side aisles and the 'gleaming courtyard' before the entrance—all seethed with the assembly of the poor waiting to be fed.[107] In the centre of the courtyard an elaborate circular fountain with four streams of water refreshed the crowds, its splendour appropriate to accompany the sacrament of salvation being enacted in the church.[108] It is remarkable how much the building and its surroundings dominated Paulinus' visualization of this occasion; the physical edifice itself became inseparable from the events which it was enveloping. Though not actually present, Paulinus imagined that he was part of the scene, and included himself in his description of those gathering at the fountain. The basilica and its approaches would certainly have been familiar from his own regular pilgrimages to Rome for the festival of Peter and Paul.[109] It is hard to resist the conclusion that the terms in which Paulinus presented Pammachius' feast were substantially those in which he annually witnessed the martyrs' celebrations. It is the description of Paulinus the pilgrim, as he observed the great congregation flocking round the basilica.[110]

[104] Jer. *Ep.* 107.9.2; cf. *V. Mel.* 5.
[105] Jer. *Comm. in Gal.* ii (*PL* 26, 355).
[106] Paul. Nol. *Ep.* 13.11ff. For such feasts and their architectural context, cf. R. Krautheimer (1960).
[107] Ibid. 13.
[108] For the analogy of fountains and salvation, cf. Eusebius' address at Tyre, above, p. 16.
[109] Cf. G. Bardy (1949), 233.
[110] *Ep.* 13.11 'I seem to see the crowds pouring into that most splendid church of renowned Peter ...'.

He would have witnessed many similar scenes at his own shrine of St. Felix in Nola.[111] The architectural features here resembled those which have dominated this chapter: a sacred precinct containing no less than three churches, linked by a central colonnaded courtyard with fountains in the middle.[112] Paulinus makes it explicit that accommodation for pilgrims was provided in rooms on an upper floor above the 'cloisters', in such close proximity to the shrine that it was possible to look into it from their windows.[113] The cloisters of the courtyard allowed for walking or taking a rest, for protection from the sun or the rain.[114] As he conducted bishop Nicetas round the site, Paulinus imagined Felix exulting from his shrine at the numbers of pilgrims flooding the precinct: 'with gladness he rejoices to see his shrine overwhelmed by the faithful crowds, the courtyards filled with the joyful throng, and the mass of people pouring out through many gates.'[115] Most of the worshippers were peasants from the local countryside, whose traditional habits of celebrating the dead with feasting and drinking Paulinus felt bound to indulge; at least their faith was not in question, and there was a hope that they might be diverted from their stomachs by feasting their eyes on the biblical scenes represented on the walls.[116] Again it is the buildings which are an integral aspect of the devotion to Felix; they both contain and merge into the crowded scene.

The first occasion when Constantine's Jerusalem buildings might be the focus of similar enthusiasm came with their dedication in September 335.[117] The imperial *notarius*, Marianus, was sent to summon the bishops then in council at Tyre to the 'new Jerusalem';[118] from all over the eastern empire assembled bishops travelling at the state's expense,

---

[111] For the texts, see R. Goldschmidt (1940). For comparison with scenes at Rome, cf. *Carm.* 14, esp. 83–5 'toto plena sui spatio spatiosaque cunctis,/credas innumeris ut moenia dilatari/hospitibus. sic, Nola, adsurgis imagine Romae'.

[112] E.g. *Carm.* 28, 7ff. 'istic porticibus late circumdata longis/vestibula incluso tectis reserantur aperto/et simul astra oculis, ingressibus atria pandunt'.

[113] Ibid. 27, 395–405; 28, 55ff.   [114] 28, 37ff.

[115] 27, 379–81.   [116] 27, 542ff., 580ff.

[117] 17 Sept., according to *Chron. Pasch.* (ed. Dindorf), 531. The annual festival was to fall on 13 Sept.: cf. below, p. 108.

[118] Socr. *Hist Eccl.* i. 33; Soz. *Hist. Eccl.* ii. 26.

and accompanied by officials of the empire.[119] As at Nicaea
they had celebrated the emperor's *vicennalia*, so now in Jerusalem they honoured the thirtieth year of his reign; but this
was no council gathered in the imperial palace, but at the
very spot from which Christianity had sprung, restored as
the centre of the faith by the emperor's own munificence.
The assembled bishops knew it was a momentous occasion:
'Having come together . . . to a great gathering which we
have held for the consecration of our Saviour's Martyrium,
which has been established to the service of God the king of
all and of His Christ by the zeal of our emperor Constantine,
most beloved of God.'[120]

The same mixture of imperial policy and ecclesiastical
aspirations which had formed the background to the emper-
or's decision to excavate the site at Jerusalem also surrounded the culmination of his building. Marianus was the
perfect imperial lieutenant, adding lustre to the occasion
with expansive largesse, gifts to the poor and donations to
the churches; while the bishops contributed homilies in
praise of the buildings, or interpretations of the Scriptures.[121]
Eusebius' own leading role in the proceedings has already
been alluded to. It was, above all, an assembly to glorify the
new buildings. Their completion was identified with the
anniversary of the emperor's reign; bishops and laymen
joined in hailing the new Jerusalem.

Theodoret tells the story of how the powerful court bishop
Eusebius of Nicomedia travelled to Jerusalem at the emper-
or's behest to inspect the widely-acclaimed building
operations.[122] The journey is suspect, for the account is not
free of chronological confusion, and it forms the setting for an
unlikely version of the deposition of bishop Eustathius of
Antioch.[123] None the less, it at least sets the Holy Land
buildings in a context far wider than the bounds of Palestine.
So, too, does that very long journey of the pilgrim from Bor-

---

[119] Eus. *V. Const.* iv. 43.
[120] The preamble to their synodical letter, quoted by Athanasius, *Apol. c. Arian.*
84.3 (= *De Synodis*, 21.3).
[121] Eus. *V. Const.* iv. 44–5.   [122] Theod. *Hist. Eccl.* i. 21.
[123] Eusebius is named as bishop of Constantinople, which he did not become until
339; cf. H. Chadwick (1948), 28.

deaux, whose simple admiration of the buildings has been registered. But if there was any doubt of the larger significance of the churches rising at the holy places it must finally have been dispelled when the emperor's own mother had set foot in Jerusalem.

2. Constantine and the Holy Land
(ii) Helena—History and Legend

HELENA was not the first Christian pilgrim in the Holy Land[1]—but legend has made her the most renowned. It is perhaps paradoxical that a tradition of pilgrimage which saw itself as founded upon the historical origins of Christianity should celebrate first and foremost an event which is without such historical foundation—and yet, it must be acknowledged from the outset that there is nothing in history to link Helena with the discovery of the true cross. The story of her 'invention' of the sacred wood is a legend which makes a sudden appearance some sixty years after her death. But such was the significance attached to the relics of the *lignum crucis* and to the 'invention' tradition in the devotion of pilgrims and the worship of the holy places that it is, almost exclusively, the Helena of legend who has been remembered, obscuring from the record the traces of the historical pilgrim.[2]

As a result, in a classic reversal of her lowly origins,[3] the reputation of Constantine's mother in the following centuries knew no limit. A feast of the 'Invention of the Cross' entered the church's calendar on 14 September, of which Helena was

---

[1] Wrongly asserted by R. Macmullen (1970), 188; cf. *JRS* 60 (1970), 216. For earlier pilgrims, cf. above, p. 4.

[2] I say nothing here of her British 'connexions'. For the ultimate in the legendary, see Evelyn Waugh, *Helena* (1950). (I have been unable to consult R. Couzard, *Sainte Hélène d'après l'histoire et la tradition*, 1911.)

[3] See Ambrose, *De Obit. Theod.* 42 'stabularia'; cf. *Anon. Vales.* 2 'Helena matre vilissima', Eutrop. *Brev.* x 2 'ex obscuriore matrimonio', Zosim. ii. 9.2 'ἐξ ἀσέμνου μητρός'.

the heroine;[4] moreover, in the East, she was celebrated as an equal partner with her son, 'like unto the apostles', sharing with him the feast day of 21 May, and honoured with the same titles.[5] Along with Constantine, Helena also found her way into the imperial acclamations addressed to her successors: while the bishops assembled at Chalcedon in 451 acclaimed the emperor Marcian a 'new Constantine, new Paul, new David', they also hailed his consort Pulcheria as a 'new Helena'—'you have displayed the faith of Helena; you have displayed the piety of Helena'.[6] The Latin version of these acclamations adds, in praise of Pulcheria, 'crucem Christi tu defendis. invenit Helena, salvavit Pulcheria!'[7] It is pertinent to add that Helena's esteem cut across political divisions; for the *Life* of the anti-Chalcedonian, monophysite bishop of Gaza, Peter the Iberian, includes a passage praising Helena for her discovery of the true cross, and her part in the Christian 'rebuilding' of Jerusalem by Constantine 'the father and patriarch of all Christian kings, in truth a new David'.[8] Helena's reputation is impeccably confirmed in the *Codes*: the twenty-eighth *Novella* of Justinian (535), in ordering the province of Helenopontus (named after his mother by Constantine), unambiguously defines her claim to fame, '....who discovered the divine symbol of the Christians'.[9]

There is no question, then, as to the basis of Helena's subsequent standing—faith was to oust facts in the tradition. But we need first to return to such facts as there are, and to the historical circumstances of Helena's journey. These deserve attention in their own right, not only in illustrating the relationship between Constantine's court and the Holy Land, but equally in setting the style of pilgrimages that were to follow.

The date of Helena's journey coincides with the period of Constantinian building in the Holy Land, i.e. after 325. The

[4] *Synax. Eccl. Constant.* (ed. Delehaye, *Acta SS. Nov.* propyl., 1902), 43–5.
[5] Ibid. 697.   [6] *Acta Conc. Oec.* ii. 1, 2 (1933), 155.
[7] Ibid. ii. 2, 2 (1936), 9. The acclamations 'a new Constantine' and 'a new Helena' were also addressed to the emperor and his consort on other occasions, e.g. at the second council of Nicaea (787): see P. Henry, *JTS* n.s. 25 (1974), 75.
[8] *V. Pet. Iber.* 40–1.   [9] *Nov.* xxviii. 1 (= *Corp. Iur. Civil.* iii, 213).

sources agree (following Eusebius) that she was an old woman at the time of her pilgrimage, and that it was not long after her return to the court that she died, around the age of eighty;[10] numismatic evidence places her death in 329.[11] The way eastwards for Constantine and his court had in the first instance been opened up by the defeat of Licinius in September 324, and we shall see that Helena travelled still in the aftermath of this victory. She journeyed as Augusta, the title with which she and Fausta had been honoured in celebration of Constantine's success at Chrysopolis: the editor of the coinage proposed 8 November 324 for their elevation, the date of the confirmation of the young Constantius as Caesar.[12]

But it needs to be remembered that we are in ignorance of the whereabouts of Helena until her emergence as a Christian pilgrim. In the interests of the dynasty, the Danubian serving-maid had given place (in 293) to the Augustus' daughter in the household of Constantine's father;[13] Constantine himself had been brought up in Diocletian's court at Nicomedia.[14] His mother, we might assume, was of the company, witnessing with her son the unleashing of persecution against the Christians—perhaps observing, too, the Christian sympathies of Diocletian's own wife and daughter.[15] She would then accompany Constantine to the West, to be at his side in his assumption of empire. There is some evidence of her presence in Trier: the ceiling frescoes representing both Helena and Fausta discovered beneath the cathedral point to her residing there at the imperial court with the rest of her family.[16] Her promotion was to go hand in hand with that of

---

[10] Eus. *V. Const.* iii. 42, 46.

[11] So P. M. Bruun, *The Roman Imperial Coinage*, vii (1966), 72–3. Seeck, *RE* vii. 2, 2822, had favoured 336.

[12] Ibid. 69. Cf. *Chron. Min.* ii, 232.

[13] See *Anon. Vales.* 1; Aur. Vict. *Caesares*, 39.25; Eutr. *Brev.* ix. 22.1; *Epit. de Caesar.* 39.2; Jer. *Chron.* s.a. 291.

[14] Lact. *De Mort. Persec.* 18.10; cf. frag. of Praxagoras of Athens (*Frag. Hist. Graec.* iv, 2).

[15] Assumed from Lact. o.c., 15.1 (cf. Moreau's note in his edition, *SChr* 39, 284–5).

[16] See E. M. Wightman (1970), 109–10. The tradition that she founded the cathedral at Trier is not earlier than the 8th cent.: E. Ewig, *Trier. Zeitschr.* 24–6 (1956–8), 147ff.

the empress Fausta—*nobilissimae feminae c.* 318, *Augustae* 324.[17] It seems from this that she accompanied her son to the East on his triumphant campaign against Licinius.

Yet it is possible that she was not in fact in the East in 324; that it was only in 326, when the emperor visited Rome for his *vicennalia* celebrations, that she returned eastwards with the court.[18] The basis for this possibility lies in the considerable body of epigraphic evidence that Helena had associations with the West as late as 326—not only in Trier, but particularly in Rome and Italy. It is from inscriptions found in the vicinity that it has been generally concluded that the Sessorian palace in Rome alongside the Porta Maggiore (site of one of Constantine's Roman churches) was a residence of Helena: one of these inscriptions, now in the church of S. Croce in Gerusalemme, is the base of a statue set up in honour of 'Fl. Iulia Helena piissima Aug.' by the *comes* Iulius Maximilianus (after 326).[19] The exiguous fragments of another stone, to be seen in the Vatican, seem to record Helena's restoration of some baths in the area.[20] Further evidence of her roots in this part of Rome is found in association with her final resting-place, the mausoleum on the old Via Labicana:[21] among Constantine's endowments for the adjoining church was a 'possessio Augustae Helenae'—an estate (including, incidentally, some baths) occupying an area beyond the Porta Sessoriana (now the Porta Maggiore).[22] The imperial properties in this corner of the city were, it appears, made over to Helena.[23]

Such indications of Helena's establishment in Rome can be supplemented by evidence of her reputation in Italy. An inscription from Salerno records her 'excellentia' and 'pietas'; it is a dedication to Fl. Augusta Helena by Alpinius Magnus, the *corrector Lucaniae et Bruttiorum*, which must be-

---

[17] On the rare *nobilissima femina* coinage, see Bruun, o.c., 493ff.

[18] As suggested by A. Piganiol (1972), 39.

[19] *CIL* vi, 1134 (= *ILS* 709); cf. 1135.   [20] Ibid. 1136.

[21] Eus. *V. Const.* iii. 47 says Helena's body was transferred to Rome, 'ἐπὶ τὴν βασιλεύουσαν πόλιν', misunderstood by Socr. *Hist. Eccl.* i. 17 as 'new Rome', i.e. Constantinople. On the tradition of her burial-place see, e.g., *Liber Pontificalis* (ed. Duchesne), 182, and the full discussion of F. W. Deichmann & A. Tschira (1957).

[22] *Lib. Pont.* 183 '....omnem agrum a porta Sessoriana...'.

[23] For imperial estates in this vicinity, see Deichmann & Tschira, 74ff.

long to 324–6 (the name of Crispus, disgraced in 326, is on the stone).[24] The conventional public sentiments of a loyal official may not count for much, but they do at least point to the standing of Helena in southern Italy in these years. As 'piissima ac clementissima Augusta' she also received statues from the senate and people of Saepinum, and likewise from the senate and people of Naples.[25]

The recollection of Helena's western connexions brings her into association with the emperor's visit to Rome in 326—and nearer to the circumstances of her pilgrimage to Jerusalem. For it is safely beyond doubt that her journey was in some way inspired by the mysterious domestic turmoil which ravaged the house of Constantine in the course of this visit to the West in 326—and which resulted in the execution of the Caesar Crispus at Pola, shortly followed by the murder of the empress Fausta.[26] We are never likely to know the full circumstances of this episode. The dynastic rivalries of Constantine's sons have been offered as one explanation;[27] or it has been suggested that the behaviour of members of his family made the emperor a 'prisoner of his own laws' on the offence of adultery.[28] Eutropius, it should be noted, alleged a conspiracy extending beyond Constantine's immediate family, adding to the list of victims 'numerous friends'.[29] Whatever had really happened, pagan authors naturally found in these events an opportunity to discredit the first Christian emperor[30]—and to lay some of the blame on his mother Helena: the *Epitome de Caesaribus* and Zosimus' source (Eunapius?) both ascribe the murder of Fausta to her promptings, allegedly outraged at the execution of Crispus and at Faus-

---

[24] *CIL* x, 517 (= *ILS* 708). Alpinius, a Sicilian from Lilybaeum, held three Italian governorships, Corsica, Lucania et Bruttii, Sicily: *PLRE* i, 534–5.

[25] Saepinum: *CIL* ix, 2446. Naples: *CIL* x, 1483–4. The name on a similar stone from Sorrento is Fausta, not Helena: *CIL* x, 678 (=*ILS* 710).

[26] The chronology of these events is uncertain. The spring of 326 was traditionally favoured, during the court's presumed halt in N. Italy: Piganiol (1972), 38, n. 6. But, modifying Seeck, Bruun (o.c., 71) prefers Sept./Oct.

[27] P. Guthrie (1966).

[28] For the adultery charges, see Seeck (1890). The phrase 'prisonnier de ses lois' is Piganiol's, o.c., 38. *CTh* ix. 7.1 (3 Feb 326) interestingly exempts from charges of adultery maidservants in inns—but not the proprietresses! Helena's background may have been a sensitive point.

[29] Eutr. *Brev.* x. 6.   [30] See F. Paschoud (1971), esp. 340–2.

ta's supposed connivance in the act.[31] It is not difficult to credit a clash between the two Augustae—even on domestic grounds alone, without recourse to the more political considerations of palace influence. Perhaps one of the elements of the feeling against Fausta has been preserved in Zonaras, who alleges that, before the defeat of Maxentius, she had urged Constantine to worship pagan idols.[32] There is nothing else to substantiate this charge, and rumours would have abounded in the ignorance of what had actually occurred in 326. We are left only with the *public* explanations put forward for Helena's pious journey.

Such explanations we may expect to find reflected in Eusebius' *Vita Constantini*. It appears from this that Helena's prayers at the holy places were presented as an act of thanksgiving for the triumph of the Christian empire, more particularly 'for so great a son, the emperor, and for his most pious sons, the Caesars' (at this date, Constantine II and Constantius);[33] St. Ambrose would carry a hint of the same explanation, in describing Helena's pilgrimage as that of the emperor's 'anxious mother'.[34] It is difficult not to see lurking behind these terms the palace crisis of 326: the stability of the Christian empire, recently affirmed at the battle of Chrysopolis, had—it might appear—been suddenly endangered; the emperor had responded with the removal of members of his family, perhaps many others besides—events which temporarily eclipsed the concord in church and state symbolized in the (almost) unified front of the council of Nicaea and in the *vicennalia* celebrations. It was surely just this situation which prompted Helena's journey: acting in concert with Constantine's own building activities in Jerusalem she was, by her prayers at Christendom's most holy place, to reaffirm God's sanction for the new order. While Constantine built the 'new Jerusalem', Helena prayed for the builder.

Helena's pilgrimage has been seen as an 'act of reparation' for a purely domestic upheaval.[35] It has to be admitted that

---

[31] *Epit. de Caesar.* 41.12; Zosim. ii. 29.2.
[32] Zonaras, xiii. 1.5. Cf. J. Vogt, in A. Momigliano (1963), 49.
[33] *V. Const.* iii. 42.
[34] *De Obit. Theod.* 41 'anxia mater pro filio, cui regnum orbis Romani cesserat'.
[35] E.g. H. Chadwick (1948), 32ff.

some such motivation had its part to play, especially when it
is recalled that not only Helena, but also Fausta's mother
Eutropia found her way to the Holy Land: it was (as we have
seen) as a result of her protests at the pagan 'pollution' of the
Mamre site that Constantine ordered the construction of his
church there.[36] Clearly whatever had transpired in the court
was sufficiently appalling to provoke the (surviving) imperial
women into this combined reaffirmation of an unambiguous
piety. Yet it was as 'emperor' and 'Caesars' that Constantine
and his sons were the subject of the Augusta's prayers; and,
although she was a mother interceding for her son, it is also
emphasized that that son had been entrusted by God with
the sole lordship of the Roman world. It was not least for the
imperial *dynasty*, for the house of Constantine, that Helena
offered her prayers. One recalls the language of the dedica-
tions: praised in this context for her 'pietas', the Augusta is
styled 'mother of Constantine ... and grandmother of the
Caesars (... Constantini et Constanti beatissimorum ac
florentissimorum Caesarum)'.[37] As such she would travel
through the eastern empire, in confirmation of her own—
and, even more so, her family's—prerogatives as God's
chosen rulers.

Of Helena's personal inclinations we shall see some suggestion in what follows;[38] but her pilgrimage is first and foremost to be viewed as a public event, seen against the background just outlined. The venture is the complement to the
emperor's building schemes in the Holy Land; indeed Sozomen would present Constantine's decision to build a church
on Golgotha in terms very similar to Eusebius' account of
Helena's motivation—as an act of thanksgiving for the
accord of the council of Nicaea, and in prayer for himself, his
sons, and the empire.[39] Interest in the Holy Land, in the
course of the century, was to be dominated by the pilgrimages of noble ladies, journeying certainly for their own
edification, but no less in the interests of families and congregations left behind; Helena, the first and most distin-

---

[36] Eus. *V. Const.* iii. 52; Soz. *Hist. Eccl.* ii. 4.6.
[37] *CIL* vi, 1134; x, 517, 1483–4.
[38] See below, p. 36.   [39] Soz. *Hist. Eccl.* ii. 1.1.

guished of this line, expressed in her pilgrimage the piety, not only of a family, but also of the Christian empire.

By the spring of 327 the court had returned to the East[40] —and Helena may then have set off on her journey to Jerusalem. That the venture was, as I have suggested, meant to be seen as a public act of state is clear from the style of Helena's passage: she left no doubt that she was the Augusta traversing the provinces.[41] Lavish munificence characterized her movements: she passed through the eastern cities amid 'the magnificence of royal power'; the townsfolk benefited extensively from her largesse—in coin, presumably, which since her proclamation as Augusta had borne her own image.[42] Even more emphatically imperial were her donatives to the soldiers *en route*, to whom she came as a reigning empress, distributing the resources of the state treasury. But besides the traditionally imperial characteristics, her journey is also presented by Eusebius as, of course, a catalogue of classic Christian beneficence: relief for the poor in the provision of money and shelter, the release of prisoners and those condemned to the mines, freedom for the oppressed, and the restoration of exiles. These items recall the fate of Christians in the age of the persecutions, and mirror the terms of Constantine's edict bringing that age to a close, issued after the defeat of Licinius.[43] Helena can here be seen supervising the enacting of this imperial proclamation of the new freedom.

Eusebius' emphasis naturally falls on the beneficent side of Helena's journey—to the neglect, it is to be assumed, of the impositions which an imperial passage meant for the cities *en route*.[44] The news of the approach of the Augusta would entail local provision for herself and her party. This may be the context of the celebrated insult caused to the emperor's mother by bishop Eustathius of Antioch, on which ground, allegedly, he was accused before Constantine.[45] As a distinguished pilgrim Helena could expect attention from the local

---

[40] Cf. Seeck (1919), 178.   [41] Eus. *V. Const.* iii. 44ff.

[42] *V. Const.* iii. 47.2 explicitly mentions her appearance on the gold coinage in association with her proclamation as Augusta.

[43] Eus. *V. Const.* ii. 24–42, esp. 30ff.

[44] Cf. the evidence discussed by Fergus Millar (1977), 28ff.

[45] Athanasius, *Hist. Arian.* 4.

bishop, especially in Antioch, the principal city on her journey; the accusation against Eustathius suggests that she failed to receive this attention—the Augusta was snubbed. The bishop, it is supposed, made disparaging comments about Helena's notoriously lowly origins.[46] We need not look far for the explanation of Eustathius' readiness to offend the empress: to the displeasure, doubtless, of the uncompromisingly Catholic Eustathius, Helena revered one of the great saints of Arianism—the martyred Lucian, teacher of Arius himself and of Eusebius of Nicomedia.[47] The precise location of the context of Eustathius' insult is no more than an attractive conjecture; he might have been accused for an unguarded remark concerning the empress, even if she were nowhere near Antioch. But at least the knowledge of her journey through the eastern provinces (to or from the Holy Land) constitutes the most probable circumstances for Eustathius' comments.

The churches in the provinces, of course, received the full benefit of Helena's generosity. Her constant attendance at the altar in Christian worship was plain for all to see, as were her glittering embellishments of the buildings. In particular, Eusebius observed that she did not overlook the churches 'even in the smallest towns'.[48] This might be seen as no more than a detailed attention to the sort of public role which I have been emphasizing; but it is also, I suspect, a reflection of some more private beliefs. Her imperial progress tends to conceal this dimension of personal piety, just as her private feelings on the circumstances of her journey are lost behind the façade of the public explanations. It is a feature of the Christian empire that its public life depended upon an underpinning of private loyalty to the faith[49]—and Helena seems to have been no exception. Most strikingly, her pilgrimage will be mirrored by that of the empress Eudocia in 438: officially an act of thanksgiving for the marriage of her

[46] Cf. H. Chadwick (1948), 34.

[47] Helena's veneration of Lucian, and the town of Drepanum where his relics lay (which was refounded as Helenopolis), is recorded only in the Arian tradition: Philostorg. *Hist. Eccl.* ii. 12 (ed. Bidez/Winkelmann (1972), 24); for other refs. see index, s.v. ʿΕλένη).

[48] *V. Const.* iii. 45.

[49] See esp. J. F. Matthews (1967), and (1975), 127–45 'Piety and Patronage'.

daughter, nevertheless its attentions to the asceticism of the younger Melania and to the relics of St. Stephen will denote an undeniably personal commitment.[50] The pilgrimage of Helena was perhaps the first prominent instance of such a combination: a predominantly public activity, carried through according to conventional patterns, but at the same time springing from an essence of individual conviction.

The most public aspect of Helena's journey is represented by her buildings at the holy places; although her precise contribution here is difficult to assess. By contrast to the trend of the later tradition (to be discussed below), at the time Helena did not have an independent role to play, but rather that of her son's partner in empire, supervising on the spot the imperial edifices of the new Christian Jerusalem.[51] There is, as we should expect, no sharp division to be drawn between churches ascribed to Constantine and those attributed to Helena; the three principal churches—at Golgotha, Bethlehem, and on the Mount of Olives—were seen as part of a unified scheme of things, essentially Constantinian in inspiration, and a traditional display of munificence to mark the new direction of imperial interest. When the pilgrim from Bordeaux visited Jerusalem in 333 he reported simply that all three churches (as well as that at Mamre) were built 'on the orders of Constantine'.[52]

Nevertheless Eusebius attributes the initiative specifically to Helena in the building of the churches at Bethlehem and on the Mount of Olives (the so-called Eleona basilica): in both cases she instigated the work, leaving it to the emperor afterwards to provide appropriate adornments and fittings.[53] By contrast there is no mention of her participating in Constantine's principal building scheme in Jerusalem, at and around the rock of Golgotha. The demolition of parts of Hadrian's city, the excavation of the site, the discovery of the Tomb, and the creation of the impressive new complex around the Holy Sepulchre—none of this activity, according

---

[50] See below, ch. 10.

[51] Cf. Egeria's description of Constantine's building 'sub praesentia matris suae': *It. Eg.* 25.9.

[52] *It. Burd.* 594, 2; 595, 6; 598, 7; 599, 5 (Mamre).

[53] *V. Const.* iii. 43. Helena's church on the Mount of Olives did not include the actual summit: see below, pp. 161ff.

to Eusebius, involved the emperor's mother; nor is she mentioned in the correspondence between Constantine and the bishop of Jerusalem. Eusebius knew of her share in the building of the other two churches; he had apparently no reason to exclude her from this central project, indeed every incentive to the contrary. The conclusion is inescapable that the Golgotha buildings were carried through, at least in their initial stages, without the intervention of the Augusta; if it is right to suppose that the operations began on the return of bishop Macarius from the council of Nicaea (325), then they will in any case have been some way advanced before Helena's arrival. She is bound to have observed the progress of the buildings (which were not dedicated until 335); but the initiative in the building scheme had not been hers.

There is thus nothing in the contemporary record to link Helena with the original excavation of the area around Golgotha and the site of the Tomb; nor is there the least mention of any discovery of the fragments of the cross. Yet it is surely beyond question that Eusebius, in his glorification of the Constantinian empire, could not have failed to exploit the appearance of the sacred wood, as an unsolicited affirmation of God's favour. Next to the Tomb itself, there could have been no more convincing sign than the actual cross of Christ (it was certainly to be interpreted as such within a very short time, by Cyril of Jerusalem). From one whose overriding concern was with the signs of the times, it is an impressively convincing silence.[54] But if this silence of Eusebius fails to persuade—and it has done so at least since Tillemont, who wrote a note on the subject in support of the tradition, 'qu' on ne peut révoquer en doute la decouverte de la Croix par Ste. Hélène'[55]—then it is only necessary to turn to the sober summary by the pilgrim from Bordeaux of what he observed in Jerusalem in 333: he saw the rock of Golgotha, the holy Sepulchre, the new basilica of Constantine—but no *lignum crucis*.

Whatever the circumstances of their origin, however, relics purporting to be those of the cross soon made their ap-

---

[54] There is nothing to suggest that the 'saving sign' referred to in the *Tricen. Orat.* means the actual wood of the cross: cf. H. A. Drake (1976), 71ff.

[55] *Mémoires*, vii, 638.

pearance (perhaps from the rubble of the Golgotha excavations).[56] For, as is familiar, in his *Catechetical Lectures* (350) bishop Cyril of Jerusalem refers on a number of occasions to the wood of the cross at this date, so it is claimed, scattered all over the Mediterranean world.[57] His claims receive confirmation from the dedication of churches in north Africa known to possess fragments of the cross.[58] Significantly, moreover, the fragments were already associated in Jerusalem with the building activity of Constantine and the revelation of the Holy Sepulchre. This is clear from Cyril's letter to the emperor Constantius, which attributes the discovery of the cross to the time of Constantine, when God's favour brought about the revelation of 'the holy places which had been hidden'[59]—an allusion, it must be allowed, to the Tomb. The belief that the fragments originated from the excavations of Constantine's builders is obviously reflected in the Jerusalem practice of celebrating *at the same time* the dedication of Constantine's Golgotha buildings (the *Encaenia*) and the Invention of the Cross: by the time that Egeria visited Jerusalem in the early 380s the celebration of the Invention coincided with the octave of the *Encaenia*, apparently superseding the latter in significance:[60] for it was because the cross was taken to have been discovered on the same day that the dedication was celebrated with such splendour.[61] Soon after Egeria's visit the Jerusalem church introduced a formal veneration of the relics, like that which occurred on Good Friday, on the day following the commemoration of the dedication of 335—and it is this which gave to the church that feast in honour of the cross which falls on 14 September.[62]

It was thus within a decade or so of the death of Constantine that Jerusalem had its *lignum crucis*, tradition associating the discovery with his clearing of the site of the Holy Sepul-

---

[56] For the *testimonia*, see A. Frolow (1961), 155ff. Eus. *V. Const.* iii. 27 mentions wood among the rubble.

[57] *Catech.* iv. 10, x. 19, xiii. 4.   [58] As early as 359: see below, p. 129.

[59] *Ep. ad Constant.* 2; cf. below, p. 156.   [60] *It. Eg.* 48.

[61] Ibid. 48.1 '.... encenia cum summo honore celebrantur, quoniam crux Domini inventa est ipsa die'.

[62] *Armen. Lect.* 68. Jerome appropriately discussed the *lignum crucis* in a sermon preached at the *Encaenia*: CC 78, 154.

chre. The memory of Helena's presence and her participation in her son's building schemes would ensure that her name would eventually come to be connected with the appearance of the remains. But before anyone could be held to have discovered the cross, some formulation of how it had come to light was required—the legend called for a logical account of the actual process of 'invention'. The earliest trace of this is to be found at Antioch, in John Chrysostom's sermons on St. John's Gospel (delivered *c*.390). He is commenting on the description of the moment of crucifixion (John, 19.17):

Jesus ... went out to the Place of the Skull ... where they crucified him, and with him two others, one on the right, one on the left, and Jesus between them.

The cross had been buried, Chrysostom continues,

but it was likely that it would in later times be discovered, and that the three crosses would lie together; so that the cross of our Lord might not go unrecognized, in the first place it would be *lying in the middle*, and secondly it was to be distinguished by its *inscription*; whereas the crosses of the robbers had no labels.[63]

Here are the, albeit implausible, beginnings of the story of the identification of the true cross from among the three which were allegedly discovered; Chrysostom must have been aware of a story of the discovery involving Pilate's inscription and the (improbable) juxtaposition of the remains as a means of recognition. This had doubtless found its way to Antioch from Jerusalem, in the wake of the fragments themselves—which had already reached Chrysostom's congregation.[64]

The insertion of Helena into the developing legend is most likely to have stemmed from Jerusalem, source both of the actual relics and of the tradition linking them with Constantine's building at the Holy Sepulchre. Moreover, there are elements in the story of her discovery, as it unfolds, which

---

[63] *Hom. in Joh.* 85.1 (*PG* 59, 461).

[64] Joh. Chrys. *Quod Christus sit Deus*, 10 (*PG* 48, 826): everyone is 'fighting over' fragments of the wood.

seem manifestly to point to a Jerusalem origin. It is the more
surprising, then, that it is from Milan that the mother of
Constantine is first heard of as the discoverer of the true
cross. In his sermon *De Obitu Theodosii*, delivered on the fortieth day after his death (25 February 395), Ambrose passes
in review the late emperor's predecessors, whose company he
now shares in another world. As the author of the Christian
Empire which Theodosius had inherited, Constantine. is
given prominence, and with him his mother 'Helena of
sacred memory', the 'bona stabularia' who herself had visited the stable of the Lord's birth.[65] At the holy places the
spirit had moved her to seek out the *lignum crucis*: 'she opened
up the earth, scattered the dust, and discovered three crosses
in disarray *(confusa)*'.[66] The true cross was not, as in Chrysostom's version, still neatly lying in the middle; but it did
retain its *titulus*, 'Jesus of Nazareth, king of the Jews'. Here
lay the means of discovery: Pontius Pilate's 'what I have
written, I have written' had been a snub to the Jews, and a
pointer for the revelation of the cross in ages to come. Helena's veneration, Ambrose is here careful to point out, was
reserved not for the actual wood ('for that is the error of
pagans and the folly of the unrighteous') but for the crucified
Christ—a passage which hints that he was no stranger to the
widespread enthusiasm for the *lignum crucis* in his day.[67]

Yet Ambrose's concern here was not with the *lignum crucis*
as such, but with the Christian empire inaugurated by Constantine and sealed by Helena's alleged discovery. In this
regard it was not only the wood, but the *nails* of the Crucifixion which had particular import. Helena sent them, so the
story goes, to Constantine, one to be incorporated in the
emperor's bridle, another in his diadem.[68] Thus in the age of
the first Christian emperor that day had dawned to which
the prophet Zechariah had looked forward, when the horse's
harness would be inscribed 'holy to the Lord'.[69] Ambrose
presents the Christian achievement of Constantine in elu-
cidation of this passage; the Helena legend provided the nails

---

[65] Ambr. *De Obit. Theod.* 41ff. On this section of the sermon, see Ch. Favez (1932),
W. Steidle (1978).
[66] Ibid. 45.   [67] Cf. below, pp. 128ff.
[68] *De Obit. Theod.* 47ff.   [69] Ibid. 40; the text is Zechariah 14.20.

of the cross, enclosed in the emperor's bridle as the 'sanctum domino' of the prophecy, and symbol of the 'imperatores credentes' of whom Theodosius was the latest. The belief that a nail from the cross was contained in Constantine's bridle was widely held; Jerome was well aware of it when he came (in 406) to comment on the verse from Zechariah, and objected to the unlearned credulity which saw in it the fulfilment of this prophecy.[70] His scepticism, however, was of little avail, and an allusion to the prophecy of Zechariah was to become a regular component of the account of the 'invention' of the cross.[71]

Thus Helena's discovery of the true cross, as it appears in Ambrose, is quite divorced from its Jerusalem context; although linked to the reign of Constantine, it is presented not against the historical background of the Jerusalem buildings, but rather to confirm the fulfilment of Old Testament prophecy. It is thus introduced to elucidate a biblical text, in the proper manner of the sermon (which is the context in which it occurs)—the narrative is summary and allusive, and embedded in the highly-wrought language of the pulpit. Ambrose clearly knew the story of Helena and the cross, but his primary purpose here was not to rehearse that—rather, by pointing to the confirmation of biblical prophecy, to glorify the Christian empire of Constantine and Theodosius.

The legend of Helena's discovery had thus found its way to the West before the return to Italy, in 397, of Rufinus of Aquileia. He had spent nearly twenty years on the Mount of Olives in Jerusalem, in the company of the elder Melania.[72] The traditions circulating in the church in Jerusalem can be expected to have permeated his translation and continuation of Eusebius' *Ecclesiastical History*, which he dispatched to bishop Chromatius *c.* 403. Of his own two additional books, continuing the narrative of Eusebius down to 395, Rufinus announces that they were based on the recollections of his own memory as well as on literary sources;[73] consequently,

---

[70] Jer. *Comm. in Zach.* iii, 14.20 (*CC* 76a, 898) 'pio quidem sensu dictam, sed ridiculam'. On the point of the text, see *The International Critical Commentary* (1912), 355–6.

[71] E.g. Soz. *Hist. Eccl.* ii. 1.9.   [72] Cf. below, pp. 170ff.

[73] See his prologue to the work (ed. Schwartz/Mommsen), 957 'quae vel in maiorum litteris repperimus vel nostra memoria attigit'.

we find the Jerusalem basis of the Helena story here coming
into prominence.

According to Rufinus Helena's pilgrimage had taken place
at the time of the council of Nicaea.[74] There is no hint of the
historical circumstances of her journey, nor anything of the
record from Eusebius' *Vita Constantini*. Encouraged on her
way by 'divine visions', Helena approached Jerusalem and
there sought out from the inhabitants the place of the Crucifixion—the dream-directed quest has here replaced the act of
thanksgiving for her son and the empire. The context is
further specified with the mention of the cross's concealment
under the pagan temple of Venus, which Rufinus has Helena
order to be demolished; this, of course, is his version of Constantine's excavation of the site to reveal the Holy Sepulchre;
into this historical setting Rufinus has woven the legend of
Helena. Yet it is now clear how this tradition might have
come about, as a result of the Jerusalem church's natural
attribution of the origin of the relics to the Constantinian
building-scheme—a belief attested as early as the middle of
the century.

The historical context which Rufinus, and the Jerusalem
Christians before him, envisaged is further confirmed by the
introduction into the narrative of Macarius, the bishop of
Jerusalem with whom Constantine corresponded on the subject of the Golgotha basilica. Macarius finds his way into
Rufinus' version of the Helena story with a suggestion to distinguish the true cross; for the *titulus* is now no longer sufficient for identification—the legend calls for nothing less
than a miracle. And so it is Macarius who persuades Helena
and the congregation to bring the three crosses to the bedside
of a distinguished lady of Jerusalem who is lying gravely ill;
the bishop prays for the true cross to be revealed, and at its
touch (it is, of course, the third to be tried) the lady is immediately cured. In response to so glorious a sign Helena
built a magnificent church over the spot where the cross had
come to light. Thus the story of Helena and the 'invention' of
the cross has become so enmeshed in the history of the Golgotha buildings that it is alleged (falsely, as Eusebius had
made clear) that she actually built the basilica. The tradition

---

[74] For what follows see Ruf. *Hist. Eccl.* x. 7–8.

—already encountered in Ambrose—that the nails were sent to Constantine recurs here in Rufinus; together with them a piece of the wood itself was transported to Constantinople, which here appears for the first time as a destination of the *lignum crucis* (evidently by the end of the fourth century the eastern capital had acquired its fragments).[75] The bulk of the find was, of course, preserved at Jerusalem, in the silver casket which Rufinus must himself have seen produced on special occasions.[76]

A further fresh element enters the tradition with Rufinus, which was to become a standard feature of the story—again it appears certain to be of Jerusalem origin. Helena is said to have waited upon the consecrated virgins she encountered in Jerusalem; inviting them to her table, dressed as a humble servant she brought them food, poured the cups, and washed their hands. The Augusta was in this way made to conform to a pattern of sanctity like that displayed (a century later) by the younger Melania, who went round her convent on the Mount of Olives attending to the needs of the sisters.[77] It must be considered a remote likelihood that such a monastic establishment existed in the Jerusalem of Helena's day.[78] Rufinus himself, on the other hand, had been one of the founding fathers of monasticism at the holy places; the sort of devotion attributed to Helena may well have been often demonstrated among the nuns of his own time. Surely he reproduces here a story which circulated among those first ascetic groups on the Mount of Olives. An interesting survival of this tradition can be detected in the *Suda*, where Helena is credited with the establishment at the holy places of a community of virgins, and the provision of their maintenance from the public revenues.[79]

The narrative of Rufinus is followed closely by Socrates.[80] Yet, interestingly, he tries to combine it with the historical

---

[75] For the later diffusion of the relics from Constantinople, cf. Frolow (1961), 73ff.

[76] Cf. Egeria's description of Good Friday in Jerusalem, below, pp. 116ff.

[77] *V. Mel.* 41.

[78] There were already those who had taken up an ascetic vocation in Cyril's congregation, e.g. *Catech.* iv. 24, xii. 33–4; cf. the 'assembly of virgins' in *Procatech.* 14. In Egeria's day the 'monazontes et partheni' led the worship, especially during the week, e.g. *It. Eg.* 24.1.

[79] *Suda* s.v. Ἑστιάδες.   [80] *Hist. Eccl.* i. 17.

material from Eusebius. Helena is alleged not only, as in Rufinus, to have built the basilica, but also to have named it the 'new Jerusalem': this will have come from Eusebius, who presented Constantine's buildings precisely as the creation of the 'new Jerusalem'.[81] Socrates also mentions, from Eusebius, Constantine's letter to bishop Macarius on the building of the Golgotha basilica, thus restoring something of the historical circumstances of the church's foundation. He goes on, again following Eusebius, with Helena's two foundations at Bethlehem and on the Mount of Olives, her donations and aid to the poor—taking care to insert, however, Rufinus' story of her waiting upon the virgins.

In the history of Sozomen the elaboration continues.[82] The context is again after the council of Nicaea, and the insertion into the account of the historical excavation of the Sepulchre is complete—for, according to Sozomen, the three crosses were found close by the Tomb. As the true explanation of Helena's discovery Sozomen favours the traditional version of God-given 'signs and dreams'; but he reports another alternative, 'as some men say', that it was a *Jew* who had pointed Helena to the spot after studying the ancient documents.[83] Sozomen's rejection of this account has considerable interest, for it can be assumed to allude to another version of the Helena legend according to which she was pointed to the true cross by a Jew named Judas, who was consequently converted to Christianity and became bishop of Jerusalem, under the new name of Cyriacus. This account, existing in Syriac, Greek, and Latin texts, has been shown to have originated in the region of Edessa *c.* 400.[84] It is in fact a conflation of the 'mainstream' of the Helena tradition with the story of the martyrdom (under the emperor Hadrian) of Judas, the last of the bishops of Jerusalem of Jewish origin.[85] This version is worth noting not merely because it was, apparently, known and discarded by Sozomen, but also be-

---

[81] *V. Const.* iii. 33.   [82] Soz. *Hist. Eccl.* ii. 1–2.   [83] Ibid. ii. 1.4.

[84] See J. Straubinger (1912), who brings this story into relation with the quite different tradition of the invention of the cross found in the Edessene *Doctrina Addai* (transl. G. Phillips (1876), 10–16), where the heroine is Protonice, alleged wife of the emperor Claudius. For speculation based on Helena's connexions with the Jews, cf. J. Vogt (1976).

[85] On Judas, see *Acta SS. Mai.* i, esp. 443–4.

cause this was the Helena story which was to gain ground in the West: Gregory of Tours reproduced it, as did the *Liber Pontificalis*,[86] and it is likely to be the 'scriptura de inventione crucis' which finds a sceptical mention—as a piece of popular reading-matter—in the so-called *Decretum Gelasianum.*[87]

Sozomen's description is notable for its air of sober reality, as in his attempt at a rational explanation of how the three crosses came to be mixed up: the soldiers who had taken down the bodies could hardly be expected to be concerned about leaving the crosses in their proper order; they would only be in a hurry to get away from the unpleasant business.[88] Noteworthy also is his reserve, as with the 'Jew' story, regarding another new element in the tradition: not only was the woman cured by the true cross, but 'it was said' that also *someone was raised from the dead*.[89] For the credulously inclined, of course, a simple cure was not enough. Sozomen acknowledges, too, that he has added to the written tradition from stories in popular circulation.[90] But he knew his Eusebius, and, like Socrates, he has grafted the Eusebian Helena on to the tradition— though more carefully than Socrates, for his account clearly distinguishes between the church on Golgotha, rightly attributed to the emperor himself, and Helena's own two churches at Bethlehem and on the Mount of Olives.[91]

In the version of Theodoret, on the other hand, Helena's assimilation into the history of the Constantinian building project has become so complete, that, after quoting from Eusebius the emperor's letter to bishop Macarius, Theodoret introduces the Augusta as actually *carrying* the letter to Jerusalem herself.[92] As in Sozomen, it was she who cleared the site of the Sepulchre, and discovered the crosses close by; while here again it was Helena who built the magnificent Golgotha basilica, admired by all the faithful of Theodoret's own day.[93]

---

[86] Greg. Tur. *Hist. Franc.* i. 34; *Lib. Pont.* (ed. Duchesne), 167 (the western chuich celebrated the Invention on 3 May).

[87] Ed. E. von Dobschütz (*TU* 38, 1912), 10.

[88] Soz. *Hist. Eccl.* ii. 1.6.

[89] Ibid. 8. [90] Ibid. 11. [91] Ibid. 2.1.

[92] Theod. *Hist. Eccl.* i. 18.1. [93] Ibid. 7.

The Helena story was not, of course, the preserve of the eastern ecclesiastical historians; it had already emerged in the West, as will be recalled, with Ambrose and Rufinus. Three years after Rufinus had returned to Italy, he was followed by his spiritual companion, the elder Melania, who came bearing some fragments of the *lignum crucis*; these she presented to her kinsman, Paulinus of Nola, who in turn sent a portion on to Sulpicius Severus in Aquitania.[94] In the letter which accompanied this gift, written in 403, Paulinus rehearsed the story of the discovery of the fragments.[95] It is a narrative significantly different in detail from that which we have been following. By its concealment the cross had escaped destruction at the hands of the Jews, only to be profaned by Hadrian's pagan temple; this state of affairs was brought to an end by Helena, who sought the authority of Constantine to clear the holy sites of this pollution. Paulinus proceeds to attribute to Helena *all* the supposedly Constantinian churches at the holy places (including the church of the Ascension on the very summit of the Mount of Olives, dating actually from the 380s—Helena, it appears, had ousted the more recent memory of Poemenia, real foundress of this church).[96] Moreover, in his version, she was led to the site of the cross by consultation not only with the Christian congregation but also with learned Jews (a foretaste of Sozomen). In Paulinus' story bishop Macarius has no place; while it is a resurrection miracle *alone* which determines the true cross.[97] Paulinus was apparently in contact with a more advanced stage of the legend, and one less rooted in the historical context, than the tradition presented by Rufinus and followed by the church historians. His anticipation of both the elements, the Jews and the resurrection miracle, which Sozomen treated as the unreliable features of the story, in popular circulation, suggests that he has got hold of a lower layer of oral tradition; Melania (or other returning pilgrims), it might be supposed, brought along with her relics some of the Jerusalem stories.

---

[94] Cf. below, p. 132.

[95] Paul. Nol. *Ep.* 31.3ff.; cf. Sulp. Sev. *Chron.* ii. 3–4. For the date, see P. Fabre (1948), 40.

[96] *Ep.* 31.4. For Poemenia, cf. below, pp. 161ff.   [97] Ibid. 5.

The persistence and elaboration of the Helena legend lie
outside the present scope; in later centuries tradition would
attribute to Helena the foundation of numerous Holy Land
churches at all the significant sites.[98] It has not escaped
notice that the legend finds a reflection in the sober pages of
PLRE, where it is stated that Helena built the church of the
Holy Sepulchre (and the Ascension!), as though that were a
historical fact to stand alongside the building of the Nativity
church at Bethlehem.[99] The entrenchment of the story in the
traditions of the Jerusalem church, already implied in the
time of Egeria, was soon to become explicit: Egeria's successors at the holy places were shown the actual spot where the
cross had been found, under the altar of the basilica[100]—fifty
steps, according to the pilgrim from Piacenza, from the rock
of Golgotha.[101] In Rome, meanwhile, Constantine's Sessorian basilica had (appropriately, as part of Helena's palace
in Rome) become the home of some relics of the cross, at
least since the early years of the fifth century, when it had
come to be known as the 'Jerusalem' church.[102] To this day,
as Santa Croce in Gerusalemme, it is a focus of devotion to
St. Helena and the *lignum crucis*.

This excursion through the literary record places it beyond
doubt that, by the time that the next pilgrim from the imperial family, the empress Eudocia, arrived at the holy places
in 438, it would be firmly held in Jerusalem that the relics of
the cross which were displayed there had been miraculously
discovered by Helena during her pilgrimage and that the
buildings on Golgotha were her response to this providential
revelation. The legend had enlarged to keep pace with the
increasing veneration of the wood of the cross. Pilgrims in
the Holy Land, eager for their fragments of the wood, were
as much attracted by the Helena of legend as by the Helena

---

[98] Over 30 in all, according to Nicephorus Callistus, viii. 30 (*PG* 146, 112ff.). Cf.
the extract from the anonymous *Vita* of Constantine (on which Nic. Call. depended)
translated by J. Wilkinson (1977), 202.

[99] *PLRE* i, 410; cf. J. F. Matthews, *Class. Rev.* 88 (1974), 105.

[100] See the Jerusalem *Breviarius*, 1, and Theodosius, *De situ terrae sanctae*, 31.

[101] Anton. Placent. *Itin.* 20.

[102] The name 'Jerusalem' first appears in the dedication set up (*c.* 425) by Valentinian III, Placidia and Honoria: De Rossi, *ICUR* ii, 435 (= *ILCV* 1775). Cf. *Lib.
Pont.* (ed. Duchesne), 179: tradition that Constantine deposited the relics there.

of history—the motivation of their kind of piety was not apt to draw such distinctions.

But the influence of the legend should not blind us to the, so far neglected, significance of her historical pilgrimage. It was, no doubt, a remarkable turn of events which saw the mother of the emperor of the Roman world, a reigning Augusta, kneeling in prayer at the holy places of Christendom; but to leave it at this would be no more than to add another confirmation of the new order which was inaugurated with Constantine. What has to be added is that the pilgrimage of Helena adapted and transformed the elements of a traditional imperial progress through the provinces to a Christian purpose. The imperial progress left its obvious marks—the foundation, for example, of a town called Helenopolis in Palestine;[103] and to the public eye Helena's journey was characterized by activities familiarly associated with the travels of any leading official or grandee—buildings and beneficence. Yet these had now become the channels for the expression of a Christian conviction which struck more deeply than the conventions. In making the transition from empress to pilgrim, Helena smoothed the way for her successors; the journeys of those who sought out the holy places became a natural element in a Christian Roman empire.

---

[103] Soz. *Hist. Eccl.* ii. 2.5—of uncertain location. The suggestion of F. M. Abel, ii (1938), 205 (followed by M. Avi-Yonah (1966), 123, 137–8) is vitiated by his acceptance of an unhistorical tradition about Helena.

3. The Journey

HELENA's illustrious pilgrimage to the holy places was a reminder that prominent Christian travellers might now be
seen making their way along the major routes of the empire
with imperial encouragement and amid much publicity.
Scarcely two years after the Milvian Bridge bishops of the
church had already been assembling for the council at Arles
with the aid of the official transport system (the *cursus publicus*), the facilities placed at their disposal by local officials on
express instructions from the emperor.[1] It was a pointer of
things to come; for there is no more graphic illustration of
the hectic ecclesiastical politics of the mid-fourth century
than Ammianus' celebrated criticism of Constantius for permitting the official transport system to be choked 'by throngs
of bishops hastening hither and thither on the public
mounts'.[2] Earlier, the eastern bishops who had gathered for
the council of Sardica in 343 had complained of the 'attri-
tion' of the *cursus publicus* caused by their use of the
facilities.[3] As the new protagonists in the high politics of the
empire Christian bishops and their entourages took their
natural place among the travelling establishment; they clearly represented, to a seasoned and himself highly-travelled
observer like Ammianus, the most obvious aspect of the
church on the move. One suspects that there might be little
to distinguish these ecclesiastical convoys from their counterparts comprising great men of state: Gregory of Nyssa was to

---

[1] So Constantine to Aelafius *vic. Afric.* (*CSEL* 26, 205–6) 'data evectione publi-
ca'; cf. Eus. *Hist. Eccl.* x. 5.23, to Chrestus bishop of Syracuse.

[2] Amm. Marc. xxi. 16.18.

[3] See ch. 25 of their synodical letter (*CSEL* 65, 64) 'cursus publicus attritus ad
nihilum deducitur'.

claim that on one such mission his state carriage was none other than a church constantly at worship—but his assertion was meant to prove the uncharacteristic nature of such behaviour, not that prelates on official business normally passed their journeys in this fashion.[4] The fact is that, as in other spheres, the absorption of Christianity by the state led to a blurring of styles: the bishop flitting between the great cities of the empire came increasingly to resemble the lofty imperial official.[5]

Among Christian travellers around the empire, however, it might be expected that those whose goal was the holy places of Palestine would be the least susceptible of being merged with the traditional 'secular' pattern of mobility; the distinctive purpose of their journey ought to ensure that Holy Land pilgrims remained recognizable as travellers in a specifically Christian setting. Yet the discussion of Helena's pilgrimage has demonstrated how the pious journey might take on familiar modes of expression from other contexts: the imperial progress was no less a characteristic of her venture than any new or distinctive form of Christian piety. Nor is there any hint that Helena would have found any contradiction in combining her pilgrimage with a journey of state. Morever, no pilgrim, whatever his social station, could always expect to find during his journey an environment congenial to the devotional purpose of his travels; there would be many stretches of the journey where he would need, like Gregory of Nyssa, deliberately to create such an environment for himself, or be content with the traditional mechanism of long journeys in the empire. Such Christian overtones as the enterprise might possess would hardly obliterate the familiar problems associated with travelling round the Roman world.

The 'traditional mechanism' of travel means first and foremost the organization and facilities of the principal routes of the empire. In this regard it was thanks to the history of the Romans' involvement in Palestine that the the way lay open for pilgrims to the Holy Land, and to Jerusalem in particu-

---

[4] Greg. Nys. *Ep.* 2.13.

[5] Cf. L. Casson (1974), 300ff. To be fair, one ought to cite the case of three impoverished British bishops who used the *cursus* to attend the council of Rimini because they could *not afford* any other means of travel: Sulp. Sev. *Chron.* ii. 41.

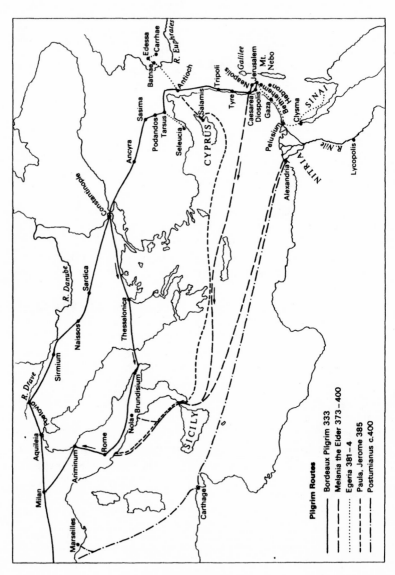

Map of Pilgrim Routes.

lar. The creation of a legionary base at Jerusalem in the
wake of the Flavian war had meant the necessity of providing
suitable communications with the provincial headquarters at
Caesarea on the coast; the coastal road which entered the
province from Syria to the north was extended inland to
Jerusalem from Caesarea, thus linking the interior and
mountainous site of the legionary camp with the principal
thoroughfare through the coastal cities.[6] Then, with the up-
grading of the province to the consular Syria Palaestina (in
the reign of Trajan) and the subsequent foundation of Hadrian's Aelia Capitolina, came further developments to the
road system: another route approached Aelia from the north,
converging with that from Caesarea, a route which joined it
to the province's second legionary base at Legio; while the
main southern approach into the province, again the major
coastal road from Alexandria, was linked to Aelia by a route
which diverged inland from Gaza.[7] A network of communication thus lay ready to hand to link the new fourth-
century Christian Jerusalem to the main routes of the
empire, and in particular to the coastal artery passing between Antioch and Alexandria; consequently, the Christian
pilgrim was provided with access to the holy places, not only
via the empire's land routes which converged on this coastal
road, but also by means of the shipping lanes issuing at the
ports of the eastern Mediterranean—most of all at Alexandria, whence the passengers disembarking from the returning
corn vessels could proceed by land into Palestine (though
probably not before taking in a visit to the monks of the
Egyptian desert).[8]

Yet the routes to which Jerusalem was linked were not
solely those leading to the coastal shores and the principal
cities of the Roman empire; for the holy places were situated
in that 'cockpit' area straddled between the Mediterranean
world and the routes to the East, to Mesopotamia and
beyond.[9] The Palestinian ports lay at the western end of

---

[6] M. Avi-Yonah (1966), 182. On Roman roads in Palestine, cf. J. Wilkinson
(1977), 20ff. (with maps).

[7] Avi-Yonah, 184ff.

[8] On sea-routes, cf. below, p. 72.

[9] Cf. Peter Brown, *JRS* 59 (1969), 96.

caravan routes from the far East,[10] and many Christian visitors were to approach Jerusalem from this direction: our
western sources, Egeria or Jerome for example, were clearly
struck by the preponderance of eastern pilgrims, many of
them monks from Mesopotamia, who flocked to the holy
city[11]—Jerome, in extravagant terms, has them from as far
afield as 'India, Persia, and Ethiopia'.[12] Such travellers to
Jerusalem were not, of course, new to the fourth century: the
New Testament has its celebrated 'wise men' from the East,
while links between Mesopotamia and Palestine had long
been prominent in the contacts between the respective Jewish communities.[13] These connexions Christian travellers
were now able to exploit. Nor was the traffic all one way;
western pilgrims also made detours to the Christian sites of
Mesopotamia. The most familiar is Egeria's excursion, on
her return from the Holy Land, to visit the monks in the
area,[14] and especially to see the city of Edessa, rich in its
associations with the apostle Thomas and the legendary correspondence between Christ and king Abgar.[15] Her journey
took her along the main route from Antioch to the Euphrates, and thence to Batnae, a town to whose importance on
this route she testifies in passing by mentioning its large
population and its resident garrison.[16] We learn more of this
from Ammianus; he had seen Batnae packed with wealthy
traders assembled for the annual fair 'to traffic in the wares
sent from India and China, and in other articles that are
regularly brought there in great abundance by land and
sea'.[17] Christian pilgrims passing between Syria and Mesopotamia clearly had busy and long-established links to follow, routes organized and protected for the interchange of
commerce and diplomacy between the Roman empire and

[10] See M· P. Charlesworth (1924), ch. 3 'Syria'; F. M. Heichelheim in T. Frank
(ed.), *Economic Survey of Ancient Rome*, iv (1938), 198–200.
[11] *It. Eg.* 49.1.   [12] Ier. *Ep.* 107.2.3.
[13] Cf. J. Jeremias (1969), 66–7.
[14] *It. Eg.* 17ff.; cf. the expedition of Rufinus, *Hist. Eccl.* xi. 8.
[15] For Christian Edessa, see J. B. Segal (1970), ch. 3. Cf. P. Devos (1967b).
[16] *It. Eg.* 19.1.
[17] Amm. Marc. xiv. 3.3 'municipium ... refertum mercatoribus opulentis ... ad
nundinas magna promiscuae fortunae convenit multitudo, ad commercanda quae
Indi mittunt et Seres, aliaque plurima vehi terra marique consueta'.

the East. Egeria's mention of the garrison at Batnae is echoed in a sermon of John Chrysostom where he remarks on the contemporary appearance of the route once followed by Abraham: busy towns, staging posts, detachments of armed guards lining the road.[18] Such would be the context of Egeria's pilgrimage to the homeland of Abraham.[19]

But it is pre-eminently a journey from the western provinces which provides the most illuminating introduction to the pilgrim on his travels. In 333 a Christian traveller from Bordeaux made the journey by land from the Atlantic coast to Jerusalem, and compiled (for the benefit of future pilgrims) a detailed record of the stages and distances *en route*, both there and back (the so-called *Bordeaux Itinerary*). The result is a very complete itinerary of his route: up the valley of. the Garonne and into Narbonensis via Toulouse, on through the Cottian Alps into northern Italy and Milan; thence on the highway across to Aquileia and into the Balkan provinces. The Danube towns—Emona, Poetovio, Mursa, Cibalae, Sirmium, Naissus, Sardica—pass by along the route to Constantinople; here was a Christian pilgrim to the Holy Land following the strategic main road which joined the eastern and western parts of the Roman empire, a route never far from the centre of great events or the passage of emperors. On from Constantinople, his road took him through the provinces of Asia Minor to the Cilician Gates and Tarsus; thus he traversed the route which linked the new capital with its eastern provinces—the road which came to be labelled by Sir William Ramsay (in recognition of these new travellers) as the 'Pilgrims' Road'.[20] He passed then via Antioch, capital of the eastern diocese, along the coast road already mentioned to Caesarea, and the northern approach to Jerusalem. There was a variant on the return journey; from Constantinople he followed, not the Danube route, but the old Via Egnatia through Thrace and Macedonia,[21] thence across the Adriatic to the heel of Italy (Hydruntum). His way northwards followed the Via Appia to Rome, then

---

[18] Joh. Chrys. *Ad Stagirium*, ii. 6 (*PG* 47, 458).   [19] *It. Eg.* 20.
[20] W. M. Ramsay (1890), 197, 240; cf. Magie (1950), ii, 1308–9.
[21] On this, and its replacement by the more northerly route (and all aspects of road travel in the empire), see W. M. Ramsay (1904), 384.

on through central Italy to the Adriatic coast at Ariminum, where he branched along the Via Aemilia north-eastwards to Milan, to rejoin his outward route.

This vast circular tour with the set purpose of visiting the Christian Palestine is considerable testimony not only to the changed perspective of the Roman empire brought about by the development of the holy places, but also to the sheer magnitude and extent of such an undertaking. It is no cosy devotional passage around the sacred sites, but a mammoth effort of travel along the major routes of the empire, a journey which would be exposed to all the hazards and discomforts which beset any kind of lengthy spell on the road. Even the final stage from Constantinople to Jerusalem, comprising some 1200 miles, passed through 58 ports-of-call—a journey of over eight weeks (assuming a night's stay at each).[22] Such a daily progress, *c.* 21 miles on average, would not be surprising in the normal conditions of private travel;[23] when this journey was repeated in 437 by the younger Melania returning from the imperial court to her cell on the Mount of Olives she completed it in about six weeks—but her biographer stresses the exceptional haste of her passage through Asia Minor, despite wintry conditions, in her eagerness to be in Jerusalem for the Holy Week liturgy.[24] The Bordeaux pilgrim was away from Constantinople in all for some seven months (he left the eastern shore of the Bosphorus on 1 June 333, and returned to Constantinople on 26 December),[25] four of which must have been spent on the journey. This, of course, is to say nothing of the first stage of his journey from Bordeaux to Constantinople, *c.* 2200 Roman miles, which, assuming the same progress as the later section, ought to have occupied at least fourteen weeks. It emerges that the pilgrim must have been away from home at the very least for over a year, and a very large proportion of this time would be consumed by travelling to and from his goal.

The journey itself thus represented a formidable element

---

[22] *It. Burd.* 601, 2.

[23] For the speed of land journeys, see Ramsay (1904), 386ff.

[24] *V. Mel.* 56–7: from the end of February to the Tuesday in Holy Week, i.e. (in 437) 6 April.

[25] *It. Burd.* 571, 6–8.

in making a pilgrimage to the Holy Land; and, as far as that of the Bordeaux pilgrim is concerned, there is nothing to suggest that it possessed a character markedly different from the conditions attending any other long journey along the public highways of the Roman empire. Indeed it is hardly a coincidence that this fourth-century record of a Christian pilgrimage serves in fact as the most revealing piece of evidence of the developed organization of transport in the empire.[26] Its detailed lists of the staging-posts (*mutationes*) and hostels (*mansiones*) which lined the roads along which the pilgrim passed, spread out at convenient intervals between the towns, are a meticulous reproduction of the contemporary state of communications along the major routes.[27] This is not to say that the pilgrim himself possessed the privilege of state travel;[28] given the strict controls which surrounded the use of the *cursus*, and the limit on the number of mounts which might be supplied,[29] it seems less than likely that a private visit to the holy places would qualify for state privileges. Bishops attending to the business of the church at the emperor's behest were a different matter; they clearly now fell into an official category, as did Gregory of Nyssa on his 'troubleshooting' mission to the church in Arabia (*c.* 380), when he was supplied with a public vehicle.[30] Or again, the younger Melania's journey to Constantinople in 436 was a summons in connexion with her uncle's presence on official business at the eastern court, and hence she and her party were supplied with public permits; yet it needed all Melania's prayers at the local *martyrium* in Tripoli to overcome the reluctance of an official there to release the mounts required for the whole entourage (and this despite laws permitting the presence of companions on an official journey).[31] The pilgrim from Bor-

---

[26] Utilized, for instance, by Pflaum (1940), 337ff., and by A. H. M. Jones, *The Later Roman Empire* (1964), 831–2.

[27] Cf. the account of Procopius, *Hist. Arcana*, 30.

[28] Assumed, for example, by B. Kötting (1950), 345.

[29] *CTh* viii. 5, *passim*: e.g. 44 (384), 54 (395), against private use; 35 (378), limit of five mounts per day.

[30] Greg. Nys. *Ep.* 2.12ff.; cf. below, p. 88.

[31] *V. Mel.* 52. For permitted entourage, see *CTh* viii. 5.4 'ad tutelam vitae vel laborem adeundum itineris'; the official faced penalties for exceeding the limits, *CTh* viii. 5.35. For more generous treatment of travellers in similar circumstances, see Greg. Thaumat. *Speech of thanks to Origen*, 69 (*SChr* 148, 122).

deaux, however, will have journeyed as a private citizen, waiting his turn to hire animals and make use of the hostels *en route* after the demands of privileged travellers had been met; such is what ordinary road users might expect to do.[32] His account of his journey reflects the elaborate organization of the public routes only because he could not escape it; apart from any private hospitality which he might secure, he would be dependent upon those· facilities which lined his road. The pilgrim from Bordeaux thus made his very long journey to the Holy Land against the background of the existing 'secular' organization of the empire's communications —and it is this which his *Itinerary* details (in contrast to the emphatically Christian core of the document devoted to the holy places themselves).[33]

In this regard it is interesting to set alongside this mammoth journey of 333 Egeria's description of her own travels in the East in the early 380s. I have already mentioned her presence along the route from Antioch to the Euphrates and Mesopotamia; to this may be added the account of her excursion from Jerusalem to Egypt and Sinai (with which the surviving portion of the *Itinerarium* opens). It is clear that she had followed the main coastal road, linking Syria and Egypt, as far as the local provincial capital of Pelusium (at the Nile's easternmost estuary), and then turned south to the Gulf of Suez at Clysma (Suez); twenty-two *mansiones* along this route separated Jerusalem and Sinai.[34] Egeria often used the term *mansio* simply as a computation of distance in her narrative (i.e. a day's journey), as in her reference to Edessa as twenty-five *mansiones* from Jerusalem;[35] but there are, by contrast, areas of her travels where *mansiones* would mean much more than mere stages on the journey, where she and her party must have had practical experience of them as hostels to put up for the night. This can be observed on her return over the desert routes of the Sinai peninsula. Taking

---

[32] For hire of horses, see Marc. Diac. *V. Porph.* 6, 14; in Procopius' day, l.c., each post had 40 mounts, so there should have been 'spare capacity'.

[33] See below, pp. 83ff.

[34] Pet. Diac. *Liber de locis sanctis*, Y4 (*CC* 175, 100)—deriving from Egeria.

[35] *It. Eg.* 17.2 (cf. Postumianus' 16 *mansiones* from Alexandria to Bethlehem, Sulp. Sev. *Dial.* i. 8). For various uses of *mansio*, see W. van Oorde, *Lexicon Aetherianum* (1929, repr. 1963), 126; G. F. M. Vermeer (1965), 35–6; P. Devos (1967a), 177 n. 3.

leave of the monks who had been her hosts at the mountain, she then found hospitality at the caravan halts along the road to Clysma and northwards to the Delta area: at the *mansio* on the shores of the Red Sea, for example, where she noted with admiration the skill with which the local inhabitants managed the difficult terrain on their camels (were she and her party required to transfer to camels?).[36] Along the four stages which separated Clysma from the *mansio* at 'Arabia' (identified as Phacusa, capital of the Arabian nome) she makes it clear that her party availed themselves of the regular facilities of this route: they had to be accompanied by an escort of soldiers, who were part of the fixed establishment of the road, garrisoned at the successive *mansiones*.[37] Their function, according to Egeria, was the maintenance of the Roman peace in these regions which she describes as 'hazardous places'; by contrast, when she joined the main road from upper Egypt to the coast as she came nearer to Pelusium there was no further need of military escort.[38] Egeria's narrative confirms that the presence of these soldiers was integral to the road which the pilgrims were following; it was not in any sense an exceptional privilege enjoyed by Egeria and her entourage.[39] Nor is there much problem in deciding why military protection was thought necessary for travellers in this area. Egeria herself, it seems, had observed the commercial importance of Clysma as the port at the head of the Gulf of Suez which funnelled goods from the far East into the Roman empire; she had noticed the huge merchant vessels on the Indian route at anchor in the harbour, and she may have remarked that Clysma was the headquarters of the official who presided over the diplomatic contacts between the Roman empire and India.[40] The route northwards from Clysma

---

[36] *It. Eg.* 6. 1–2.

[37] Ibid. 7.2. For identification of 'Arabia', see J. Wilkinson (1971), 216.

[38] Ibid. 9.3 '...milites, qui nobis pro disciplina Romana auxilia praebuerant, quamdiu per loca suspecta ambulaveramus'; cf. 7.4.

[39] Hence no argument for using the *cursus publicus*.

[40] Pet. Diac. *Liber de locis sanctis*, Y6 (*CC* 175, 101). These details may derive from Egeria, but the official's suspiciously Byzantine title ('logothetes') suggests some later interpolation. On Clysma, cf. Anton. Placent. *Itin.* 41 'civitas modica, quae appellatur Clisma, ubi etiam et de India naves veniunt', with A. C. Johnson & L. C. West, *Byzantine Egypt: Economic Studies* (1949), 137–8, and E. H. Warmington (1974), 95ff.

towards the Delta was hence a vital thoroughfare to the
Mediterranean for this eastern trade; and therein would lie
the necessity for military protection against any desert
marauders. We recall the similar organization along the
caravan route which Egeria followed on her way to Edessa.

These are characteristics of Egeria's travels which belong,
as with the Bordeaux pilgrim, to the existing 'map' of the
Roman empire: elements in the description of her journeys
which are indicative of the contemporary organization of the
routes along which she passed, and which contribute nothing
distinctively Christian to her movements. (It may be
observed that by the time that, in the sixth century, the pilgrim from Piacenza visited Sinai, the organization of the
route had taken on a more obviously Christian character.)[41]
Yet Egeria's *Itinerary* is a thoroughly Christian document: it
is permeated by the fervour and excitement of her 'desiderium' to witness the holy places, which was not easily
extinguished.[42] Consequently, it is the Christian overtones of
her travels which predominate in the narrative; her stays in
desert outposts, the escorts of Roman soldiers—these fall into the background in face of her enthusiastic gratitude to the
devoted bands of monks who escorted her party round Sinai, and gave them lodging and hospitality in their
monasteries.[43] Egeria is extravagant in her praise of these
holy men, who met all her needs as a pilgrim, showing her
the biblical sites, conducting appropriate acts of worship on
the spot, escorting her on her way with parting gifts
(*eulogiae*).[44] She is equally enthusiastic on behalf of those
monks who were her hosts in Mesopotamia.[45] No less than
monks, of course, the local bishops were assured of a prominent place in Egeria's recollections: despite her reference to
the *mansio* at 'Arabia', it appears in fact to have been the
bishop in the town who furnished hospitality to the party of
pilgrims.[46] Egeria had encountered him on her earlier excur-

---

[41] Anton. Placent. *Itin.* 41: e.g. Magdalum (cf. *It. Eg.* 7.4), now with a church and
two *xenodochia* 'propter transeuntes'.

[42] *It. Eg.* 16.3 'ut sum satis curiosa'.   [43] Ibid. 5.12.

[44] On these gifts, cf. below, p. 130.   [45] *It. Eg.* 21.3.

[46] Ibid. 8.1, 9.1 ('mansio Arabiae'). Phacusa is known to have had a bishop in the
4th cent.: Wilkinson, l.c.

sion up to the Thebaid, and she was now welcomed with
enthusiasm on her second visit; she describes her host, a former monk, as a man of saintly character and well-versed in
the Scriptures, and one who knew how to look after
visitors.[47] He conducted them round all the sites, and could
offer them the convenient bonus of sharing with his congregation the celebration of the festival of Epiphany.[48] Egeria
left behind here more than just her escort of soldiers; it is as
if the whole 'secular' context of her travels in this area faded
away into a totally Christian environment—holy bishop, holy places, Christian hospitality, church festival. The same
might be said of her presence among the saintly 'confessor'
bishops of Mesopotamia.[49] During her three-day stay in
Edessa it was the bishop (again, like his counterpart in 'Arabia', commended for his hospitality) who acted as her host
and conducted her to the shrine of Thomas and other *martyria* in the neighbourhood, as well as taking her to visit the
surrounding monks.[50] The memorials of king Abgar had
pride of place in the tour, particularly his celebrated correspondence with Christ, a copy of which Egeria received as a
parting-gift from the bishop (a fuller version, she avows, than
the one she possessed at home).[51] Egeria was shortly to receive the same attention from the nearby bishop of Carrhae,
who was able to offer sites rich in the memory of Abraham;[52]
and here, as earlier in Egypt, she struck lucky with a local
saint's festival (Helpidius) which, much to her gratification,
attracted a rare and splendid assembly of remote monks to
participate in the celebrations.[53] The monks around Carrhae,
and their demeanour towards her, provoked the same kind of
enthusiastic gratitude from Egeria as had those of Sinai.

[47] *It. Eg.* 8.4 'suscipiens peregrinos valde bene'; cf. 9.2.
[48] 6 Jan. 384: see P. Devos (1967b), 184–5.
[49] On the identification of these, see below, p. 165.
[50] *It. Eg.* 19.5.
[51] Ibid. 19.19. The version of the correspondence that Egeria knew in the West
was presumably that preserved by Eus. *Hist. Eccl.* i. 13, which lacks an additional
sentence to be found in the Edessene (Syriac) *Doctrina Addai*: see J. B. Segal (1970),
73–4 (though with wrong dating for Egeria), and J. Wilkinson (1971), 151.
[52] *It. Eg.* 20.2 'episcopum loci ipsius...qui mox nobis omnia loca ibi ostendere
dignatus est quae desiderabamus'.
[53] Ibid. 20. 5–6.

Yet beneath all her Christian devotion there emerge occasional glimpses of the more practical realities confronting Egeria as a pilgrim in this far-flung corner of the empire: the observation, for instance, completely counter to the impression conveyed by the narrative as a whole at this point, that Carrhae was a city of pagans, and its bishop presided over a tiny following of clergy and monks;[54] or the bishop's reminder to Egeria just how far from home she was, with the Persian frontier only five *mansiones* distant, and Abraham's home of Ur now inside Persian territory and inaccessible to Roman travellers.[55] The Christian enthusiasm which pervaded Egeria's movements and united her in faith to the holy men and holy places which she encountered cannot totally efface the massive process of uprooting and dislocation which a journey taking her more or less from the Atlantic to the Euphrates must have entailed; the Christian emphasis, though the dominant element in her record, still had to contend with the exigencies of travel at the edges of the empire.

The imposition of this Christian character on the pilgrim's journey was a conscious development which came with the consolidation of the Christian empire and the increasing vogue for pilgrimage itself. It is an evolution highlighted by the contrasting atmosphere of the Bordeaux itinerary, with its emphasis on the public facilities of the empire, and Egeria's description of her pilgrimage overlaid by a Christian pattern of travel and hospitality in which the principal role falls to bishops and monks. These were heirs to a tradition of attention to the needs of strangers and travellers which went back to the origins of Christianity, and which, by the fourth century, had come to be incorporated into the regular organization of the church.[56] A high place among the duties falling to the local bishop went to his role as a host for Christian travellers[57]—abundantly documented in connexion with in-

---

[54] 20.8; for confirmation of this, cf. Theod. *Hist. Eccl.* iv. 18.14 'a city full of pagan thorns'.

[55] 20.12 (hence the *terminus post quem* of her journey was 363, Jovian's truce with Persia).

[56] See, in general, D. Gorce (1925b), 146ff.; id. (1972), and art. 'Gastfreundschaft', *RAC* 8 (1972), 1110ff.

[57] Cf. Ambrose, *De Off. Ministr.* ii. 103ff., 'christianising' Cicero by adducing the precedent of Abraham.

dividual journeys of pilgrimage, as has already been observed in the case of Egeria. If the Bordeaux pilgrim was received by local bishops in the course of his journey (and surely he cannot have escaped the attention of church leaders in those towns which had considerable Christian congregations) he chose rather to record only the bare details of his itinerary; this in itself might suggest that in 333 there was no system of Christian hospitality sufficiently evolved to make an impact on his travels. But when the younger Melania followed the same road from Constantinople to Jerusalem a century later she was met by 'the bishops of Galatia and Cappadocia';[58] doubtless these receptions were partly in response to the reputation of her ascetic life (which must have stood high after her twenty years in Jerusalem), as well as to the official nature of the mission on which she had been engaged—yet as Christian traveller returning to the holy places Melania had no less claim on the bishops' hospitality. When she and her family had first made their way to Jerusalem from north Africa they had been welcomed in Alexandria by the great bishop Cyril himself.[59] Nor were such episcopal receptions reserved for the wealthy and well-connected; it was Cyril's predecessor, Theophilus, who had received the Gallic monk Postumianus when he disembarked at Alexandria.[60]

The responsibility for attention to travellers went far beyond the person of the bishop himself. The Christian empire saw the frequent establishment of hostels (*xenodochia*) supervised by clergy or monks.[61] The importance of such individuals in the local hierarchy is clear from the prominence of some of them in the ecclesiastical politics of their day: Isidore, the *xenodochus* of Alexandria, who first received Palladius in Egypt, was to cross swords with his bishop, Theophilus, over the disposal of funds for charity.[62] The provision of facilities for visitors was soon invested with the spurious authority of canon law, finding a place among the

---

[58] *V. Mel.* 56.   [59] Ibid. 34.

[60] Sulp. Sev. *Dial.* i. 7 (Postumianus was deterred from staying by the troubles with 'Origenist' monks).

[61] See B. Kötting·(1950), 366ff.; L. Casson (1974), 320ff.; O. Hiltbrunner, art. 'Xenodochium', *RE* ii. 18, 1490ff.

[62] Pall. *Hist. Laus.* 1; cf. id. *Dialogus*, 35, and Soz. *Hist. Eccl.* viii. 12.6.

many canons falsely attributed to the council of Nicaea.[63] It became, too, a regular and prominent aspect in the activities of monastic communities, as is clear from the experience of Egeria—a picture of hospitality mirrored wherever there were concentrations of monks. Palladius, for example, observed the *xenodochium* alongside the church at Nitria, where the monks provided hospitality for their visitors for up to a week (any who stayed longer were set to work for their keep).[64] In a later chapter there will be much to say of visitors to two such hostels in particular, those attached respectively to the monastic establishments on the Mount of Olives and to the foundation of Jerome and Paula in Bethlehem: the visitors' hostel at the roadside in Bethlehem was one of the principal buildings of the monastery, and the concerns of hospitality were (as we shall see) to loom large among the preoccupations of Jerome.[65] The Bethlehem hostel was only one among many which came to be established in the vicinity of the holy places; travellers (like the younger Melania) were able to stay in close proximity to Constantine's buildings at the Holy Sepulchre, and the church authorities in Jerusalem became increasingly concerned with the reception of pilgrims—by the sixth century there were *xenodochia* attached to many of the principal sites which attracted visitors.[66] There were similar developments at other centres of pilgrimage; the extensive complex of buildings at Telanissos, associated with the fame of Symeon Stylites, included pilgrim hostels;[67] while Paulinus has left a description of the accommodation at Nola from which the pilgrims could gaze into the shrine of Felix.[68] Another famous shrine which had its adjacent hostel was that of Cyprian on the harbour-front at Carthage, where Monica lodged on the night that her son Augustine set sail for Italy.[69] Such a facility at Carthage is

---

[63] Canon 75 (Mansi, *Sacr. conc. nova et ampl. coll.* ii, 1006). On these spurious canons, see Hefele/Leclercq, *Histoire des conciles*, i (1907), 511ff.

[64] *Hist. Laus.* 7.　　　　[65] See below, pp. 173ff.

[66] Anton. Placent. *Itin.* 23 'xenodochia virorum ac mulierum, susceptio peregrinorum, mensas innumerabiles, lecta aegrotorum amplius tria milia'. For examples in Jerusalem, see Cyril Scyth. *V. Sabae*, 31, and below, pp. 228, 239.

[67] Cf. G. Tchalenko, *Villages antiques de la Syrie du Nord*, i (1953), 208–9, and now L. Reekmans (1980).

[68] Above, p. 25.　　　　[69] August. *Confess.* v. 8.15.

an indication that there came to be specifically Christian
establishments of this kind at the important ports of the
Mediterranean: and nowhere more celebrated than at the
harbour of Rome, where the hostel founded by Pammachius
and Fabiola was known to voyagers, according to Jerome,
'the world over'.[70]

This preoccupation with Christian hospitality meant the
increasing availability of an alternative, and explicitly
Christian, framework for travel around the Roman empire,
which imposed its own pattern on a journey, in contrast to
that provided by the existing state facilities; the existence of
such a Christian network was frankly acknowledged in a
canon of the council of Nîmes (396) which sought to prevent
the abuse, 'on the pretext of pilgrimage', of the charity of
local churches.[71] The 'Pilgrims' Road' through Asia Minor
provides some confirmation of this development of a Christian context for the journey. I have already noted the change
implied by the contrast between the journey of the Bordeaux
pilgrim in 333 and that of Melania a century later: whereas
the former gives the impression of having passed from *mansio*
to *mansio*, Melania was welcomed by a succession of bishops
and their congregations, and lodged in the Christian
hostels.[72] There is explicit recognition of the organization of
Christian hospitality in this area in the pagan programme of
charitable works which Julian despatched to his high priest
in Galatia, endeavouring to evoke the same concern among
pagans by recalling the Homeric tradition of hospitality to
strangers—charity should not be the preserve of the 'impious
Galileans'.[73] This Christian network was to receive much
further impetus through the influence and example of bishop
Basil at Caesarea;[74] his contemporaries viewed with admira-

[70] Jer. *Ep.* 77.10 'xenodochium in portu Romano situm totus pariter mundus audivit'; cf. *Ep.* 66.11.
[71] Canon 5 (*SChr* 241, 128) 'multi sub specie peregrinationis de ecclesiarum con-
latione luxoriant...'.
[72] *V. Mel.* 56.
[73] Julian, *Ep.* 22 (Loeb), 430b–31b; cf. his *Fragment of a Letter to a Priest*, 291b.
The imitation of Christian practice was dwelt upon by Greg. Naz. *Orat.* iv. 111 (*PG*
35, 648), and Soz. *Hist. Eccl.* v. 16.2 (it is Soz. who preserves the text of Julian's
letter).
[74] See S. Giet (1941), 417ff.

tion the extensive establishment which he erected to cater for
the demands of travellers (and other categories of the needy),
a building which was to be named 'Basileias' after its
founder;[75] and under his influence the *chorepiscopi* throughout
central Asia Minor themselves founded hostels modelled on
that of their master (Basil was able to use his political influence to appeal to the authorities for tax exemptions on their
behalf).[76] Travellers along the Pilgrims' Road towards the
Cilician Gates would be able to benefit from these developments, which all contributed towards the creation of the
appropriately Christian context to surround the pilgrim on
his way to the Holy Land. Basil's creation of new bishoprics
would also help towards the provision of Christian facilities
for the route: both Sasima and Podandos, towns along the
road from Ancyra to Tarsus (and *mansiones* through which
the Bordeaux pilgrim had passed), now acquired Christian
bishops.[77] The earlier pilgrim was presumably denied the
possibility of the organized Christian hospitality which the
new bishops would undertake for future travellers; the
bishops of Sasima and Podandos would be among those
'bishops of Galatia and Cappadocia' who greeted Melania as
she passed in 437. A final chapter of evidence confirms the
prevailing pattern of Christian facilities for travellers along
this main route through Asia Minor: when Palladius returned from his Egyptian exile to his homeland of Galatia in
the second decade of the fifth century, to assume the bishopric of Aspuna (two days' journey out on the road from
Ancyra), he saw at close quarters some of the charitable
organization under the wing of the church in Ancyra.[78]
Among the distinguished practitioners whose conduct he records, one example may be singled out: the deaconess Magna, who made provision for 'hostels, beggars, and travelling
bishops'.[79]

---

[75] Greg. Naz. *Orat.* 43.63 (*PG* 36, 577) referring to the building as a 'new city';
Basil, *Ep.* 94. For the name, Soz. *Hist. Eccl.* vi. 34.9.

[76] Basil, *Epp.* 142–3.

[77] W. M. Ramsay (1890), 293–4 (Sasima), 348–9 (Podandos). Cf. *It. Burd.* 577,
4; 578, 4.

[78] *Hist. Laus.* 66–8. For Aspuna along the route, see *It. Burd.* 575, 12.

[79] Ibid. 67.

Developments such as these in the organization of local churches along the main pilgrim routes established the Christian context for the journey. But the pilgrim himself might contribute a good deal to the atmosphere surrounding his expedition according to the extent to which he endeavoured deliberately to impose a Christian character on his travels.[80] It is appropriate to recall at this point Gregory of Nyssa's state carriage, which assumed, according to him, the features of church and monastery, its passengers 'joining in psalms throughout the whole journey, and fasting for the Lord'.[81] Paulinus also vividly imagined the sound of hymns and psalms echoing from the vessel which conveyed bishop Nicetas of Remesiana home from a visit to Nola.[82] Such continuous practice of the Christian liturgy was an obvious and explicit 'label' of the pious nature of the enterprise; there would even be well-to-do lay pilgrims who transported their own clergy among their entourage—bishops included.[83] Services of worship, as a matter of rule, always accompanied Egeria's halts at Christian sites; and the central place was given to the reading of the appropriate passage of the Bible.[84] Egeria's Bible was her constant travelling-companion—as it was for the younger Melania, who, according to her biographer, never let it go from her hands.[85] A more spectacular instance of this kind is recorded by Palladius among his encounters with Egyptian monks: he accompanied one Hero the forty miles through the desert to Scetis, who in the course of his journey took no refreshment and strode off ahead of his companions reciting by heart sections of the Bible. This, of course, was to turn the journey into a prodigious ascetic feat:[86] weaker brethren like Palladius himself had to stop twice over the distance for food, and three times for drink (Palladius might console himself with the observation that Hero was clearly overdoing it—he was later to succumb to the temptations of city-life in Alexandria).[87] Yet the long and

---

[80] See D. Gorce (1925b), 125ff.   [81] Greg. Nys. *Ep.* 2.13.
[82] Paul. Nol. *Carm.* 17, 109ff. (with the dolphins listening in!)
[83] See below, p. 77.   [84] *It. Eg.* 4.3, 10.7.
[85] *V. Mel.* 21 (as aspect of her 'askesis').
[86] For asceticism and Bible reading hand in hand, cf. the achievements of Ammonius (*Hist. Laus.* 11) and Melania (ibid. 55), with generally D. Gorce (1925a), 63ff.
[87] *Hist. Laus.* 26: the nadir was an affair with an actress.

arduous journeys which pilgrims undertook obviously were a suitable opportunity for the display of an aggressive brand of asceticism by those so inclined—a readiness, for example, to embark on mammoth expeditions on foot: Palladius himself claims to have endured—indeed welcomed— the discomfort of journeys of up to sixty days tramping the Roman empire in search of holy men;[88] while long treks into the demon-ridden desert (like the expedition to Scetis) were a regular element in the asceticism which he encountered. Macarius of Alexandria, for instance, told him of one foray of his when he had made his way for nine days in the desert guided only by the stars, and placing reeds at intervals to mark his return (reeds which the demons, in relentless war against the holy man, removed).[89] With the same endeavour, the Galatian presbyter Philoromus had been on pilgrimage to Rome, Alexandria, and Jerusalem—and all on foot.[90] For the habitual ascetic, naturally, the discomforts of the journey itself were no bar to the continuance of a customary pattern of behaviour: the snows of Anatolia could not induce the younger Melania to break her fast;[91] and when a small company of travellers from Jerusalem, including the elder Melania and Palladius, arrived at Pelusium escorting the pilgrim Silvia into Egypt, there was a rebuke for the young deacon Jovinus as he bathed his hands and feet after the journey—although in her sixtieth year, Melania claimed that she had not washed her face or her limbs, except the tips of her fingers (a concession to the liturgy?); nor had she rested on a bed, or ridden anywhere in a litter.[92]

Such ascetic extravagance, or the more sedate practice of Christian worship and Bible reading, could leave no doubt that the pilgrim on the road saw himself as engaged in an enterprise of pious devotion, and as clearly set apart from his surroundings. This might be emphasized by his attention to Christian shrines on, or close by, his route (we recall this aspect of Helena's pilgrimage). Egeria would not return from the Holy Land without making the (obligatory) detour to Edessa, any more than she would pass through Cilicia with-

---

[88] *Hist. Laus.* prolog. (Butler, 11) 'ἠσμένισα τὴν κακουχίαν τῆς ὁδοιπορίας . . .'.
[89] *Hist. Laus.* 18 (Butler, 49–50).   [90] *Ibid.* 45.
[91] *V. Mel.* 56.   [92] *Hist. Laus.* 55.

out pausing at the shrine of Thecla by Seleucia;[93] Melania spent the night of her stay at Tripoli on her knees before the remains of the local saint, Leontius.[94] Better still if such sacred remains could actually accompany the journey itself and ensure the protection of the traveller: Peter the Iberian, for example, would travel to the Holy Land with a fragment of the cross enclosed in a copy of St. John's Gospel.[95] By such numerous devices the Christian 'style' might pervade the pilgrim's journey, giving it a character and an emphasis aimed to insulate it from the worldliness of the environment. Demonstrations of piety of varying intensity *en route*, the increasing development of recognized patterns of reception and hospitality by clergy and monks—these stamped on the pilgrimage its unmistakably Christian label. There is no misunderstanding the faithful conviction in which Egeria on returning to Constantinople passed from church to church in the capital pouring out her gratitude to God for the opportunity of her travels: 'Next day I crossed the sea and reached Constantinople, giving thanks to Christ our God for seeing fit, through no deserving of mine, to grant me the desire to go on this journey, and the strength to visit everything I wanted and now to return again to Constantinople'.[96]

Yet a qualification has to be entered. Egeria's enthusiastic response represents a view of her pilgrimage as she would have it—a journey conceived and undertaken in thoroughly Christian terms which did not countenance any intrusion from the contemporary secular world; evidence of such intrusion, as I have indicated, is rare in her narrative and is not allowed to detract from the predominant emphasis. To this extent the development of an insulated Christian network of travel was an aim which was idealized as part of the pilgrim's *desiderium*, rather than perfected in the actual conditions of the journey. This is not, of course, to deny the reality of the advance towards a Christian scheme of travel and hospitality, or its obvious manifestation in particular areas and at frequented sites; but it is to suggest that the more precise

[93] *It. Eg.* 17.2 'nullus Christianorum est qui non se tendat illuc gratia orationis', 22.2 (Thecla).
[94] *V. Mel.* 52.   [95] *V. Pet. Iber.* 29–30; cf. below, pp. 227–8.
[96] *It. Eg.* 23.8–9 (transl. J. Wilkinson).

impression of the Christian pilgrim on his way towards the
Holy Land will be the one which recognizes that the journey
was undertaken not in any Christian 'cocoon', but under
conditions where the Christian style had to mingle with that
of the world. This can be seen at its most extreme in Gregory
of Nyssa's advice to intending monks and virgins on the
hazards of going on pilgrimage. The danger of travel, argues
Gregory, is that it introduces confusion and an absence of
distinctions ('ἀδιαφορία') into a life (i.e. the monastic life)
which should be characterized by an ordered singleness of
purpose: on the road men and women cannot be secluded
and keep themselves to themselves; the women need help in
getting on and off their mounts or at difficult parts of the
journey; even more so in the hostels and inns the personnel is
indiscriminate, emotions which should be under control risk
being brought to the surface—'how is it possible to pass im-
passively through places where passions lurk?'[97]

Gregory's remarks here are aimed at dissuading from
travel a particular group of Christians who aspire to high
standards of ascetic perfection. Yet his vivid portrait of the
perils inherent in making a journey does highlight the obvious fact that travellers on pilgrimage could not expect
always to journey in Christian isolation, in circumstances in
which they were discriminated from others on the road (in
any age travelling may bring together unlikely companions);
the Bordeaux pilgrim will have encountered in his *mansiones*
all sorts and conditions of men on the move. These and related establishments, every variety of inns and hostels, had
never enjoyed a high reputation among the respectable folk
of antiquity, and the Christian authorities continued to view
them with suspicion.[98] Church canons forbade the clergy to
enter such places, although one exception significantly allows
for the necessities of the road:[99] there might, in the last resort, be no alternative—as along the shores of the Red Sea.

---

[97] Greg. Nys. *Ep.* 2.5–7 'πῶς ἔσται δυνατὸν ἀπαθῶς παρελθεῖν τοὺς ἐμπαθεῖς τόπους;'
For this letter, cf. below, p. 91.

[98] See T. Kleberg (1957), 91–6.

[99] Laodicea Canon 24 (Hefele-Leclercq, *Histoire des conciles*, i, 1012–3) forbids
clergy to enter inns; for the exception, on grounds of 'necessity', see *Apostolic Constitutions* (ed. Funk, 1905), viii. 47.54.

From the scattered archaeological evidence of *mansiones* it is possible to imagine the indiscriminate and crowded conditions which might have characterized a typical establishment along one of the main routes of the empire: the pilgrim would most likely be faced with a structure built around a central courtyard, with stabling and other facilities for the animals leading off this on the ground floor—for his own accommodation he would be provided with rooms above, along with all his fellow-travellers (and their army of grooms and attendants).[100] The remains of the *caravanserais* still to be seen in Turkey convey a vivid impression of the principal features of such transit-posts: very substantial structures enclosing large courtyards surrounded by the space for the animals— with the floor above to house their passengers.[101] The confusion of which Gregory warned would not be limited to the *mansio* itself. Many of the smaller communities along the 'Pilgrims' Road' in Asia Minor must have been virtually whole towns on the move: even as long ago as the beginning of the second century the traffic problems of some of these places had been pressing, as is evidenced by Pliny's reference to Trajan of the difficulties of the congested border-post of Iuliopolis caused by the great numbers of travellers passing through.[102] There was a similar atmosphere at Sasima in Cappadocia, which contributed to the reluctance of Gregory of Nazianzus to become its first bishop; he found the place all hustle and bustle, everything on the move: 'all is dust and noise and carriages....the people are all strangers and travellers'.[103] The establishment of the imperial capital at Constantinople and the frequency of contacts at all levels with the eastern provinces must have greatly exaggerated this density of traffic on the main route to the East; Christian pilgrims making for the holy places would hardly have the road to themselves.

---

[100] See evidence assembled by Pflaum (1940), 361ff., and comparable *hospitia* at Pompeii, Kleberg, 31ff. For an example in the Holy Land, R. Beauvery (1957), 86–94.

[101] E.g. the fine Seljuk *caravanserai* at Sultan Han, between Aksaray and Konya: *Les Guides Bleus, Turquie* (1965), 612.

[102] Pliny, *Ep.* x. 77.

[103] Greg. Naz. *De vita sua*, 443–5 (*PG* 37, 1060).

If it was thus difficult for the Christian traveller on land to maintain the distinctiveness of his pious undertaking, then it would have been even more so for those who approached the Holy Land on board ship.[104] In the confined conditions with which sea passengers had to contend there would be little scope for the definition of categories among those on board; it was the perfect setting for Gregory's damaging 'ἀδια-φορία'.[105] The sea-going pilgrims from the West arrived via the coastal ports of Palestine, or the great harbours of Alexandria and Antioch.[106] In the ports of southern Gaul or Italy the pilgrim would have no shortage of vessels to convey him eastward:[107] among Jerome's visitors in Bethlehem, for instance, were those who had sailed from Gaul, including Postumianus and his companions—they had found a ship at Narbonne to carry them to Carthage, thence on to Alexandria; on their return they were to pick up a vessel at Alexandria sailing for Marseilles.[108] Similarly Justus, the fourth-century bishop of Lyons who retired from office to seek the ascetic life in the desert, simply sailed for Egypt from the port of Marseilles.[109] The sea-voyage, of course, if all went well, was completed much more quickly than the many months involved in travel by land; with the advantage of north-westerly winds in the eastern Mediterranean the fastest sailings from Italy to Alexandria might take little over a week, and not much more than a fortnight might be needed for the voyage from the Gallic ports[110] (even the return journey, without the winds in its favour, could be accomplished to Italy in three weeks, to Gaul in four).[111] The contrast with

[104] See D. Gorce (1925b), 97ff.   [105] Cf. J. Rougé (1966), 362ff.

[106] On these ports, see Rougé, 126ff.; cf. the contemporary witness of the *Expositio Totius Mundi et Gentium* (ed. Rougé, *SChr* 124), 29, on the commercial links between Ascalon, Gaza, and 'Syria and Egypt'.

[107] For evidence of direct contacts between Gaul and Palestine, Rougé (1966), 96–7.

[108] Sulp. Sev. *Dial.* i. 1.3, 3.1–2; cf. Jer. *Ep.* 121 'Apodemius.... longa ad nos veniens navigatione'.

[109] *Acta SS. Sept.* i, 373.

[110] On the speed of voyages, Rougé, 99ff.; L. Casson (1971), 281ff. The *locus classicus* (for speeds under favourable conditions) is Pliny, *Hist. Nat.* xix. 3–4. On the advantages of winds in sailing to Alexandria, see Philo, *Flacc.* 26.

[111] Melania, Caesarea to Rome in 20 days: *Hist. Laus.* 54. Postumianus, Alexandria to Marseilles in 30 days, 'prospera navigatio': Sulp. Sev. *Dial.* i. 1.3. The return journey was unpredictable—Lucian's Isis, after 70 days out from Alexandria, had still only reached Piraeus: *Navigium*, 9.

the land journey is most graphically demonstrated by setting
the two months which occupied the Bordeaux pilgrim in
travelling from Constantinople to Jerusalem against the ten
or twelve days required for the sail from the capital to the
coast of Palestine.[112] Yet the comparative shortness of the
journey would hardly be compensation for its discomfort. Pilgrims like Postumianus and his colleagues (following the normal procedure for sea-travel in the Roman empire) had to
look round the harbour for a vessel and a willing captain
about to sail to their destination;[113] after paying over an
agreed fare they would find themselves quartered in ram-
shackle accommodation on the deck, if not actually out in the
open and fully exposed to the elements.[114] Although the hor-
rors of sea-travel were a congenial theme to the classical writers and a fruitful subject for entertaining elaboration, we
can salvage enough detail from the famous accounts of dis-
astrous voyages at least to savour what circumstances might
be expected to arise in hard times at sea—Synesius' hair-
raising trip along the coast of north Africa, for instance (the
route taken, in the reverse direction, by Postumianus' ship),
with the passengers huddled on the deck, men and women
separated by a torn-off piece of sail; or Aristides returning
from Italy to Asia through a continuous deluge of wind and
waves.[115] Such accounts may be compared with the factual
narrative of Paul's voyage to Rome in the *Acts of the Apostles*,
a less likely context for the traditional embellishments of the
seafaring theme;[116] here we encounter passengers and crew
debating the desirability of continuing the voyage in unfavourable conditions, and then all hands being put to work
to protect the vessel when it was driven off course by violent
gales.[117] The centurion and his prisoners were by no means

---

[112] See Marc. Diac. *V. Porph.* 27 (10 days), 55–8 (12 days in all, storm delay).

[113] For the procedure, see Rougé (1966), 364; L. Casson (1974), 153. Postumianus: Sulp. Sev. l.c. Cf. Mark the deacon, whose master had provided a sum for
the fare, *V. Porph.* 6. At Constantinople Libanius went round enquiring about vessels for Athens: *Orat.* i. 31; cf. ibid. 15 (captain persuaded by mention of a fare).

[114] See Casson (1971), 175ff.

[115] Synes. *Ep.* 4 (*PG* 66, 1329), and Ael. Arist. *Orat.* 48.64–8 (= C. A. Behr,
Aelius Aristides and the 'Sacred Tales' (1968), 237). On the literary tradition, see, e.g.,
Nisbet/Hubbard, *Commentary on Horace Odes I* (1970), 43ff.

[116] The classic treatment is James Smith (1880).

[117] Acts 27.9ff. (debate), 14ff. (storm measures).

alone among the passengers on this Alexandrian vessel *en route* to Italy, who may have numbered (according to one tradition) 276 souls;[118] at least they managed to avoid coming to grief, in contrast to the experience of Josephus on a voyage to Rome—on this occasion six hundred people were left to swim for their lives when the ship foundered in the Adriatic.[119]

Sea-travel, therefore, in these conditions hardly allowed for social divisions; passengers shared each other's fortunes in the course of a voyage, and might be expected, in difficulties, to join in saving their belongings, the ship, and—ultimately—themselves. Christians on their way to visit the desert fathers or the holy places of Palestine would be unable to isolate themselves from the demands of the voyage; for all his *desiderium* the pilgrim could not direct the winds, as Postumianus discovered when his ship lay becalmed off the coast of Africa.[120] Pilgrims confronted other familiar problems: there would be those who could not afford the fare, and actually worked their passage as members of the crew;[121] the monk Hilarion was lucky enough to find a sympathetic captain who, in lieu of a fare, was happy to take a copy of the Bible.[122] Presumably there were few who adopted the sheer audacity of Palladius' Sarapion, whose ascetic habits alone secured his passage from Alexandria to Rome: five days out from Alexandria the crew noticed that he had never taken anything to eat, and it came to light that he had nothing for his fare; 'Take me back whence you found me' was Sarapion's answer to their dilemma, confident that the crew would not welcome the prospect of turning back—he got to Rome for nothing![123]

A glimpse at the ordinary conditions of sea-travel which the Holy Land pilgrim might encounter thus points in the same direction as our consideration of the corresponding circumstances on land; all suggests the mingling and confusion

[118] Ibid. 37 (the *Vaticanus* has 'about 76').

[119] Joseph. *Vita*, 15.

[120] Sulp. Sev. *Dial.* i. 3.2; cf. the younger Melania's thwarted attempts to call at Nola, *V. Mel.* 19.

[121] Rougé (1966), 364.

[122] Jer. *V. Hilar.* 35.

[123] Pall. *Hist. Laus.* 37 (Butler, 112–3).

of individual travellers inherent in undertaking long journeys. Christian pilgrims could not expect to assert throughout their journeys (even with the growing network of 'purpose-built' hospitality) the particular identity of their enterprise. Such confusion has so far emerged as imposed by the existing conditions of travel; but an examination of another category of sea voyagers will indicate that some pilgrims might deliberately adopt a mode of travel which in itself had nothing distinctively Christian about it, but which was taken over from a 'secular' context and merely decked out with Christian trimmings—this recalls again the atmosphere of Helena's imperial progress through the eastern provinces.

Sea-travel had always presented the opportunity for a greater differentiation of style than was allowed on the sort of vessels discussed above.[124] For the voyager who was concerned to 'keep up appearances', even on the high seas, the slow coastal progress was to be preferred, avoiding the hazards of the open sea, and allowing repeated halts both to replenish supplies and to pay leisurely calls. Such would naturally be the style adopted by the emperors in presenting themselves to their subjects around the Mediterranean.[125] It is instructive, in this regard, to note the contrasting circumstances of their return to the West of Vespasian and Titus after the victory of the Flavian cause: Vespasian, having crossed from Alexandria to Rhodes on an ordinary merchant-vessel, then transferred to a fleet of triremes for a triumphant progress back to Italy, greeted with ovations everywhere he landed;[126] while Titus (precisely, it is alleged, to dispel suspicion of his imperial ambitions) arrived discreetly at Puteoli —as any ordinary traveller would—on board a cargo ship from Alexandria.[127] The point had been appositely presented by Cicero at the time of his own journey to his province: for a Roman official to land abroad from a small cargo vessel and without much luggage was 'not decorous enough'.[128] The

[124] For what follows, see J. Rougé (1953).

[125] So Philo, with reference to a projected voyage to Egypt by Caligula: *Legat. ad Gai.* 250ff.

[126] Joseph. *Bell. Jud.* vii. 21–2.

[127] Suet. *Titus*, 5; for the arrival of Alexandrian vessels at Puteoli, cf. Seneca, *Ep.* 77.1–3.

[128] Cic. *Ep. ad Att.* v. 9 'non satis . . . . . decorum'.

same punctilious regard for the decorous, with all its overtones of Roman senatorial dignity, emerges in the voyages of
well-to-do western pilgrims; not for them the cramped quarters on the deck of a grain vessel, or the perilous voyage in all
weathers. Her aristocratic relations saw off Paula and her
companions from the quay as she sailed for the East in the
summer of 385; it was to be a progress through the
Mediterranean which had all the marks of a leisured style,
with sightseeing and social calls *en route*.[129] The calls were
naturally emphatically Christian: the island of Pontia, sacred
to the memory of Flavia Domitilla (traditionally a pioneer
among Christian converts from the ranks of the Roman
nobility);[130] and the monasteries of Cyprus, where her host
was the bishop of Salamis, Epiphanius—whose hospitality
returned that he had earlier received from Paula in Rome.[131]
Yet however Christian the content of her voyage, its style
was that which flowed from her social station, and which she
inherited from long-established aristocratic habit. We can
see it in practice again (in a non-Christian setting) in the
voyage home from Rome in 417 of the Gallic senator Rutilius
Namatianus, who, despite the barbarian crisis at home, still
found time to pay calls on his friends who had villas near the
Italian coast.[132] The elder Melania, too, on returning to
Rome from the Holy Land in 400 stopped off her voyage at
Naples in order to pay a visit to her kinsman Paulinus at
Nola.[133]

Clearly such voyages implied the means and independence
to hire one's own vessel and sail at leisure from port to port,
accompanied by a private retinue. Among Christian pilgrims
the style is seen at its most demonstrative in the splendid
journey up the Nile of the noble lady Poemenia (whom we
shall later encounter in Jerusalem).[134] The motive of her
voyage was one of eminent piety, to visit the hermit John at

[129] Jer. *Ep.* 108.6.3ff. Cf. J. N. D. Kelly (1975), 116–17.

[130] For the Christian tradition on Domitilla, see Eus. *Chron.* s.a. 96 (ascribed to a
certain 'Bruttius'), and *Hist. Eccl.* iii. 18.4; according to Cassius Dio, lxvii. 14, she
was banished by Domitian to Pandateria for 'atheism'.

[131] Jer. *Ep.* 108.7.2–3.

[132] Rut. Namat. *De Reditu Suo*, 453ff., 491ff., 541ff.

[133] Paul. Nol. *Ep.* 29.12.

[134] See P. Devos (1969), and below, pp. 160ff.

Lycopolis in the Thebaid and seek from him the cure of an ailment, but its manner was anything but that of discreet and private devotion. She had sailed into Alexandria 'in her own boats' (we note the plural), and there transferred to a fleet of local ships to take her up river; her entourage of attendants included, apparently, eunuchs and Moorish slaves, as well as a complement of bishops and priests.[135] The notoriety of this grand procession on the Nile arises from an incident on the return journey to Alexandria when some of the local inhabitants of the town of Nikiupolis were involved in a brawl with Poemenia's followers, resulting in injury and even death among her company, abuse and threats directed at herself, and 'the most holy bishop Dionysius' being toppled into the river.[136] The Egyptians, clearly finding this army of visitors less than welcome, successfully disturbed the aristocratic decorum which had thus far characterized Poemenia's voyage. This array of boats on the Nile, the entourage of a single noble pilgrim, arouses interest. Poemenia was making devotional visits to Egyptian hermits, and she would go on to found a church on the Mount of Olives; yet, save for the presence of Christian clergy in her party, she was travelling with all the grandeur and style associated with the rich and leisured—far from being singled out as a distinctively Christian enterprise, her journey displays an almost aggressive intrusion of an aristocratic *panache*, the carrying over into a Christian pilgrimage of habits of travel which belong to a long 'secular' tradition. The sight of Poemenia and her boats on the Nile can hardly have been significantly different, say, from that of the emperor Hadrian's entourage in 130, or of any other of the celebrated visitors to the sights of Egypt who had preceded her. She is explicitly linked to this long line of distinguished tourists by her wish to visit Alexandria 'to investigate the city'.[137] 'ἱστορία', the spirit of learned curiosity, had brought tourists to Egypt ever since Herodotus, and was still effective in Poemenia's day[138]—two instances, from many, may be cited.

---

[135] Devos, 194.   [136] Pall. *Hist. Laus.* 35 (Butler, 106).
[137] Pall. l.c. 'ἱστορῆσαι τὴν πόλιν'.
[138] On tourism in Egypt, see L. Friedländer, *Darstellungen aus der Sittengeschichte Roms* (9th. edit. rev. Wissowa), i (1919), 421–44; N. Hohlwein (1940).

There had been the visit, at the behest of Constantine, of the pagan priest Nicagoras 'in the steps of Plato', attested among the inscriptions from the Tombs of the Kings;[139] while later another pagan and native of Egypt, Olympiodorus the diplomat and historian, would travel up the Nile 'in the interests of ἱστορία'.[140] Poemenia's trip to the Thebaid, despite its motive of Christian piety, thus reflected much of a tradition which lay outside Christianity, in long-standing travelling habits of antiquity.

The style of Poemenia's movements might well be compared with the journey of one Theophanes, an official on the staff of the *praefectus Aegypti*, who (*c.* 320) had travelled on government business to Antioch. A set of papyrus documents records his itinerary and the accounts for the journey, giving details of the equipment and supplies which his party required.[141] It was none other than Nikiupolis, the scene of Poemenia's riot, which was the starting-point for his journey to the easternmost estuary of the Nile and the coastal route to Antioch. Theophanes' expense accounts furnish a vivid illustration of the manner of travel which he and his party adopted, from the abundant variety of clothing supplied to the minute details of the menus served to the travellers (making full use of the local produce of Syria—figs, apricots, damsons, etc.);[142] the height of delicacy seems to have been reached at Byblos, where the purchase of some snow is recorded—presumably to keep the wine cool for the table.[143]

The provision for Theophanes' comfort on his journey reinforces the picture of Poemenia visiting holy places surrounded by the entourage and attention which went with her station in life. Christian pilgrim she may have been, but rather than adopt a mode of travel which might be thought to suit an enterprise of devotion, she conducted her pilgrimage with all the display which characterized the public behaviour of members of her class: the maintenance of the right

---

[139] See Fergus Millar, *JRS* 59 (1969), 17 ἱστορήσας τὰς θείας σύριγγας ἐθαύμασα.

[140] Olympiod. fr. 37 (*Frag. Hist. Graec.* iv, 66); cf. J. F. Matthews, *JRS* 60 (1970), 79ff.

[141] See C. H. Roberts (1952), B. R. Rees (1968).

[142] Clothing: Roberts, 117ff.; food, *passim* (e.g. notes at p. 131).

[143] Roberts, 141 (1.331).

style was paramount. This had always been a pre-eminent requirement in the movements of the upper classes of the Roman empire. Despite the long journeys dictated by their official careers, they had traditionally been a group which affected to dislike the discomfort and dislocation imposed by travelling, and which set boundaries no further than their own villas and estates.[144] Poemenia's contemporaries were no exception: the much-travelled Ammianus poured scorn on the Roman senators who found even a journey from Rome to Spoletium a superhuman effort, and a visit to their estates a labour equalled only by the travels of Alexander or Caesar;[145] Symmachus' own correspondence, in confirmation, documents his leisurely peregrinations around resorts in Campania.[146] What was all-important was that there should be no diminution of status in moving around: an extravagant carriage, extensive retinue—these sustained dignity and were the insulation against the intrusive difficulties of travelling; they were a way of life on the move, which could not be discarded as long as the traveller was in the public eye.[147] Seneca confesses that he once tried to make a journey as a simple traveller, taking with him just a few slaves (only as many, he concedes, as would fill one carriage) and only the clothes he was wearing; he rode in a rustic cart, drawn by poor old mules ('only by walking do the mules show that they are alive') and one bare-foot muleteer.[148] But, despite his efforts, he was unable to conceal his embarrassment on meeting the usual processions of noble travellers: 'I dare not parade frugality in public'.[149] Little, save for the Christian purpose of her movements, separates Poemenia from this maxim; the scene evoked by her passage down the Nile clear-

---

[144] Hence southern Italy is the limit of the restlessness of which Seneca complains among his peers: *De Tranquil. Animi*, 2.13.

[145] Amm. Marc. xiv. 6.24, xxviii. 4.18.

[146] See the convenient table in the introduction to the edition of Seeck (1883), lxvi; cf. J. A. McGeachy, *Quintus Aurelius Symmachus and the Senatorial Aristocracy of the West* (Chicago, 1942), 115–17.

[147] So Seneca, *Ep.* 123.7 'Omnes iam sic peregrinantur, ut illos Numidarum praecurrat equitatus, ut agmen cursorum antecedat; turpe est nullos esse qui occurrentis via deiciant, aut qui honestum hominem venire magno pulvere ostendant'.

[148] *Ep.* 87.2–4.

[149] Ibid. 5 'nondum audeo frugalitatem palam ferre; etiamnunc curo opiniones viatorum'.

ly displays that same *penchant* for self-advertisement which
Seneca had unsuccessfully sought to suppress. A similar pattern is revealed in a familiar chapter of Jerome. In presenting
(to Furia) a scheme of perfect Christian widowhood, he referred to the scandal associated with an unnamed female pilgrim visiting the holy places amid worldly luxury and a
splendid retinue:

> I have lately seen a scandalous object flitting this way and that
> through the East. Her age, her style, her dress, her gait, the indis-
> criminate company she kept, and the regal pomp of her elaborate
> dinners, all proclaimed her a fitting bride for Nero or
> Sardanapallus.[150]

His complaint about this showy affair centred, as might be
expected, on the reputation of the lady concerned, not on the
suitability or otherwise of such a style for travelling around
the Holy Land. Jerome's pilgrim, it seems, fitted into the
same mould as Poemenia; to her pilgrimage around the
Christian sites she transferred the assumptions of extravagance and show traditionally associated with upper-class
travel.

An uncompromising expression of aristocratic habits, then
(just as, from a different perspective, a congenial organization of Christian hospitality), might afford to the pilgrim on
his journey some kind of protective insulation from the
harshness of a long journey. Yet in the last resort such insulation should not be allowed to detract from the magnitude
of the pilgrim's enterprise—that vast land journey from Bordeaux to Jerusalem, or Egeria forging her way through the
desert of Sinai. The scale of these undertakings can only be
re-emphasized. A hardened traveller like Ammianus, even when
in flight from the Persian enemy, found a walk of ten miles
the limit of his endurance—he was unaccustomed, he confess-
ed, to going on foot.[151] Egeria, by contrast, accompanied by

---

[150] Jer. *Ep.* 54.13.3 (transl. Loeb, adapted). Jerome's mention of 'Nero or Sardanapallus' suggests someone associated in his eyes with the monastery of Melania the
elder on the Mount of Olives: see below, p. 171.

[151] Amm. Marc. .xix. 8.6 'incedendi nimietate iam superarer ut insuetus in-
genuus'.

the monks who were her guides, overcame the labour of reaching the summit of Sinai on foot, a height which, according to Postumianus, was inaccessible and 'almost touched the sky'.[152] Mount Nebo, too, was scaled by Egeria, most of the way on donkeys, but the final stages on foot.[153] It was, she affirms, her unremitting *desiderium* to visit the holy sites which conquered the difficulties involved,[154] and which would drive her on over long detours and hard desert terrain.

This is a spirit far removed from the comfortable assumptions of Poemenia's mode of travel. Whereas she conducted her pilgrimage according to a familiar worldly pattern, Egeria's was a determinedly unwordly assertion of her pious goals. The contrast between the two approaches is nowhere more strikingly presented than in Paulinus' account of the elder Melania's arrival at Nola on her return from Jerusalem in 400.[155] Mounted on a slender horse 'worth less than an ass', she was met by all the pomp of a senatorial reception: her rich relations flocked to greet her, the Via Appia 'groaning' beneath bedecked horses and gilded carriages. This splendid and opulent company confronted the woman of God returning from the Holy Land, dressed in simple garb and surrounded by a small band of saintly followers. Paulinus exulted that here was no fusion of contrasting styles, but rather the total 'confusion' of the worldly pattern in face of the display of Christian holiness: 'I witnessed the confounding of this world as was fitting to God, purple silk and golden ornaments doing service to old black rags.' He did not fail to exploit the potential of this *adventus*;[156] cast in precisely the terms of a traditional welcome for a high secular official,[157] yet its central character was here a model of Christian humil-

---

[152] Sulp. Sev. *Dial.* i. 17.2; for Egeria's ascent, *It. Eg.* 3.2 'cum grandi labore, quia pedibus me ascendere necesse est'.

[153] *It. Eg.* 11.4.

[154] Ibid. 3.2 'non sentiebatur labor, quia desiderium, quod habebam, iubente Deo videbam compleri'.

[155] Paul. Nol. *Ep.* 29.12–13.

[156] On Christian reinterpretations of the *adventus*, see S. MacCormack (1972).

[157] Compare Paulinus' account with, e.g., Pacatus' description of Theodosius' reception in Emona (*Paneg.* 37): 'festum liberae nobilitatis occursum, conspicuos veste nivea senatores, reverendos municipali purpura flamines, insignes apicibus sacerdotes . . . . .'.

ity 'outshining' the vain splendour of her former aristocratic
peers. The familiar pattern was overturned at its focal point,
and what might have been a great ceremony in 'secular'
terms became instead for Paulinus a triumphant expression
of Christian piety; a studied display of *humilitas* replaced
the arrival of a grandee. Such scenes evoked a similar response elsewhere. The Roman lady Fabiola arrived in Jerusalem to a huge reception, but immediately imported a distinctively Christian element into the occasion by withdrawing to the hospitality of the Bethlehem monastery.[158] Paula
had earlier waived the official reception in Jerusalem and the
proconsul's offer of hospitality, in favour of a 'humble cell'.[159]
The same robust presentation of Christian piety accompanied her departure from Antioch when on her way to the
holy places: bishop Paulinus escorted her on the road riding
on a donkey, 'the noble lady who earlier was used to being
carried by the hands of eunuchs'.[160] Like Paulinus, Jerome
here made the most of the 'confusion' of secular values inherent
in this scene.

Such set-piece descriptions as these episodes at Nola, Jerusalem, and Antioch might be dismissed as careful literary
presentations in which Paulinus and Jerome indulged in im-
aginative elaboration of the scenes which they had witnessed.
It is less easy to thrust aside the picture of Egeria labor-
iously ascending the mountain of Sinai. Here was an authentic expression of Christian purpose before which the obsta-
cles of the journey dissolved—the goal was all-important.
What drove Egeria towards the summit of Sinai in this determined fashion was the place's association with momentous
events from the Old Testament. By her resolve to reach, at
all costs, the place where the Lord had come down to speak
to Moses she was confirming that the Christian character of
her journey rested ultimately on biblical foundations. The
pilgrim's destination was the land of the Bible.

---

[158] Jer. *Ep*. 77.7.1.   [159] Id. *Ep*. 108.9.2.   [160] Ibid. 7.3.

4. Pilgrims and the Bible (i) The Holy Places

OUR earliest known pilgrim journey to the Holy Land, that of Melito of Sardis, had been an essentially *biblical* quest, to establish an accurate canon of the Old Testament—to this end Melito had sought the authority of the land 'where these things were preached and done'.[1] In this he was pointing the way to the fundamental impetus which was to underlie the concentration of pilgrims at the holy places—and to drive Egeria on to the summit of Sinai. Whatever the varied experiences of the journey which brought them there, we can be certain that it was the same basic *desiderium*, rooted in the Bible, which impelled them all towards Palestine. Whether it was the solid literalism of those who expected to see every line of the Scriptures brought to reality before their eyes, or the sober and learned interest of a biblical scholar such as Origen, it was always the Bible which inspired their enterprise, and indeed shaped their whole conception of the Holy Land.

This can be amply demonstrated from the detailed record of his visit to the holy places in 333 left us by the pilgrim from Bordeaux. After his long journey across the breadth of the Roman empire, his arrival at his destination plunged him at once into an exclusively biblical world. Each of the sites which he records having visited in the Holy Land was labelled by its precise Scriptural associations, neither more nor less; to the names of the places where he halted he appended a bald statement of the biblical event which was there com-

[1] Eus. *Hist. Eccl.* iv. 26.14. Cf. above, p. 3.

memorated. This is more often than not an item of Old
Testament history—and 'history' it was, for the pilgrim always acceded without demur to the biblical traditions cultivated at a particular spot. The past which he went in search
of was the narrative of the Bible, and this he expected to see
mapped out in contemporary Palestine. Only a handful of
non-biblical reminiscences appear to have caught the pilgrim's attention on his travels: the tomb, for example, of
Hannibal at Libyssa, the memorials of the sage Apollonius
at Tyana, or the burial-place of Euripides.[2] Perhaps most
strikingly of all, he passed through the city of Rome on his
return from the East without even the briefest mention of
anything that was to be seen there. *Urbs Roma* was, for the
pilgrim, only a stage on the return journey—nothing of its
great past seems to have stirred his enthusiasm.[3]

By contrast, his narrative is crowded with the biblical past
evoked by the sites of the Holy Land. I quote a few examples. As he approached Jerusalem, he saw the village of
Bethar; nearby was Bethel, where Jacob as he journeyed to
Mesopotamia experienced his vision of the ladder rising up
to heaven; here too the prophet who had disobeyed the word
of the Lord was killed by a lion (and the pilgrim provides a
summary of the story from I Kings).[4] Again, on his way
down to the Jordan, the pilgrim passed through Jericho, now
the third town on this historic site; here was the house of
Rahab and the scene of Joshua's triumphant assault on the
walls, while not far away lay the twelve stones which the
tribes of Israel had removed from the bed of the Jordan as
they crossed.[5] Another excursion took him to the south of
Jerusalem and to Hebron, rich in memories of Abraham and
the patriarchs.[6] But it was, of course, not solely the history of
the Old Testament which captivated the visitor from Bor-

[2] *It. Burd.* 572, 4 (tomb of Hannibal); 578, 1 (Apollonius); 604, 7 (Euripides).
Other non-biblical points: 564, 9; 606, 1.
[3] Ibid. 612, 4. Cf. Jer. *Ep.* 121, Apodemius visited Bethlehem from Gaul 'Roma
praeterita'.
[4] Ibid. 588, 9ff. (cf. Genesis, 28.12, 32.24; I Kings, 13). By Jerome's day a
church had been built here: *Onomastikon*, 7. On this, and all Holy Land sites, see the
useful *Gazetteer* in J. Wilkinson (1977), 149ff.
[5] 596, 10ff. (cf. Joshua, 2.1ff., 4). For the three cities of Jericho, see Eus. *Onomastikon*, 104 'ἑτέρα ἐκ τρίτου συνέστη εἰς ἔτι νῦν δεικνυμένη πόλις'.
[6] 599, 8 (cf. Gen. 23), with J. Jeremias (1958), 90ff.

deaux. Jerusalem, particularly, was full of the memorials of the events of Holy Week, Christ's Passion and Resurrection, from Golgotha and the Tomb itself to the remains of the house of Caiaphas or the column of the Flagellation on Mount Sion.[7] Among other memories of the New Testament he would view the place of the Nativity at Bethlehem, and the scene of the encounter with the woman of Samaria at Jacob's Well.[8]

Even this bare (and selective) catalogue cannot conceal the total prominence of the Bible motivating the Bordeaux pilgrim in the Holy Land. His rigidly historical approach to the events of the Scriptures was prepared not only to behold *in the Jerusalem of the fourth century* Zacchaeus' sycamore-tree or the palm-tree whose branches were strewn on the road at the Triumphal Entry,[9] but even to see a surviving stone among the Temple ruins as 'the stone which the builders rejected' of Psalm 118.[10] There was no limit to the possibilities of bringing the Bible to life before his eyes; the biblical associations (no matter how fragile) constituted the credentials of a pilgrim site, distinguishing it as a holy place. The traveller depended for these local traditions on the monks and clergy who had charge of the site; they transmitted its biblical import to the pilgrim, often with no lack of the pious credulity of the 'simpliciores fratres' to which Jerome was later to allude—and indeed on precisely a point where the Bordeaux pilgrim was (as always) convinced, namely that the bloodstains of Zechariah could still be seen on the Temple site.[11] Our pilgrim, furthermore, seems to have been told, erroneously,—and accepted—that the scene of Christ's Transfiguration lay on the Mount of Olives.[12]

[7] 592, 4ff. (Sion); 593, 4ff. (Golgotha). On New Testament sites generally, see C. Kopp (1959–63).

[8] 598, 6 (Bethlehem); 588, 2ff. (Jacob's Well: cf. John, 4).

[9] 596, 5–6 (Zacchaeus); cf. Anton. Placent. *Itin.* 15. 595, 1 (palm-tree), also mentioned by Cyril, *Catech.* x. 19, and Pet. Diac. *Liber de locis sanctis* I (*CC* 175, 96).

[10] 590, 3 (cf. Psalm 118.22).

[11] 591, 2; cf. Jer. *Comm. in Matt.* 23.35 (*CC* 77, 220) 'non condemnamus errorem qui de odio Iudaeorum et fidei pietate descendit', with F. M. Abel (1920), 142–4.

[12] 595, 6ff; cf. the belief among the 'simpliciores fratres' that the Beatitudes belonged on the Mount of Olives, 'quod nequaquam ita est', Jer. *Comm. in Matt.* 5.1 (*CC* 77, 24). By the middle of the century Mt. Tabor had settled as the site of the Transfiguration: Cyril, *Catech.* xii. 16. On the errors of the 'sanctorum locorum . . . . . monstratores', cf. Jer. *Comm. in Esai.* xi, 38.4ff. (*CC* 73, 445).

After the stark narrative of the Bordeaux pilgrim, Egeria's description of her pilgrimage furnishes a more penetrating glimpse into the devotion of the Christian traveller. It can be illustrated from her movements in the desert of Sinai, around the sites associated with the experiences of Moses and the children of Israel. She was shown, for example, the bush from which the Lord had spoken to Moses in the fire, 'the bush which is still alive and sprouting';[13] she was shown where the golden calf had been erected during Moses' absence on the mountain ('where a large stone was set in the ground and still stands'), a mountain which still dominated the scene wherever Egeria looked, as it had done in the days of the Exodus;[14] she was shown the huge rock against which Moses in his anger had broken the tablets of the Law; the remains of the dwellings of the children of Israel in the desert; the place where the Seventy elders were endowed with the Spirit by Moses; where part of the camp of the Israelites was consumed by fire; where the camp was covered with quails, and the manna fell from heaven. The list does not end here, but it may be summed up in Egeria's own words:

So we were shown everything which the Books of Moses tell us took place in that valley beneath holy Sinai, the mount of God.... it may help you, loving sisters, *the better to picture what happened in these places* when you read the holy books of Moses.[15]

Egeria here makes explicit the relationship between familiarity with the text of the Bible and the desire to visit the holy places of Palestine. The pilgrim was accorded the privilege of seeing in reality what his fellow-Christians at home or in the local congregations always saw in the imagination as the biblical narratives were read; for the pilgrim it was a visualization, in the contemporary setting, of the familiar texts. Such was the enticement which Jerome held out to encourage visitors to the holy places:

[13] *It. Eg.* 4.6–5.2 'qui rubus usque in hodie vivet et mittet virgultas' (cf. Exodus, 3).
[14] Ibid. 5.3ff. (cf. Exod. 32).
[15] Ibid. 5.8 (transl. J. Wilkinson (1971), 97–8).

To worship at the place where the feet of the Lord have stood is the task of faith (*pars fidei*), and to have set eyes on the traces of the Nativity, the Cross and Passion, as though they were newly-made.[16]

Marcella was urged to come to the Holy Land and re-live before her eyes the Gospel narratives.[17] But it was the pilgrimage of Paula above all which demonstrated this enthusiasm to 'see more clearly' the biblical past: in a hectic burst she traversed the holy places, at every turn witnessing the life of Christ unfold before her—at one moment prostrate before the cross, 'as though she looked upon the Lord hanging there',[18] at another standing in the cave of the Nativity affirming to Jerome that she beheld there the child in the manger, the Magi and shepherds adoring, and the star shining above.[19] Characteristically, it was no ordinary eyesight, but the 'eyes of faith' which supplied Paula with these images. With similarly vivid (and credulous) devotion Egeria traced out in the desert of Sinai, 'according to the Bible', the erratic steps of the children of Israel, scarcely comprehending the irregularity of their route.[20]

The Bible was both Egeria's guide-book and the dominant influence on the language and presentation of her narrative.[21] All that she saw was in response to her demand to be shown the settings of the events of the Bible—an impetus which was as clear to the Spanish monk Valerius writing of Egeria in the seventh century as it is to readers of what survives of her narrative today.[22] At one point only does Egeria display a hint of scepticism with regard to what was pointed out to her: the place where the pillar of salt into which Lot's wife had been transformed had allegedly stood was visible from the summit of Mount Nebo, but according to the local bishop the pillar itself had several years earlier

---

[16] Jer. *Ep.* 47.2.2. Cf. J. Wilkinson (1977), 40ff.

[17] Id. *Ep.* 46.13; cf. ibid. 5.3 '....iacere in sindone *cernimus* salvatorem...rursum *videmus* angelum sedere ad pedes eius'.

[18] Id. *Ep.* 108.9.2.

[19] Ibid. 10.2; cf. the comments of J. N. D. Kelly (1975), 123–4. On Paula's pilgrimage, see below, pp. 171ff.

[20] *It. Eg.* 7.2–3.   [21] See J. Ziegler (1931b).

[22] *Ep. Valerii*, 1 'cuncta igitur veteris ac novi testamenti omni indagatione percurrens volumina...' (*Anal. Boll.* 29 (1910), 394).

been washed away by the Dead Sea. Only the actual pillar, however, would have convinced Egeria: '. . . we did not see it, and I cannot pretend we did'.[23]

It is clear that Egeria herself saw her pilgrimage as an endeavour intimately related to her understanding of the Bible. For her the central feature of the worship which she and her companions conducted at each holy site was always the reading of the relevant passage of the Bible. Thus, for instance, at the cave on Mount Horeb where Elijah was said to have fled from king Ahab, the appropriate portion of I Kings was read at the service.[24] This association of Bible reading and pilgrimage sites runs right through Egeria's narrative —from her own private devotions at each stopping-place to the public liturgy of the church in Jerusalem. What impressed Egeria (as will be noted) was the observation that biblical lessons in the Holy Land could always be appropriate to the place where the faithful were assembled and to the event commemorated, 'apta diei et loco'.[25] The Bible reading to which she was accustomed in the West, by contrast, was remote from the physical context of the narrative and, as a result, would have seemed disembodied—whereas the visible holy places of Jerusalem and Palestine formed precisely that element of secure reality which was missing elsewhere.

Just before Egeria visited the Holy Land, the Cappadocian bishop Gregory of Nyssa was also touring the holy places.[26] In a letter to three ladies of his congregation he recorded his impression of what he had seen.[27] For Gregory the great New Testament sites were *symbols* of the salvation that lay in Christ, analogous to the Christian life as a whole.[28] To follow Christ anywhere was to be born with him in Bethlehem, to be crucified with him on Golgotha, to roll away the stone from the tomb of mortal life, and rise with him to the life immortal. For the true Christian Bethlehem, Golgotha, the

---

[23] *It. Eg.* 12.6–7. The column came and went: cf. J. Wilkinson (1971), 219–20.

[24] Ibid. 4.3 (I Kings, 19.9); cf. 10.7.

[25] E.g. 47.5; cf. below, pp. 120ff.

[26] Returning from a diplomatic mission to the church in Arabia *c.* 380; Greg. Nys. *Ep.* 2.12 (for the date, cf. P. Maraval, *SChr* 178, 65–6).

[27] *Ep.* 3.1–2.

[28] For similar language, cf. *V. Macrinae*, 1 (ed. P. Maraval, *SChr* 178, 138), and *Ep.* 2.2.

Mount of Olives and the empty Tomb should always be before his eyes as spiritual pointers to the godly life. Gregory rejoices that he sees in the Christian conduct of his correspondents precisely such spiritual signs of the holy places which he himself had witnessed with his own eyes.[29]

So where Egeria had seen the solid manifestation of a biblical narrative, Gregory saw a stimulus to the Christian life. Egeria's response to the holy places was, primarily, one which viewed them as a visible witness to historical events, whereas for Gregory the physical remains were important only as an indication of that inner spirituality which should be the possession of Christians anywhere. Such a contrast is emphasized by a comparison of Egeria's pages on her wanderings through the desert of Sinai and the same Gregory of Nyssa's *Life of Moses* (written *c*.392). This is a work of spiritual instruction (sub-titled 'Treatise on Perfection in Virtue'), of which the first part is presented as a historical treatment of the story of Moses, 'just as we have learnt from holy Scripture', while the second, and much more substantial, part unfolds its symbolic interpretation as a rule for the perfect Christian life.[30] Gregory may have travelled to Sinai while he was in Palestine; certainly he will have met those who had been there; yet his historical exposition never once relates the life of Moses to the fourth-century pilgrim sites. It would never be realized, for instance, in reading the *Life of Moses*, that the bush from which the Lord spoke to Moses out of the fire was actually being shown to pilgrims like Egeria at the time that Gregory was writing.[31] Again, at the close of the *Life*, Gregory records the final ascent of Moses 'up a lofty mountain' to behold the Promised Land, before his death 'leaving no sign or memorial of his departure';[32] there is no mention here of Mount Nebo in Transjordan, where a shrine on the summit covered the spot where Moses was believed to be buried. Egeria was among the visitors to this place.[33]

---

[29] *Ep.* 3.3.   [30] See *V. Moysi*, 15.   [31] Ibid. 20.

[32] Ibid. 75 (cf. Deuteron. 34.6 'but no man knows the place of his burial till this day').

[33] *It. Eg.* 12.1–2: to reconcile the presence of a tomb with the biblical tradition, Egeria reported the story that Moses had been buried by angels. Later, an alternative explanation arose: *V. Pet. Iber.* 88 (= J. Wilkinson (1977), 57). For the remains, see S. J. Saller (1941), 23ff., and Avi-Yonah (ed.), *Encyclopedia*, iii, 923–6.

From here the pilgrims could, as Moses before them, view the Promised Land spread out beneath their feet. While Egeria was able to follow, step by step, the wanderings of the children of Israel, for Gregory the historical life of Moses was a stimulus to Christian behaviour—a rule of conduct:[34] it was necessary to 'see through' history to find the model to be imitated.[35] In this work he was in no way concerned to locate the events on the map of fourth-century Palestine. The same might be said of Fabiola's learned interest in the travels of the children of Israel in the desert, which was to be satisfied by an exposition from Jerome of the symbolic interpretation of the stages recorded in Numbers ch. 33;[36] there is no indication that she sought to follow Egeria in actually tracing the route for herself.

Fabiola, and Gregory, were not, of course, the first Christians to view the Exodus narrative in this light; such symbolic interpretations went back to the New Testament and St. Paul.[37] We may suspect that it came down to Gregory via the work of Origen, who had preceded him in seeing the fortunes and progress of the children of Israel as a model of spiritual illumination and instruction.[38] Origen was, of course, the prime exponent of an exegetical tradition which, while it recognized the importance of the historical interpretation of biblical texts,[39] nevertheless set more store by their allegorical significance; the immediate and literal sense was only a key with which to reveal the full spiritual meaning concealed in every word of the Scriptures.[40] But the biblical associations of the holy places (at least as illustrated in the reactions of Egeria or the pilgrim from Bordeaux) belonged unmistakably to this literal realm; the scholar interested in the deeper meaning of the Bible would find here

---

[34] For his historical exposition as *moral edification*, see Daniélou's introduction to his edition of *V. Moysi* (*SChr* 1, 3rd edit. 1968), 17ff.

[35] *V. Moysi*, 14.

[36] See Jer. *Ep.* 78.1 on the search for the 'spiritual' meaning.

[37] Cf. J. Daniélou, *From Shadows to Reality* (Eng. transl. 1960), 153ff.

[38] E.g. Orig. *De Principiis*, iv. 3.12; *In Exod. Hom.* 5.

[39] Cf. *De Princ.* iv. 3.4 'πολλῷ γὰρ πλείονά ἐστι τὰ κατὰ τὴν ἱστορίαν ἀληθευόμενα τῶν προσυφανθέντων γυμνῶν πνευματικῶν'.

[40] Ibid. iv, *passim*, e.g. 2.9 'ἀποκρύπτων ἀπὸ τῶν πολλῶν τὸν βαθύτερον νοῦν...'.

only the simple faith of the multitude, a faith which could not penetrate through the world of sensible realities to the eternal mystery which, lay beyond.[41] This was a mystery which was not to be confined to a narrow tract of land in Palestine:[42] Christianity (so it was argued) had swept away the locally-based worship of the Jews, tied to the Temple in Jerusalem, and had replaced it with a universal faith—which demanded no resort to any holy places in Jerusalem, but the sincere worship of a true follower of Christ, 'in spirit and in truth', irrespective of place.[43]

Such a line of argument, decisively at odds with the pilgrims' literalistic regard for the actual holy places, was effectively employed in two letters of advice to professed ascetics by Gregory of Nyssa himself and by Jerome (writing to Paulinus of Nola), in which they sought to *dissuade* their correspondents from undertaking a pilgrimage to the Holy Land. The letters have become the classic statement of the 'spiritual' objections to the would-be pilgrim's 'literal' enthusiasm for the biblical remains.[44] Gregory and Jerome appeal to the condition of a man's soul, that he should be open to the Spirit 'blowing where it wills'.[45] His location is immaterial: 'non Hierosolymis fuisse, sed Hierosolymis bene vixisse laudandum est'. Jerome adduces the armies of monks who had never seen Jerusalem—yet the 'door of Paradise' lay open for them; for Gregory it was the numerous altars of Cappadocia—were they to be held to be ineffectual?[46] In all it is the irrelevance of place for Christian devotion which is stressed: a man must carry his cross everywhere, and be risen with Christ every day; no bonus came from the wooden

[41] Cf. H. Crouzel (1961), 239–49. On the association of pilgrimage with the literal sense of the Bible, cf. Paul. Nol. *Ep.* 49.14 'simplici sensu secundum litteram... non abutendum est'.

[42] Cf. Jer. *Ep.* 58.3.1 'non audeo dei omnipotentiam angusto fine concludere et artare parvo terrae loco, quem non capit caelum'.

[43] Orig. *Hom. in Josh.* (*SChr* 71), 17.1; Eus. *Dem. Evang.* i. 6 (e.g. 39–40, 44, 57); Jer. *Comm. in Esai.* v, 23.18 (*CC* 73, 223) 'servire autem domino... non est loci, sed meriti'.

[44] Greg. Nys. *Ep.* 2; Jer. *Ep.* 58 (Jerome and Gregory had met in Constantinople in 381: Kelly (1975), 71). Cf. B. J. Kötting (1959). Gregory's letter was at the centre of controversy in the church in later centuries, and its authenticity questioned.

[45] Greg. *Ep.* 2.16ff., Jer. *Ep.* 58.3.

[46] Jer. *Ep.* 58.3.4, Greg. *Ep.* 2.8–9.

relics, or from the sight of the actual Tomb.[47] Jerome would choose the occasion of an annual veneration of the cross to elaborate precisely these themes in a sermon:

> By the cross I mean not the wood, but the Passion. That cross is in Britain, in India, in the whole world. . . . Happy is he who carries in his own heart the cross, the resurrection, the place of the Nativity of Christ and of his Ascension.[48]

(We are very close here to Gregory's rationalization of his own pilgrimage.) Views like this belong to the same kind of intellectual tradition as the allegorical exegesis of Origen and his followers; they appear to leave little room for the historical claims of the holy places.

And yet there is at least one unambiguous hint in his writings that Origen did not neglect completely the biblical remains in the Holy Land. In a famous passage discussing John 1.28, he raises the question of the place where John was baptizing—'at Bethany beyond Jordan' according to the received text. But the Bethany that Origen knew was the village on the slopes of the Mount of Olives two miles out of Jerusalem, home of the family of Lazarus; and he was persuaded that the reading in this verse of John should be, not Bethany, but 'Bethabora'. This was a village on the banks of the Jordan where there was a tradition that John had baptized, as he had discovered on a visit to the area, 'in search of the traces of Jesus and his disciples and the prophets'.[49] Origen, it would seem from this passage, travelled round some parts of Palestine with the pilgrim's eye for the vestiges of the historical Bible. He certainly knew his topography, though we can hardly say how much of the knowledge was acquired from personal travel and observation; he affirmed that the so-called 'Gadarene' swine had nothing to do with Gadara, but rather belonged to the town of Gergesa on the shores of lake Galilee, where the location of their careering over the cliff was 'shown' to visitors;[50] he was aware of the

---

[47] Jer. *Ep.* 58.3.3.   [48] *Tract. de Ps. xcv* (*CC* 78, 154).

[49] *Comm. in Joh.* vi. 40 (ed. C. Blanc, *SChr* 157, 284ff.). On Bethany-Bethabora, see C. Kopp (1963), 113ff.

[50] Ibid. vi. 41. The place is Kursi, site of a 5th cent. church and monastery: C. Kopp (1959), 284ff., and *Rev. Bibl.* 79 (1972), 409ff.

cave of the Nativity, familiar to pilgrims to Bethlehem,[51] and of the tomb of Rachel on the road into the village;[52] he knew, too, of the Tomb of the Patriarchs at Hebron;[53] and had apparently seen the famous wells of Ascalon allegedly dug by Abraham—he comments on 'their strange and extraordinary style of construction in comparison with other wells'.[54] (Significantly, Eustathius of Antioch was to complain of Origen's allegorical interpretation of these wells 'when even to this day they are still to be seen'.)[55]

Thus, even if the intellectual tradition to which Origen belonged, and his emphasis on the deeper meaning of Scripture, would not dispose him to appeal to the existence of the holy places, he can nevertheless be seen to have displayed a detailed interest in the physical location of the biblical events. But there was much more to this than the visual realism and simple faith of the pilgrim. In part it was a further aspect of exegesis, for Origen inherited from the Jewish tradition a propensity for the allegorical interpretation of Hebrew place-names;[56] thus his identification of 'Bethabora' is supported by his (mistaken) understanding of its meaning as 'house of preparation' (appropriate for the place of Christ's baptism), whereas 'Bethany' was interpreted as 'house of obedience', fitting the home of the dutiful family of Mary and Martha. Similarly 'Gergesa', meaning 'residence of those cast out', was a name appropriate to the incident of the swine.[57] An interest in the location of the biblical place-names obviously went hand-in-hand with this concern for their correct interpretation. The point was to be made explicit in a passage of Jerome:

---

[51] *C. Cels.* i. 51.

[52] *Comm. in Matt.* fr. 34 (*GCS* 41, 29).

[53] *De Princ.* iv. 3.4.

[54] *C. Cels.* iv. 44; cf. H. Chadwick, *Origen: Contra Celsum* (1965), 219, and Eus. *Onomastikon*, 168.

[55] *De Engastrimytho*, 21 (ed. Klostermann, *Kleine Texte* 83, 1912)—the whole treatise is an attack on Origen's allegorical method.

[56] Cf. Jerome, *Liber Interpret. Hebraic. Nominum*, pref. (*CC* 72, 59): Origen and Philo. See N. R. M. De Lange (1976), 117–21.

[57] Orig. *Comm. in Joh.* vi. 40–1 'he who wishes fully to understand holy Scripture must not neglect accuracy with regard to the names'. For discussion of Origen's interpretations, see Blanc, l.c.

...The man who has seen Judaea with his own eyes, and who knows the sites of ancient cities, and their names whether the same or changed, will gaze more clearly upon Holy Scripture.[58]

The context in which this citation occurs opens up a wider perspective against which to set the biblical scholar's interest in Palestinian topography. For Jerome places it in the tradition of the learned tourism of the past which had sought out the sites of classical history and literature; he evokes the student of Greek history visiting Athens, or the Virgilian scholar following the voyage of Aeneas through the Mediterranean. In similar vein, elsewhere, Jerome found in the Holy Land the 'studiorum fastigium' of the Christian, equivalent in significance to the position of Athens at the centre of Greek learning.[59] Thus the interest in the holy places of the Bible was here assimilated to a long-standing tradition of travel for intellectual and scholarly purposes. Origen implied such a view by his use of the term 'ἱστορία' to label his movements in Palestine, a word which summons up habits of learned tourism going back to Herodotus.[60] Against this background Christians journeying in search of the biblical remains might have recalled, for example, those second-century travellers who went, Pausanias in hand, to seek out the sites of classical Greece.[61]

The activities of pilgrim and scholar, at first apparently divergent, are now seen to share common ground. The topographical precision necessary for an accuracy of text and interpretation of the Scriptures, together with a wider framework (inherited from its classical background) of intellectual investigation 'on the ground', ensured that the biblical sites after all had some place in the scholarly tradition. As far back as the reign of Caracalla, Alexander, the future bishop of Jerusalem, had come to the holy places from Cappadocia 'for the purpose of prayer and investigation', thus combining the devotion of the pilgrim with the spirit of intel-

---

[58] *Praef. in Lib. Paralip.* (*PL* 29, 401). For the conclusion, however, that Jerome had no extensive personal experience of Palestinian topography (beyond his own pilgrimage), see J. Wilkinson (1974).

[59] Jer. *Ep.* 46.9.   [60] Cf. above, pp. 77–8.

[61] Cf. the introduction to J. G. Frazer's translation of Pausanias (1913), xxiv.

lectual curiosity.[62] Both strands came together in the Holy Land precisely because of its remains of the biblical past, which answered to both piety and learning.

It was Jerusalem which had pride of place in this biblical past. In Origen's day, of course, much of this past was obscured by the Roman colony of Aelia Capitolina—but this fact only fostered the biblical perspective in which Origen viewed the city which he must often have visited from Caesarea.[63] The destruction of the physical heart of Judaism, the desolation of the Temple and the termination of the cult, had, naturally, a profound significance for Christians: Origen saw it as marking the end of all the paraphernalia of the cultic worship of the Jews, instituted by Moses in the desert, which the advent of Christ had superseded; the destruction of the earthly Jerusalem had opened the way to the establishment of the heavenly city.[64] The whole history of the people of God, as represented in the Bible, culminating in Christ's inauguration of the new Covenant, thus found its echo in the fate of the Jewish capital. In seeing biblical history represented in the contemporary state of Jerusalem Origen was exploring ideas which would be given their fullest expression by another scholar of Caesarea, bishop Eusebius.

Eusebius of Caesarea was the foremost biblical scholar of his time.[65] His was a study of the Bible which could not be divorced from contemporary history. In his own lifetime he had seen the church survive a period of violent persecution to emerge in triumph, its opponents vanquished, and with a Christian emperor on the throne. The palpable facts of the success of Christianity had, in Eusebius' eyes, superseded the whole course of the debate between Christian apologists and their pagan opponents:

. . . . all words are superfluous, when the works are more manifest and plain than words—works which the divine and heavenly pow-

---

[62] Eus. *Hist. Eccl.* vi. 11.2.

[63] Epiphanius, *Panarion*, 64.2, mentions Origen preaching in Jerusalem; cf. P. Nautin (1977), 71.

[64] E.g. *Hom. in Josh.* 17.1, *Hom. in Levit.* 10.1, *Comm. in Matt.* 16.3, *C. Cels.* iv.22.

[65] See D. S. Wallace-Hadrill (1960), 59ff., citing *testimonia* from *Nicene and post-Nicene Fathers*, i (1895), 57ff.

er of our Saviour distinctly exhibits even now, while preaching good tidings of the divine and heavenly life to all men.[66]

His presentation of the faith is profoundly *historical*:[67] the Scriptural prophecies to which the Christians laid claim had been validated in the course of history, by the birth of the 'universal' empire of the Romans, by the disasters which had been inflicted on the Jewish nation, and, triumphantly, in the appearance of Constantine. His Christian panorama saw a historical continuum encompassing Abraham and Constantine, taking in on the way the Old Testament prophets, the events of the Gospels, the growth of the Roman empire and the destruction of the Jews. His view of the events of his own day was thus firmly rooted in the Bible; history had vindicated the claims of Scripture.

This theme lies at the base of all Eusebius''apologetic' works, including both the *Chronicle* and the *Ecclesiastical History*.[68] But it is to be seen most fully set out in the *Demonstratio Evangelica* (compiled in the second decade of the fourth century). Here, having established that the prophecies of the Old Testament may justifiably be claimed as their own by the Christians, Eusebius proceeds to his 'demonstration' of the faith ('ἀπόδειξις') by pointing to the historical fulfilment of these prophecies in the life of Christ and the progress of the Christian church. The picture is dominated by the preoccupation, already presaged in Origen, with the fate of the Jews and the destruction of the Temple, which, by a good deal of chronological licence, is brought into association with the advent of Christ and the establishment of the Augustan *pax Romana*—this alone provided the stage for the universal spread of Christianity.[69] For Eusebius this was a preoccupation fostered by the evidence of his own eyes: 'in our own time we have seen Sion ploughed with yokes of oxen by the Romans and utterly devastated'—as the prophet Micah had

[66] *Praep. Evang.* i.3 (transl. E. H. Gifford (1903), 8).

[67] So Wallace-Hadrill, 168ff. 'The Purpose of God and Human History'.

[68] See H. Berkhof (1939), 39ff. 'Eusebius als Apologet'; cf. now R. M. Grant, *Eusebius as Church Historian* (1980), ch. ix.

[69] E.g. among many passages, *Dem. Evang.* iii. 7.30ff., vi. 18.4ff., viii. 1.51. The synchronization of Christ and Augustus was a theme of the Apologists, cf. Melito of Sardis in Eus. *Hist. Eccl.* iv. 26.7.

proclaimed, 'Sion shall be ploughed as a field'.[70] He had seen inhabitants of Jerusalem pillaging stones from the ruins; the very stones of the Temple had gone to build pagan shrines and theatres.[71] He will have stood with Christian pilgrims congregating on the Mount of Olives to behold with satisfaction, across the Kidron valley, the 'Abomination of Desolation' (as from that very spot Christ had predicted, recalling the words of the prophet Daniel) standing on the site of Solomon's Temple[72]—in fact the two statues of Jupiter and the emperor Hadrian which surmounted the Temple rock in Roman Aelia.[73]

Thus it becomes clear how the evidence of the physical remains in Jerusalem could serve for Eusebius as an extension of his 'demonstration' of the Christian faith; they were a readily observable, and historical, verification of the claims of the Bible. A great part of Eusebius' literary output was concerned precisely to uphold these claims, and the holy places could be marshalled in support—they served both to secure and to augment the testimony of the Scriptures.

The import which Eusebius attached to the holy places emerges at its clearest in his topographical guide to the place-names of the Bible, the so-called *Onomastikon*.[74] This work was dedicated to Eusebius' fellow-bishop, Paulinus of Tyre—at a date, it is recognized, before the Christian development of the Holy Land; perhaps even at the very beginning of the century.[75] It was the last in a series of geographical works, following on a translation into Greek of the Hebrew names in the Bible for the nations of the world, a description of ancient Judaea and its twelve tribes, and a plan of Jerusalem and the Temple; none of these predecessors survives, yet Eusebius' summary of them confirms his interest in the biblical topography of Palestine. It was his

---

[70] *Dem. Evang.* vi. 13.17, cf. viii. 3.9.

[71] Ibid. viii. 3.11–12. Jerome too saw ruins of the Temple in his day: *Tract. de Ps. cxvix* (*CC* 78, 247).

[72] *Dem. Evang.* vi. 18.23, with viii. 2.121ff. (cf. Matthew, 24.15; Luke, 21.20). (Note also the Christian satisfaction at the annual return of the Jews to mourn the loss of the Temple: Jer. *Comm. in Soph.* i. 15 (*CC* 76a, 673–4)).

[73] Cf. above, pp. 1–2.

[74] Cf. Wallace-Hadrill, appendix 'Eusebius and the Topography of Palestine'.

[75] See P. Thomsen (1903), 101, and T. D. Barnes (1975).

concern in the *Onomastikon* to relate this biblical setting to the map of contemporary Palestine:

> ... to extract the names of the towns and villages mentioned in the Bible, describing the location of those places and the names by which they are known today—whether these are the same as of old or have been changed.[76]

Such a purpose recalls the interests of the biblical scholar in the details of topography and nomenclature (Jerome echoed Eusebius' words in a passage already cited);[77] and that Eusebius was no stranger to this tradition is confirmed by his incorporation into the *Onomastikon* of Origen's identification of Bethabora and Gergesa.[78]

Yet Eusebius' guide is more widely related to the development of the holy places.[79] In seeking to bring together the locations familiar from the Bible and their counterparts in the Palestine of the fourth century he is answering directly to that historical and visual approach to the Scriptures characteristic of the pilgrim. Such an approach aimed precisely to locate the biblical narratives in the contemporary surroundings. Thus Eusebius' method was to superimpose the biblical setting, as represented by its place-names, on to the organization of the Roman province in which he lived. As he went through the books of the Bible extracting the names and assembling them in alphabetical order he added to each its biblical context and, often, a note on the meaning of the name; finally, wherever possible (Eusebius only succeeded in about a third of the cases), the place was given its contemporary location. The information which Eusebius used—routes, distances, military dispostions—will have been available to him in the records at Caesarea (the provincial headquarters).[80] As the pilgrims went in search of their biblical history, a handbook such as the *Onomastikon* would

---

[76] See his preface to the *Onom.*　　　[77] Above, p. 94.

[78] See *Onom.* 58, 74. For Eusebius' use of Origen, cf. E. Klostermann (1902), 13–14.

[79] *Pace* Barnes, 413 'By its very nature the *Onomasticon* has less relevance to the Palestine of Eusebius' own day than to biblical times'.

[80] See Thomsen, 140, and, on documents to which Eusebius may have referred, J. Wilkinson (1974), 249–54.

be an important aid in tracking it down. That Eusebius'
work functioned in this way is confirmed by its early translation into Latin (before Jerome turned his attention to it)[81]
—a translation which may have been familiar to Egeria.[82]
Eusebius thus showed himself aware of the biblical impetus which was central to the piety of the holy places. But
the *Onomastikon* has added significance in relation to his view
of the 'apologetic' potential of the sites. The reader is struck
by the repeated use of the verb 'δείκνυται', 'is shown' (or
its various parts); from the remoteness of the remains of
Noah's Ark, still alleged to be visible ('δείκνυσθαι') on
Mount Ararat,[83] to the solid memorials of the Old Testament figures to be seen spread around the Holy Land, or the
towns and villages of the Gospel narratives, Eusebius is always concerned to stress what there was to *see* in the Palestine of his day. The inference is clear: anyone disposed to
doubt could behold the Scriptures set forth in unchallenge-
able terms, in the evidence of the surrounding landscape.
The 'δείκνυται' of the *Onomastikon* is but a more concrete
extension of the 'ἀπόδειξις' of the *Demonstratio Evangelica*; the
testimony of the holy places is to substantiate and supple-
ment the testimony of the Bible. It is a combination which
will reappear (*c.* 350) in the *Catechetical Lectures* of Cyril of
Jerusalem. His presentation of the faith to his baptismal
candidates was based firmly in Holy Scripture,[84] but he also
called into service the 'evidence' ('μαρτυρία') of the holy
places which surrounded him as he spoke in Constantine's
basilica on Golgotha. Take, for instance, the list of
'μαρτυρίαι' of Christ in x.19: the Scriptural 'witnesses' are
there, the angel Gabriel, Symeon, Anna the prophetess, John
the Baptist, etc.; but so too are those 'witnesses' which his
hearers could see around them—from Bethlehem and
Galilee, to the Mount of Olives, Gethsemane and Golgotha,
where they were standing at the time; there was the actual

---

[81] Jer. preface '.... quidam vix primis imbutus litteris hunc eundem librum ausus
sit in Latinam linguam non Latine vertere'.
[82] On the *Onom.* as a source for Egeria, see J. Ziegler (1931a)—although, if our
dating of her pilgrimage is correct, she could not have known Jerome's translation
(as Ziegler suggests).
[83] *Onom.* 2–4; on the use of 'δείκνυται' see B. J. Kötting (1950), 87.
[84] Cf. below, p. 122.

sacred wood of the cross, which had carried its testimony round the world; there was the Saviour's Tomb, and the stone which had covered the entrance. If any were inclined to deny the truth of the Crucifixion, Cyril would refute them by reference to the site of Golgotha itself, and to the wooden relics of the cross;[85] he would add, among other witnesses, the ruined house of Caiaphas, and Pilate's deserted *praetorium*.[86] 'Reverence the *place*,' he had urged his baptismal candidates, 'and learn from *what you see*'.[87] Such plain confidence in the visible testimony of the holy places was shared even by Jerome, in his enthusiastic reaction on first arriving in Jerusalem: 'I saw many wonders; and what previously I had heard by report, I verified *by the evidence of my own eyes*'.[88] By the middle of the fifth century, as will be observed, the irrefutable witness of the Holy Land sites would be marshalled as a powerful ally for the cause of Catholic orthodoxy.[89]

Eusebius, then, would not be alone in exploiting the holy places in this way. For him, the sites had a decisive position in his essentially biblical view of history in that they confirmed, in visible fashion, the truth of the Christians' biblical claims. We are not here concerned only with strengthening the conviction of the faithful—with the satisfaction of Jerome's 'task of faith' by the sight of the holy places; we have also to reckon with the proclamation of a victorious religion to its opponents, Jews and pagans, in the most convincing terms available. Once again, Eusebius had taken his cue from Origen, who deployed this particular line of argument in writing, for instance, of the site of the Nativity:

If anyone wants further proof to convince him that Jesus was born in Bethlehem besides the prophecy of Micah and the story recorded in the Gospels by Jesus' disciples, he may observe that, in agreement with the story in the gospel about his birth, the cave at Beth-

---

[85] *Catech.* iv. 10, xiii. 4.   [86] Ibid. xiii. 38, 39; cf. *It. Burd.* 592, 4; 593, 2–3.

[87] Cyril, *Procatech.* 4.

[88] Jer. *Apol. c. Ruf.* iii. 22 '. . . . quae prius ad me fama pertulerat, oculorum iudicio comprobavi'.

[89] See below, p. 246.

lehem *is shown* where he was born and the manger in the cave where he was wrapped in swaddling clothes.[90]

A contemporary of Origen, the martyr Pionius, spoke in similar vein in defending his faith before the authorities in the agora at Smyrna. Pionius reveals how he had travelled widely in the Holy Land, and presents the evidence of his own eyes as proof of Christian claims: 'I saw the land which to this day *bears witness* to the wrath of God'.[91]

For Eusebius, the potential of the holy places as a witness to the faith was most effectively realized in the rediscovery of the Holy Sepulchre, beneath the temples of Aelia Capitolina. His exuberant account[92] of the clearing and excavation of the site, leading to the miraculous appearance of the Tomb, is couched in an elaborate imagery of light and darkness; the vital point for him was one of *vision*, that it was now possible to *see* the tomb from which the Saviour had risen from the dead—and thus, following a line of reasoning now familiar, the *fact* of what had occurred was plain for all to behold, 'events speaking louder than all words'.[93] The very word 'μαρτύριον' which Eusebius uses to describe the newly-discovered Tomb makes explicit that here was a witness to the truth of the faith (and the term entered regular usage as the name for Constantine's basilica alongside).[94] For one who had already seen the possibilities of the holy places as vehicles for the proclamation of Christianity, the emergence of the Holy Sepulchre was abundant confirmation.

Constantine himself showed that he too was no stranger to this view when, in writing to bishop Macarius after the discovery, he referred to the long hidden Tomb as the 'means of knowing (γνώρισμα) Christ's suffering'. [95] The revelation had brought with it the knowledge of the truth. We may suppose that Constantine came to be influenced in his own attitudes

---

[90] *C. Cels.* i. 51 (transl. Chadwick, 47). Cf. Eusebius on the cave of the Nativity: *Dem. Evang.* iii. 2.46ff.; vii. 2.15, 43.

[91] *Mart. Pionii* (ed. Knopf/Krüger), 4.18 'γῆν ἕως τοῦ νῦν μαρτυροῦσαν.........'.

[92] Eus. *V. Const.* iii. 25ff.   [93] Ibid. 28.

[94] For 'μαρτύριον' used of the Sepulchre, see Eus. *Comm. in Psalm.* 87.13 (*PG* 23, 1064), and Athanasius, *De Synodis*, 21.2 (synodical letter of bishops at Jerusalem in 335).

[95] Eus. *V. Const.* iii. 30.1.

to the holy places by Eusebius, who, after his 'rehabilitation' at Nicaea, was a guest in the imperial palace and counted himself a friend of the emperor.[96] Certainly Constantine's letter to the bishops of Palestine on the subject of the shrine at Mamre takes on an added colour when associated with the views of Eusebius. Ordering the destruction of every vestige of paganism and the building of an appropriate Christian basilica, the emperor concluded:

> For you are not unaware that there the God of the universe first appeared to Abraham and conversed with him. There first the observance of the divine Law began; there first the Saviour himself with the two angels vouchsafed to Abraham a manifestation of his presence; there God first appeared to men; there he gave promise to Abraham concerning his future seed, and straightway fulfilled that promise; there he foretold that he should be the father of a multitude of nations.[97]

So Constantine, recalling Genesis ch.18, presented the weighty biblical justification for a proper Christian veneration of the site—and in terms all the more significant in the light of Eusebius' presentation of the Christian empire of Constantine as reviving the age of Abraham and the patriarchs.[98] The age which had witnessed the victory of Christianity had seen, on this view, a return to the pure religion of the patriarchs, undiluted by the inferior (and temporary) provisions of the Mosaic law; moreover, the destruction of the Jewish cult and the spread of Christianity through the *pax Romana* was represented as the fulfilment of God's promise to Abraham 'that he should be the father of a multitude of nations'. Eusebius' 'sacred history' was framed by the figures of Abraham and Constantine, with Christ at the centre; and it was not difficult to see in the first Christian emperor an echo of the patriarch, especially when he had already been hailed as a second Moses, vanquishing Maxen-

---

[96] Ibid. i. 28 ('when I was deemed worthy of his acquaintance and friendship'); iv. 7, 24 (Eus. among the bishops in the palace). On his role in shaping imperial attitudes to the holy places, cf. F. L. Cross, *St. Cyril of Jerusalem's Lectures on the Christian Sacraments* (1951), introd. xv, n. 2 'giving earthly Jerusalem ideological significance'; J. Lassus (1967); Wallace-Hadrill (1960), appendix.

[97] Eus. *V. Const.* iii. 53.3.

[98] See esp. *Dem. Evang.* i, and *Hist. Eccl.* i. 4.

tius at the Milvian Bridge as the Egyptians had been destroyed at the Red Sea.[99] With this view in mind, it is possible to appreciate some of the importance which Constantine attached to the Mamre site. As a figure acutely conscious of a historic destiny, one foreshadowed above all in both Old and New Testaments of the Bible,[100] he would see a striking opportunity to bind together the memorials of Abraham and the Christian empire of the fourth century. In endeavouring to turn Mamre into a purely Christian holy place, and to encourage the worship of Christian pilgrims, he was not merely emphasizing the biblical foundation of the site's credentials, but furthermore he was pointing to that fulfilment of the promise to Abraham in the Christian empire —just as the creation of the 'new Jerusalem' symbolized the hope of the New Testament.

But if the encouragement of the Christian veneration of Mamre was an aspect of the new ideology of the Christian empire, the site nevertheless was still capable of arousing that 'simple' faith of the pilgrim with which this chapter opened. It is nowhere better put than in a sermon of the Cappadocian Asterius of Amasea, who compared his own devotion to the cult of the martyr Phocas with the faith of the pilgrims at the oak of Mamre and the tombs of the patriarchs at Hebron:

With the sight of the holy places they renew the picture in their thinking, and behold in their minds the faithful patriarch...they reflect too on his descendents Isaac and Jacob, and with the recollection of these men they become spectators of the whole history concerning them.[101]

Here again are those 'eyes of faith' with which Paula saw the scene at the manger in Bethlehem. The narrative of Genesis 18 came readily to life in the imagination of the pilgrim at Mamre, who became a spectator, not only of the shrine that he could see before him, but of the whole succession of biblical 'history' associated with the spot.

[99] Eus. *Hist. Eccl.* ix. 9; cf. *V. Const.* i. 38.
[100] E.g. E. Becker (1910), I. Gillman (1961), H. Montgomery (1968).
[101] *Hom.* (ed. C. Datema, 1970), ix. 2.

The pilgrim's imagination was aided, according to Eusebius, by a picture, which was to be seen at Mamre, of Abraham greeting the three strangers.[102] This isolated mention of
a visual representation of a biblical scene is worth pausing
over. Our knowledge of the internal decoration of Holy Land
churches in this period is very scanty—Eusebius says nothing of paintings or mosaics in his description of the Golgotha buildings, nor is much to be gained from Egeria's
general reference to 'mosaic' among the splendours of Constantine's churches (we have to wait until Choricius of Gaza
in the sixth century for detailed mention of church
decoration);[103] otherwise we might with some confidence
have concluded that the pilgrim's characteristic capacity to
visualize the biblical past owed something, not only to the
fact of his presence at the site, but also to what he saw depicted on church walls and apses. There is evidence from
elsewhere that such visual decoration was capable of making
a forceful impact on worshippers: Prudentius, for example,
was moved by the portrayal of the martyr's death which he
saw at some of the shrines he visited;[104] we might also cite
Paulinus' justification of the biblical wall-paintings at Nola,
that they diverted the minds of those intent on less reverent
pursuits (similarly St. Nilus of Ancyra was prepared to allow
that representations of Old and New Testament scenes might
be an aid for the ignorant).[105] Paulinus and Nilus expected
the paintings of biblical scenes to be noticed. Despite this, it
has to be admitted that, if pilgrims at the holy places really
had remarked what covered the interior walls of the churches
in which they worshipped, we should have expected them to
have provided more detail in their descriptions.[106]

But the pilgrim's intention of visualizing the biblical
narrative in the holy places which he visited did have consequences in another area of visual decoration. For just as

[102] Eus. *Dem. Evang.* v. 9.7–8.
[103] J. W. Crowfoot (1941), 109–16; cf. *It. Eg.* 25.9.
[104] *Peristeph.* 9, 9ff.; 11, 123ff. Cf. Greg. Nys. on wall-paintings at shrine of Theodore, *PG* 46, 737–40.
[105] Paul. Nol. *Carm.* 27, 511ff. ('qui videt haec vacuis agnoscens vera figuris/non
vacua fidam sibi pascit imagine mentem'); Nilus, *Ep.* 4.61 (*PG* 79, 577–80).
[106] Cf. C. Dauphin (1978), 29ff.

the pilgrim saw, in the setting of fourth-century Palestine, the familiar biblical events, so an iconography of the Bible episodes was to develop (originating, we must conclude, in the Holy Land itself) which centred them, not in any idealized portrayal of a scene contemporary with the episodes themselves, but in a representation of the holy places *as they actually appeared to the early pilgrims*.[107] Its most familiar instance is found on the *ampullae* in which sixth-century pilgrims carried back their holy oil to the West from Jerusalem, where the centre-piece of the portrayals of the Nativity, Crucifixion, and Resurrection is in each case the appropriate contemporary memorial—the 'aedicules' over the cave in Bethlehem and over the Tomb on Golgotha, and the actual wooden relic of the cross.[108] Thus the visible holy places themselves, their reputation disseminated by pilgrims, had come to represent the biblical episodes. But such iconography is not confined to the specifically Palestinian *ampullae*. It can be traced too in other, western, representations of biblical scenes, which seem to have owed their inspiration to the influence of this iconography generated by the holy places. The Roman apse mosaic of S. Pudenziana has been mentioned in an earlier context.[109] To return to Mamre, it may be noted that the sixth-century mosaic of Abraham and his three visitors in S. Vitale at Ravenna has been taken to depict the contemporary holy site: its realistic oak-tree can be contrasted with the more stylized version to be seen in S. Maria Maggiore in Rome.[110] The Ravenna mosaicist may well have been influenced by the contemporary pilgrim's view of Mamre. The pilgrim background is certainly detectable in Prudentius' *Tituli Historiarum*, his verse captions for a series of biblical scenes decorating (presumably) the walls of a basilica;[111] not only does their style recall the biblical 'labelling' of sites characteristic of the pilgrim records, but it is sometimes possible to trace in them the description of a contemporary location (which would have been portrayed in the accom-

---

[107] Cf. K. Weitzmann (1974).   [108] See A. Grabar (1958), 50ff.
[109] See above, p. 17.
[110] C-O. Nordström, *Ravennastudien* (= *Figura*, 4, 1953), 95–8.
[111] Cf. A. Baumstark (1911). Similar verse captions are attributed to Ambrose: *PL* Suppl. i, 587–9.

panying scene)—as in the case of the oak of Mamre, or the cave which was the tomb of Sarah.[112]

The readiness to elide the gap between the present day and the biblical past thus finds distant confirmation in the wall-paintings of western churches—as does the far-reaching visual impact of the holy places on those who visited them. Whether pilgrim, scholar, or apologist of the Christian empire, all for their different purposes drew satisfaction from the *sight* of the biblical remains. The pilgrim in particular, for whom faith and history coincided, hoped for nothing more than to see the contents of the Scriptures in the setting of contemporary Palestine: 'no other feeling draws men to Jerusalem, save to see and touch the places in which Christ was bodily present'.[113]

---

[112] Prudent. *Tit. Histor.* 4, 5 (*CC* 126, 391).
[113] Paul. Nol. *Ep.* 49.14.

5. Pilgrims and the Bible (ii) The Liturgy

THE new Christian holy places, as it turned out, had still more to contribute to the pilgrims' expectations. In the course of the fourth century they became the setting for a church liturgy which evolved its distinctive character (in part at least) in response to that particularly historical kind of biblical understanding which pilgrims displayed in their travels round the Holy Land. We are confronted by the emergence at the holy places, for the first time, of an annually recurring cycle of liturgical festivals in commemoration of the life of Christ—the familiar 'church's year' which subsequently came to dominate the pattern of Christian worship far and wide.[1]

One instance will serve to trace the outline of this development. The Constantinian building programme at the holy places had been brought to a conclusion in the celebrations for the dedication of the Golgotha basilica in 335. The dominant theme of these events had been an imperial one, the · thirtieth year of the reign; the bishops had assembled on the orders of the emperor; an imperial official had presided; it had been Constantine's own achievements, symbolized in the spectacular new buildings, which had been the subject of

---

[1] The first study of Egeria's evidence on the Jerusalem liturgy was F. Cabrol (1895); see also A. Bludau (1927), 41–190, with the summary of J. Wilkinson (1971), 54ff. Jerusalem also has a central place in G. Dix (1945), ch. 11 'The Sanctification of Time'. The best modern work is that of A. Renoux on the *Armenian Lectionary* (which reflects the Jerusalem liturgy): see esp. his introduction, with bibliography, in *PO* 35, fasc. 1 (1969) (cf. also Wilkinson, 253ff.). On terminology, see A. A. R. Bastiaensen (1962).

acclaim.[2] For Eusebius, it was natural to make the comparison with that other episcopal gathering which had distinguished an earlier milestone in the emperor's reign, the council of Nicaea[3]—as with its predecessor, there may have been nothing to suggest that the assembly in Jerusalem was anything other than a single occasion to honour the Christian emperor.

By the last quarter of the fourth century, however, the imperial anniversary of 335 had been transformed into the liturgical celebration of the 'dies encaeniarum', the feast of the dedication of the Golgotha buildings.[4] It had settled into the regular pattern of the church's year in Jerusalem, its observance in September enlivening that long period of liturgical inactivity which fell between the feast of Pentecost in May/June and the celebrations of Christ's Nativity (the Epiphany) on 6 January.[5] Egeria describes with excitement the crowds which she observed assembling for the Dedication festival. Long before the day monks began to gather for the celebrations from their traditional haunts in Egypt, Syria, or Mesopotamia, as well as from elsewhere in the eastern provinces; pious lay men and women converged from far afield; while at least 'forty or fifty' bishops were in attendance, accompanied by their numerous clergy. Absence from the celebrations, according to Egeria, was a lapse of duty ('maximum peccatum') which only the most pressing commitment could excuse.[6]

The festival itself was observed with ceremonies similar to those which marked the celebrations of Epiphany, Easter, and Pentecost. The 'dies encaeniarum' was the starting-point for eight days of special liturgy, enveloping the holy places of Jerusalem. The surviving portion of the *It. Eg.* breaks off in the middle of the account, after mentioning the celebrations of the first two days at the Golgotha basilica, and the third at the Eleona church; we are left to surmise that at least the

---

[2] See above, pp. 25–6.   [3] Eus. *V. Const.* iv. 47.

[4] *It. Eg.* 48–9; cf. Jerome, *Tract. de Ps. xcv* (*CC* 78, 155), with Bludau, 185ff.

[5] The date in *Armen. Lect.* 67 is 13 September.

[6] *It. Eg.* 49.1–2. (It may have been the crowds around the Golgotha buildings assembled for this festival who witnessed the clash between bishops Epiphanius and John in 393 (Jer. *C. Ioh. Hier.* 11): P. Nautin (1973), 72–3.)

great church on Mount Sion would be included in the round
of worship, perhaps also the basilicas at Bethany and Bethlehem. At all events, Egeria found the churches decorated
for the *Encaenia* as magnificently as for the other ecclesiastical
festivals in Jerusalem.[7]

The church historian Sozomen (himself born in the Holy
Land) was also familiar, in his own day, with the Dedication
festival in Jerusalem. He notes that the worshippers 'assembled for services' for a period of eight days, and that the
festival was instrumental in bringing to the holy places many
pilgrims from all over the world. To him we owe the additional detail that the *Encaenia* had become one of the seasons
of the year at which baptisms took place.[8]

Thus what had begun as a celebration of imperial achievements and a cementing of the union between emperor and
church had been fully incorporated into the Jerusalem liturgy; it had become thoroughly 'ecclesiastical', taking on the
same characteristics as the other church festivals, even to the
extent of being regarded along with Easter and Pentecost as
a suitable time to present candidates for baptism. In the process the *Encaenia* festival had attracted associations other
than those of the Constantinian buildings: Egeria invoked
the description of the dedication of Solomon's Temple in the
Old Testament;[9] while the prescribed reading for the festival
liturgy was a passage from St. John's Gospel referring to the
Jewish festival of the Dedication which had been instituted in
the Maccabean period.[10] Even the season of the year at
which the fourth-century festival occurred could be used to
summon up biblical parallels.[11] In the Bible, too, lay the
model for the extension of the proceedings to eight days

---

[7] Ibid. 49.3.

[8] Soz. *Hist. Eccl.* ii. 26.4 (writing in the 440s) 'οἵ καθ᾽ ἱστορίαν τῶν ἱερῶν
τόπων πάντοθεν συντρέχουσι....'.

[9] *It. Eg.* 48.2. The Latin Bible would have made the word 'encaenia' familiar to
Egeria: Bastiaensen, 119–20.

[10] *Armen. Lect.* 67 (John, 10.22ff.); cf. I Maccabees, 4.52ff. For the suggestion that
the Jewish festival was actually the origin of the Christian *encaenia*, see M. Black
(1954), 84; and for further discussion on Jewish resemblances, J. Wilkinson (1979).

[11] Jer. *Tract. de Ps. xcv* (*CC* 78, 155) 'semper encaenia in tempestate sunt, in plu-
viis sunt, in hieme sunt'; cf. John, 10.23. Yet the fact remains that, whereas the new
Christian festival fell in September, the biblical Dedication had occurred in December.

(Eusebius gives no hint of the duration of the celebrations of 335), the period which had marked this, and other, Jewish festivals.[12] Even without these precursors, however, the Jerusalem *Encaenia* might well have been expected to take on the octave of observances traditional to the other Christian festivals: here the prototype lay in the Gospel account of Christ's two Resurrection appearances to the disciples, separated by eight days.[13]

Despite its roots in the reign of Constantine, the *Encaenia* had thus readily assumed links with biblical antiquity. In common with the rest of the liturgy evolving at Jerusalem, it both drew its inspiration from, and was expressed through, the reading of the Bible. The *Encaenia* may also be taken as representative in its inclusion of the several holy places in the course of the celebrations: we shall see how worshippers in Jerusalem were expected to be on the move (for long periods at a time) from church to church not only in the city itself, but even as far as the six miles to Bethlehem. In addition, the fact that this was a pilgrims' festival, attracting participants from far afield, makes clear the tight connexion between the nature of the liturgical round in Jerusalem and the expectations of those who came to visit the city. That capacity (explored in the previous chapter) vividly to recall to the imagination the scenes from the biblical narrative at the contemporary holy places naturally found no less satisfaction in the liturgical re-enactment of those events *in situ*. The re-creation, in the round of services, of the Gospel account of Christ's presence on earth directly answered to the pilgrims' visual demands; the Jerusalem liturgy as it developed was founded upon, and made explicit, such biblical realism.

It is again to Egeria's acute eye for observation, already displayed re-living the biblical account of the experiences of the children of Israel in the Sinai desert, that we owe our knowledge of the liturgy of the holy places. As she set out to describe for her western readers those features of church

---

[12] I Maccabees, 4.59; cf. the feast of the Tabernacles (II Macc. 10.6, Levit. 23.36).

[13] John, 20.26; cf. below, p. 112. On the tradition of the octave, see G. Löw, *Enciclopedia Cattolica*, ix (1952), 451ff.

worship which impressed her as unfamiliar,[14] her record concentrates on the local peculiarities of the Jerusalem liturgy. After a lacuna in the manuscript (the description of the beginning of the ecclesiastical year is lost) Egeria's text is resumed as she is recounting the procession returning from Bethlehem to Jerusalem on the night of the Epiphany festival;[15] the movement is slow, for the monks are on foot; Jerusalem is not reached until 'the hour when one man can recognize another', just before dawn. Then, after a blessing from the bishop in the *Anastasis*, the congregation (but not the monks) takes a brief rest before the main celebration in the Golgotha basilica 'at the beginning of the second hour'. Egeria emphasizes the appropriateness for the day of the hymns, readings, and preaching at this service, which occupied the congregation at Golgotha for as long as four hours.[16] The same celebrations were repeated there on the second and third days of the octave, followed on successive days by services on the Mount of Olives, at Bethany, and on Mount Sion, returning at the end of the week to the *Anastasis* and the Cross. Here, as elsewhere, Egeria notes the crowds of monks and lay people who assembled in Jerusalem for these proceedings.[17] The festival had begun on the eve of the Epiphany at Bethlehem; and after the departure of the main congregation it was maintained there with the same pomp throughout the week by the presbyters and monks. The inclusion of Bethlehem in the Epiphany celebrations is a reminder that Egeria would find that it was Christ's Nativity which was commemorated at this feast in Jerusalem, a divergence from western practice which she may well have remarked on in the lost pages of the text.[18] Having travelled from the west, she would have been familiar with the alternative tradition of the observance of Christmas as the celebra-

---

[14] Not the Sunday Eucharist, for instance: 'fiunt omnia secundum consuetudinem, qua et ubique fit die dominica' (25.1).

[15] 25.6ff. Cf. Bludau, 68ff.

[16] 25.10 'omnia tamen apta ipsi diei'.   [17] 25.12.

[18] For the evidence on the divergent traditions, see Bludau, 70ff. There have been numerous monographs, e.g. H. Usener, *Das Weihnachtsfest*[2] (1911), B. Botte (1932), and for a brief summary O. Cullmann, *Weihnachten in der alten Kirche* (1947). It was bishop Juvenal, in the 5th cent., who first introduced 25 December in Jerusalem: see *PG* 85, 469.

tion of the Nativity;[19] and she would certainly have encountered it on her way as a feast newly introduced into the churches of Asia Minor and Syria.[20] Yet in recounting her journey from Sinai along the shores of the Red Sea she found no cause to mention 25 December—the celebration of the Epiphany, by contrast, provided a welcome break.[21]

The physical presence of the Holy Sepulchre ensured that the celebration of the Resurrection was never far from the centre of the Jerusalem worship; there was little new to add when it came to marking the festival of Easter. Much of what Egeria observed was familiar, 'which is also the custom among us'[22]—the Easter vigil, the nocturnal ceremonies of baptism, the observance of the octave. As at Epiphany, the principal celebrations rotated round the holy places during the week.[23] Most distinctively, however, to Egeria's eyes, the Easter celebrations were framed by two gatherings after Vespers at the basilica on Mount Sion, on Easter Day itself and again on the following Sunday.[24] On these two days the whole congregation, singing hymns, conducted the bishop to this church to the south of the city, to commemorate there the two appearances of the risen Christ to the disciples assembled in the Upper Room, with the appropriate readings of the story of Thomas from St. John's Gospel.[25] This Sion church was none other than the traditional site of the Upper Room: 'on the same day in the very place ('eadem die...in eodem loco') where the church of Sion now stands, the Lord came in to his disciples through the closed doors'.[26] Egeria here isolates the unique potential of the Jerusalem liturgy: gatherings of the faithful charged by the awareness of their presence at the very site of the events commemorated.

[19] The earliest evidence is the Roman *Chronographer of 354*, which may indicate that Christmas had been kept in Rome as early as 336 (Botte, 32ff.). Jerome's *Sermon on the Nativity* (*CC* 78, esp. 527ff.) was a defence of the western date against the Jerusalem practice.

[20] E.g. in his *Homily on the Nativity* (386) Joh. Chrys. defends the recent introduction of the western usage at Antioch: *PG* 49, 351ff. For other evidence, see J. Mossay (1965).

[21] According to P. Devos (1967a), 188ff., 25 December would find her at the station on the shores of the Red Sea (*It. Eg.* 6.1); for Epiphany, *It. Eg.* 9.1.

[22] *It. Eg.* 38.2.   [23] Ibid. 39.2.   [24] 39.4–5, 40.2.

[25] Confirmed by *Armen. Lect.* 45, 52 (John, 20.19ff.).   [26] *It. Eg.* 39.5.

The period of fifty days following Easter, marked by an absence of fasting, ended with the celebration of 'the day of Pentecost'. This was the only liturgical 'season' which had any history before the fourth century.[27] By the time of Egeria's pilgrimage the liturgy of Pentecost had developed into an elaborate and demanding ritual, exploiting to the full the possibilities of localized devotion and of peripatetic worship.[28] The normal Sunday Eucharist on Golgotha was brought to an end earlier than usual, so that the whole congregation might then ceremonially accompany the bishop to the church of Sion, for the commemoration of the descent of the Holy Spirit at the first Christian Pentecost. As at Easter, the scene was again the traditional site of the Upper Room; here they listened to the narrative from the *Acts of the Apostles* recounting the events which had occurred (so they believed) at this very spot.[29] When this celebration was concluded, the archdeacon announced the afternoon procession to the summit of the Mount of Olives. After a brief respite every Christian in Jerusalem, according to Egeria, made the ascent; they sat down (in the open air) with the bishop and clergy to hear readings appropriate to the Ascension of Christ—the mark of whose last footprints on earth could be seen at the place where they were assembled, 'from where the Lord ascended into heaven'.[30] From this, the second commemoration of the day,[31] the procession descended towards the city, with a halt for Vespers at the Eleona church; at the city gate they were met with candles—not until the 'second hour of the night' did they reach the Golgotha basilica. But all was not over yet, for after services at the holy places on Golgotha the congregation 'to a man' now escorted the bishop again to Sion

---

[27] Ibid. 41. Cf. R. Cabié (1965); the fifty days were celebrated in effect as one long Sunday (Cabié, 49ff.).

[28] *It. Eg.* 43.1 'qua die maximus labor est populo'; cf. 43.9.

[29] 43.3; cf. *Armen. Lect.* 58 (Acts, 2.1–21).

[30] 43.4–5; for these (indestructible) footprints, see Paul. Nol. *Ep.* 31.4, Sulp. Sev. *Chron.* ii. 33.7.

[31] The celebration of the Ascension in Jerusalem had yet to be moved to the Fortieth Day after Easter, a transference which, to judge from its appearance in *Armen. Lect.*, occurred soon after Egeria's visit; cf. below, n. 34, on the Fortieth Day in Bethlehem. For the (predominantly Jewish) background to the twin commemoration of Pentecost in Jerusalem, see G. Kretschmar (1954–5).

for the last observance of the day,[32] including further
appropriate readings;[33] it was the middle of the night before
the faithful were finally dismissed to their homes. Thus ended a day of worship which had begun, as normally on a
Sunday, before cock-crow, and had continued, with only a
single break, until well into the following night.

Such exertions highlight the degree of complexity which
the festival liturgies of fourth-century Jerusalem had
attained. The desire to embrace all the principal holy places
in the course of the celebrations, combined with the possibility of commemorating the events of the Gospel at the actual
places where they were believed to have occurred, produced
a form of worship distinguished by its constant movement
and its arduous length. The processions in which the throng
of the faithful, led by the clergy and monks, accompanied
the bishop to and from Sion or the Mount of Olives emphasized the totality of the holy places, by including them in an
all-embracing public ceremonial. This was made to extend as
far as Bethlehem, where the bishop attended at least twice in
the year in the formal context of the liturgy.[34] Against the
background of this unified emphasis, each festival concentrated attention on one principal site (or, in the case of
Pentecost, on two), the actual scene of the event commemorated; here lay Jerusalem's opportunity for the development
of a liturgy which could evoke, as nowhere else, a dramatic
realization of the Gospel narrative. The pattern of the liturgy
and its ritual gave visual substance to the biblical recollections at each spot.

At the centre of the pilgrims' interest, as at the hub of the
liturgy, were the group of Constantinian buildings on Golgotha. The round of the daily offices was conducted in the

---

[32] *It. Eg.* 43.8 'usque ad unum'.

[33] Ibid. 43.9; Acts 2 again? (cf. *Armen. Lect.* 58).

[34] Once on the eve of the Epiphany (above, p. 111), and again on the Fortieth
Day after Easter: *It. Eg.* 42. On this occasion the preaching was 'apta diei et loco',
but the nature of the commemoration is uncertain—it is unlikely, in view of the
celebration at Pentecost, to be the Ascension. The chapter has generated many
attempts to identify the festival: see views discussed by P. Devos (1968a), and also J.
Crehan, *Theological Studies*, 30 (1969), 315–16. I favour the caution of J. Wilkinson
(1971), 77–8.

Anastasis;[35] here, too, every Sunday morning before dawn the bishop solemnly read the 'Resurrection Gospel' at the mouth of the Tomb.[36] At dawn the congregation gathered in the basilica for the Sunday Eucharist.[37] The setting of these regular acts of worship points to the centrality of Christ's Passion and Resurrection in the evolution of the Jerusalem liturgy; and nowhere is this more apparent than in the intricate pattern of the worship for Holy Week (the week before Easter), which in two respects has made its mark on the rest of Christendom—in the celebration of the Triumphal Entry, and in the Good Friday veneration of the True Cross.[38]

At the close of the Eucharist on the Sunday which opened the 'Great Week' the archdeacon announced the afternoon assembly on the Mount of Olives.[39] There, after services in the Eleona church and at the place of the Ascension, the climax came 'at the eleventh hour' with the reading of the Gospel narrative of Christ's entry into Jerusalem.[40] Then began the procession into the city, the whole congregation going on foot before the bishop, singing hymns and chanting 'Blessed is he that comes in the name of the Lord'; all the children, even the smallest who had to be carried on their parents' shoulders, waved branches of palm and olive.[41] The bishop was led at a slow pace all the way into the city to the *Anastasis*; so notable was the occasion that even persons of rank joined the procession on foot.[42] Egeria naturally understood, in the Jerusalem context, that this Palm Sunday ceremony was a reproduction of Christ's entry into Jerusalem along the same route—with the bishop assuming the role of

---

[35] *It. Eg.* 24.1–7. On the daily worship, see Bludau, 43ff., and Dix, 328ff.; for its structure, R. Zerfass (1968), 7ff.

[36] 24.10; cf. below, pp. 122–3.   [37] 25.1.

[38] Triumphal Entry: A. Baumstark (1958), 148ff., and Bludau, 124ff. Adoration of the Cross: Baumstark, 142ff., and (for 7th cent. Constantinople) Arculf, *De Locis Sanctis*, iii. 3 (= J. Wilkinson (1977), 113). On the Holy Week liturgy generally, see J.-B. Thibaut (1926).

[39] *It. Eg.* 30.2.   [40] 31.2.

[41] The stress on the role of the children in the Palm Sunday procession is not warranted by any of the biblical accounts, although its origin can be detected in the allusion to Psalm 8.2 ('Out of the mouths of babes and sucklings....') at Matthew, 21.16: cf. J. Ziegler (1931), 188–9.

[42] 31.4 'matronae.... aut domini'; the upper classes were reluctant pedestrians, cf. above, p. 80.

Christ himself: 'and thus the bishop is accompanied in the very way that the Lord was then accompanied'.[43] Yet in one, perhaps embarrassing, particular she remained silent—the bishop of Jerusalem, it is tempting to believe (to complete the visual replica), was led into his city riding on a donkey.[44]

The observances of the 'Great Week' reached their climax on Good Friday with the exposure and veneration of the relics of the True Cross. This was the one occasion (soon to be joined by a second at the *Encaenia* festival in September)[45] on which the closely guarded fragments were presented to public view; at other times only the specially favoured among pilgrims might be allowed a private showing by the bishop.[46] Good Friday, however, as the commemoration of the Crucifixion, could not pass without the sight of the actual wood of the cross.

After only a brief rest from a night of services, 'at the second hour' on Good Friday morning the congregation crowded into the courtyard on Golgotha as the preparations were made for the ceremony. The bishop's *cathedra* was placed in the chapel behind the rock surmounted by the replica of the cross; there on a table in front of him was placed the precious reliquary. He removed the wooden fragments and the inscription, taking care when laying them out to keep hold of them with his fingers, while the deacons stood round in a circle. Then the whole congregation filed past one by one; kneeling before the bishop, they kissed the sacred wood in turn, never touching it with their hands. (The deacons standing guard were necessary, so Egeria had heard, to prevent the recurrence of a notorious incident of theft.)[47]

---

[43] 31.3 '.... in eo typo, quo tunc Dominus deductus est'. Cf. H. J. Gräf, *Palmenweihe und Palmenprozession in der lateinischen Liturgie* (1959), 4: 'Hier ist der Bischof der Typus des feierlich in Jerusalem einziehenden Christus. Man suchte also mit Bedacht bei dieser Feier den Herrn *sichtbar* bei sich zu haben.'

[44] This would seem to follow from 'in eo typo quo...', and was assumed by Thibaut, 23 'assis sur une humble monture'; certainly Athanasius entered Alexandria thus (see below, p. 126). In a context so dominated by the biblical associations, it would hardly seem outrageous that the bishop should, like Christ, ride a donkey, yet there is no trace of this in the early sources for the Jerusalem practice (cf. Gräf, 1–9). At any rate, by the 13th cent. the patriarch of Jerusalem was observed to ride a donkey: G. Ostrogorsky, *Seminarium Kondakovianum*, 7 (1935), 198.

[45] Cf. above, p. 39.

[46] Paul. Nol. *Ep.* 31.6 'quasi in pretium longinquae peregrinationis'.

[47] *It. Eg.* 37.1ff.; for the details, cf. below, p. 128.

After the cross came other relics—the ring of Solomon and the horn from which the kings of Israel had been anointed.[48] The column of the faithful was moving past the objects for as much as four hours. When the ceremony was completed the congregation reassembled in the open air in the courtyard, packed so tightly that the gates could not be opened;[49] the bishop took his seat before them, and for three hours presided over a continuous series of readings on the Passion, from the Psalms and the Prophets, to the Epistles and Gospels, unfolding the fulfilment of God's purpose in the last hours at this spot on Golgotha: 'for these three hours all the people are told that nothing which took place had not been foretold, and all that was foretold was completely fulfilled'.[50] The readings and prayers were accompanied by what Egeria described as 'remarkable' displays of tearful emotion among the congregation.[51] At the culmination, the ninth hour itself, the description of the moment of Christ's death on the cross was read from St. John's Gospel (John 19.30).

This studied recollection of the Gospel narrative, its vividness emphasized in the emotional reactions aroused, represents a climax in the process of assimilating the form of the liturgy to the historical realism inspired by the holy places. Yet it had not always been so. The scenes which Egeria witnessed in Jerusalem in re-enactment of the stages in the life of Christ were the successors of a much less historical sense of the holy places, which had centred on the three 'core' sites acknowledged before the arrival of Constantine's builders— at Bethlehem, Golgotha, and on the Mount of Olives. Here principally, so it appeared, God had been revealed to men through Christ, in the Nativity, the Resurrection, and the Ascension; the revered caves were the scene of the 'theophanies' of the New Testament, as in earlier times the sacred oak at Mamre had witnessed God's appearance to Abraham.[52] The individual historical events in the life of Christ counted for less than the fact that the three caves isolated instances of

---

[48] Cf. the Jerusalem *Breviarius*, 2. The ring figured in the apocryphal story of Solomon's contest with the demons: see J. Wilkinson (1971), 156, n. 4.

[49] *It. Eg.* 37.4.

[50] Ibid. 37.6; for the readings, cf. *Armen. Lect.* 43.

[51] 37.7 'tantus affectus et gemitus totius populi est, ut mirum sit'.

[52] Cf. A. Grabar (1946), i, 240ff.; ii, 129ff.

divine revelation; that the sites were distinguished from each other by separate historical claims faded into relative insignificance in face of their common association with the mysteries of God.[53] A similar notion may be reflected in Eusebius' failure to mention (as we noticed earlier) the site of the Crucifixion on Golgotha in his account of the Constantinian building—an omission perhaps explicable by analogy with liturgical practice: when Eusebius wrote, the dissolution of the celebration of Easter into a series of historical commemorations had yet to come; the church's thinking still concentrated on the total mystery summed up in the empty Tomb, and the commemoration of the Passion as an event separate from this mystery was as yet unfamiliar.[54]

Such an emphasis on the common characteristics of the holy places was still maintained alongside the increasing particularization which occurred in the course of the century. It can be seen reflected, for instance, in the intercessions of the *Liturgy of St. James:*

We give thee thanks, O Lord, for thy holy places, which thou hast glorified by the appearance (θεοφανείᾳ) of thy Christ and by the visitation (ἐπιφοιτήσει) of thy Holy Spirit....[55]

This prayer originated in Jerusalem, probably in the fourth century.[56] It is interesting, moreover, that bishop Cyril, to whose influence the developed historical liturgy has been traced,[57] and who certainly showed himself aware of the individual testimony of each of the holy places,[58] nevertheless

---

[53] So Eus. *Tricen. Orat.* 9.17 'χώρας τρισὶν ἄντροις μυστικοῖς τετιμημένας'.

[54] Cf. above, p. 12. I am influenced here by Baumstark (1958), 157: '.... the great Feasts of primitive Christianity were by nature not historical commemorations of such and such an episode in the sacred history, but were instituted rather to give expression to great religious ideas.' For his treatment of Easter as originally a 'Feast of Idea', see 164ff.: 'a Feast expressive of the great Idea which holds in union the remembrance both of the death and resurrection of Christ' (173). For a similar approach to the evolution of Pentecost and the Ascension, see Cabié (1965), esp. 163–78 on the Jerusalem evidence. Cf. also J. G. Davies (1954), arguing for an 'unhistorical' celebration of the Ascension (?) at Bethlehem, justified by *theological* associations with the Nativity.

G. Dix (1945), 349, laments the 'disintegrating effects' of the historical commemoration of Easter.

[55] Ed. Mercier, *PO* 26 (1946), 206.

[56] Ibid. 124.   [57] Dix, 350ff.   [58] See above, pp. 99–100.

retained a strong sense of their unity; the passage is worth quoting in full:

We know the holy spirit which spoke in the prophets and at Pentecost descended on the apostles in the form of tongues of fire here in Jerusalem in the upper church of the Apostles. For the chief claims of all are ours. Here Christ descended from the heavens; here the holy spirit descended from the heavens. And assuredly it were most fitting that, as we read of Christ and Golgotha here on Golgotha, so we should read of the holy spirit in the upper church. But since that which descended there partakes of the glory of him who was crucified here, so we also speak here of the spirit which descended there—for the worship of God knows no division.[59]

Cyril, conscious of the developing fragmentation of the Jerusalem liturgy, here reasserts in conclusion the essential indivisibility of the holy places—all bore witness to the glory of God. This is all the more striking when it is reflected that Cyril, who was bishop of Jerusalem until 387, will have been the very bishop whom Egeria observed at the centre of the historical liturgy. His insistence on the inseparability of worship gives substance to the view expressed earlier that the elaborate movement and ceremonial described by Egeria served to hold together the holy places in their totality, a feature which would otherwise have been lost in the localized commemorations of particular biblical events.

This localizing tendency must go back to the Constantinian period, when the new buildings erected carried with them an inevitable concentration on the individual claims of each site. Each became a focus of attention for the crowds who were able to gather in the courtyards in front of the churches, while the edifice itself emphasized the independent status of the site as a holy place. With the solidity of buildings came the firmer definition of the particular *locus*. This was accompanied by certain practical developments in the organization and control of the holy places, which again reinforced their individuality. The supervision of the sites must have entailed the emergence of a number of appropriate officials: a Theodosian law addressed to the *comes Orientis* sin-

---

[59] Cyril, *Catech.* xvi. 4 'ἀμέριστος γὰρ ἐστιν ἡ εὐσεβεῖα'.

gles out 'custodes ecclesiarum . . . . vel sanctorum locorum' for
tax exemption;[60] while we also hear of members of the Jerusalem clergy who held the important office of 'guardian of
the cross'.[61] Crowd-control, too, was an inevitable product
of the increasing numbers of pilgrims and worshippers. Egeria noticed that the crowds which kept vigil every Saturday
night before the *Anastasis* were not admitted to the church till
cock-crow: 'the custom is that the holy places are not open
before cock-crow'.[62] Significantly, too, the younger Melania
found herself forced to leave the *Anastasis* when it was closed
for the night.[63] Even such restriction of access, paradoxically,
will have further emphasized that each site had particular
claims to be visited.

But the main impetus here, as in so much else, was the
influence of the Bible. The particularity of each site was
naturally determined by the increasing concentration on its
biblical associations, and formally confirmed in the liturgical
reading *in situ* of the appropriate passage: the local acts of
worship in which Egeria engaged, with their focal biblical
reading, were an integral contribution to the historical definition of the sites which she visited.[64] Similarly in Jerusalem,
the role of the Bible in the formal surroundings of the liturgy
was crucial to the transformation from the affirmation of
ideas to the celebration of historical events.

The impression made on Egeria by the 'appropriateness'
of the forms of service to the places where they occurred runs
through her narrative. Time and again she returns to stress
the novelty of hymns, prayers and readings which were 'apta
diei et loco':

And what I admire and value most is that all the hymns and anti-
phons and readings they have, and all the prayers the bishop says,
are always relevant to the day which is being observed and to the
place in which they are used. They never fail to be appropriate.[65]

---

[60] *CTh* xvi. 2.26 (31 Mar. 381).
    [61] E.g. Porphyry, future bishop of Gaza (Marc. Diac. *V. Porph.* 10), and Cosmas,
future bishop of Scythopolis (Cyril Scyth. *V. Euthym.* 37).
    [62] *It. Eg.* 24.8: was she accustomed to churches always open?
    [63] *V. Mel.* 36.   [64] Cf. R. Zerfass (1968), 4–6.
    [65] *It. Eg.* 47.5 (transl. J. Wilkinson).

The extent of the innovation involved in such a practice, at
least for a westerner like Egeria, can be gauged from the fact
that it is not until the middle of the fifth century that anything is heard, in the West, of a concern for the liturgical
appropriateness of biblical extracts.[66] It then appears as a
new element in the liturgy; the accomplishments of Claudius
Mamertus, presbyter of Vienne (died *c.* 470), included the
composition of an annual lectionary[67]—while at a similar
period in Marseilles the learned presbyter Musaeus compiled
for his bishop an arrangement of lessons to suit the liturgical
year.[68] Such works were obviously novelties.

Yet the introduction of a lectionary related to the church
calendar had originally been no less of an innovation in the
East—and it is to the Holy Land that we must look for its
origin. The very appropriateness which so caught Egeria's
attention was a refinement of the eastern liturgy brought
about by the biblical precision possible only at the holy
places.[69] The regular daily worship of the East had known
nothing at all of lessons from the Scriptures;[70] it was only
their introduction in Jerusalem to mark the special commemorations of the year which was eventually responsible
for their diffusion in the eastern liturgy. It is to be stressed
that it was precisely the Scriptural element which distinguished the worship of these special occasions ('feast-days')
from the regular daily offices—in this way the timeless and
unending round of devotions was arrested in a historical concentration on a particular biblical commemoration. On these
occasions the lessons were at the centre of the services; they
were the anchor securing the contemporary liturgy to past
events recollected. Thus, to take a notable instance (already
referred to), the centrepiece of the Good Friday solemnities
included three hours of lessons on the Passion; but this was

---

[66] The West favoured the monastic tradition of *lectio continua*, Bible reading as
'Erbauung': R. Zerfass (1963), 164–6.

[67] Sidon. Apoll. *Ep.* iv. 11.6 'hic sollemnibus annuis paravit/quae quo tempore
lecta convenirent'.

[68] Gennadius, *De Vir. Illustr.* 80 'excerpsit ex Sanctis Scripturis lectiones totius
anni festivis aptas diebus'.

[69] I am indebted here to R. Zerfass, both (1963) and esp. (1968).

[70] As can be observed in Egeria's description of the daily office (24.1–7), which
makes no mention of biblical lessons—apart from the psalter.

only the culmination of a week which had seen the whole biblical narrative of the events leading up to the Crucifixion rehearsed in the course of a liturgy which was itself a conscious portrayal of those events.

But the prominence of the Bible in the Jerusalem services went further. It is clear that Egeria found a much greater emphasis on *preaching* about the Scriptures in the regular Sunday Eucharists than she had been accustomed to: not only did the bishop himself deliver a sermon, but this was preceded also by homilies from all those presbyters who wished to contribute, 'so that the people are always learning about the Bible and the love of God'.[71] Such lengthy exposure to biblical instruction was a continuation of the emphasis of the lectures which the faithful would have received from the bishop before baptism: this *catechesis* (as Egeria observed) ran through the whole of the Bible from the very beginnings of the Old Testament, offering both 'literal' and 'spiritual' interpretations.[72] From bishop Cyril's surviving *Catechetical Lectures* it is clear that the theme of the unity of Old and New Testaments was to the fore: the prophecies of Israel found their fulfilment in Christ.[73] Such was the import, as we have seen, of the readings for Good Friday. Egeria noticed the pervasive influence of this catechetical training: the congregation in Jerusalem always attentively followed the Bible when it was read in church.[74] Those local worshippers who could not understand Greek, the language of the liturgy, were able to benefit from an Aramaic interpreter.[75]

The introduction of the biblical element into the regular liturgy was, then, a development fundamental to the unique situation of the Jerusalem church. Its prototype is to be found in the vigil which preceded the Sunday services.[76] At cock-crow the *Anastasis* was opened, to allow the crowd which had been gathering outside to pour into the church, now ablaze with lamps; the bishop descended into the Sepul-

---

[71] *It. Eg.* 25.1. For this 'multiple' preaching, cf. *Apostolic Constitutions*, ii. 57.9 'let the presbyters one by one, *not all together*, exhort the people'.
[72] Ibid. 46.2.
[73] See A. Paulin (1959), 99ff.; cf. esp. *Catech.* iv. 33, xvi. 4.
[74] *It. Eg.* 46.3.
[75] 47.3–4; on the local languages, see below, pp. 152–3.
[76] See J. Mateos (1961).

chre itself, while the clergy led the congregation in psalms and prayers; then, as the church filled with the aroma of incense, the bishop came to the mouth of the Tomb and read from the Gospels of the Passion and Resurrection of Christ. So moving was the occasion, according to Egeria, that even the most unfeeling ('quamvis durissimus') of the congregation were brought to tears.[77] This ceremony, clearly in origin akin to the other particular commemorations of the liturgical year, had by the date of Egeria's pilgrimage become a feature of the worship of *every* Sunday—it was to prove an important influence on the liturgy not only more widely in the East, but even in certain aspects of western church life.[78]

This Sunday morning occasion is a measure of Jerusalem's liturgical contribution. Into the regular round of daily observances, originating from the discipline of the monastic life, was injected a lively sense of place and time. The reading of the Bible focused the attention of the congregation on *where* they were and on the unique historical significance of the spot. The truth which Eusebius had found miraculously confirmed in the discovery of the Tomb was formally reasserted every Sunday when the bishop read the Resurrection narrative. The congregation thus came again and again to the Sepulchre in recollection of that first visit of the women in the Gospel; as the angel announced to them that Christ had risen, so the bishop regularly proclaimed the news to the faithful. It was the representation of this scene, the women visiting the empty Tomb, which dominated the early iconography of the Resurrection;[79] at the centre of the portrayal, significantly, was no rock-tomb in a garden, but a reproduction of the actual Holy Sepulchre as it appeared, or was imagined to appear, in contemporary Jerusalem[80]—a compression of time which united the women at the Tomb and the congrega-

---

[77] *It. Eg.* 24.9ff. Although Egeria mentions only the Resurrection, it is clear from the reaction of the congregation ('ut quamvis durissimus possit moveri in lacrimis Dominum *pro nobis tanta sustinuisse*') that the Passion must have been included in the reading: Baumstark (1958), 40, n. 2.

[78] Cf. Mateos, 304ff., on its influence in the West; for the East, see *Apost. Const.* ii. 59.3, reproducing the Jerusalem usage (cf. Zerfass (1968), 44ff.).

[79] See R. Louis (1954).

[80] As on the *ampullae*, above, p. 105. Contrast the representation on western ivories in Munich, Milan, and the British Museum: J. Villette (1957), 59–87, esp. 72ff. (*ampullae*), 83ff. (ivories), with pls. xxxviii-xli.

tion hearing their bishop. Jerusalem offered this unique possibility of a liturgy where the faithful could entirely enter into the biblical heritage, and, by moving round the holy places and hearing the Scriptures read, actually involve themselves in the historical life of Christ. The emotional scenes which Egeria describes as accompanying the ceremonies go some way towards demonstrating the evident reality of this involvement; the treachery of Judas or the sufferings on the cross were for the faithful no remote events of the past, but, through the medium of the location and the readings, vividly recalled in the present.[81]

The particular attraction of celebrating events in Christ's life at the places where they were believed to have occurred is amply demonstrated in the crowds which gathered in Jerusalem for the great festivals of the year. Egeria, it has been observed, noted an element of obligation in the urge to attend the *Encaenia* celebrations. The importance attached to being present at the Jerusalem festivals has been used to effect by Devos in his arguments for dating Egeria's pilgrimage to 381–4; it was his calculation that, on this dating, her departure from Jerusalem would fall on 25 March 384—in that year, Easter Monday.[82] This invites the conclusion that Egeria may have deliberately waited until after taking part in the liturgy of the 'Great Week' and Easter Day before setting out on her journey. Devos is able to corroborate this by reference to the younger Melania, who in 437 hastened back from Constantinople through unprecedentedly wintry conditions in Anatolia in order to reach Jerusalem in time for Easter —where she in fact arrived on the Tuesday of Holy Week. Defying all the bishops who would have detained her on the way, she had only one desire: 'to celebrate the Passion of the Lord in Jerusalem'.[83]

The concern of pilgrims to witness and involve themselves in the liturgy of the holy places is reflected in the widespread interest in the ecclesiastical practices of Jerusalem. Egeria knew that the sisters for whom she was writing would be eager to hear about the worship of the holy places;[84] while an

[81] For the Judas reading, see *It. Eg.* 34. [82] P. Devos (1967a), 177–8.
[83] *V. Mel.* 56–7; cf. Devos, 176, n. 4. [84] *It. Eg.* 24.1.

earlier visitor to the Holy Land, Firmilian bishop of Caesarea in Cappadocia, had regarded the observances of Jerusalem as a standard against the liturgical deviations of Rome.[85] It may reasonably be supposed that a wish to adopt elements of the Jerusalem liturgy into local usage was a consequence of this interest.

The influence of the liturgy of the holy places on the rest of Christendom has proved a well-worked theme.[86] I have already chosen to emphasize the crucial role played by Jerusalem in introducing biblical lessons into the offices of the eastern church. As is well-known, the ancient *Lectionaries* of the Armenian and Georgian churches preserve the tradition of the lessons as read in Jerusalem, 'in the holy places of Christ'; and the early Syriac liturgy of Edessa was also influenced from Jerusalem.[87] Other notable features of the liturgy witnessed by Egeria (as we have seen) found their way into the church at large: the Triumphal Entry of Palm Sunday, the Adoration of the Cross. More particularly, the characteristic 'stational' liturgy of papal Rome, in which the clergy and people would proceed on great festivals to the basilica announced by a deacon, to greet there the pope arriving in state, or to accompany him in procession to another church, has an obvious affinity with fourth-century Jerusalem;[88] as does also the Roman practice of celebrating Christmas with a nocturnal mass at S. Maria Maggiore followed by a morning mass at St. Peter's, reproducing the double celebration of the Nativity at Bethlehem and Jerusalem—a parallel rendered even closer when the relics of the manger from Bethlehem came to be preserved at S. Maria Maggiore.[89] Interesting, too, is the insistence in the *Rule of St. Benedict* that the abbot read the Gospel at Sunday Matins—this had been taken as a

---

[85] [Cypr.] *Ep.* 75.6 'nec observari illic omnia aequaliter quae Hierosolymis observantur'. For Firmilian's visits to Origen in the Holy Land, see Eus. *Hist. Eccl.* vi. 27, and Jer. *De Vir. Illust.* 54 ('sub occasione sanctorum locorum').

[86] E.g. Dix, 328ff., 348ff.; Baumstark, 39ff., 140ff., 154ff. Cf. G. Kretschmar (1956), 46 '(the combination of liturgy and biblical history) war auch ein Reichtum, der Ost und West befruchtet hat'.

[87] F. C. Conybeare, *Rituale Armenorum* (1905), 516. For Edessa, cf. F. C. Burkitt, *Proc. Brit. Acad.* 10 (1921–3), 323–4.

[88] Cf. Ch. Pietri (1976), i, 575ff.

[89] See L. Duchesne (1919), 265; Baumstark, 154ff.

legacy of the bishop's Sunday reading at the Holy Sepulchre.[90]

These last-mentioned instances of supposed borrowings from Jerusalem are, as it happens, traceable only several centuries after the pilgrimage of Egeria; and similarity of practice is not a conclusive argument for the dependence of one on the other. In considering, for instance, the antecedents of 'stational' worship at Rome it is important not to overlook the evidence of the fourth century for the celebration there of the festivals of apostles and martyrs.[91] It cannot be established, moreover, precisely how the observances of Jerusalem found their way into the liturgy of other churches. Certainly pilgrims like Egeria, who would return home to a position of considerable prestige in the local community, must have been important in disseminating the pattern of worship from Jerusalem; but it is unlikely that all pilgrims would share her acute powers of observation. It is tempting to believe that a greater role should be assigned to the clergy in the spread of liturgical practice; those 'forty or fifty' bishops, for example, whom Egeria observed attending the *Encaenia* celebrations in Jerusalem might be expected to have carried back to their own churches some of the pattern of worship which they encountered in the Holy Land.

Despite its influence elsewhere, the essential character of the Jerusalem liturgy—as a biblical replica *in situ*—could not be recreated away from the holy places. Only there was the local background of biblical history and tradition which gave vivid point to the ceremonies. There is an interesting contrast to be drawn with an incident in Alexandria in 346. The bishop, Athanasius, returned in triumph to his city, riding on a donkey and accompanied by cheering crowds, who spread precious clothing on the road before him.[92] This was clearly

---

[90] *Benedicti Regula*, xi. 9 (*CSEL* 75 (1960), 58) '.... cum honore et timore stantibus omnibus'.

[91] Cf. Jer. *Comm. in Galat.* ii, pref. (*PL* 26, 355) 'ubi alibi tanto studio et frequentia ad Ecclesias et ad Martyrum sepulchra concurritur?' For Jerome's own experience as a young man in Rome, see *Comm. in Hiez.* xii, 40.5 (*CC* 75, 556) '.... diebus dominicis sepulchra apostolorum et martyrum circumire...'. N. B. also Prudentius, on the festivals of Hippolytus (*Peristeph.* 11, 195ff.) and Peter and Paul (ibid. 12, 57ff.).

[92] Greg. Naz. *Orat.* 21.27-9 (*PG* 35, 1113-17) describes the occasion.

a deliberately staged effort at reproducing, in Alexandria, the biblical account of Christ's entry into Jerusalem: by this means the bishop sought to outdo the recognized pattern of ceremonial *adventus* into the cities of the empire.[93] But Alexandria was not Jerusalem, and while Athanasius' standing in the city might make the imitation of an imperial arrival appropriate, the biblical echoes were mere presumption. A bishop of Jerusalem might well have been affronted by the extravagance of Athanasius' return, which had neither the biblical credentials of the holy places, nor the ritualized context of a liturgy to justify it—and it was upon these two supports that the uniqueness of his own Palm Sunday ceremony rested.

.What Alexandria could not reproduce was that indissoluble link between place and piety which gave to the Christian Holy Land its particular appeal. The entire conception which I have sketched—buildings, holy places, liturgy—represents a unity inspired by a common basis in the Bible, and expressed in a complex re-creation of this biblical past in the Palestine of the present. In observing and participating in the progress of the church's year in Jerusalem the Christian pilgrim was displaying a devotion which not only was unique to the Holy Land but the very essence of which was derived from the appropriateness of place and season: to visualize and re-enact the biblical narrative in itself required no special context; but only the holy places of Palestine provided that particular stimulus to pious conviction summed up by Egeria's 'eadem die... in eodem loco'.

[93] Ibid. 29 'εἰκὼν καὶ αὕτη τῆς ἐπιδημίας Χριστοῦ'. For *adventus*, cf. above, p.81.

6. Jerusalem or Babylon? Relics, Tourism, and Wealth

As the pilgrim Egeria observed the passage of the liturgical year in the church of Jerusalem one particular detail of the Good Friday ceremonies caught her attention: the wood of the cross, displayed on this day for public veneration, was kept (it will be recalled) under heavy guard—the bishop never letting his hands off it, and a posse of deacons encircling it. Egeria was told the reason for these precautions: in times past one zealous worshipper, on kissing the sacred wood, had bitten off a portion to keep for himself.[1] This incident well illustrates several facets of the pilgrims' impact at the holy places. Most obviously it exemplifies the sheer practical difficulties which arose in coping with the numbers of visitors; the church authorities in fourth-century Jerusalem were clearly having to contend with problems of security and crowd control such as would be familiar today to the guardians of any much-frequented tourist attraction. The evidence suggests that Jerusalem was less than successful in controlling would-be purloiners of its prize relic. The Syrian city of Apamea, for example, came to possess—and to treasure—a piece of the wood ('a cubit in length' according to Procopius) which had been stolen by a pilgrim;[2] while, as early as the middle of the fourth century, bishop Cyril's repeated references to the widespread distribution of the fragments around the Mediterranean world raise inevitable questions about the means of their acquisition: not all of them

---

[1] *It. Eg.* 37.2.
[2] Procop. *Bell. Persic.* ii. 11.4: the fragment was instrumental in protecting the city against Chosroes.

can have originated with those privileged enough, like the elder Melania, to receive a portion from the hand of the bishop of Jerusalem himself.[3] It was not long before the Jerusalem church made a virtue of necessity, and invested the wood of the cross with miraculous qualities of regeneration: no matter how much was removed by pious enthusiasts, it was always remarkably replaced.[4]

Yet the urge to possess fragments of the cross is symptomatic of something more than the mere souvenir-hunting inevitably associated with crowds of visitors. It can be shown to stem from the same enthusiasm for the visible remains of biblical history which has emerged so prominently in previous chapters. Any relics originating from the Holy Land (I shall suggest) were treasured possessions precisely because they were capable of arousing that kind of vivid reaction which the holy places themselves stimulated, and which the church's liturgy mirrored. The possibility of acquiring Holy Land relics represented a substantial development, in that the response of the pilgrim visiting the sites, typified in Paula's 'eyes of faith', was no longer confined uniquely to the Holy Land, but, through the mobility of relics in the hands of returning pilgrims, capable of being recreated far afield among local Christian congregations.

The wood of the cross was the principal agent of this process, the most widely circulated of the physical remains of the biblical past.[5] Almost every area of the Roman empire yields evidence of the presence of fragments of the cross by the beginning of the fifth century: Syria, Asia Minor, Italy, Gaul, Africa.[6] In the last case a *martyrium* dedicated as early as 359 (at Tixter in Mauretania) boasted a collection of relics which included a fragment of the cross in addition to remains of local martyrs and Peter and Paul; it laid claim, moreover, to earth from the Holy Land, 'de terra prom-

---

[3] Paul. Nol. *Ep.* 31.1; cf. Cyril, *Catech.* iv. 10, x. 19, xiii. 4.

[4] Paul. Nol. *Ep.* 31.6 '...detrimenta non sentiat et quasi intacta permaneat...'.

[5] Cf. A. Frolow (1961), 155ff.

[6] E.g. Joh. Chrys. *Quod Christus sit Deus*, 10 (*PG* 48, 826) (Antioch); Greg. Nys. *V. Macrinae*, 30 (Asia Minor); Paul. Nol. *Ep.* 31.1 (Italy/Gaul—cf. the fragment at the Sessorian basilica in Rome, above, p. 48); *CIL* viii, 9255 (Mauretania, cf. J. F. Matthews, *Class. Rev.* 88 (1974), 104, and next note).

issionis ubi natus est Christus'.[7] Such soil from the holy places was another species of Holy Land relic eagerly transported by returning pilgrims; spots specifically alleged to have borne Christ's own footprints were particularly susceptible to plunder, notably the place of the Ascension at the summit of the Mount of Olives (as with the wood of the cross, an endless quarry thanks to miraculous regeneration).[8] There is more evidence from Africa: the ex-official Hesperius in the neighbourhood of Hippo had a lump of earth which a friend had brought back from the Holy Land hanging in his bedroom to ward off misfortune (when later transported to a public shrine it became a source of healing miracles);[9] while Augustine pointed the finger at the Donatists who venerated earth from the Holy Land and yet insisted on the rebaptism of any Christians who came from there.[10]

Individual pilgrims would treasure their own *eulogiae*—mementos rendered precious by contact with holy places (or holy men).[11] Egeria's, for instance, were the small private gifts of locally cultivated produce (fruit from Mount Sinai or the 'garden of John the Baptist') presented to her by the monks as they escorted her on her travels[12]—not relics in the strictest sense, but none the less having the special *imprimatur* of originating from the land of the Bible. Perhaps the handiest—and eventually the most popular—of these portable links with the holy places were small flasks of the oil which kept alight the lamps at the Holy Sepulchre. The collections dating from the sixth century at Monza and Bobbio in north Italy, with their realistic iconography of the holy places in miniature, are the most celebrated examples of these pilgrims' *ampullae*[13]—and it is to the record of the unknown pilgrim from neighbouring Piacenza that we owe the only eye-witness account of the oil which they contained being sanctified through contact with the wood of the cross: the oil

[7] *MEFR* 10 (1890), 440–68 (= *CIL* viii, suppl. iii, 20600).
[8] Paul. Nol. *Ep.* 31.4, Sulp. Sev. *Chron.* ii. 33.6–8.
[9] August. *Civ. Dei*, xxii. 8 (*CC* 48, 820).   [10] Id. *Ep.* 52.2.
[11] Cf. B. Bagatti (1949); B. J. Kötting (1950), 403–13; A. Stuiber, *RAC* 6 (1966), 925ff.
[12] *It. Eg.* 3.6, 11.1, 15.6, 21.3; cf. G. F. M. Vermeer (1965), 76.
[13] See A. Grabar (1958).

in the flasks, the pilgrim alleges, boiled so furiously on touching the fragments that the caps had to be replaced to prevent all the liquid being spilled.[14] In taking away oil from the Sepulchre pilgrims were only echoing the veneration which surrounded any martyr's tomb, where oil from the burning lamps was one of the mementos which worshippers might make their own;[15] yet with the additional credential of contact with the cross oil from the Holy Land became a portable representative of the holy places, capable of being transported to distant congregations.

The range of Holy Land relics was considerably extended with the sudden awakening, towards the end of the fourth century, of the impetus to discover hitherto unsuspected remains:[16] thus revelations unearthed a succession of Old Testament prophets, Habakkuk, Micah, Zechariah, to be capped only by the emergence, in December 415, of the tomb of the first Christian martyr, St. Stephen. Within less than three years of this event, the presbyter Orosius had carried relics of Stephen from the Holy Land to North Africa and, surprisingly, to the island of Minorca.[17]

A description of the translation of some remains of one Old Testament figure points the way to setting this export of sacred articles from the Holy Land in the dominant biblical context of pilgrimage. In the pamphlet which Jerome wrote against Vigilantius in defence of the veneration of relics, he pictured the scene as relics of the prophet Samuel were transported to the court of Arcadius at Constantinople: the whole route, he would have us believe, was lined by the faithful, linking the Holy Land to the Hellespont in a unison chorus of acclamation.[18] The typical response in the Holy Land, the vivid realization of biblical history, was seen through the reaction of the crowds to be transmitted along the journey to Constantinople; the relics were representative of the biblical

---

[14] Anton. Placent. *Itin.* 20. Cf. the oil which poured from Peter the Iberian's relic of the cross, *V. Pet. Iber.* 29–30. On the oil's miraculous qualities, see Cyril Scyth. *V. Sabae*, 27: the saint cleared the demons from Mt. Castellium by sprinkling holy oil.

[15] Cf. Joh. Chrys. *Hom. in Martyres* (*PG* 50, 664) 'ἔλαβε ἔλαιον ἅγιον ...'.

[16] See esp. H. Delehaye (1933), 68ff.

[17] See below, pp. 211ff.

[18] Jer. *C. Vigilant.* 5. For Samuel's arrival in Constantinople, see *Chron. Pasch.* s.a. 406 (Dindorf, 569).

prophet, and the faithful *en route* responded as though to his physical presence ('quasi praesentem viventemque') just in the way that pilgrims in the Holy Land visualized biblical events at the holy places the visited. The 'eyes of faith' here were focused, not on the fixed landscape of Palestine, but on a moving target—on portable remains which carried their biblical credentials with them, without territorial restriction. Some remarks of Paulinus of Nola are instructive. In a passage where he is outlining the pilgrim's satisfaction at seeing the holy places of Palestine in recollection of the biblical past he includes the acquisition of portions of earth from the Holy Land and of the wood of the cross as the concomitant of such visual satisfaction.[19] The theme is more fully discussed in the letter he wrote (in 403) to Sulpicius Severus to accompany a fragment of the cross which he was sending for the dedication of Sulpicius' new church at Primuliacum (Paulinus had himself received some of the wood brought back from Jerusalem by his kinswoman Melania). The emphasis again is firmly on vision. All that Severus will see with the naked eye is a few scraps of wood; but this is only a stimulus to the wider lens of his 'interior eyesight' ('interna acies') which will summon up a picture of the whole series of biblical events surrounding the Crucifixion, and their implications for Christian belief ('with his interior eyesight he will see the whole meaning of the cross in this tiny fragment').[20] These visual consequences of the possession of the fragments are, following Paulinus' argument, to be a reward for the Christian conviction which Severus has displayed in the past without the aid of such obvious confirmation. Paulinus' interpretation here amounts to a reproduction, through the portable medium of the relics, of the immediate and visual reaction displayed by the pilgrims at the holy places *in situ*. Severus' 'interior eyesight' and Paula's 'eyes of faith' are one and the same. In the possession of fragments of the wood of the cross, Paulinus in Italy and Sulpicius Severus in southern Gaul (and their local congregations) shared in the pilgrims' experience of confronting Christian history face to face.

[19] *Ep.* 49.14.
[20] *Ep.* 31.1; cf. *Ep.* 32.11 (from lines inscribed at Nola) 'totaque in exiguo semine vis crucis est'.

Such an interpretation of the interest in physical remains from the Holy Land, as an extension of the pilgrims' biblical realism, is mirrored more widely in the Christian enthusiasm to possess relics of apostles and martyrs. There is no doubt that bones, ashes, or some object associated with the saint, were taken to be representative of his presence among the local congregation—a *praesentia* essential to his effective intercession on their behalf.[21] But the *praesentia* was no mere abstraction: the fragmentary remains were taken as visible testimony of the saint to whom they belonged. A classic text here is the sermon *De Laude Sanctorum* by Victricius bishop of Rouen, friend of Paulinus and another enthusiastic collector of relics: Victricius argues along lines which are identical to the interpretation which Paulinus places on the fragments of the cross—the physical remains, the 'blood and dust', are what the eye sees; yet this visual experience opens the 'eyes of the heart' (another variant of the 'eyes of faith') to apprehend the presence of the saint himself, 'ubi est aliquid, ibi totum est'.[22] Where Paulinus envisaged the whole import of the cross flooding before Severus' eyes at the sight of the mere fragments, Victricius proclaimed that the sight of nothing but scraps of dust would stimulate vision of the saint whole and entire. The theme is common to sermons on the martyrs.[23] It is particularly vividly expressed, for example, by Gregory of Nyssa, preaching in honour of the martyr Theodore.[24] He pictures the faithful approaching a casket of relics:

those who behold them embrace them as though the actual body, applying all their senses, eyes, mouth, and ears; then they pour forth tears for his piety and suffering, and bring forward their supplications to the martyr as though he were present and complete . . .

---

[21] E.g. Jer. *C. Vigilant.* 6, 10 ('. . . . quomodo in vilissimo pulvere et favilla, nescio qua, tanta signorum virtutumque praesentia'); cf. Ambrose, *Ep.* 22.11, and below, p. 213 (Stephen).

[22] *De Laud. Sanct.* 10 (*PL* 20, 452); on Victricius' relics, cf. ibid. 6.

[23] Cf. Theodoret's defence of the cult of relics in his *Cure of Pagan Ills*, viii. 11 (indivisibility of the martyr), with e.g. Gaudentius of Brescia, *Tract.* 17. 35–6 ('pars ipsa, quam meruimus, plenitudo est'); Chromatius of Aquileia, *Serm.* 26.1; Paul. Nol. *Carm.* 27, 440ff.

[24] *PG* 46, 740a-b.

The sheer visual realism here portrayed is exactly that of the pilgrim at the holy places, now evoked by scraps of a saint's remains.[25] The conclusion is simple, but effective: through the circulation of relics, no matter how meagre, the saint could be present, and above all be seen to be present, in any number of places at once—'hic et ubique'. Likewise, through the diffusion of remains from the Holy Land—wood of the 'cross', soil from the holy places, oil from the Sepulchre—the visual enthusiasm typical of the pilgrim on the spot could be disseminated and shared by congregations far and wide.

The urge to leave the Holy Land with some relic in hand has so far been interpreted as an aspect of the Christian pilgrim's understanding of his enterprise, regarding the holy places as a fundamentally biblical objective. Yet the movement of relics from the Holy Land, as Egeria's Good Friday anecdote confirms, is by no means entirely explained in such terms: it inevitably reflected as well other trends not unique to the holy places, nor indeed specifically Christian. Interpretations (like that offered by Paulinus of Nola) founded on Christian conviction held the field side by side with less exclusive reactions to the possession of a relic such as a fragment of the cross. Worn or carried everywhere by its owner, a piece of the wood could be held to act primarily as a talisman—a potent guarantee of good fortune akin to the power traditionally exercised throughout antiquity by magical amulets (and still widely effective in the Christian empire).[26] It was to this end, for example, that Macrina, the sister of Basil and Gregory of Nyssa, wore round her neck a fragment of the cross encased in a metal ring;[27] similarly, we shall observe Peter the Iberian making his way to Jerusalem from the court of Theodosius II under the protection of a piece of the cross carried inside a copy of St. John's Gospel.[28] In the

---

[25] Cf. Asterius of Amasea on the devotion to the martyr Phocas, cited above, p. 103.

[26] Cf. A. A. Barb, 'The Survival of Magical Arts', in A. Momigliano (1963), 100–25. For popular superstition and the *lignum crucis*, see Joh. Chrys. *Quod Christus sit Deus*, 10 (*PG* 48, 826), and Jer. *Comm. in Matt.* iv, 23.5 (*CC* 77, 212) on the 'superstitiosae mulierculae'.

[27] Greg. Nys. *V. Macrinae*, 30 (ed. P. Maraval, *SChr* 178, 238ff.), with F. J. Dölger (1932).

[28] See *V. Pet. Iber.* 29–30 (below, pp. 227–8).

same vein, when a relic of the cross formed the centrepiece of a church dedication, as at Primuliacum, language depicting its protective power was prominent: Sulpicius' relic was thus 'a guarantee of present safety and a pledge of eternal salvation'.[29]

The wood of the cross, although especially esteemed, had no monopoly of such potency. It can be observed, for example, in connexion with the devotion to Symeon Stylites, a holy man perched on his column who was the focus (according to his biography) of pilgrim journeys from all over the world; in his case it was the small statues of the saint, brought back by the returning faithful, which functioned as talismans—examples were to be seen erected at the entrances of workshops in Rome.[30] The mention of such effigies introduces the inevitable commercial interest which was exploited in response to the pilgrims' hunger for relics and mementos—replicas of Symeon were obviously being manufactured to meet the visitors' needs, as for the same purpose were medallions showing a representation of the stylite saint on his column (some of these survive).[31] There seems here to be clear recognition of the commercial potential involved in the manufacture of tourist souvenirs for the pilgrim market —again a feature far from unique to the holy places of Christianity. It is worth recalling that one of the promotions mounted in the second century by the new Asclepius cult of Alexander of Abonuteichus had been the manufacture of paintings and effigies of the god to be circulated by pilgrims.[32]

As for the Holy Land, it is easier to assert than to demonstrate in detail that the enthusiasm of pilgrims at the holy places had economic consequences of the kind attested around Symeon's pillar. That there was commercial gain to be achieved from the transport of martyrs' relics from the eastern part of the empire is implied by Theodosius' law addressed to Maternus Cynegius endeavouring to prohibit,

---

[29] Paul. Nol. *Ep.* 31.1; cf. ibid. 32.8 'ad cotidianam tutelam atque medicinam...'. The portion of the cross preserved at Constantinople was a talisman for the preservation of the city: Socr. *Hist. Eccl.* i. 17.

[30] Theodoret, *Hist. relig.* 26.11 'φυλακήν ... καὶ ἀσφάλειαν ἐντεῦθεν πορίζοντας'.

[31] See J. Lassus (1932).   [32] Lucian, *Alexander*, 18.

among other things, 'traffic' in relics ('nemo mercetur').[33] It is perhaps safe to assume that a good deal of such traffic may have contributed to the early circulation of alleged relics of the cross: the many pieces of wood which cannot legitimately have originated from the hands of the bishop of Jerusalem may have been, if not stolen by pilgrims, then at least purchased in the vicinity of the holy places. At a later period the profusion of *ampullae* is sufficient indication of the readiness to manufacture objects for the pilgrim market; but as early as the reign of Constantine there is an isolated mention of ikons of Christ available in the Holy Land—Eusebius wrote to the emperor's sister rebuking her for seeking to obtain one for herself.[34]

The most substantial evidence of the development of a commercial interest at a site frequented by pilgrims comes, not from Jerusalem, but from Mamre. This sacred spot was the focus of a long tradition of pilgrimage, revered not only by Jews and Christians for its memories of Abraham, but also as a centre of pagan worship; in ordering the building of a church here Constantine, as a Christian emperor, had sought to monopolize this devotion. But the application to the site of a Christian label was hardly enough to eradicate the habits which had come to characterize the motley gatherings at the shrine. Mamre was celebrated for its annual fair, when local inhabitants and visitors from farther afield in Palestine and Arabia conveniently exploited a religious assembly to exchange their wares (recalling, for instance, the traders in the Temple forecourt at the Jewish Passover);[35] the fair was a long-standing institution which, for the Jewish pilgrims at Mamre, evoked a painful memory—of the sale into slavery of many thousands of their people captured in the revolt against Hadrian.[36] It continued to persist long after Constantine's attempt to Christianize the shrine: Jerome was familiar with the annual 'crowded market', while Sozo-

---

[33] *CTh* ix. 17.7 (386); cf. Augustine, *De Opere Monach.* 36, on bogus monks who dealt in relics.

[34] Eus. *Ep. ad Constantiam* (*PG* 20, 1545). The letter's authenticity is open to doubt: Sr. C. Murray, *JTS* n.s. 28 (1977), 326ff.

[35] Soz. *Hist. Eccl.* ii. 4. For the association of fairs and religious gatherings, see R. Macmullen, *Phoenix*, 24 (1970), 336ff.

[36] Jer. *Comm. in Zach.* iii, 11.4 (*CC* 76a, 851); id. *Comm. in Hier.* vi, 18.6 (*CC* 74, 307); *Chron. Pasch.* (ed. Dindorf), 474.

men attests the continuing vitality of the gathering in his day.[37] Sozomen implies that the manifestations of pagan worship, libations and sacrifices, had come to an end with Constantine's intervention; yet archaeological finds in and around the sacred well, including numerous lamps and coins (objects specifically mentioned by Sozomen as offerings which had customarily been thrown into the well), far from indicating a termination of traditional practices, suggest rather an increased intensity in the period after Constantine.[38] The Christian emperor, it would appear, failed to deprive Mamre of its long-established associations.

The holy city itself, it may be assumed, must have witnessed commercial developments to accompany the boom in pilgrimage. It is possible to identify, for instance, the growth of small trades appropriate to the pilgrim demand. Thus Porphyry, having disposed of his fortune in Jerusalem, was able to earn a living as a shoemaker—a trade doubtless owing as much to the needs of the footsore visitors as to Porphyry's monastic training in Egypt.[39] His biographer, Mark the deacon, had similarly taken up the occupation of calligraphy in Jerusalem.[40] Furthermore, there was always the need for guides at the holy places, who would no doubt expect payment for their services: the 'simpliciores fratres' were ready to oblige with their rehearsal of the local traditions which, however erroneous, helped to satisfy the pilgrims' urge to seek out the location of the biblical narratives.[41]

Yet there were economic consequences for the Holy Land on a far larger scale than is implied merely by a consideration of the limited commercial developments associated with pilgrimage in its 'tourist' guise. The Christian focus on the holy places was the signal for a marked infusion of wealth into the region, as the donation of funds for pious ends became an established habit.[42] Imperial munificence and the new enthusiasm for a renunciation of worldly fortune concentrated on the Holy Land; here emperors and aristocratic

---

[37] Jer. *Comm. in Zach.* l.c., Soz. l.c.
[38] See E. Mader (1957), 107, and 151ff. for detailed survey.
[39] Marc. Diac. *V. Porph.* 9. Shoemaking was one of the activities of the Pachomian monks observed by Palladius: *Hist. Laus.* 32 (Butler, 96).
[40] *V. Porph.* 5.   [41] Cf. above, p. 85.
[42] See the fundamental study of M. Avi-Yonah (1958).

ladies would pour out extravagant donations to the church
and the charitable institutions which it supported; monasteries would spring up on the proceeds of landed estates, the
products of the increasing momentum to dispose of vast
wealth in obedience to the Lord's command. Alongside the
dramatic renunciations were the less spectacular workings of
wealthy patronage, providing a durable support for the institutions of the church in the Holy Land. While as a constant accompaniment to this outward show of the new interest in the land of the Bible there flowed the continuing
stream of lesser men, monks and pilgrims with their modest
offerings to be deposited at the holy places.

The desire to dispose of ancestral wealth was pursued with
unrelenting (and improvident) rigour. When the Roman
widow Paula died at Bethlehem in 404, her daughter Eustochium, left in charge of the monastery in Bethlehem, found
herself faced with a huge debt as a consequence of her
mother's vow that she would die a beggar.[43] The younger
Melania, who had arrived in Jerusalem little better than a
pauper,[44] handed over her last fifty *solidi* to the bishop
announcing that she would not even keep so paltry a sum
from her vast patrimony[45]—which had once yielded an
annual revenue of 120,000 *solidi* (*c.* 1700 lb. of gold).[46] More
modest fortunes, too, like the 1400 gold pieces which Porphyry had to distribute in the Holy Land, were soon li-
quidated; Porphyry himself (as we have noted) had to find a
living in shoemaking.[47]

The political circumstances of the western empire at the
end of the fourth century helped towards this direction of
wealth into the Holy Land church. At a period subject to the
constant threat of barbarian invasion the insecurity confronting the owners of landed property was to overcome, for the
few who inclined to some act of pious renunciation, the inherent senatorial reluctance to part with the possessions which
lay at the basis of their status:[48] that the estates of senators

[43] Jer. *Ep.* 108.15.6–7, 30.   [44] *V. Mel.* 35.
[45] Ibid. 30.   [46] Ibid. 15.
[47] The money was Porphyry's share in the family property: *V. Porph.* 6.
[48] Cf. M. T. W. Arnheim (1972), 143ff. A good instance is Ausonius' incompre-
hension in the face of Paulinus' disposal of his estates: e.g. *Ep.* 27 (Loeb), 110ff.

might fall victim to the barbarians was a prospect which touched the most sensitive nerves of aristocratic possessiveness. Melania's liquidation of her estates in the West was thus carried out in the teeth of the Gothic raids, precisely to forestall their falling into the hands of Alaric while still in her possession.[49] Some property in Spain had, however, to be left unsold until after she had arrived in Jerusalem (*c.*417), when part of it raised a small sum of gold 'snatched from the jaws of the lion', which was handed over to the church.[50]

The principal beneficiaries of this liberality were, of course, the church and its institutions: buildings and furnishings assumed a showy opulence, while the funds made available by rich benefactors were employed in the maintenance of monasteries and the diverse charitable activities associated with the holy places. The silks and silver which had adorned luxurious houses became instead altar-hangings and church plate;[51] when Melania the younger began to dispose of her estates lavish gifts of money were distributed through the eastern provinces in a rush of almsgiving— 15,000 *solidi*, for instance, to Palestine, and another donation of 45,000 *solidi* to an unknown destination.[52] She was following in the steps of her grandmother, whose generosity had borne comparison with the wealth of Persia.[53] Porphyry gave away all to those in need, and was a 'second Abraham' in his hospitality to visitors to Jerusalem.[54]

Such emphasis on the more spectacular displays of individual munificence tends to overshadow the longer-term provisions which the founders of churches and monasteries made for their maintenance and upkeep, in the form of annual re-

[49] Pall. *Hist. Laus.* 61; cf. *V. Mel.* 19 'happy are those who have sold their belongings before the assault of the barbarians'.

[50] *V. Mel.* 37 (cf. the similar expression at *Hist. Laus.* l.c.).

[51] E.g. for the younger Melania, *Hist. Laus.* l.c., *V. Mel.* 19; cf. Marc. Diac. *V. Porph.* 9 (silver plate).

[52] Compare the lists in *Hist. Laus.* 61 and *V. Mel.* 15; for the 45,000 *solidi*, *V. Mel.* 17 (it provoked an encounter with the devil!).

[53] *Hist. Laus.* 54 '(her generosity) is not mine to recount, but rather a task for those who dwell in Persia'. Butler understands this to mean that the Persians were among the beneficiaries—which is how the expanded 'B' text interpreted it (*PG* 34, 1226).

[54] Marc. Diac. *V. Porph.* 9.

venues from estates and properties transferred to them.[55] It is obvious that the continuing support of a regular income was necessary if the influx of aristocratic wealth was to be anything more than an extravagant and short-lived gesture; by the sixth century it would be laid down in a law that no new church could be consecrated without adequate endowments for repairs, lighting, maintenance, etc.[56] Of the endowments of the early foundations, however, we are unaware; only in connexion with the church in Gaza is the ownership of property alluded to—the deacon sent to a neighbouring village to collect revenues owing to the church was attacked by the local pagan inhabitants.[57]

How best to dispose of funds in accord with the Gospel message was an issue widely debated in the early church;[58] the authorities who had the responsibility for the maintenance of buildings or the upkeep of charity would be concerned to check that desire for a wholesale dispersal of their fortunes which gripped the wealthy pioneers of the ascetic life. This could only result in the sort of poverty which is alleged to have beset Melania and Pinianus on their arrival in Jerusalem, who, having given away the money realized from the sale of their estates, even considered having themselves enrolled on the list of the poor to be supported by the church.[59] It is reported by one source that Pinianus earned a living by selling wood which he had transported from the desert, Melania by spinning wool (we recall Porphyry's shoemaking)[60]—even so, her second monastery could only be founded with the aid of a gift of 200 *solidi*.[61] The cautious voice of the authorities is heard in the advice of the three African bishops, Augustine, Alypius, and Aurelius, who sought to restrain the instinct of Melania and Pinianus to sell

---

[55] On this, and other aspects of church finances, see J. Gaudemet (1958), 288ff., and A. H. M. Jones, *The Later Roman Empire* (1964), 894ff.

[56] Justinian, *Nov.* lxvii. 2 (538) (= *Corpus Iuris Civilis*, iii, 345).

[57] *V. Porph.* 22.

[58] Cf. the anecdote of Paesius and Isaiah in Pall. *Hist. Laus.* 14, and the dispute over the disposal of revenues between bishop Theophilus and Isidore in Alexandria: id. *Dialogus*, 35 (cf. Soz. *Hist. Eccl.* viii.ǀ12.6).

[59] *V. Mel.* 35.   [60] *V. Pet. Iber.* 33ff.

[61] *V. Mel.* 49. With the penury of Melania and Pinianus in Palestine can be contrasted their wealth in Africa, ·allegedly the reason for the attempt to detain Pinianus as a priest at Hippo: see August. *Ep.* 125.2, 126.7ff.

all their African properties and distribute the proceeds in charity: 'the money which you now distribute to the monasteries will soon be spent; but if you wish to leave an everlasting memorial in heaven and on earth, then give to each monastery *premises and an income*'[62]—here were the two basic necessities of any foundation, which the senatorial landlord was best equipped to provide by transferring to the church the ownership of his estates. The advice seems to have been heeded at any rate in Africa where, alongside the usual gifts to the church of Thagaste of precious plate and hangings, Melania handed over a rich estate, larger (it is affirmed) than the town itself, and the two monasteries established there were each endowed with an adequate income.[63]

The problems created by extravagant beneficence can be illustrated from the experience of Jerome in Bethlehem. He had not far to look to behold the expensive silver which adorned, and obscured, the simple clay manger in which Christ was believed to have been born;[64] yet amidst this unproductive affluence it would be necessary to dispatch his brother to Dalmatia to sell off what was left of their family property after the barbarian raids in order to find the funds to cope with the visitors to his monastery.[65] Paula, it will be recalled, died leaving a huge debt, and this despite the fact that, according to Jerome, she had been cautious in her generosity.[66] The liberality of the elder Melania must have been exceptionally disciplined if, as Palladius affirms, she was able to sustain her acts of charity for thirty-seven years.[67]

The pace for this private munificence in the Holy Land was set by the imperial example of Constantine and Helena. The flow of wealth from the court continued under Constan-

---

[62] *V. Mel.* 20.

[63] Ibid. 21–2 (the details of the estate are found in the Latin version). Pall. *Hist. Laus.* 61 says that Melania reserved her properties in Sicily, Campania, and Africa for the 'provision of monasteries'.

[64] *Hom. de Nativ. Domini* (*CC* 78, 524): 'O si mihi liceret illud praesepe videre, in quo Dominus iacuit! Nunc nos Christi quasi pro honore tulimus luteum, et posuimus argenteum'.

[65] Jer. *Ep.* 66.14 (in 398).

[66] *Ep.* 108.16 'non divitiarum magnitudine, sed *prudentia dispensandi*'.

[67] *Hist. Laus.* 54, presumably referring to the period from her withdrawal from Rome in 372 until her death.

tine's successors, and was to reach a new intensity with the activity of Eudocia, the empress of Theodosius II. Our evidence about this material involvement of the emperors is sparse, and again is limited to the public show of imperial largesse to the churches of the Holy Land, without conveying anything of the more settled financial arrangements which must have accompanied such individual gifts. Certainly the resources of the province were mobilized for the support of the church, whether for building activities,[68] or in the form of grants for the maintenance of charity;[69] when Porphyry of Gaza and the bishop of Caesarea visited the court of Arcadius they came away with a grant of 20 lb. of gold each 'from the revenues of Palestine'.[70] Not, however, until the middle of the fifth century and the activities of Eudocia do we hear anything of the provision of regular income for imperial foundations.[71]

Hardly better documented is the continuing tradition of the public display of imperial munificence. Cyril of Jerusalem could gaze on the gold, silver and precious stones which adorned the basilica on Golgotha where he was lecturing his catechumens, ascribing this grandeur to the sons of Constantine.[72] It is clear that the rich embellishment of the churches established by Constantine was continued after his death; although future generations would not recognize the magnificence of the Holy Land churches as anything other than the work of the first Christian emperor.[73] The only particulars we possess of an early imperial foundation (after Constantine) concern the church at Gaza founded on the site of the destroyed temple of Marnas. Arcadius' empress, Eudoxia, gave to bishop Porphyry 200 lb. of gold for the building of the church, with the promise of more if necessary; the foundation was to include a hostel for visitors, with provision for them to stay three days. Her donation included some

---

[68] E.g. Eus. *V. Const.* iii. 31 (the Golgotha basilica).

[69] Theod. *Hist. Eccl.* i. 11.2–3 mentions grants from provincial revenues for the support of widows, virgins, etc.; cut off by Julian, these were subsequently restored, though only at one-third of their original level.

[70] Marc. Diac. *V. Porph.* 54.

[71] See below, pp. 239ff.

[72] *Catech.* xiv. 14; cf. the '*βασιλικὴ φιλοτιμία*' mentioned at xiv. 9.

[73] So Egeria: *It. Eg.* 25.9.

church plate, and was followed up by a gift of 32 columns of Carystian marble.[74]

There is no mistaking the appearance of opulence displayed by the Holy Land churches, and especially by those in and around Jerusalem. The silver adornment of the manger in Bethlehem, for example, or the glittering cross which topped the church of the Ascension on the Mount of Olives[75] were the focus of a new wealth and prestige, displayed to its fullest potential in the great liturgical festivals of the church in Jerusalem: Egeria was overawed by the richness of the decorations, the gold and silver, the jewels, the silk hangings, to say nothing of the fabric of the churches themselves, which shone with gilding, mosaic, and marble.[76] Such a show of wealth is reminiscent of the magnificence of the fourth-century Roman church, which attracted the attention of a number of notable outsiders—including the distinguished pagan senator Praetextatus,[77] as well as the historian Ammianus, both of whom were struck by the worldliness of the bishop of Rome and of the church over which he presided.[78] The property endowments of the Constantinian churches in Rome, recorded in the *Liber Pontificalis*, amounted to an annual revenue of some 400 lb. of gold[79]—which, although it will have grown during the century with further donations and legacies, represents a modest sum by comparison with the known resources of some Roman senators, the wealthiest of whom could command an annual income of 4000 lb. of gold, and those of the second rank 1500 or 1000 lb. of gold.[80] (The younger Melania's estates, we have seen, yielded c.1700 lb.) The income of landed senators, however, was largely surplus wealth, to be consumed in

---

[74] *V. Porph.* 53, 84 (marble columns).

[75] See Jer. *Comm. in Soph.* i. 15 (*CC* 76a, 673) '...de Oliveti monte quoque crucis fulgente vexillo'. Cf. *Ep.* 108.12.1, and *Comm. in Hiez.* iii, 11.23 (*CC* 75, 125).

[76] *It. Eg.* 25.8–9.

[77] See his celebrated observation of the standing of the bishop of Rome: Jer. *C. Ioh. Hier.* 8.

[78] Amm. Marc. xxvii. 3.14–15: his unfavourable comparison of the ostentation of the Roman church with the modest conduct of provincial bishops. Cf. Jerome's satire on the Roman clergy (esp. *Ep.* 22): D. S. Wiesen (1964), 69ff.

[79] Ed. L. Duchesne, i, 170ff. Cf. Ch. Pietri (1976), i, 79ff.; Fergus Millar (1977), 186–7.

[80] See Olympiodorus, fr. 44 (*Frag. Hist. Graec.* iv, 67–8).

occasions of lavish public display;[81] the revenue required for the actual running of estates would be only a small proportion of these total sums. Whereas, in the case of the church, the amount of surplus revenue (if any) is likely to have been small; the 400 lb. of gold probably represents a sum close to the income needed to meet the expenses of maintenance and charity. The opulent style of the Roman church which so impressed observers can no doubt be accounted for in additional donations of vestments and treasures: the lists in the *Lib. Pont.*, for example, abound with the precious ornaments of gold and silver which Constantine presented to the churches.

The material situation of the church in Jerusalem cannot have been much different from that in Rome: a revenue from endowments supplemented by individual donations of church plate or furnishings. Regrettably no document has survived comparable to that preserved by the *Lib. Pont.*, and hence any estimation of the real wealth of the Jerusalem church in the fourth century becomes hazardous. The Constantinian foundations we must assume to have been suitably endowed; the fact that the Roman basilicas of St. Peter and St. Paul were presented with properties entirely in the eastern half of the empire makes it not unlikely that the church in Jerusalem, too, benefited from the revenues of imperial domains in the East.[82] In Palestine itself the emperors had held property since the dissolution of Herod's kingdom, and this will have accumulated as a result of the two Jewish wars;[83] the later empire saw imperial *saltus* in the south of the province,[84] while the empress Eudocia certainly possessed

---

[81] Cf. the remarks of R. P. Duncan-Jones in *PBSR* 31 (1963), 160ff. For expenditure on public games, see Olympiod. l.c. The Republican background: I. Shatzman, *Senatorial Wealth and Roman Politics* (1975), ch. 4.

[82] For these eastern estates (in Syria, Egypt, Mesopotamia) see Duchesne, 177ff.

[83] Imperial bequests from the family of Herod are mentioned in Joseph. *Antiq. Jud.* xviii. 31; Vespasian is said to have declared the territory of Judaea his own property, id. *Bell. Jud.* vii. 216–17 (from which Joseph. benefited: *Vita*, 422, 425); the balsam estates at Jericho and Engeddi were imperial possessions, Pliny, *Hist. Nat.* xii. 54.

[84] The *Saltus Gerariticus* and the *Saltus Constantinianus* (?): see A. H. M. Jones, *The Cities of the Eastern Roman Provinces*² (1971), 281, 464 n. 74, with A. Alt, *ZDPV* 69 (1953), 68–70; M. Avi-Yonah (1966), 123.

estates in the vicinity of Jerusalem.[85] Constantine's foundations in Jerusalem may well thus have received endowments
of nearby imperial properties, not to speak of any further
afield in the eastern provinces. Added to which, the Jerusalem church will also have had its share of the general restoration of church property which followed on the victory
over Licinius.[86]

The income needed to sustain the additional demands on
its resources as a centre of pilgrimage must have been considerable. At Antioch, for example, in John Chrysostom's
day the church's revenue was equivalent to that of one of the
city's wealthier, but not the very wealthy, inhabitants; with
these resources, John claimed, the church was able to meet
all the demands of charity, including the maintenance of
3000 widows and virgins.[87] That the Jerusalem revenues, by
contrast, were not always adequate to meet the extra commitments is suggested by the charges alleged against bishop
Cyril by his opponents, that during a period of famine he
had sold church treasures to raise money for the needy, including—the particular cause of offence—a gilded vestment
presented by Constantine to bishop Macarius for use in the
baptismal ceremony.[88] By the reign of Justinian the commitments of the *Anastasis* church in sustaining the crowds of
pilgrims were recognized in a law addressed (in 535) to the
archbishop of Jerusalem, in which it was partially exempted
from the general prohibition on the sale of church property,
and which compared the task of attending to the needs of the
'boundless number' of pilgrims with Christ's miraculous
feeding of the five thousand.[89] The emperor, advised that
there were pilgrims who would pay handsomely for dwellings
in proximity to the holy places (up to fifty times the annual
revenue that they produced), permitted the sale of properties
belonging to the church (though the exemption was not extended to church lands). This law was aimed at enabling the

---

[85] See below, p. 239.
[86] Cf. Eus. *V. Const.* ii. 39.
[87] Joh. Chrys. *Hom. in Matt.* 66.3 (*PG* 58, 630).
[88] Soz. *Hist. Eccl.* iv. 25.3–4; Theod. *Hist. Eccl.* ii. 27.1–2. The dancer who subsequently wore the garment to grace his act was reportedly struck dead.
[89] Justinian, *Nov.* xl (= *Corpus Iur. Civil.* iii, 258–9).

church of the *Anastasis* to pay off those creditors with the aid
of whose loans it had purchased a property for 380 lb. of gold
(which in turn was yielding an annual revenue of 30 lb. of
gold). It is clear that by this date the Jerusalem church had
become a property owner of some means: in the reign of
Anastasius the churches were faced with a tax demand for
100 lb. of gold, which the imperial officials had transferred
to them from citizens less able to pay. Despite the monk
Sabas' appeals at court against these exactions, relief only
came in the reigns of Anastasius' successors, Justin and
Justinian.[90]

In addition to this regular income as an owner of property
the church of Jerusalem could also, of course, count on the
offerings of the faithful.[91] Lucinus, for example, despatched
from Baetica financial contributions to the churches of Jerusalem and Alexandria;[92] while Sisinnius came to Bethlehem
bringing the church collections of the Christians in Toulouse
to be distributed among the monks of Palestine and Egypt
—and he was eager to be off to Egypt precisely for that
purpose.[93] This practice of sending contributions for charity
to the Holy Land was among the pious habits attacked by
Jerome's critic Vigilantius, although when he visited the holy
places he had himself not come without alms to distribute.[94]
Jerome's answer to Vigilantius' attack on these offerings was
naturally to invoke the New Testament and the injunctions
of St. Paul; he was at pains to point out that these resources
were expended in charitable enterprises, and not in filling the
coffers of the Jerusalem church.[95] His emphasis was different,
however, in his polemic against the establishment centred
around Melania and Rufinus in Jerusalem (by whose generosity the clergy were supported), where he pointedly re-

[90] Cyril Scyth. *V. Sabae*, 54.

[91] See A. H. M. Jones, *The Later Roman Empire* (1964), 894–5.

[92] Jer. *Ep.* 75.4.

[93] Id. *C. Vigilant.* 17 'propter sanctorum refrigeria'; cf. *Ep.* 119.2, and *Comm. in
Zach.* ii, pref. (*CC* 76a, 795) 'frater Sisinnius ire festinat ut odorem bonae fragran-
tiae, qui a te missus est fratribus, illuc quoque perferat'.

[94] *C. Vigilant.* 13 'qui tanta cunctos largitate donasti, ut nisi venisses Hierosolymam et tuas vel patronorum tuorum pecunias effudisses, omnes periclitaremur
fame'.

[95] l.c. 'non in avaritiam, sed in refrigerium'.

turned on a number of occasions to the theme of the divergence between their ascetic professions and the extravagance
of their way of life.[96] In this context the offerings of the faithful were presented as enriching the pockets of the bishop of
Jerusalem: 'you who abound in riches and profit from *the
faith of the whole world*'.[97]

That Jerome could portray the bishop of Jerusalem making a healthy profit from the offerings of pilgrims is an indication of how far the discussion has shifted from the ideal
conception of a holy city, a recreation of the biblical past in
the Palestine of the present, to the contemporary reality—a
city thronged with visitors and vulnerable to the possibility
of economic gain. The pilgrims' 'eyes of faith' were naturally
closed to all that surrounded the holy places, their field of
vision encompassing only the biblical scene which they had
come to witness; but Constantine's new Jerusalem, despite
the claims of Eusebius, remained a group of buildings
erected in the midst of a pre-existing city, and it is unlikely
that the pious attention which they aroused among Christian
visitors would be immune from the reality of their surroundings. The economic exploitation which we have been examin-
ing was but one instance of this intrusion of earthly matters
into the pilgrims' expectations of a 'heavenly' city.

The new Jerusalem and the old were, of course, one and
the same; and the Christian buildings were not a hermetical-
ly sealed enclave. Even in Eusebius' eulogy of the 'new' Jerusalem, the passers-by who glimpsed the magnificence of Constantine's buildings through the *propylaea* on the main street
are a reminder that its surrounding wall was all that separated the Golgotha precinct from the Roman *colonia* of Aelia
Capitolina.[98] The only significant transformation of the city
lay-out, in the fourth century, had been the demolition of
pagan temples and the creation of the Christian Golgotha; all
the other principal sites which were the focus of Christian
attention lay outside the boundary of Aelia—on the Mount
of Olives, Mount Sion, or away at Bethlehem. The Con-

---

[96] E.g. *Ep.* 57.12.5 'si quis e nobis inter Croesi opes et Sardanapalli delicias de sola
rusticitate se iactet...'; cf. other refs. at p. 171, n. 89.

[97] Jer. *C. Ioh. Hier.* 14.

[98] Eus. *V. Const.* iii. 39; cf. above, p. 14.

stantinian buildings, therefore—the physical presence of Christianity in fourth-century Jerusalem—although centrally placed, are unlikely to have appeared to outsiders to be the dominating characteristic of the city that is presented by the Christian sources (as revealed in my first chapter). We need to take account of the continued existence of much of the urban environment which had been laid out by the Hadrianic planners, save only for the temples which had fallen victim to the onset of the Christian Jerusalem. Regrettably the subsequent rebuildings of Jerusalem have obliterated from the archaeological record all but a few traces of this phase in its history (remains of the Forum, for example, and of monumental arches such as that known as *Ecce Homo*);[99] yet it must be supposed that Roman Aelia would have displayed the predictable range of public buildings and facilities associated with any other provincial city in the eastern Roman empire (especially as it was the location of a legionary camp). The Forum, of course, alongside the Golgotha buildings is noticed and referred to by Christian visitors—as in Egeria's allusion to the 'market-place'.[100] As for other features of Hadrian's colony, our knowledge depends on a list, difficult to interpret, of some of its buildings which survives in the *Chronicon Paschale*.[101] It includes two 'δημόσια', which have been taken to be 'public baths'—there is little to support such a designation, except that pools and watering-places are known to have been a feature of the city in the fourth century, which Christian guides (like the Bordeaux pilgrim's escort) sought to identify with those mentioned in the Gospels;[102] Jerome, too, confirms the presence of cisterns around Jerusalem to sustain the water-supply.[103] It is not improbable that buildings erected as part of the water-supply of Roman Aelia were being shown to Christian visitors as biblical monuments. This assumption is supported in the case of another building named in the *Chron. Pasch.* as the

---

[99] Cf. K. Kenyon (1974), 256ff., and Avi-Yonah (ed.), *Encyclopedia*, ii, 610ff.
[100] *It. Eg.* 43.7.
[101] Ed. Dindorf, i, 474. The basic discussion is still Vincent/Abel (1914), 6ff.
[102] See *It. Burd.* 589, 7–11; 590, 6–7; 592, 1–3. On Bethsaida, cf. Eus. *Onomastikon*, 58, with C. Kopp (1963), 307ff. For the suggestion that the 'δημόσια' are 'forums', see J. Wilkinson (1976), 78.
[103] *Comm. in Esai.* xiii, 49.14 (*CC* 73a, 543).

'τετράνυμφον', apparently a Nymphaeum with four porticoes; when this is placed alongside the Bordeaux pilgrim's description of the pool of Siloam, 'habet quadriporticum', it looks likely that the Hadrianic Nymphaeum and Christian monument are one and the same (there is evidence of Hadrianic building at the traditional site of Siloam).[104] Among other buildings in the list, the 'θέατρον' is less mystifying: despite the (almost universal) reticence of Christian visitors, we may presume that fourth-century Jerusalem still had its theatre—indeed Eusebius had claimed to have seen stones from the ruins of the Temple used to build 'pagan shrines and theatres'.[105] The mention of baths and theatre alone is sufficient reminder that Jerusalem cannot have been transformed in its entirety into the holy city of the pilgrims' imagination; the Christian focus of Golgotha was planted in what was a Roman colony, which retained many of the physical features characteristic of a Roman *urbs*. Even its Hadrianic name 'Aelia' failed to be supplanted by the Christian Jerusalem, but remained alongside it in the official designations of Byzantine lists.[106] In the *Onomastikon* Eusebius had used both names indiscriminately, but the influence of 'Aelia' is strong, as the name which he would have encountered in his official sources on the provincial organization;[107] most tellingly of all, it appears where it might be expected that the biblical Jerusalem would spring most immediately to mind—in the location of Golgotha 'in Aelia, to the north of Mount Sion'.[108]

The most incisive portrayal of the realities of urban life in Jerusalem in contrast to the Christian ideal comes, as might be expected, from the pen of Jerome. Having first arrived in

---

[104] *It. Burd.* 592, 1; for the excavations, see Vincent/Abel, 860ff., and Kopp (1963), 315ff. A church covered the site by the middle of the 5th cent.: A. Ovadiah (1970), 90ff.

[105] *Dem. Evang.* viii. 3.12 'τὰ τῶν πανδήμων θεαμάτων κατασκευάσματα'.

[106] Hierocles, 718, 8; Georgius Cyprius, 998 (ed. Honigmann, *Forma Imp. Byzant.* fasc. i, 41, 66). *Notit. Dign. Or.* 34.21 has 'Aelia' alone, as *Conc. Nicae.* Can. 7.

[107] As the official designation, 'Aelia' was the point of reference for routes and distances in contemporary Palestine: e.g. the road from Aelia to Jericho (*Onom.* 24), where we might have expected the biblical Jerusalem; but Rachel's tomb was at the fifth milestone 'from Jerusalem' (82).

[108] Ibid. 74. Even Egeria admitted Aelia at one point (in a context of routes and *mansiones*), *It. Eg.* 9.7 'regressa sum in Helia, id est in Ierusolimam'.

the Holy Land as a Christian haven after what he termed the
'Babylon' of Rome, he was in the course of time (in circumstances to be discussed later) to become disenchanted with
Jerusalem too.[109] Writing to Paulinus of Nola (in 395) from
the 'solitude' of Bethlehem he would see in Jerusalem the
traditional vices of life in the town; in tones worthy of Juvenal he confirmed the existence there, not only of the theatre,
but of all the paraphernalia of urban living. Jerusalem
was 'a crowded city, with its council, its garrison, its prostitutes, actors, jesters, and everything which is usually found in
other cities'; the dregs of the whole world gathered there—
'men of every race and so great a congestion of both sexes
('tanta utriusque sexus constipatio') that you are forced to
endure there everything that you seek to escape from
elsewhere'.[110] It is hard to believe that this thronged congestion of all sorts and conditions of men (and women) is the
same as the scene of Egeria's pious assemblies of Christian
pilgrims; there were certainly no prostitutes in her Jerusalem! Yet Jerome's remarks, for all their overstatement, do
at least furnish a glimpse of otherwise neglected aspects of
contemporary Jerusalem: its *curia* of city fathers, for example
—how far, one wonders, was this body percolated by Christianity, and how did it view the rival dominance in the city of
bishop and church?[111] The answer eludes us. There is corro-
borative evidence, however, for Jerome's 'garrison': the *Notitia
Dignitatum* records among the dispositions of the *dux Palaestinae* a division of cavalry described as 'Mauri Illyriciani' sta-
tioned in Jerusalem.[112]

Jerome's criticism lays emphasis on the motley and indiscriminate population; a point confirmed by the presence in
the city of a garrison whose name suggests that it had originated (in part at least) from north Africa. Diversity will have

[109] For the move from 'Babylon', see *Ep.* 45.6, and the preface to the translation
of Didymus' *De Spiritu Sancto* (*PL* 23, 101).

[110] *Ep.* 58.4.4; for even stronger language about Jerusalem, cf. Greg. Nys. *Ep.*
2.10. D. S. Wiesen (1964), 38–41, makes little of Jerome's comments here. On
Jerome and Jerusalem generally, see F. M. Abel (1920), and (along with other
towns) P. Antin (1961), 299ff.

[111] Cf. the study of this aspect of social change in Antioch, J. H. W. G. Liebeschuetz (1972), 224ff.

[112] *Notit. Dign. Or.* 34.21; for a *dux Palaestinae* in Jerusalem, see below, p. 166.

been a hallmark of the population since the foundation of Aelia, when colonists came from far and wide in the East to replace the Jews expelled by Hadrian.[113] There seems no reason to suppose that Christianity would predominate among this cosmopolitan population until the full impact of the Constantinian developments had its effect—there were certainly few parts of Palestine at the beginning of the fourth century which were extensively Christianized, and Eusebius picked out only a handful of Christian villages in the *Onomastikon*.[114] The likelihood of a considerable population of non-Christian onlookers observing the creation of the 'new Jerusalem' raises intriguing, if only speculative, questions: how would they react to the new buildings, to the crowds of Christian visitors, and, above all, to the ceremonial of the church festivals which must have enveloped the city at certain periods of the year?

The establishment of the Christian Jerusalem contributed enormously to the cosmopolitan nature of the city's inhabitants. The Constantinian foundations brought builders and artisans from all over the eastern empire,[115] to say nothing of the visitors and pilgrims attracted to the Holy Land. The diversity of their origins did not escape observers: bishop Cyril saw parallels with the great assembly of the Jewish Pentecost in Acts 2;[116] while Jerome claimed every nation to be represented at the holy places.[117] Against the general background of this international presence at the holy places, it is possible to isolate particularly close links over a broad zone to the east of the Mediterranean; the predominant 'catchment area' for worshippers at the Jerusalem festivals was the band of territory stretching from Egypt through to Syria and Mesopotamia, with Palestine at its centre. This was a region bound together by both commercial and cultu-

---

[113] Cassius Dio, lxix. 12.2; cf. Jer. *Comm. in Esai.* x, 34.8ff. (*CC* 73, 422–3) 'de diversis gentibus adductas Hierusalem colonias...', and id. *Hom. de Nativ. Dom.* (*CC* 78, 528).

[114] *Onom.* 26 (Anea), 108 (Iethira), 112 (Caraiatha). On the general level of Christianisation in the region, see Liebeschuetz (1978), id. (1979).

[115] Eus. *V. Const.* iii. 30.

[116] *Catech.* xvii. 16.

[117] *Ep.* 108.3.3 'cuius enim gentis homines ad sancta loca non veniunt?'; cf. *Ep.* 46.10, the 'flower' of all the churches assembled in the Holy Land.

ral ties,[118] to which Christianity had added the further bond of monasticism: when Egeria and Jerome referred to pilgrims from those areas whom they encountered assembling in Jerusalem it was monks in particular that they had in mind[119] —and a later chapter will demonstrate the important contacts between the holy places and monastic Egypt.[120]

The natural expression of the diversity of Jerusalem's population was, of course, the variety of the prevailing languages. For the Christian visitor, this was most obviously reflected in the church's liturgy. The Jerusalem services witnessed by Egeria were conducted in Greek, which was interpreted, for the benefit of the main body of the congregation, into what she calls 'Syriac', i.e. the local Aramaic dialect; while for those who knew only Latin, there were bi-lingual brethren on hand ('fratres et sorores grecolatini') to translate for them.[121] The same pattern characterized the services in the church of the Nativity at Bethlehem: at the funeral of Paula the psalms resounded in the three languages.[122] The presence of Greek and Aramaic spoken at the holy places is what we might expect to find: the local dialect of Palestine existing, as in other parts of the eastern empire, alongside the Greek of the educated, urban community;[123] the bishop, according to Egeria, knew his Aramaic, but still it was only Greek which was regarded as appropriate for the church's worship. The implication that the majority of the congregation spoke 'Syriac' confirms the affinities with the Aramaic and Syriac-speaking belt of Syria and Mesopotamia,[124] the place of origin of many of the visitors to the holy places. The inclusion in the liturgy of Latin, however, points also to a considerable presence of non-Greek-speaking westerners

---

[118] Cf. above, p. 53. On the cultural links, see the remarks of P. Brown, *JRS* 59 (1969), 96.

[119] E.g. *It. Eg.* 49.1 (*Encaenia*) 'de Mesopotamia vel Syria vel de Egypto aut Thebaida, ubi plurimi monazontes sunt...'.

[120] Below, pp. 185ff.   [121] *It. Eg.* 47.3–4.

[122] Jer. *Ep.* 108.29; cf. *Ep.* 147.4 '...in diversarum gentium linguis unus in laudem dei spiritus concinebat', and *Ep.* 46.10.3 'vox quidem dissona, sed una religio'.

[123] For detailed evidence, Fergus Millar, *JRS* 61 (1971), 5–8; in general, R. Macmullen, 'Provincial Languages in the Roman Empire', *Amer. Journ. Phil.* 87 (1966), 1–17.

[124] Cf. Millar, art. cit., 2ff.; Brown, l.c.

among the pilgrims. Such a description could not be applied
to the great western figures whose presence dominated Jerusalem towards the end of the century, Melania, Rufinus, and
their côterie—they were steeped in the Greek Fathers (Melania is said to have gone through the works of Origen and
others seven or eight times),[125] and presumably would find
no difficulty with Greek as the language of the church; they
were in regular touch with bishop John of Jerusalem, contacts which Jerome was perhaps wrong in assuming to have
taken place in Latin[126]—certainly, when Paula lay on her
death-bed, she was to converse with Jerome in Greek.[127] For
those western visitors in Jerusalem, on the other hand, who
(as Egeria herself) knew little or no Greek,[128] the services of
interpreters would enable them to participate to the full in
the demands of the liturgy.

The triple language of the Jerusalem church reflects the
cosmopolitan city which encased the new Jerusalem. The
mixture of tongues which the influx of visitors and pilgrims
contributed brings into fuller perspective the setting in which
Jerome could accuse the bishop of Jerusalem of being en-
riched by the religion 'of the whole world'. However the
faithful might imagine otherwise, his city was in practice an
international meeting-place which did not shrink from drawing material profit from its growing status as a religious
capital. As if in confirmation of this, bishop John himself acquired a reputation for worldliness from which he could not
escape. A tradition preserved in an eastern church calendar
reinterpreted the circumstances of his celebrated dispute
with Epiphanius (over the theological beliefs of Origen) entirely in terms of a disagreement about material wealth:[129]
they had grown up in the monastic life together, it was recalled, but Epiphanius was grieved to see his old colleague neg-
lecting his charitable duties in favour of more worldly habits,
dining off silver tableware. His visit to Jerusalem was seen as

---

[125] Pall. *Hist. Laus.* 55.
[126] Jer. *Ep.* 82.7 'assidua confabulatione et cotidiano Latinorum consortio'.
[127] Id. *Ep.* 108.28.2.
[128] Egeria seems only to have had the fragmentary Greek of a tourist: *It. Eg.* 7.7,
8.4, 13.4, 15.3 (although there is no mention of interpreters in her conversations
with local bishops).
[129] *Synaxarium Aethiopicum*, 7 June (*PO* i, 602ff.).

a crusade to recall John to his earlier virtues and asceticism; but Epiphanius found the former monk unrepentant, and when John challenged him for having, by a ruse, sold his tableware to raise alms for the poor, he was struck blind. Only then did he realize the error of his ways, and began to devote himself to a life of piety and charity.

It cannot be fortuitous that the eastern church preserved a story concentrating on the material wealth of bishop John, which only knew of his passage-of-arms with Epiphanius as a disagreement about the value of ascetic renunciation. The tradition is likely to have had its roots in an unease, in some quarters of the church, at the visible wealth of the bishop of Jerusalem. True, Jerome's polemic is only properly seen in the wider context of his dispute with the bishop; but his strident criticisms of the worldliness of Jerusalem as a city are an indication that he was only too conscious of the extravagant exploitation of the holy places and the showy wealth of local churches which the vogue for pilgrimage had introduced. The Christians' Holy Land could not simply be the re-creation of the biblical background which the pious wanted to visualize—any more than the relics which they took away were purely portable extensions of this conception. As the movement of relics came to be permeated by the 'tourist' trade, so on a larger scale the Holy Land became the inevitable object of the—now Christian—largesse of emperors and wealthy individuals who adorned the holy places with the opulent memorials of their piety. Jerome had it right when he remarked that such behaviour belonged to the pagan tradition of expansive munificence; the essence of Christianity would have left the Bethlehem manger unadorned, as a reminder of the true nature of Christ's birth.[130] But the Christian Jerusalem was contaminated by its times, and in reality it could hardly be imagined that Babylon was left behind when Jerome set sail from Rome.

---

[130] *Hom. de Nativ. Domini* (*CC* 78, 525) 'Argentum et aurum meretur gentilitas; Christiana fides meretur luteum illud praesepe'.

7. The Age of Theodosius: Mount of Olives and Bethlehem

THE worldly realities of contemporary Palestine cannot be said to have diminished the credentials of the Christian Holy Land. In the middle of the fourth century, indeed, there were supernatural indications which only seemed to confirm its exceptional status— and bishop Cyril of Jerusalem was able to inaugurate his episcopate with a spectacular display of the divine favour which was bestowed upon the holy places.[1] In 351,[2] during the season of Pentecost (on 7 May), for most of one day the sky over Jerusalem was seen to be filled with a shining light, which appeared (so it was confidently asserted) in the form of a cross; the gleam was so powerful that it outshone the rays of the sun. Everyone alike in Jerusalem was said to have observed this phenomenon, stretching from the sky above the Christian monuments of Golgotha eastwards as far as the Mount of Olives; the reaction of all, Christian and non-Christian, was unanimous—to flock to church and affirm their faith in Jesus Christ.[3]

[1] It would be welcome to be able to include here the revelation in the Cedron valley, also in 351, of the tomb of James the Lord's brother (together with Symeon and Zechariah), as recorded in a 10th cent. Latin MS. (see *Anal. Boll.* 8 (1889), 123ff.). But the details of the dream appearances which provoked the revelation, as well as of what followed (including the role of the bishop of Jerusalem), bear suspicious similarities to the account of the discovery of the remains of St. Stephen in 415 (see ch. 9), and the authenticity of the episode seems to me to be open to question. Certainly by the later 4th cent. there *was* a tradition of James's burial in the Cedron valley (rejected by Jerome in *De Vir. Illust.* 2), which had hardened by the 6th cent. (Theodosius, *De situ terrae sanctae*, 9), but the account of the revelation is more likely to have succeeded, than to have instigated, this tradition. Cf. F. M. Abel (1919).

[2] The year is problematical, though it should be at the time of the war against Magnentius: cf. G. Kretschmar (1971), 190, n. 86. J. Vogt (1949) argued for 353.

[3] Cyril, *Ep. ad Constantium*, 4; cf. Soz. *Hist. Eccl.* iv. 5.

According to Sozomen, pilgrims returning home from the holy places spread the news of this remarkable occurrence.[4] But it was best known from the account of the incident which bishop Cyril reported in a (surviving) letter to the emperor Constantius. The emperor, so the bishop argued, by this manifestation was blessed with conclusive proof of divine support for his rule and for his campaigns against his enemies (the allusion was to the war against Magnentius, the western usurper). Even the favours which God had disposed upon his father Constantine were outclassed: whereas he had been given a mere earthly sign in the discovery of the relics of the cross, Constantius could now lay claim to no less than a sign from heaven.[5] In describing what had occurred Cyril appropriately recalled the prophecy of Christ in St. Matthew's Gospel, 'and then will appear in heaven the sign that heralds the Son of Man'—and thus drew attention to the expectations of the Second Coming which had traditionally been associated with the Mount of Olives.[6] The light across the sky revived the belief that the Christian Holy Land had not only seen Christ's earthly presence but equally was still the expected setting of his final return at the end of time; and it was certainly this thought which impressed itself on the congregation in Jerusalem, which chose to include in its annual commemoration of this appearance of light the reading both of Cyril's letter to the emperor and also of the biblical promises of the Second Coming.[7]

A further boost to Christian assurance in the Holy Land must have accompanied the abandonment (in May 363) of Julian's project to rebuild the Jewish Temple.[8] Christian writers gleefully provided miracles and marvels to embellish the earthquake and subsequent fire which brought the building operations to a halt;[9] and it is not difficult to imagine the exultation with which the fate of the scheme would be

---

[4] *Hist. Eccl.* iv. 5.4.   [5] Cyril, o.c., 2–3.

[6] Matthew, 24.30; cf. Cyril's use of the text in *Catech.* xv. 22. On the Mount of Olives and the Second Coming, cf. above, p. 3.

[7] *Armen. Lect.* 55.

[8] For the best account, M. Avi-Yonah (1976), 191ff. Recent evidence on the date: S. P. Brock (1976), and G. Bowersock, *Julian the Apostate* (1978), 120–2.

[9] The soberest description is Amm. Marc. xxiii. 1; for further details, Rufin. *Hist. Eccl.* x. 38–40.

greeted. Julian's plan, had it been carried through, would
have struck at the heart of the Constantinian Jerusalem, in
which the Temple site had pointedly been left abandoned to
evoke reminders of the past and the fulfilment of biblical
prophecy. Now the apostate emperor had proposed to recre-
ate a Jewish Jerusalem centred upon the rebuilt Temple, and
thus to reverse Constantine's foundation of his new Christian
Jerusalem;[10] even the procedures which Julian adopted, placing the work in the hands of a trusted senior official, the
Antiochene Alypius, with the assistance of the local provincial governor, recall directly the actions of Constantine in
initiating the building at the Sepulchre.[11] In trying to recover
Jerusalem for the worship of the Jews Julian was challenging
Christian claims about the holy places, and in particular
Constantine's efforts to solidify those claims in his new
Christian buildings. The failure of Julian's challenge can only have enhanced the position of the 'new Jerusalem', and
further encouraged the concentration of Christian pilgrims
visiting what were now indisputably *their* holy places.

With the reign of Theodosius (379–395) it becomes possible to chart, through the identification of individual participants, the outline of this movement towards the Holy Land.
As earlier with Constantine, the starting-point is the imperial
court; for the last twenty years of the fourth century were an
age when the influence of the emperor (and, more particularly, of his entourage) led the field in enterprises of Christian
devotion. The role of the predominantly western court at
Constantinople in leading the crusade against paganism and
in promoting an unambiguous Christianity, through, for example, the patronage of monasticism or the acquisition of
saints' relics, now stands clearly on record.[12] In so far as the
eastern provinces of the empire were the stage which saw the
working-out of this 'demonstrable piety',[13] we may be confident that the holy places of Palestine would have their part
to play as an obvious sphere of attention. It is with the acti-

---

[10] Cf. the conclusion of Julian's letter to the Jews (*Ep.* 51, Loeb): '... I may
rebuild by my own efforts the sacred city of Jerusalem'.

[11] Amm. Marc. xxiii. 1.2–3.

[12] See John Matthews (1975), 127–45 'Piety and Patronage'.

[13] Id. (1967), 439.

vities of Theodosius' supporters that the holy sites are
brought once again into the ambit of the imperial court, in
the way which had been presaged by the journeys of members of Constantine's family.

Theodosius, it seems, never visited the Holy Land as a
pilgrim. While those who surrounded him were free to travel
the provinces and indulge their distinctive tastes in devotion,
the emperor could not leave his post; wars and diplomacy
would not wait on piety. From a distance he would consult
with an Egyptian hermit on the outcome of his campaigns;[14]
and he found himself confronted by the truths of Christianity
not in Jerusalem, but nearer home in Milan—in the person
of bishop Ambrose. Not until the late compilation of Georgius Cedrenus (11th–12th century) do we find a tradition
that Theodosius did actually visit Jerusalem:[15] he arrived at
the gates of 'the holy *Anastasis*' disguised as a private
citizen, but when the door was opened for him the candles,
which had all been extinguished, miraculously burst into
light, 'as at a church festival'. The bewildered attendant led
the stranger to the bishop, who, recognizing him as the
emperor, was gratified that he had come to worship at the
holy places in so humble a manner. The only solid piece of
evidence associating the emperor with the Holy Land
appears relatively prosaic by comparison with this attractive
little story: the law (of 381) extending tax exemptions to the
'custodes ecclesiarum . . . vel sanctorum locorum'.[16] Alongside this must be noticed the tradition ascribing to Theodosius the foundation of the church on the slopes of the Mount
of Olives, at the site of Christ's 'agony' in the garden of
Gethsemane.[17] At the time of Egeria's visit the spot was
occupied by an 'attractive church', a building which must
have been of recent construction, in view of Jerome's insertion into his translation of Eusebius' *Onomastikon* (*c*.390): 'and
now a church is built over the spot'.[18] It is unlikely that Eger-

---

[14] On Theodosius and John of Lycopolis, see below, p. 163.
[15] Ed. Bekker, i, 567.   [16] *CTh* xvi. 2.26 (31 Mar. 381).
[17] Recounted (in Arabic) by Eutychius of Alexandria (quoted in Vincent/Abel
(1914), 306, n. 1). On the site, to be distinguished from that of the Betrayal, see C.
Kopp (1963), 345ff.
[18] *It. Eg.* 36.1 'ecclesia . . . elegans'; cf. *Onomastikon*, 75. For this church, see Vin-
cent/Abel, 328ff.

ia, who always remarked on the Constantinian foundations, would have overlooked to mention the name of the emperor of the day, if it had been associated with this church. Later tradition attributed to the emperor the foundation of a church which clearly dated from the later years of the fourth century, but the details of its origins were unknown. At least one other church on the Mount of Olives, as we shall see, may perhaps be linked with Theodosius—through a member of his entourage.[19]

If not the emperor himself, then certainly some of those close to him set off for the holy places.[20] In September 394, before an assembly of eastern bishops in Constantinople, the praetorian prefect Flavius Rufinus dedicated his *martyrium* containing the relics of Peter and Paul, brought back from Rome; it is likely that Rufinus, at the time *de facto* regent of the eastern empire during Theodosius' absence on the campaign against the usurper Eugenius, also marked the occasion by his own baptism in the new church.[21] Witnessing these events will have been the prefect's sister-in-law, Silvia, who some time afterwards travelled on a pilgrimage to the Holy Land and Egypt.[22] She shared her brother-in-law's interest in the acquisition of relics: it transpires from a letter of Paulinus of Nola that, on returning from the Holy Land, she promised Victor, friend of Sulpicius Severus, the remains of 'many martyrs from the East' for the new basilica at Primuliacum.[23] The last years of her life were spent, it seems probable, at the centre of the local congregation at Brescia, in northern Italy—where tradition honoured a saint Silvia.[24] Gaudentius, the local bishop, shared with Silvia the experience of a pilgrimage to Jerusalem (from which he had been

---

[19] Poemenia: below, p. 162. The Jerusalem church commemorated Theodosius (like Constantine) in its liturgy, *Armen. Lect.* 12.

[20] For what follows, see E. D. Hunt (1972).

[21] Hunt, 360, with E. Honigmann, 'Le concile de Constantinople de 394', *Subs. Hag.* 35 (1961), 11ff. The baptism depends on the 5th cent. 'B' recension of *Hist. Laus.* 11 (Butler, 35, 192–3), where these events are erroneously associated with the Egyptian Ammonius (cf. J. F. Matthews, *Class. Rev.* 88 (1974), 105).

[22] Pall. *Hist. Laus.* 55. On the date of her pilgrimage, see Hunt, 355ff., with P. Devos (1973), 110ff., and below, p. 190.

[23] Paul. Nol. *Ep.* 31.1 (403).

[24] Hunt, 362ff.; P. Devos (1974). Cf. below, pp. 198–9.

prevailed upon to return to assume the see of Brescia).[25] Passing through Caesarea on his way he had obtained relics of the Forty Martyrs of Sebaste, heroes of the Cappadocian churches; the saints then accompanied him as the 'faithful companions' of his pilgrimage, and returned to pride of place in the new basilica which he constructed at Brescia.[26] Our scanty knowledge of Silvia evokes a world of expressive devotion, a strain of piety which embraced pilgrimages and relics, arising from the heart of Theodosius' court. Fl. Rufinus' enthusiasm was communicated to other members of his family besides Silvia: it is not to be forgotten that after his assassination on 27 November 395 it was Jerusalem that his wife (presumably the sister of Silvia) and daughter chose as their place of exile—an explicit intervention of court politics in the life of the holy city which occasioned the only acknowledgement by a pagan source of the new prestige of the Christian Jerusalem.[27]

Silvia met in Jerusalem the elder Melania, the aristocratic Roman widow who then presided over a monastic establishment on the Mount of Olives.[28] It was Melania and the monk Palladius who escorted Silvia on her way to Egypt, to continue her pilgrimage there among the fathers of the desert.[29] The close contacts between the holy places of Jerusalem and the monks of Egypt had already been exemplified in considerable style by the noble Poemenia, whom we have earlier encountered surrounded by her flotilla of boats and distinguished array of retainers, sailing up the Nile to visit the hermit John in the Thebaid.[30] That expedition, it will be recalled, ended in a fracas with the local population. But there is more to tell. Thanks to Fr. Devos' publication of a previously unknown fragment of a Coptic *Life* of John of

[25] See Gaudent. *Tract.* 16.2, 17.14.

[26] Ibid. 17.14ff. The story of their martyrdom, following sermons of Basil and Greg. Nys., is the principal subject-matter of Gaudentius' dedication sermon. The cult was much in vogue in Cappadocia: P. Franchi de' Cavalieri, 'I santi Quaranta Martiri di Sebastia', *Studi e Testi*, 49 (1928), 155–84. I take it this was their first introduction to western congregations.

[27] Zosim. v. 8.2 (Eunapius) 'ἀπὸ δὲ τῆς Κωνσταντίνου βασιλείας ὑπὸ Χριστιανῶν τιμωμένην οἰκοδομήμασιν';cf. *Chron. Min.* ii.64.

[28] Cf. below, pp. 168ff.

[29] The journey mentioned at the beginning of *Hist. Laus.* 55.

[30] See above, p. 77.

Lycopolis it is now possible to affirm beyond doubt that the Poemenia who visited, and was cured by, the hermit in the Thebaid was the like-named lady whose activities *in the Holy Land* have long been familiar from the *Life* of Peter the Iberian.[31] The fragment of the Paris MS. reveals that on leaving John Poemenia intended, before she returned home, 'to go to the holy city Jerusalem, and to pray at the holy tomb of Christ, as well as Golgotha, the *Anastasis*...'.[32] This avowal that Poemenia planned to travel to the Holy Land provides (as Devos observed) the otherwise missing link between the visitor to the Thebaid and the lady mentioned in the *Life* of Peter the Iberian.[33] Poemenia is introduced into Peter's story after a mention of the two Melanias: they were preceded to Jerusalem, the narrative continues, by a lady 'famous for her family and her fortune' named Poemenia (or Pomnia?) whose manner of life they strove to imitate. Two of her actions are then recorded: the building of the church of the Ascension, and the destruction of an idol on Mount Gerazim in Samaria, which had been venerated by the local inhabitants up to that time.[34]

There have been those disposed to disbelieve that it was Poemenia who was responsible for the church of the Ascension at the summit of the Mount of Olives, around the very spot bearing Christ's last foot-prints.[35] The traditional ascription to Helena, and the assumption that the Constantinian building on the Mount of Olives embraced the summit in a single precinct, is persuasive.[36] Eusebius' description of Helena's church is notoriously unclear, and will certainly bear the interpretation that he had two buildings in mind, one at the summit and the other at the nearby cave.[37] Yet the evidence of Eusebius' day suggests (as we have seen) that

---

[31] P. Devos (1969), 200ff., for the previously unpublished fragment. Cf. *V. Pet. Iber.* 35.

[32] Devos, 203.

[33] Ibid. 204 '... celle que nous savons maintenant être *une unique Poemenia*'.

[34] *V. Pet. Iber.* 35. Was this part of Hadrian's temple to Jupiter? (Cf. R. J. Bull, *Amer. Journ. Arch.* 71 (1967), 387–93; id. *Rev. Bibl.* 75 (1968), 238–43.)

[35] Notably A. Grabar (1946), i, 284ff.

[36] Cf. above, p. 47.

[37] *V. Const.* iii. 43.3 'ἱερὸν οἶκον ἐκκλησίας ..... νεών τε κἀνταῦθα προσευκτήριον'. Cf. Vincent/Abel (1914), 379ff., and L.H. Vincent (1957), answering Grabar.

the cave was regarded as the site of the Ascension as much as of the eschatological teaching, and that there was *no* separate tradition attaching to the actual summit.[38] Eusebius is unambiguous that it was the sacred cave alone which was the object of the Constantinian building. By the time that Egeria visited Jerusalem in the early 380s the tradition of the separate site of the Ascension was well established; and she is consistent in her distinction between what she knew as the Imbomon, the *locus* from which Christ ascended, and the Eleona, the *ecclesia* above the cave where Christ had taught the disciples.[39] She evidently saw no sacred precinct embracing both the summit and the cave, and her unvarying distinction of the *locus* on the one hand and the *ecclesia* on the other invites the conclusion that the church of the Ascension was yet to be built. The first evidence of its existence is to be found in Jerome's *Commentary on Zephaniah*, completed before 392, where he refers to the cross which surmounted it glistening at the summit of the Mount of Olives.[40] Poemenia will fit into the gap between 384 and *c*.390, as the foundress of the church of the Ascension. Her role was already recognized by Pères Vincent and Abel in their standard work;[41] although their reconstruction of her church as an octagon (as the mosque which has succeeded it) has had to be modified, in the light of more recent discoveries, to a circular structure of the kind described by the seventh-century pilgrim Arculf.[42]

If, as the *Life* of Peter the Iberian asserts, Melania in fact emulated the behaviour of Poemenia, the two women must have met in Jerusalem: Poemenia could hardly in any case have founded her church on the Mount of Olives without attracting the attention of the monastic leadership close by. Like Silvia, she seems likely then to have been associated with the establishment of Melania the elder. She may also, like Silvia, have had connexions with the imperial court. Poemenia's passage up the Nile has already suggested wealth and leisure; the former is confirmed by the foundation of a

---

[38] Above, p. 3.   [39] *It. Eg. passim.* esp. 39.3. Cf. Devos, 208–12.

[40] *Comm. in Soph.* i. 15 (*CC* 76a, 673).   [41] Vincent/Abel, 382.

[42] Ibid. 360ff., corrected by J. T. Milik, *Rev. Bibl.* 67 (1960), 557, with V. Corbo, *Liber Annuus*, 10 (1959–60), 206ff. Cf. Arculf, *De Locis Sanctis*, i. 23 (= J. Wilkinson (1977), 100–1).

church distinguished by its location overlooking Jerusalem, and close by one of the three Constantinian basilicas at the holy places.[43] Attention then turns to the background of this lady 'famous for her family and her fortune'. Père Devos also noted the entry for John of Lycopolis in the Ethiopian *Synaxarium*, a résumé of material found in the Coptic *Life*: according to this, an unnamed 'noble woman *of the royal family*' visited John and was cured of a malady.[44] There is no doubt, given the other matching pieces of evidence, that this unnamed lady is Poemenia; though how far the assertion that she belonged to the emperor's family can be trusted remains uncertain. It is impossible to determine if it is merely an assumption from the evidence of her worldly stature, or whether it is a genuinely new piece of information lost from the earlier tradition. Her announcement to John of Lycopolis that she visited him 'from a distant land' is hardly convincing evidence of a Spanish origin;[45] yet her action in destroying a pagan idol is distinctively reminiscent of the behaviour of Theodosius' supporters in the eastern provinces.[46] Moreover John's support of the Theodosian regime by his well-known prophecies of the successful outcome of the campaigns against Maximus and Eugenius links the hermit to the court at Constantinople;[47] it must have been visitors to the Thebaid like Poemenia who fostered such links. Certainly it is difficult to avoid the conclusion that the visit to the Thebaid of an obviously aristocratic (and western) lady in the middle of Theodosius' reign is not unconnected with the network of pious enterprise which fanned out from the court.

This network is also likely to have embraced the best documented of all fourth-century pilgrims, Egeria. Two assumptions, now generally accepted, have lain behind her

---

[43] Poemenia's church and Helena's close by were seen together as 'duae... ecclesiae celeberrimae' in the account attributed to 'Eucherius': see *CC* 175, 238.

[44] Devos, 204ff.   [45] Ibid. 195.

[46] Pre-eminently Maternus Cynegius and his wife: John Matthews (1975), 140ff. Compare the exploits of Serena in Rome, below, p. 165, n. 58.

[47] Pall. *Hist. Laus.* 35 (Butler, 100–1); *Hist. Monach.* 1.1, 64; Rufin. *Hist. Eccl.* xi. 19, 32; August. *Civ. Dei*, v. 26. There is also a suggestion of John's connexion with Theodosius in the story of a circus riot which is a doublet of the 'riot of the statues' (at Antioch) and the massacre of Thessalonica: P. Peeters, *Anal. Boll.* 54 (1936), 363–6.

constant reappearance in earlier chapters: firstly, that the
three years ('tres anni pleni') which she spent in the Holy
Land and Egypt were precisely the years 381–4;[48] and,
secondly, that her country of origin was the region of Galicia,
north-western Spain.[49] Valerius, the seventh-century hermit
of Vierzo, clearly had no doubt that his heroine Egeria belonged to the same area of Spain as himself and the monks to
whom he was writing;[50] and somewhere on the western fringes of the Mediterranean would seem to be implied for her
origins by the bishop of Edessa's recognition that her journey
had brought her 'de extremis... terris'.[51] Three years,
moreover, to roam around the holy places of Palestine and to
visit the Egyptian monks suggests indeed a lady of leisure,
and, not least, a lady of means—'une très grande dame'.[52]

Amid all the uncertainties of Egeria's background, certain
points are not to be missed. The base for her eastern journeys was undoubtedly Constantinople; she returned there in
the spring of 384 by the land route across Asia Minor which
she had taken on her way out.[53] At the time she wrote to her
'sisters' she was spending some time in the capital, before
embarking on a further pilgrimage to the shrine of St. John
at Ephesus.[54] A pious lady from north-western Spain (the
emperor's own homeland), setting out from Constantinople
on an extended pilgrimage to the Holy Land in 381—it is
hard to deny some connexion with Theodosius and his predominantly Spanish entourage.[55] On 24 November 380 the

---

[48] Established in a series of articles by P. Devos (1967a,b), (1968a) (although this
last attaches too much importance to *It. Eg.* 42 as decisive for dating).

[49] Particular milestones in the voluminous literature are M. Férotin (1903), and
A. Bludau (1927), 232–44. On the Galician context, cf. H. Chadwick (1976), 166–
7.

[50] *Ep. Valerii*, 1 'huius occiduae plagae... extremitas' (*Anal. Boll.* 29 (1910), 393);
ibid. 4 'extremo occidui maris oceani litore exorta' (398). For similar language of
Galicia, cf. on Orosius, below, p. 214, n. 60.

[51] *It. Eg.* 19.5.

[52] The phrase is Dom Lambert's, *Revue Mabillon*, 27 (1937), 34.

[53] *It. Eg.* 23.7 '...faciens iter iam notum per singulas provincias, quas eundo
transiveram...'.

[54] Ibid. 9–10.

[55] First argued by Férotin (1903). One view called her 'Eucheria', and related her
to Theodosius' uncle Fl. Eucherius: Dom Wilmart, *Rev. Bénédict.* 25 (1908), 458–67,
followed by G. Morin, ibid. 30 (1913), 174–86.

emperor had entered Constantinople;[56] his arrival in the East
was accompanied by a well-defined group of Spanish supporters, characterized by Piganiol in a famous phrase as a
'côterie espagnole pieuse';[57] Egeria's own arrival in the capital is concurrent with this drift of the emperor's supporters
from his western homeland. Devout ladies of Egeria's stamp
were to be found in immediate association with Theodosius:
the pious empress Aelia Flacilla, and his niece Serena, an
implacable opponent of paganism.[58] It is unlikely that Egeria
would have stood right outside this group of western Christian devotees in the eastern capital. Her involvement, whatever its nature, is indefinable; but her narrative, we may take
it, is an authentic witness of 'Theodosian' Christianity.

The arrival of Theodosius and his court marked, of course,
the end of the Arian domination of the eastern church, and
the establishment of the Catholic faith. Imperial policy, it is
acknowledged, was in line with, some would say determined
by, the enthusiasm of the emperor's supporters.[59] Flacilla, for
example, was a resolute opponent of Arianism, regarding it
as a heresy matched only by idolatry.[60] Against such a
background Egeria's contacts with the Catholic bishops of
the East fall naturally into place. She was warm in her
admiration of the three 'confessor' bishops in Mesopotamia
(Batnae, Edessa, and Carrhae):[61] two of these at least, Eulogius of Edessa and Protogenes of Carrhae, had earned that
title for their resistance to the Arians—they had been exiled
to upper Egypt by the officials of Valens.[62] Nor is it insigni-
ficant that the year in which it appears that Egeria traversed

---

[56] For the date, Socr. *Hist. Eccl.* v. 6.   [57] A. Piganiol (1972), 238.

[58] For the piety and charitable works of Aelia Flacilla, see the *epitaphium* of Greg.
Nys. (ed. Jaeger/Langerbeck, 1967), e.g. 487ff., and Theod. *Hist. Eccl.* v. 19; cf.
Ambrose, *De Obit. Theod.* 40 ('fidelis anima deo'), and *Suda* s.v. Πλακίλλα. The
enthusiasms of Serena are clear from her assaults on pagan statues in Rome (Zosim.
v. 38), and from her patronage of Melania and Pinianus (*V. Mel.* 11ff.); she also
embellished with African marble Ambrose's shrine of Nazarius in Milan (*CIL* v,
6250 = *ILCV* 1801).

[59] Cf. the observation that Theodosius 'led his regiment from the rear': Peter
Brown, *The World of Late Antiquity* (1971), 106.

[60] Greg. Nys. o.c., 489.   [61] *It. Eg.* 19.1, 5; 20.2.

[62] Cf. Theod. *Hist. Eccl.* iv. 18, v. 4.6. For the identification of these two figures
with Egeria's unnamed bishops, see P. Devos (1967a), 169–76 (following Baumstark).

the eastern provinces *en route* to the Holy Land was precisely
that in which, in May, the eastern bishops assembled for the
council of Constantinople (a gathering which included not
only the Mesopotamian bishops, but also a delegation from
Palestine, headed by Cyril of Jerusalem).[63] Egeria can hardly
have been unaware of the impending assembly as she set out
for the holy places, probably in the spring of 381. As the
eastern bishops converged on Theodosius' capital to confirm
the establishment of Catholic Christianity, the devout pilgrim was beginning her journey around the Holy Land and
Egypt.

Though hardly in the strictest terms a pilgrim, Theodosius' loyal Iberian supporter, the *comes* Bacurius, may be introduced here. Known to Libanius both as a soldier and a
man of culture, he was to be famed for his brave exploits in
command of a barbarian contingent at the Frigidus (where,
according to Zosimus, he met his death).[64] To Christian
sources he was familiar, moreover, as a man of religious
conviction.[65] Rufinus of Aquileia had encountered Bacurius
during his tour of duty as *dux Palaestinae*, when he was a frequent visitor to Rufinus' monastery on the Mount of Olives
—to one of these meetings we owe the traditional story of the
conversion to Christianity of the Iberian kingdom in the time
of Constantine.[66] It would be surprising if the devout general
did not take the opportunity of this posting in Palestine to
visit the holy sites.

The roll-call of distinguished visitors to the Holy Land
from the emperor's entourage would be incomplete without
mention of the deacon Evagrius[67]—who had penetrated, if
not the imperial palace, certainly the society which sur-

[63] See the list of signatories in C. H. Turner, *JTS* 15 (1913–14), 168.

[64] Liban. *Ep.* 1043–4, 1060; Rufin. *Hist. Eccl.* xi. 33; Socr. *Hist. Eccl.* v. 25.13;
Zosim. iv. 57.3, 58.3.

[65] Rufin. *Hist. Eccl.* x. 11, *ad fin.* 'cui summa erat cura et religionis et veritatis'.

[66] This is the substance of Rufinus' chapter; cf. Socr. *Hist. Eccl.* i. 20.20, with P.
Peeters, 'Les débuts du christianisme en Géorgie', *Anal. Boll.* 50 (1932), 5–58, esp.
27ff. Peeters, 35–6, denies the identification of the Iberian Bacurius with the correspondent of Libanius whom (as *PLRE* i, 144) he 'evidently regarded as a pagan'; but
it need not follow from this that Libanius' correspondent actually *was* a pagan—and
his military reputation certainly matches that of the Iberian.

[67] For virtually all that we know of his life, see Pall. *Hist. Laus.* 38, summarized
conveniently by A. Guillaumont in *SChr* 170, 21–8.

rounded the court at Constantinople. Originally from Ibora
in Pontus, he had arrived in the capital as the deacon of
Gregory of Nazianzus (when he became bishop); on Gregory's departure Evagrius continued to serve his successor,
Nectarius, when his principal *forte* was in arguing the faith
against heretics. He rose to fame in this role—but only to
succumb to the temptations of the high life: Evagrius later
told Palladius how, after an affair with the wife of a prominent citizen, he had been forced to flee to the protection of
Jerusalem, and to the monastery of the elder Melania on the
Mount of Olives.[68]

We are ignorant of the circumstances which led the young
Palladius himself to abandon his home in Galatia and, like
Evagrius, to take up residence on the Mount of Olives. He
later wrote that he had lived there 'for three years' (from
*c.*385) in the company of the presbyter Innocent.[69] Palladius
thus came into contact with one whose sojourn in Jerusalem
(he tells us) went back to the time of the emperor Constantius, under whom Innocent had forsaken an official career for
the life of a monk at the holy places, taking with him his son
who was serving in the palace bodyguard.[70] He is revealed as
a man of Italian origin, and one of a group of monks settled
on the Mount of Olives: they were sufficiently well-known far
afield to be in correspondence with both Basil and
Athanasius.[71] It may well have been from the bishop of Alexandria that Innocent acquired the relics of John the Baptist
for which he built a *martyrium* on the Mount of Olives.[72]

It was not only Innocent and his companions who were
receiving visitors in Jerusalem. Early letters of Jerome, for
instance, indicate that some of his old friends from the dis-

---

[68] Pall. l.c. (Butler, 117ff.).

[69] Pall. *Hist. Laus.* 44. These three years will hardly fit anywhere in the career of
Palladius except—where Butler placed them—prior to his arrival in Egypt (certainly 388: see below, p. 185). The alternative proposed by D. F. Buck (1976), 295, is,
as he acknowledges, 'cramped' (301).

[70] On Innocent, see Butler's notes, 219–21.

[71] Basil, *Ep.* 258.2, 259; Athan. *Ep. ad Pallad. presbyt.* (*PG* 26, 1168). Confusingly,
it emerges that another Palladius (not the future author of *Hist. Laus.*) had earlier
been residing with Innocent: see Butler, l.c.

[72] *Hist. Laus.* 44. The remains had been rescued from the ravages of Julian's men
at Sebaste and sent to Athanasius by monks from the monastery of 'Philip' at Jerusalem (Rufin. *Hist. Eccl.* xi. 28)—might Innocent have been among them?

persed community at Aquileia were provided with hospitality in Jerusalem (in the early 370s) by another Italian monk residing there, Florentinus—Jerome wrote acclaiming his attention to visitors.[73] But it was to be the monastic establishment presided over by Melania the elder and Rufinus of Aquileia, her 'companion in the way of the spirit',[74] which would emerge (as we have already detected) as a focal point for visitors to the holy places—not least those who originated from court circles in the eastern capital.

What of the circumstances in which Melania and Rufinus had themselves come to settle in the Holy Land?[75] Melania's background, part-Roman, part-Spanish, is recognizably that of the governing aristocracy of the western empire: eulogies of her pious conduct make the point that the nobility of her secular standing was surpassed only by that of her Christian calling, 'ennobled with consuls as grandfathers she made herself yet more noble by despising external nobility'.[76] The consular grandfather here referred to was Antonius Marcellinus, proconsul of Africa, praetorian prefect of Italy, and consul in 341—a man 'of distinguished family', according to a dedication from the senate of Bulla Regia.[77] Melania's husband, in like vein, was a member of the extensive *gens Valeria*, most probably Valerius Maximus *pf. urbi* 361–2 (he owed his post to his relationship to the influential Vulcacius Rufinus).[78] Predictably, Melania's renunciation of this heritage in favour of the spiritual life provoked the resistance of

[73] Jer. *Ep.* 5.2 'ceteros hospitio recipis, solacio foves, sumptibus iuvas', cf. id. *Chron.* s.a. 377 'tam misericors in egentes fuit, ut vulgo pater pauperum nominatus sit'; among Florentinus' guests had been Jerome's friend Heliodorus, Jer. *Ep.* 4.

[74] Paul. Nol. *Ep.* 28.5. On western monasticism generally at the holy places, see G. D. Gordini (1961).

[75] On Melania, see F. X. Murphy (1945), 32ff.; id. (1947); D. Gorce, in *SChr* 90, 20ff.; *PLRE* i, 592.

[76] Paul. Nol. *Ep.* 29.6; cf. Jer. *Ep.* 39.4, *Chron.* s.a. 374. For her Spanish background, Pall. *Hist. Laus.* 46, with Gorce, o.c., 110–11; Melania's family had Spanish properties to dispose of, *V. Mel.* 37.

[77] *PLRE* i, 548, with *CIL* viii, 25524. Melania is correctly identified as his granddaughter (Pall. and Jer. make her his daughter) by Paul. Nol. *Ep.* 29.8, and Rufin. *Apol. c. Hier.* ii. 29.

[78] Pall. *Hist. Laus.* 46 'some man of high rank, whom I forget'. For the identification (first made by Rampolla) see Murphy (1947), 64; on Valerius Maximus, A. Chastagnol (1962), 154ff.

her family (as it would again in the case of her grand-daughter); like other ascetic converts, she found powerful opposition from the solidarity of the aristocratic clan—'all the influence of her noble relatives was employed to prevent her resolve and tried to obstruct her departure'.[79] Those who knew Melania had no doubt of the specific motivation of her pious venture—they traced it back to the experience of a suc-cession of bereavements, the death of her husband closely followed by the loss of two of her children.[80] Such domestic tragedy fractured family bonds, and made possible the kind of social uprooting on which Melania embarked (widow-hood, it may be observed, is a recurring factor impelling other noble Roman ladies—Paula, Fabiola, Marcella—to abandon their secular surroundings and turn to forms of asceticism). Her withdrawal, however, was not at the total expense of commitments to her family. She took care to leave behind in Rome her one surviving son and ensure that he was not destitute[81]—he was to grow up a devoted Christian but one who never forsook the public trappings associated with senatorial wealth and dignity, and who only on his deathbed became reconciled to his own daughter's plans to follow in her grandmother's footsteps.[82] After thus attending to her son's future and the continuity of public life in her family Melania was ready to set sail for Alexandria and the holy men of the Egyptian desert (and still with enough funds to support more than a quarter of a century of charity).[83] It was only some six months before she was caught up in the ecclesiastical disturbances which ensued after the death of

---

[79] Paul. Nol *Ep.* 29.10.   [80] Jer. *Ep.* 39.5, Paul. Nol. *Ep.* 29.8.

[81] On Publicola, see *PLRE* i, 753. There are divergent traditions about what hap-pened to him on his mother's departure: Pall. (*Hist. Laus.* 46) has him handed over to a 'guardian' ¦('*ἐπίτροπον*'). Paul. Nol. (*Ep.* 29.9) prefers 'into the bosom of Christ'; the puzzling statement of Jer. *Chron.* s.a. 374 ('unico practore (?) tunc urba-no filio derelicto') may be corrupt—see E. Schwartz (1937), 167. On the wealth left to Publicola, cf. Jer. *Ep.* 39.5.5 'omni quam habebat possessione concessa'.

[82] For his social standing, see Pall. *Hist. Laus.* 54 '*ἐντὸς τῶν κοσμικῶν ἀξιωμά-των ἐγένετο*' and Paul. Nol. *Ep* 45.2–3 'necdum illum descruerat senatoriae dignitatis ambitio'. Death-bed reconciliation: *V. Mel.* 7.

[83] For her departure, see *Hist. Laus.* 46, Paul. Nol. *Ep.* 29.10, Jer. *Ep.* 39.5.5 'ingrediente iam hieme'. This will have been late in 372: Murphy (1947), 66. Jer. and Paul. Nol. have her destination as Jerusalem, but Jer. *Ep.* 4.2 knew that she was in Egypt.

Athanasius in 373: when the leadership of the Nitrian monks was exiled by the prefect of Egypt she accompanied this group to Diocaesarea in Palestine.[84]

Melania may have encountered in Egypt the man who was to be her companion on the Mount of Olives, Rufinus of Aquileia. When Jerome was in Antioch (*c.* 374) he heard rumours that they were both on their way to the Holy Land,[85] but in the event it was only Melania who arrived (with the party of exiled monks); Rufinus was to remain among the monks in Egypt (as their 'ally in suffering' according to his own account) for eight years in all, before he finally came to join Melania at the holy places.[86] The reasons which had led to his departure from Italy in the first place are unclear. He was one of a group of aspiring Christian devotees (Jerome included) gathered at Aquileia, which suddenly broke up *c.*372 as individuals went their separate ways to continue their ascetic vocations elsewhere. Jerome speaks of the 'sudden whirlwind' which parted him from his dear friend Rufinus without alluding to the circumstances; yet the capacity to cause offence which the rest of his life was to reveal may suggest that on this occasion too Jerome was no innocent partner in this parting of friends.[87]

Melania and Rufinus thus came to settle at the holy places with certain common experiences which they could share. Both had broken away from tight social groupings in order to pursue their ascetic callings; and more recently both had seen at first hand and participated in the troubles of the Egyptian monks at the hands of the authorities. Nor did Melania escape by fleeing to Palestine. Her generosity towards the exiled monks here brought her into conflict with the provincial governor, who was reluctant to punish her, according to Palladius, only because of her aristocratic

---

[84] On her patronage of these exiles, Pall. *Hist. Laus.* 46 and Paul. Nol. *Ep.* 29.11.

[85] Jer. *Ep.* 4.2 'Rufinus qui cum sancta Melania ab Aegypto Hierosolymam venisse narratur'. For Rufinus in Egypt, cf. id. *Ep.* 3.1 'audio te Aegypti secreta penetrare, monachorum invisere choros et caelestem in terris circuire familiam'.

[86] For the eight years, see Rufin. *Apol. c. Hier.* ii. 15 '...sex annis...et iterum, post intervallum aliquod, aliis duobus'. On Rufinus and the monks, see also Jer. *Ep.* 3.1 (previous note), Rufin. *Hist. Eccl.* xi. 4, id. *Apol. ad Anast.* 2 (with Jer. *Apol. c. Ruf.* ii. 3); Murphy (1945), 40ff.

[87] Jer. *Ep.* 3.3; cf. J. N. D. Kelly (1975), 33ff.

connexions.[88] Yet this was not to stop her keeping open house on the Mount of Olives for visitors to the holy places. The hospitality of Melania and Rufinus has been made notorious by Jerome's jibes at the lavishness of Croesus or Sardanapallus;[89] but it was this which made the Mount of Olives into the focal point of the 'Theodosian' Jerusalem which has emerged in this chapter. Those Holy Land pilgrims who came as visitors from the emperor's entourage and the fringes of the court could expect to be made welcome in the monasteries of Melania and Rufinus.

But Jerusalem and the Mount of Olives, of course, could claim no monopoly of Holy Land visitors. There was always that other western establishment close by the church of the Nativity in Bethlehem, the foundation of Jerome and Paula.[90] It was in August 385 that Jerome turned his back on the Roman Babylon, and set sail for Jerusalem.[91] Paula, it seems, had already made known her intention to follow—indeed Jerome attributes her resolve to her meeting with bishops Epiphanius of Salamis and Paulinus of Antioch when they came to Rome for the synod of 382: she had already sailed eastwards with them 'in spirit'.[92] By the time that Jerome reached Antioch, Paula was with him;[93] it was here, it will be recalled, that Jerome observed his noble companion riding from the city on a donkey, with the bishop as her escort.[94] Then began their pilgrimage around the holy sites, catalogued by Jerome as a breathless outburst of biblical enthusiasm.[95] As Christian pilgrim, Paula explicitly rejected the governor's hospitality in Jerusalem (offered to her

---

[88] *Hist. Laus.* 46, cf. Paul. Nol. *Ep.* 29.11.

[89] E.g. *Ep.* 57.12.5 'inter Croesi opes et Sardanapalli delicias...', *Ep.* 125.18 Rufinus 'a Nero at home, a Cato abroad'; cf. other refs. at F. Cavallera (1922), i, 200 n. 3, with Murphy (1945), 61–4. For a more sympathetic appreciation of their hospitality, see Pall. *Hist. Laus.* 46.

[90] Cf. Cavallera, i, 127ff.; Gordini (1961), 90ff.; Kelly (1975), 129ff.

[91] *Ep.* 45.6 (to Asella, from on board ship). For his description of the journey, see *Apol. c. Ruf.* iii. 22 'mense Augusto'.

[92] *Ep.* 108.6 'ipsa voto cum eis et desiderio navigabat'. She was still in Rome when Jerome left, *Ep.* 45.7, although her resolve was clear, ibid. 2.

[93] Compare Jerome's account of his own journey (above, n. 91) with the matching description of Paula's, *Ep.* 108.6–7.

[94] *Ep.* 108.7.3.

[95] Ibid. 8ff. Cf. Kelly, 177ff., and above, p. 87. For translation and maps, see J. Wilkinson (1977), 46ff.

as a family friend), favouring instead an appropriately humble cell—there were monastic cells alongside the Sepulchre.[96] From there Paula's devotion carried her from site to site, torn between the desire to linger and eagerness to be on her way:[97] Golgotha, the Tomb, Sion, Bethlehem, the cave of the Nativity, Hebron, Bethany, Jericho, the Jordan; northwards to Galilee, then south into Egypt, and to the monks of Nitria —hers was the complete 'grand tour' of the pilgrim.[98]

Jerome's description of Paula's journey of devotion was composed some twenty years after the event, in the idealized context of an *epitaphium*;[99] its theme, predictably, is the faith and perseverance of his heroine. He did not admit any hint of the dissension in the Holy Land which had marred the intervening years[100]—nor that he himself had shared this pilgrimage with Paula.[101] A similar silence surrounds Paula's presence in Jerusalem: no word of any visit to the monastery on the Mount of Olives. She and Jerome must have made the ascent of the hill several times: the gleaming cross which surmounted the church of the Ascension more than once caught his attention;[102] and certainly as they followed the road down into the Jordan valley they would have passed over the hilltop to Bethphage and Bethany.

It would be an unaccountable gap if the succession of visitors on the Mount of Olives had not included Jerome and Paula. In embarking for Jerusalem Paula, herself a widow, cannot have been unaware of the precedent of Melania, with whose name her own vocation had been linked;[103] and, in consoling Paula on the loss of her daughter Blesilla, Jerome had quoted the example of Melania's resilience in bereavement.[104] Some contact between Jerome himself and Melania during his 'student' days in Rome is suggested by

---

[96] Ibid. 9.2; Kelly, 120, identifies the governor as Fl. Florentius. For the cells, cf. above, p. 22.

[97] Jer. l.c. 'cuncta loca tanto ardore ac studio circumivit...'.

[98] Ibid. 13.6 'dies me priusquam sermo deficiet, si voluero cuncta percurrere, quae Paula venerabilis fide incredibili pervagata est'.

[99] Paula died on 26 Jan. 404 (*Ep.* 108.34).

[100] This forms the background to ch. 8 below.

[101] So the brief summary of his journey in *Apol. c. Ruf.* iii. 22.

[102] See above, p. 143, n. 75.

[103] Jer. *Ep.* 45.4–5.   [104] *Ep.* 39.5.4–5.

the presence of one of her household in his company on his arrival in Antioch *c*.374.[105] As for Rufinus, his friendship with Jerome was regarded as a model of Christian *amicitia*. In the days when they had become estranged, Augustine was to look back on their association with warm regard: '...what friend will not be afraid of becoming an enemy if this rift which we mourn could arise between Jerome and Rufinus?'[106] Jerome for his part, writing of their days together at Aquileia, could speak of the 'affection' which united him to Rufinus, while awaiting with excitement the prospect of meeting him again.[107] Against such a background a visit to the Mount of Olives by Jerome and Paula goes without saying. Yet by the time that he came to compose his *epitaphium* for Paula, Jerome had already contemptuously removed Melania's name from his *Chronicle*;[108] small wonder that he now declined to mention any meeting in Jerusalem.

Some of the monks who sailed from Rome with Jerome did, it seems, settle in Jerusalem;[109] as Jerome himself might well have expected to do (although in embarking for 'Jerusalem' he seems to have looked as much to a spiritual as to a geographical destination, the counterweight to the Roman Babylon).[110] Yet it was not in Jerusalem, but at Bethlehem that Jerome and Paula came to rest, surrounding themselves with communities of monks and nuns, and daily welcoming visitors to their hostel conveniently situated at the roadside.[111] Here Jerome claimed to find the true 'solitude' in search of which he had fled from Rome, 'all is simplicity and—apart from the psalms—silence'[112]—an idyll of devotional calm which it is hard to credit when set aside his continuing complaints about the distractions resulting from the flood of visitors.[113] The reasons for this withdrawal to

---

[105] *Ep.* 3.3.2 'erat nobiscum et Hylas sanctae Melaniae famulus'.

[106] August. *Ep.* 73.6 (= Jer. *Ep.* 110), written in 404 ('...tam caras familiaresque personas *cunctis paene ecclesiis notissimo amicitiae vinculo* copulatas').

[107] Jer. *Ep.* 3.3.1, 4.2.1.

[108] Rufin. *Apol. c. Hier.* ii. 29. Jerome was not successful in obliterating her name from the tradition: see his *Chron.* s.a. 374.

[109] Jer. *Apol. c. Ruf.* iii. 22 '...qui nunc Hierosolymae commorantur...'.

[110] *Ep.* 45.6; cf. *Ep.* 22.30 'Hierosolymam militaturus pergerem', and generally the preface to the translation of Didymus' *De Spiritu Sancto*, PL 23, 101.

[111] *Ep.* 108.14.4 'iuxta viam'.   [112] *Ep.* 46.12.3.

[113] E.g. *Ep.* 66.14, 71.5 '...frequentia commeantium et peregrinorum turbis...'.

Bethlehem can be no more than speculation; but there is a strong impression, fostered by the tensions of the following years, that the establishment in Bethlehem functioned (if not by design then certainly in its practical effects) as a *rival* to the Mount of Olives. The circumstances of the Mount were mirrored in Bethlehem: western foundations, with 'twin' monasteries for men and women, opening their doors to the stream of visitors to the Holy Land. Away from the shadow of the earlier arrivals in Jerusalem, Jerome and Paula could at least make Bethlehem, the 'villula Christi', their own pre-serve, and there exercise the kind of patronage denied them in the holy city itself.

The nucleus of the establishment in Bethlehem will have been those monks and virgins who were the companions of Jerome and Paula on their pilgrimage. Paula's family had been left behind on the quay at Ostia, leaving only her daughter Eustochium to accompany her on her enterprise, 'companion both in her resolve and in her voyage'.[114] It emerges also that 'many virgins' travelled with them through the Holy Land and Egypt[115]—and would continue to sur-round them in Bethlehem. As for Jerome, he had sailed from Italy accompanied by a group of monks, together with his younger brother Paulinianus and the presbyter Vin-centius.[116] This is the first indication of his brother's pre-sence at Jerome's side; Vincentius, on the other hand, was a friend from his days in Constantinople, with whom he had discussed the problems facing a translator (he was the de-dicatee of translations of some of Origen's sermons).[117] Both these fellow-travellers to the holy places would find them-selves caught in the centre of the ecclesiastical storm which broke over Jerusalem and Bethlehem in the 390s (the theme of the next chapter). In 398 Paulinianus returned to the West to dispose of the remains of the family's ravaged estates in Dalmatia, to raise funds for the Bethlehem monastery.[118] He

[114] *Ep.* 108.6.4 'quae et propositi et navigationis eius comes est'.

[115] Ibid. 14.4.

[116] Jer. *Apol. c. Ruf.* iii. 22 'cum sancto Vincentio presbytero, et adolescente fratre, et aliis monachis qui nunc Hierosolymae commorantur'.

[117] See the introduction to the *Chron.* For the sermons (on Jeremiah and Ezechiel), see *PL* 25, 583–6.

[118] Jer. *Ep.* 66.14; cf. *Apol. c. Ruf.* iii. 24, *Ep.* 81.2.

was accompanied on this trip by another of the circle of Jerome's friends, Eusebius of Cremona. This man, who had been of some standing in his home-town in north Italy, had embarked on a career in public life, like many other promising young men of his day—most likely as an advocate.[119] The prospect of advancing his fortunes amid the society of the imperial court will have attracted him to the neighbouring city of Milan. It is likely that it was here that he encountered, and embarked on a friendship with, the young Gallic aristocrat Meropius Pontius Paulinus, who in the early 380s was returning to Aquitania from his period of office as *consularis* of Campania.[120] Paulinus was later to attribute some of his own inclination to the ascetic life to this spell in Milan and to the influence of bishop Ambrose (who had wanted to ordain Paulinus into his clergy);[121] a similar, and more celebrated, testament to the spiritual forces unleashed in Milanese court society in these years by the powerful bishop is, of course, the experience of the professor of rhetoric, Augustine.[122] It may be possible to add to these names the aspiring advocate from Cremona, who evidently about the same time discarded any intentions of secular promotion in favour of the monastic life. Whereas Paulinus was ultimately to reject a journey to the Holy Land and settled instead at his shrine in Nola, Eusebius determined to make for the holy places and there became a loyal disciple of Jerome: at the height of the 'Origenist' controversy with Rufinus his skills at advocacy would be employed again in his master's behalf.[123]

This group of Jerome's colleagues from Bethlehem reveals something of the loyalty and cohesion of a close-knit fraterni-

---

[119] Id. *Ep.* 57.2 'vir apud suos haut ignobilis'. The nature of Eusebius' secular career is alluded to by Rufin. *Apol. c. Hier.* i. 19 '...in foro positus vel in negotiis saecularibus...quia saecularem iam vitam reliquit...'. Yet (Jer. l.c.) he remained ignorant of Greek.

[120] For Eusebius and Paulinus, see Jer. *Ep.* 53.11.1 'amantissimum tui fratrem'; cf. P. Courcelle (1947), 264–6. For the young Paulinus alongside others of his 'mould', see John Matthews (1975), 73–5, 151–3, and W. H. C. Frend (1969).

[121] Paul. Nol. *Ep.* 3.4.

[122] For the background, see Matthews, ch. 8.

[123] Having returned to Italy with Paulinianus (Jer. *Apol. c. Ruf.* iii. 24). To Rufinus he was 'quasi calumniandi peritissimus', *Apol. c. Hier.* i. 19; cf. ibid. i. 21 '...per totam me Italiam criminari, instigare turbas, conturbare ecclesias, aures quoque polluere sacerdotum...'.

ty, in contrast to the widespread and influential circle of visitors who came and went on the Mount of Olives. A loyal group of followers stands out against the list of persons from high places who were identified enjoying the hospitality of the Jerusalem monasteries. It is certainly more difficult to establish for Jerome's community in Bethlehem any of the connexions with Theodosius' entourage which distinguished the settlement on the Mount of Olives. Two names appear promising. During his stay in Constantinople c.380 Jerome had encountered the Spanish courtier Nebridius, a relative of the empress Flacilla, who became *comes rei privatae* in 382, rising to become prefect of Constantinople in 386.[124] Writing of their friendship years afterwards (in 400), Jerome looked back on it as a close relationship;[125] but it can have been no more than a distant memory, for Nebridius was long dead. Jerome only resumed contact with his family when he wrote a letter of consolation to the widow of his son, a young man of exemplary piety; it is clear that he had never met Salvina, and felt constrained to justify his addressing of this *consolatio* to her.[126] Another of the emperor's Spanish supporters, Nummius Aemilianus Dexter, son of the bishop of Barcelona, was counted among Jerome's 'amici';[127] 'distinguished in the world and devoted to the faith of Christ', Dexter urged on Jerome the composition of the *De Viris Illustribus*, and received the dedication in 392 (or 393).[128] It is possible, as has been suggested, that Dexter actually visited Jerome in Bethlehem during the period in which he held office in the East (*procos. Asiae* 379–87, *comes rei privatae* 387);[129] but the manner of his appearance in the pages of the *De Viris*, with its air of studied

---

[124] For Nebridius, in his context among the supporters of Theodosius, see Matthews, 109–10, 132.

[125] *Ep.* 79.1.4.

[126] l.c. 'cur ego ad eam scribimus, quam ignoramus?'. In the circumstances of 400, we may think of the politics surrounding John Chrysostom, of whom Salvina was a committed supporter (Pall. *Dialogus*, 61)—was Jerome trying to win her over? Cf. below, pp. 195ff.

[127] Jer. *Apol. c. Ruf.* ii. 23 'Dexter amicus meus...'. For his career, Matthews, 111–12, 123.

[128] *De Vir. Illust.* prolog.; cf. ibid. 132. Controversy surrounds the date: P. Nautin (1974), 280–4, reasserted 393 after T. D. Barnes, *Tertullian* (1971), 235–6, had argued for 392.

[129] Matthews (1967), 440, hinted again in (1975), 133.

remoteness regarding Dexter's literary accomplishments as a historian, fails to convince of any direct personal contact.[130] Certainly by 395 (when, as we shall see, Jerusalem's contacts with Constantinople were at their most effective), Dexter had returned to the West with Theodosius, and was in office as *ppo Italiae*.[131]

Contacts between Bethlehem and the court, then, remain elusive. Not so the links between Jerome and his devotees in the West. The Roman widow, Fabiola, finding inadequate scope for her pious donations in the city and among the monks of the off-shore islands, took ship for Jerusalem in the company of Oceanus (*c*.394–5);[132] from a crowded reception in the holy city she withdrew to enjoy Jerome's hospitality, where she indulged her taste for holy scripture with a flood of enquiries on points of biblical exegesis.[133] Jerome, regrettably, does not reveal whether her interest in the account of the progress of the children of Israel out of Egypt was accompanied by a pilgrimage to the sites concerned; but it seems unlikely in view of the shortness of her stay in Bethlehem, which was curtailed by the rumours of barbarian invasions threatening the Holy Land and by the 'local war' raging then against the establishment in Jerusalem.[134] Fabiola, unable to match Jerome's attachment to the holy places, sailed away to pursue her charitable works in Rome.[135] Fabiola's stay in Bethlehem coincided with that of another western pilgrim, Vigilantius, a presbyter of Barcelona;[136] he arrived in the course of 395, bearing a letter from Paulinus seeking Jerome's advice on his new spiritual vocation, and a copy of Paulinus' recently composed oration in praise of the 're-

[130] *De Vir. Illust.* 132 '...fertur ad me omnimodam historiam texuisse, *quam necdum legi*'.

[131] First attested 18 Mar. 395 (*CTh* viii. 5.53).

[132] Jer. *Ep.* 77.7 (*consolatio* addressed to Oceanus). That Oceanus was with her emerges from *Apol. c. Ruf.* iii. 4, and *Ep.* 61.3.3 (Oceanus in Bethlehem).

[133] *Ep.* 77.7. The request for the exegesis of Numbers, 33, the catalogue of the Israelites' *mansiones*, was fulfilled posthumously, in *Ep.* 78.

[134] *Ep.* 77.8 'domestica bella'; for the 'quaedam apud nos dissensio', cf. below, p. 191. The invasions were those of the winter of 394–5, during the absence of Theodosius' army in the West (ibid. 8.2).

[135] Including the foundation, with Pammachius, of the *xenodochium* at Portus: *Ep.* 77.10, cf. 66.11.

[136] Jer. *Ep.* 58.11.3.

ligiosissimus princeps', Theodosius.[137] Vigilantius, as we
shall see, was soon to fall out of favour with Jerome, and
made a hasty departure for Egypt.[138]

The Spaniard Lucinus, from the province of Baetica, may
well have intended to make a pilgrimage. His contacts with
Jerome seem to have had more than just a literary interest,
and were as much the product of a pious attachment to the
Holy Land; for, besides the six *notarii* who were sent to make
copies of Jerome's translations, Lucinus also dispatched contributions to the churches of Jerusalem and Alexandria,
together with personal gifts for Jerome himself.[139] His death
was to prevent him fulfilling the invitation to visit the Holy
Land;[140] but it may be that his widow Theodora took up the
invitation in his stead—if so, no record survives of her
reaching the holy places.[141]

Jerome's Roman friends, other than Fabiola, were less
inclined to follow the example of Paula and Eustochium. The
long letter which he composed in their name to Marcella, in
an attempt to persuade her to embark for the Holy Land,[142]
did not succeed in dislodging her from the suburban retreat
which she had made her own 'Jerusalem';[143] nor, so far as we
are aware, did Desiderius and his wife Serenilla take up the
invitation from Bethlehem, '...to pray where the feet of the
Lord have stood...'.[144]

Other would-be pilgrims emerge fleetingly in the correspondence. The blind Pannonian Castricianus, a 'land-
lubber' ('terrenum animal') who braved the waters of the
Adriatic and the Aegean, but was turned back by family ties;
Jerome at least found satisfaction in his intention, even if he
failed to complete his journey.[145] Or the soldier Exsuperantius, with whom Jerome embarked on a correspondence in
anticipation of his arrival in Bethlehem: 'I have knocked at

---

[137] Ibid. 8ff. For the date, see P. Nautin (1973), 230ff.   [138] Below, pp. 191–2.

[139] *Ep.* 71.5, 75.4; for the gifts, 71.7. Jerome responded appropriately, with four
goat's-hair tunics and a work expounding the visions of Isaiah.

[140] *Ep.* 71.4.1, 75.1 '...quem in brevi tempore huc venturum esse credebam'.

[141] *Ep.* 76.3 '...ut in coepto itinere non lassetur, ut ad terram sanctam multo per
heremum labore perveniat'; as much else in this paragraph, this may well be figurative.

[142] I.e. *Ep.* 46.   [143] Cf. *Ep.* 127.8 '...Romam factam Hierosolymam'.

[144] *Ep.* 47.2.2 'adorasse, ubi steterunt pedes Domini, pars fidei est...'.

[145] *Ep.* 68.1.

the door of friendship; if you open it, you will find ready hosts'.[146] It is possible that Exsuperantius reached the Holy Land: it was to be alleged that one of that name, described as an 'Italian', was driven away from Bethlehem by Jerome's quarrelsome disposition.[147] One visitor at least who arrived at Jerome's door stayed in the monastery, full of admiration for his host, for six months—the Gallic pilgrim Postumianus, who fled from the dissension in the Egyptian church (c.400) to the hospitality of Bethlehem; this was evidently his second visit, for Postumianus claims that Jerome was known to him from an earlier pilgrimage.[148]

In the reception of visitors to the Holy Land in the years of Theodosius' reign the monastery dominating Jerusalem from the Mount of Olives thus had its equivalent in Jerome's establishment in Bethlehem, which also functioned as a haven for foreign arrivals (though more vulnerable, as will become clear, to the storms of ecclesiastical dispute than its counterpart in Jerusalem). His passing comments on the numbers of visitors to his monastery are given some substance by the catalogue of names here outlined. It is a group of people more disparate and far-flung than the markedly homogenous 'Theodosian' connections of the Mount of Olives; western aristocrats, clergymen, soldiers—their common links with Bethlehem were not solely those of a shared attachment to the holy places but as much a personal association (in not a few cases quick to transform into an equally personal antipathy) with Jerome himself, forged through his correspondence and *clientela*. The public prestige of holy city and imperial entourage is counterbalanced in Bethlehem by the personal dominance of the biblical scholar surrounded by the sites which were integral to this study. Both are facets, as earlier chapters have shown, of the position of the Holy Land in the Christian empire. It was a position which, sooner or later, would place it in the full glare of ecclesiastical controversy; and when that came, in the 390s, the fragility of the Bethlehem links would emerge in the face of the robust dominance of the Mount of Olives.

---

[146] *Ep.* 145.1. [147] Pall. *Hist. Laus.* 36 (Butler, 108).
[148] Sulp. Sev. *Dial.* i. 8–9. The authenticity of Postumianus' pilgrimage, which had been denied by Babut, was reaffirmed by H. Delehaye, *Anal. Boll.* 38 (1920), 84ff., followed by J. Gribomont (1961).

8. Pilgrims and Politics (i) Palladius

To focus the lens, as the previous chapter has done, on the two western monastic establishments in Jerusalem and Bethlehem may appear at first sight to distort the picture of pilgrimage to the Holy Land in the later years of the fourth century: an overwhelming inbalance of evidence (it may well be argued) has led to an exaggerated concentration on a small, untypical, and exclusively privileged band who, in virtue of their education and influence, were aloof from the majority of pilgrims at the holy places. Moreover, had not Melania, Rufinus, Jerome and Paula and their friends long since ceased to be pilgrims at all? After an initial display of enthusiasm for the holy sites in the conventional tour, they settled down in their monastic surroundings into long-term residence—it was more than a quarter of a century before Melania or Rufinus returned to Italy, while Jerome and Paula never again saw the western part of the empire. The holy places, and the piety which they inspired, might seem a largely irrelevant background to the regime of monastic life being conducted on the Mount of Olives and among the community in Bethlehem.

Yet the flow of travellers which we have recounted belies any assumption that the western monasteries in the Holy Land had little part to play in the general pattern of pilgrimage to the holy places. Foremost among the concerns of both establishments, it has emerged, was the reception of visitors and pilgrims: this was placed first by Palladius in his summary of the activities of Melania and Rufinus on the Mount of Olives, and its prominence is implied by Jerome's carping on their hospitality; similarly in the case of his own establish-

ment in Bethlehem, attention to visitors strained the resources to the extent (as we have seen) of having to sell up
the remains of the family estates to raise funds.[1] It is clear
that the monasteries, far from being irrelevant, were in fact
in the forefront in meeting the demands created by the concentration of pilgrims—it could hardly be otherwise when
they were deliberately sited in the proximity of the leading
holy places.

These establishments were inevitably drawn into the public and liturgical life of the church in the Holy Land (which
was observed and participated in by large numbers of pilgrims). Jerome himself regularly preached in the church of
the Nativity at Bethlehem, and it was expected that he and
his friend Vincentius, as ordained presbyters, would carry
out their priestly duties accordingly (although, in Jerome's
eyes, the performance of these duties conflicted with the dic-
tates of monastic solitude);[2] at all events, some of Jerome's
community took their part in the worship of the neighbouring holy places.[3] The integration of the western establishment on the Mount of Olives with the public life of the
church in Jerusalem is clearly recorded—from the fact of
their lavish material patronage and wealthy donations to
their full participation in the round of worship. The monks
and nuns, for instance, whom Egeria observed maintaining
the elaborate liturgy in Jerusalem must surely have included
many from the monasteries of Melania and Rufinus.[4]
Rufinus himself was a presbyter in the Jerusalem clergy, and
staunchly loyal to bishop John;[5] John in his turn was
evidently closely in touch with the monastic leadership on
the Mount of Olives.[6] Moreover Palladius' puzzling reference

---

[1] Jer. *Ep.* 66.14. For the Mount of Olives, see Pall. *Hist. Laus.* 46 'δεξιούμενοι ....
τοὺς παρατυγχάνοντας ἐν τοῖς Ἱεροσολύμοις εὐχῆς ἕνεκα ...'.

[2] Cf. Sulp. Sev. *Dial.* i.8 (Postumianus) 'ecclesiam loci illius Hieronymus presbyter regit'; although Jerome and Vincentius had been reluctant to carry out priestly
duties, see Jer. *Ep.* 51.1.5ff. For the incompatibility with monasticism, *Ep.* 58.4.

[3] E.g. the satirical portrait of the monk Sabinianus conducting an illicit love-
affair during services in the church of the Nativity: *Ep.* 147.4.

[4] E.g. the Latin interpreters, 'fratres et sorores grecolatini': *It. Eg.* 47.4.

[5] For Rufinus as presbyter, see Pall. *Hist.l Laus.* 46, and Jer. *Ep.* 51.6.4. On his
loyalty to his bishop, see the prologue to his translation of Pamphilus' *Apology* (*CC*
20, 234), with *Apol. c. Hier.* i. 13.

[6] Jer. *Ep.* 82.7 '... assidua confabulatione et cotidiano Latinorum consortio'

to Melania and Rufinus 'healing the schism of Paulinus' and returning four hundred monks to the fold of the church, however interpreted, confirms the impression that the Mount of Olives community wielded solid support for the ecclesiastical structure of Jerusalem.[7]

Yet the role played by the establishments in Jerusalem and Bethlehem was not merely local to the surrounding holy places. The fact that the leaderships not only kept open their own channels of communication with friends further afield but through the coming and going of pilgrims in their hostels had a ready means of contact with distant parts of the Mediterranean world meant that they were instrumental in consolidating the position of the Holy Land as a pivot of the Christian empire. This becomes especially evident when the controversy over the orthodoxy of Origen raged around the holy places in the last years of the fourth century. This fierce quarrel about the theological standing of the Alexandrian scholar was instigated in the Holy Land (in 393) with the arrival there of the heresy-hunting bishop of Salamis in Cyprus, Epiphanius—who had earlier influenced Paula's ascetic resolve in Rome and had been host to her and Jerome on their journey to the Holy Land. Epiphanius' criticisms were aimed at the 'intellectualizing' tendency of Origen's theology which, by questioning fundamental doctrines such as the resurrection of the body, appeared to threaten the real bedrock of the Christian faith.[8] The issue was to divide the monasteries at Bethlehem and in Jerusalem. Jerome apparently set more store by friendship with Epiphanius than by his recently avowed admiration of Origen, and eagerly joined in the condemnation of Origen's views; while Rufinus (and bishop John) championed their orthodoxy.[9] Because this dispute centred upon the two 'western' communities, it was from the start very much more than a local argument in the Holy

---

[7] Pall. l.c. Butler and others have followed Tillemont in suggesting that Pall. was referring to 'Paulinianus', Jerome's brother, and the dispute between Jerusalem and Bethlehem over his ordination: cf. J. N. D. Kelly (1975), 200ff.

[8] Cf. above, p. 90, on Origen's allegorical exegesis.

[9] On this contentious episode it is now adequate to cite only Kelly, ch. 18. For the transmission of the quarrel further afield see esp. P. Brown (1970). There is also a narrative of events in P. Nautin (1971–2, 1972–3). On Jerome's praise of Origen, cf. *De Vir. Illust.* 54 'immortali eius ingenio'.

Land: first imported to the holy places by Epiphanius, the quarrel was largely sustained by foreign residents, through whose agency it was disseminated to other corners of the empire. The movement of pilgrims to and from the holy places was an essential component in this grid; drawn into the ambit of one or other of the contending parties by their reception in Jerusalem or Bethlehem they would find it hard to escape identification with one side of the case, and through their travels would spread the controversy to a wider arena. It is a measure of the true impact of Melania, Jerome, and their circles of friends on the life of the holy places that it became difficult for their visitors to adopt a pious indifference or neutrality—pilgrims found themselves turned into political partisans.

The absorption of an outsider into the political conflicts of the Holy Land, and his participation in the wider transmission of these conflicts, is to be observed most effectively through the career of the Galatian monk and bishop, Palladius.[10] The *Historia Lausiaca*, despite its avowed intention to edify and its reticence with regard to the political involvements of holy men,[11] none the less remains an individual record of the personalities encountered by Palladius during his travels in Palestine and Egypt, and further afield.[12] It is a first-hand account of the associations and loyalties of a visitor to the Holy Land—and of his gradual shift from detached observer to committed participant.[13]

When Palladius arrived at the holy places (*c*.385) and joined the monk Innocent on the Mount of Olives,[14] he could hardly have predicted that his move would be anything more than a stage *en route* to the ascetic life; yet in settling in Jerusalem he found himself drawn into contacts which were to shape the course of his future career. His association with Melania is the most pervasive to emerge from the pages of

[10] What follows in this chapter is a modified version of E. D. Hunt (1973).

[11] On the reticence of the *Hist. Laus.*, see E. Schwartz (1937), 197ff.

[12] Cf. D. F. Buck (1976).

[13] C. H. Turner (1904–5), 345–6, long ago recognized Palladius' share in the 'personal jealousies and party passions which cloaked themselves under the mask of zeal for orthodoxy'.

[14] Above, p. 167.

the *Hist. Laus.*:[15] 'thrice-blessed Melania' is not only the subject of three chapters in the work, but also the source for stories of some of the Egyptian monks, notably Or and Pambo of Nitria (who had died by the time Palladius himself arrived in Egypt).[16] As Melania and Palladius were neighbours on the Mount of Olives, it is unlikely that his own decision to travel to the Egyptian desert did not owe something to their conversations about these holy men. In his meetings with Melania Palladius also could not fail to encounter her colleague Rufinus, who earns high praise from him for his 'knowledge' and 'reasonableness'.[17] Such commendations carries an unmistakable implication that Rufinus had attained the 'gnosis' which lay at the summit of the spiritual life as Palladius conceived it (a judgement in remarkable contrast to Jerome's stream of invective aimed at Rufinus).[18]

Palladius also came to know of Jerome during his years on the Mount of Olives, when he stayed for a while in Bethlehem with the monk Posidonius (who had emigrated to the Holy Land from Egypt).[19] About the same time Jerome and Paula had arrived in Bethlehem to begin the establishment of their own monastic foundations. When he came to write the *Historia Lausiaca*, Palladius spoke with admiration of Paula's spiritual endeavours[20]—but he held that her aims were thwarted by the 'evil influence' of Jerome, whose great command of Latin letters, which Palladius acknowledged, was vitiated by irredeemable faults of character.[21] This harsh verdict on Jerome, written some thirty years after Palladius' own stay in Bethlehem, would hardly be surprising in the light of what was to intervene—the 'Origenist' dispute and

---

[15] On Palladius and Melania, see Turner, 351–4, and Schwartz, 165ff.

[16] *Hist. Laus.* 46, 54, 55 (the ascription of the last to Melania has been accepted since the arguments of Turner, cf. Hunt (1972), 352). Melania is quoted as a source in *Hist. Laus.* 5, 9, 10.

[17] Ibid. 46 'οὗ γνωστικώτερος καὶ ἐπιεικέστερος ἐν ἀνδράσιν οὐχ εὑρίσκετο'.

[18] On Palladius and Evagrian 'gnosis', cf. below, n. 35. For samples of Jerome's language about Rufinus, see F. Cavallera (1922), ii, 131–5.

[19] Pall. *Hist. Laus.* 36. Schwartz, 162–3, reasserted Tillemont's location of the period with Posidonius *before* the departure for Egypt, *contra* Butler, 244, and recently Buck, 299–300.

[20] Ibid. 41: Pall. admits he had not met her daughter Eustochium—he may not actually have encountered Paula herself.

[21] His word is 'βασκανία' (cf. ibid. 36, Butler, 108).

the subsequent differences over John Chrysostom;[22] it is the judgement of one who was to become identified with Jerome's principal opponents. Yet this process had begun as early as his reception into Melania's company on the Mount of Olives, and the disdain lurking in the phrase 'a certain Jerome from Dalmatia' may well have had its origins in these first years of Palladius in Jerusalem. The criticism of Jerome's influence over Paula echoes that which had surrounded his recent departure from Rome, when his authority among the ladies of certain senatorial households had become the subject of scandal, no less in avowedly Christian circles than among traditional pagans.[23] These charges, it appears, pursued Jerome to the Holy Land—where they were taken up again by Palladius.

This coolness towards Jerome, conditioned by his relations with the Mount of Olives community, places Palladius in effective contrast to the Gallic pilgrim Postumianus, who visited Jerome on two occasions, the second time (*c.*400) as a refugee from the anti-Origenist upheavals in Egypt, when he enjoyed his hospitality for six months. For Postumianus, besides being a man of incomparable learning,[24] Jerome was a resolute fighter against heresy and a ceaseless critic of the faults of the clergy; his was a 'universal learning and sound teaching', such that he was a proper object of admiration and affection for all right-thinking men.[25] Like Palladius' judgement of Rufinus, this is the voice of a pilgrim caught up in political divisions, and of identifiable loyalties; as visitors at the holy places, both men found themselves drawn inextricably into the factions dividing the two communities in Jerusalem and Bethlehem, unable to remain outside the conflicts which dominated the world into which they had entered.

When Palladius travelled on from Jerusalem to Egypt, and was met by the presbyter Isidore at Alexandria in 388,[26] he was treading a path familiar to pilgrims moving between the

---

[22] Cf. below, pp. 195ff.   [23] Jer. *Ep.* 45.4. Cf. Kelly (1975), 107ff.

[24] Sulp. Sev. *Dial.* i. 8.3 '... ut se illi in omni scientia nemo audeat comparare'.

[25] Ibid. 9.4–5 'plane eum boni omnes admirantur et diligunt'.

[26] *Hist. Laus.* 1 'the second consulship of Theodosius'—the only firm date in the work.

holy places and the holy men of the Egyptian desert. In the journeys of Egeria and Paula, for example, we have already met the 'grand tour' extending from the Holy Land into Egypt, a pattern which was repeated on numerous occasions in this period.[27] The traffic was not all one way—Egyptian monks too were often to be seen on pilgrimage and participating in the worship of the holy places.[28] Such ready movement between Egypt and Palestine was to some extent a Christian reflection of the close cultural and commercial ties across the eastern Mediterranean; yet Palladius' journey is also indicative of a more particular association which developed between the community on the Mount of Olives and the desert fathers, stemming from the loyalties already demonstrated by Melania and Rufinus during the years of Arian dominance. Palladius' removal to Egypt was matched by other such journeys in the period of Melania's presence in Jerusalem: there was, for example, the tour of the monastic sites in Egypt in 394 by a group of seven monks from the Mount of Olives—described in the *Historia Monachorum*.[29] Most important of all had been the withdrawal of Evagrius of Pontus from the Mount of Olives to the Nitrian desert (*c.* 382).[30] Evagrius typifies most strikingly the Egyptian connexions of the communities on the Mount. Having withdrawn to Jerusalem (as we have seen) from an influential position as deacon in the church at Constantinople, he had been welcomed at the holy places by Melania—and to prove to her his vocation to the ascetic life he had moved on to settle in the Egyptian desert. His may have been the precedent which encouraged Palladius in his own withdrawal to

[27] It is implied in Antony's question of visiting monks, 'Are they from Egypt or Jerusalem?' (*Hist. Laus.* 21, Butler, 66). This distinction came to be figurative, see R. Draguet (1947), 6.

[28] E.g. John Cassian, *Inst.* iv. 31 'qui ad loca sancta de Aegypti partibus orationis causa convenerant'; or the monks from Egypt who came to the Jerusalem *Encaenia* (*It. Eg.* 49.1). Cf. Jer. *Ep.* 3.2 on the 'crebra commeantium multitudo' passing between Egypt and Palestine. Porphyry, future bishop of Gaza, first arrived in the Holy Land from Egypt 'to worship at the holy places': Marc. Diac. *V. Porph.* 4.

[29] The monks' visit to Egypt coincided with the battle of the Frigidus, *Hist. Monach.* 1.64.

[30] *Hist. Laus.* 38 (Butler, 120); cf. Socr. *Hist. Eccl.* iv. 23.34ff. On Evagrius, see A. Guillaumont (1962), esp. 47ff.

Egypt. Evagrius gathered round him a distinguished entourage, among them the renowned 'Tall Brothers', pupils of the
Nitrian Pambo, who had been in the company of those who
fled with Melania to Palestine under the Arian onslaught in the
reign of Valens.[31] This was the group of monks who, under
Evagrius' leadership in Egypt, were to be the champions of
the teachings of Origen—and in this too kindred spirits of
their friends on the Mount of Olives.[32] Having followed in
Evagrius' footsteps from Jerusalem, Palladius naturally
gravitated to this monastic circle: when visiting John of
Lycopolis he announced that he came from 'the company of
Evagrius';[33] while the chapter devoted to Evagrius ('a man
who lived as the apostles') in the *Hist. Laus.* is the principal
source for his life—and a centrepiece of the work 'for the
edification of the reader and the glory of the goodness of our
Saviour'.[34] The influence of Evagrius, in both language and
thought, has been detected throughout the pages of the *Hist.
Laus.*[35]

Evagrius and those around him still looked back from
Egypt to Jerusalem and the Mount of Olives: a correspondence, for example, on spiritual matters passed between him
and Melania;[36] while Rufinus himself was a follower of Evagrian monasticism.[37] It is worth noting that in the prologue to
his *Praktikos* Evagrius addresses an Anatolius, who had written to him in Egypt 'from the sacred mountain' with an in-
quiry about the significance of the monastic habit;[38] we can
surmise that Anatolius had in fact been writing from Jeru-

[31] See above, p. 170. (Palladius mistakenly included Pambo himself among the
fugitives: Butler, 191.)

[32] On this group, see Guillaumont, 51ff., and O. Chadwick (1968), 24ff. Already
in 377 Epiphanius, *Panarion*, 64.4, had seen the threat of Origenism among the 'most
distinguished' of the monks in Egypt. For Melania's reading of Origen, see Pall.
Hist. Laus. 55.

[33] *Hist. Laus.* 35 (Butler, 102); cf. a meeting with Dioscuros in the company of
Evagrius, ibid. 12, and Socr. *Hist. Eccl.* iv. 23.79 (Pall. a 'pupil of Evagrius').

[34] *Hist. Laus.* 38 (Butler, 116).

[35] See R. Draguet (1946), (1947).

[36] Jer. *Ep.* 133.3.5 'scribit ad eam, cuius nomen nigredinis testatur perfidiae
tenebras'. For editions of Evagrius' so-called 'Letter to Melania', see W. Frankenberg
(1912), 613–9, and G. Vitestam (1963–4).

[37] Jer. l.c. Cf. Pall. on Rufinus, above, p. 184.

[38] *PG* 40, 1220 (cf. *SChr* 171, 482).

salem, the city of the sacred mountain of Sion.[39] There may
be more to the contacts between Evagrius and Jerusalem
than exchanges of letters. It is reported that Theophilus of
Alexandria wanted to ordain Evagrius to a bishopric;[40] indeed a Coptic version of the *Hist. Laus.* supplies the see in
question (Thmuis) and the information that, to avoid this
unwelcome elevation, Evagrius fled to Palestine.[41] As the
Mount of Olives would be for him an obvious place of refuge,
we cannot rule out the possibility that Evagrius returned to
Jerusalem at some point during his seclusion in Egypt.

As for Palladius, it is an attractive (but little substanti-
ated) hypothesis that he may have been the messenger who
carried letters from Evagrius to Melania in Jerusalem—
among Evagrius' letters is one referring to 'our dear brother
Palladius' who had delivered some correspondence, but the
name of the addressee is unknown.[42] It was certainly on
Evagrius' behalf that Palladius embarked on his eighteen-
day journey up the Nile to investigate the renown of the hermit John at Lycopolis;[43] and it may have been Palladius'
reports on his return to his master which encouraged the
seven visitors from the Mount of Olives to make the same
trip to the Thebaid.[44] The presence in Egypt of these monks
serves to confirm the continuing relations between the
Mount of Olives and the desert communities around Nitria;
they were hospitably received, and observed the life of the
monks around them—both Ammonius (leader of the 'Tall
Brothers') and Evagrius were among those whom they met.[45]

This was late in 394.[46] By this date there is a strong likelihood that Palladius himself (despite the diplomatic silence of

---

[39] Sion was the 'sacred mountain' *par excellence* for Evagrius, as the symbol of
'contemplation' (e.g. *Kephal. Gnostic.* v. 88, vi. 49). The suggestion (*SChr* 171, 483) of
the identity of this Anatolius with a Spanish official mentioned in a Coptic version
of *Hist. Laus.* will not work—the latter is unlikely to be historical (cf. John Matthews (1975), 144, n. 4).

[40] Socr. *Hist. Eccl.* iv. 23.75.   [41] Cf. Butler, i, 144.

[42] Frankenberg, 599.   [43] *Hist. Laus.* 35 (Butler, 101–2).

[44] I.e. the journey described in *Hist. Monach.* 1. Palladius recounts that, on his
return to Evagrius, he met other monks who went on to visit John 'two months'
later (Butler, 104–5).

[45] The Nitrian section of *Hist. Monach.* begins at 20.5; Rufinus' Latin is fuller at
this point (21–30), *PL* 21, 443ff.

[46] Cf. n. 29, above.

the *Hist. Laus.*) had returned for a visit to Jerusalem, perhaps
encouraged by the arrivals in Egypt from the Mount of
Olives. The evidence is to be found in a letter addressed to
bishop John of Jerusalem by Epiphanius, bishop of Salamis
in Cyprus, towards the middle of 394. The 'Origenist' storm
has broken over the holy places, exposing the dissension between the church in Jerusalem and the monks of Bethlehem.
Epiphanius, the leading participant in the campaign for
orthodoxy, warned the bishop of Jerusalem against the
teachings of Origen (his letter was later translated by
Jerome),[47] and concluded by advising him of the danger
from Palladius—with a strong implication that Palladius was
either on his way to, or in, Jerusalem at the time:

Beware of the Galatian Palladius, who once was a friend but now
is in need of God's mercy because he is preaching and teaching the
heresy of Origen, lest perchance he lead astray some of the people
who are entrusted to you into the perversity of his own error.[48]

Along with Rufinus, mentioned earlier in the letter,[49] Palladius is here alleged to pose a threat to bishop John's congregation *in* Jerusalem: the people 'entrusted' to John could
only be his parishioners at the holy places.[50] Epiphanius is
unlikely to have uttered this warning if he did not have good
reason to believe that Palladius was in Jerusalem and joining
ranks with Rufinus.

The affiliations of Palladius on the Mount of Olives and
in Egypt make such an alliance entirely predictable. Epiphanius' dismissal of Palladius, an erstwhile friend, as an
'Origenist' sets the seal on his absorption into the party of
Rufinus, Melania, Evagrius, and Ammonius; it was a commitment which would be recalled on two more occasions, in

---

[47] I.e. Jer. *Ep.* 51. On the date, see P. Nautin (1973), 76–8.

[48] *Ep.* 51.9.3. For this much-discussed passage, see E. Preuschen, *Palladius und
Rufinus* (1897), 242–3; Butler, i, 293ff., ii, 240ff.; id. (1920–1), 153; E. Schwartz
(1937), 163–5.

[49] *Ep.* 51.6.4.

[50] *Pace* Butler's later view (favoured by Schwartz), Epiphanius' remarks must im-
ply Palladius' imminent presence *in* Jerusalem: the phrase 'populus...creditus'
matches that used in connexion with Rufinus, who certainly *was* in Jerusalem, and
where Epiphanius specifies 'omnes fratres *qui tecum* (sc. John) *sunt*'.

accusations against him at the 'Synod of the Oak' in 403,[51] and by Jerome writing in 415, contrasting his own ruthless defence of orthodoxy with the heresy of his opponents—in his eyes both Rufinus and Palladius were guilty of the same error.[52] Having travelled to the Holy Land in the first place as an aspirant to the monastic life, Palladius had been drawn into the surrounding controversy; the associations which he had formed on the Mount of Olives had hardened into a political alliance.

Returning to Jerusalem in 394, Palladius would be arriving at the period when his friends on the Mount of Olives scored their most notable success over the community in Bethlehem. It was at this time that the bishop of Jerusalem, who had excluded Jerome and his colleagues from communion, went so far as to invoke the 'secular arm' against them: threats of banishment emanated from official circles in Constantinople.[53] The execution of the sentence appears only to have been averted by the distraction of the barbarian invasions of the winter of 394–5, and the political changes at court surrounding the fall of the praetorian prefect, Fl. Rufinus, who was assassinated on 27 November 395. This was the man, *de facto* regent at the eastern court after Theodosius' departure for the West in May 394, whom Jerome saw as the source of the action against him—and he was soon to greet Rufinus' gruesome end with satisfaction.[54] But Jerome was clear that the real initiative in the move to banish him lay with his opponents in Jerusalem: here may well have been an occasion when the church establishment at the holy places actually exploited for political ends the contacts with the imperial court made available by well-placed pilgrims.[55] Only with the aid of such influential channels

---

[51] In the *Acta* preserved by Photius (*Bibliotheca*, cod. 59), Palladius is among those denounced as 'Origenists'.

[52] Jer. *Prolog. ad Dial. adv. Pelag.* (*PL* 23, 497) 'Palladius servilis nequitiae eandem haeresim instaurare conatus est'. On the question of Palladius' orthodoxy, see Butler, i, 173–8, and Coleman-Norton's introd. to his edition of the *Dialogus*, xx ff.

[53] Jer. *Ep.* 82.10, *C. Ioh. Hier.* 43. Cf. P. Nautin (1973), 78–9; id. (1971–2, 1972–3); Kelly (1975), 203–4.

[54] Jer. *Ep.* 60.16.1 (severed head and hand); cf. Claudian, *In Rufin.* ii. 405ff., and Zosim. v. 7.6. For his 'regency', Zosim. iv.57.4.

[55] Cf. above, pp. 159ff. I am no longer sure that the pilgrimage of Silvia (Rufinus' sister-in-law) is relevant here—her journey may be as late as 399–400. Cf. the arguments of P. Devos (1973), 113ff., against my conjectures in (1972), 357ff.

would Jerusalem have been able to secure from the court the threat of exile and seriously to menace the position of Jerome and his colleagues in Bethlehem.

The impact on Bethlehem of this turn of events can be assessed by considering the cases of some pilgrims at Jerome's monastery. It was in the course of 395 that Fabiola was fleeing from Bethlehem amid rumours of barbarian invasions. But a threat much nearer at hand also contributed to her departure: 'there was at that time *disagreement among ourselves* and local conflicts counted for more than battles with barbarians'.[56] Jerome's allusion to the divisions enveloping the holy places is a hint that Fabiola was caught up in the surrounding politics; this is amplified in his polemic against Rufinus, where he alleges that the thieves of his translation of Epiphanius' letter to bishop John (a work undertaken privately for Eusebius of Cremona, with damaging implications, if made public, for Jerome's relations with his bishop), thieves whom he holds to have been instigated by Rufinus, actually planted the document in the lodging of Fabiola and Oceanus—before it made its way to his opponents in Jerusalem.[57]

The involvement of Fabiola, who was in Bethlehem as pilgrim and (as we have seen) student of the Bible, in these political manoeuvres illustrates the difficulty of staying outside the prevailing dissension. The reports of invasion doubtless provided an opportunity to withdraw from the tense atmosphere; the innocent pilgrim packed her bags. Another hurried departure in this crowded year of 395 was that of the presbyter Vigilantius. His initially enthusiastic reception of an anti-Origenist sermon by Jerome on the resurrection of the body was before long turned into an attitude of hostility towards the Bethlehem monks and an early withdrawal to Egypt.[58] Like Fabiola, Vigilantius in visiting the holy places was caught in the cross-fire between Jerusalem and Beth-

---

[56] Jer. *Ep.* 77.8.4.

[57] Id. *Apol. c. Ruf.* iii. 4 'cuius artificio, et a cuius ministris in sanctae Fabiolae hospitio, et viri Christiani et prudentis Oceani, inventus est codex *quem illi numquam viderant?*' For this theft, see *Ep.* 57.3.

[58] For Vigilantius' change of heart, see Jer. *Ep.* 61.3.3; and the hasty withdrawal, *Ep.* 58.11.3. The relevant sections of P. Courcelle (1947) have been superseded by P. Nautin (1973), esp. 231–4.

lehem. Arriving in the Holy Land with the recommendation of Paulinus,[59] he naturally presented himself on the Mount of Olives, and enjoyed there the hospitality of Paulinus' relative, Melania.[60] In the prevailing situation, this was enough to damage his credit with Jerome, who looked on him as a mere instrument of the Jerusalem establishment.[61] Courcelle's suggestion that Vigilantius was implicated with Rufinus' followers to the extent that he was himself the thief of Jerome's incriminating translation has now been discounted;[62] none the less, he clearly found himself labelled as a supporter of Melania and Rufinus and, as far as Jerome was concerned, squarely on the wrong side. The pilgrim had become a political figure, who, one suspects, was glad to escape to the relative calm of the Egyptian desert—leaving to Jerome the task of explaining the turn of events in his reply to Paulinus: in the end he preferred a diplomatic silence.[63]

Jerome's changing relations with Paulinus can perhaps be clarified in terms of the circumstances of 395.[64] Having in the previous year urged the ascetic recruit Paulinus to devote himself to the study of the Scriptures, and moreover under his own tutelage in Bethlehem,[65] he replied to Paulinus' second letter by attempting to dissuade him altogether from any pilgrimage to the holy places.[66] To some extent, Jerome's altered advice was confirming a change of heart on Paulinus' part; he had in the meantime found his holy place nearer at hand and channelled his enthusiasm into the shrine at Nola. But the situation in the Holy Land will not have

[59] Ep. 61.3.4 '...illius (sc. Paulinus) super nomine tuo non putavi errare iudicium'.

[60] Nautin (1973), 231ff.

[61] Jer. *Apol. c. Ruf.* iii. 19 'ego in Vigilantio tibi (sc. Rufinus) respondi'.

[62] Nautin, 234, n. 107: the theft took place when Vigilantius would already have left Bethlehem.

[63] Ep. 58.11.3 'qui (sc. Vigilantius) cur tam cito profectus sit et nos reliquerit, non possum dicere, *ne laedere quempiam videar*'.

[64] I follow the chronological order of *Epp.* 53 and 58 as they appear in Hilberg's edition. Since Cavallera, ii, 89–91, it had been customary to reverse them, but Nautin (1973), 213ff., has argued the case for keeping Hilberg's order; cf. Kelly (1975), 192–4.

[65] Compare *Ep.* 53.6 '...te in scripturis sanctis *sine praevio et monstrante* semitam non posse ingredi', with the invitation to Bethlehem, ibid. 11.

[66] *Ep.* 58.2–4; for the arguments, cf. above, p. 91.

been irrelevant to Jerome's change of mind;[67] his experience with Fabiola and Vigilantius pointed to the current tendency. The dissension between Jerusalem and Bethlehem was pervasive, and Jerome's own position was seriously weakened: the Mount of Olives enjoyed powerful support, while the monks of Bethlehem were out of communion with their bishop and threatened with banishment. On arriving in the Holy Land Paulinus might naturally have been expected to turn, not to Bethlehem, but to the monastery on the Mount of Olives and to his relative Melania.[68] This was the direction which future contacts were to follow: Paulinus established a fruitful literary friendship with Rufinus,[69] and it was Melania whom he proudly welcomed to Nola in 400.[70] Paulinus' projected pilgrimage would surely have indicated the same alignment.

The behaviour of Jerome's visitors in 395 thus reflects the surrounding political dissension at the holy places, and their assimilation into the conflict. In the course of a year in which Bethlehem was noticeably at a disadvantage, Fabiola and Vigilantius deserted, Paulinus stayed at a safe distance, and Jerome's one known friend in high places, Nummius Aemilianus Dexter, was away at the western court.[71] Before long, however, it was the turn of Palladius and his friends to scatter far afield. Within five years the leadership on the Mount of Olives would have dispersed, and Melania and Rufinus returned their separate ways to Italy. Palladius remained in Egypt till the early months of 399;[72] but he then forsook the desert (on medical advice) for another brief sojourn in the Holy Land, *en route* to Bithynia and his consecration as bishop of Helenopolis (in the spring of 400).[73] At the same

[67] Cf. Nautin, 235.

[68] For their relationship, see Paul. Nol. *Ep.* 29.5 '... noster sanguis propinquat'; Melania's Spanish background may provide the link with the Aquitanian family of Paulinus, but see the cautious conclusion of D. Gorce, *SChr* 90, 111 'il faut donc se résigner à ignorer leur parenté exacte'.

[69] See Paul. Nol. *Ep.* 28.5 ('intima mihi affectione coniunctus'), with P. Courcelle (1947), 274ff., F. X. Murphy (1956), and C. P. Hammond (1977), 380–2, 413ff.

[70] Above, p. 81.   [71] Above, p. 177.

[72] Although it is uncertain whether he was present at Evagrius' death at Epiphany 399: cf. D. Buck (1976), 293ff.

[73] *Hist. Laus.* 35 (Butler, 105). He was consecrated bishop in time to be present at the Constantinople synod in May 400: see *Dialogus*, 87.

period (in 399) many of his monastic associates in Egypt,
notably Ammonius and the other 'Tall Brothers', were
driven from their heartlands by the vigorous hounding of
Theophilus, the bishop of Alexandria, who in a sudden *volte
face* turned against the 'Origenist' monks and forced them
into exile.[74] Against the background of collaboration between
Jerusalem and the Egyptian monks which we have already
detected, the Holy Land now offered the obvious prospect of
refuge;[75] but nowhere proved secure against the energetic diplomatic offensive being conducted by Theophilus (with an
enthusiastic ally in Jerome). While Theophilus complained
to bishop John of Jerusalem about the reception in his diocese of fugitives from the authority of Alexandria, the Egyptian exiles slipped away on board ship for Constantinople.[76]
It must have been at this time that Melania, too, set sail for
the West.[77]

For a glimpse of a pilgrim's reaction to this upsurge of
anti-'Origenism' and to the violence which it aroused we can
turn to the comments of Postumianus, an unwilling witness
of the heavy-handedness of the bishop of Alexandria against
fellow-Christians: despite the bishop's generous hospitality
the visitor preferred not to linger 'where the smart of strife
between brothers still stung fresh', and travelled instead to
the company of Jerome in Bethlehem.[78] His attitude is reminiscent of that of Fabiola in Bethlehem a few years earlier.
But others like Palladius only saw their departure from
Egypt as an opportunity to carry further afield the political
conflict in which they were enmeshed; in his case the pilgrim
had long since ceased to stand aloof. With the removal of the
monks to Constantinople, and of Palladius himself to neigh-

---

[74] See Pall. *Dial.* 35ff., with Schwartz (1937), 168ff., and A. Favale (1958), 93ff.

[75] Pall. *Dial.* 39. They intended to settle in Scythopolis, Soz. *Hist. Eccl.* viii. 13.1.

[76] Jer. *Ep.* 92.1 (Theophilus) '...cum quibusdam peregrinis, qui in Aegypto
parumper habitant, ad vestram provinciam transmigrasse...'. Even Jerome was
stirred to the defence of his bishop, claiming that he had hastily offered hospitality,
not knowing of the turn of events in Egypt: *Ep.* 86.2. For their departure, see *Ep.* 90
(Theophilus) 'didici enim, quod calumniatores verae fidei...Constantinopolim
navigaverint'.

[77] From Caesarea: *Hist. Laus.* 54. For the date of her arrival at Nola as 400 (when
Paul. Nol. wrote *Ep.* 29), see P. Fabre (1948), 38.

[78] Sulp. Sev. *Dial.* i. 7.5–6. On Postumianus' account of events in Alexandria, cf.
J. Gribomont (1961).

bouring Bithynia, the cause with which they were identified shifted to focus on the bishop of Constantinople, John Chrysostom—who now inherited the hostility which Theophilus of Alexandria had earlier reserved for the 'Origenist' monks.[79] There is a direct line of descent from the alignments which had prevailed in the Holy Land and Egypt to the party which now came to surround the embattled Chrysostom, and among his most prominent supporters were many monks who had fled from Egypt before the violence of Theophilus.[80] The 'Tall Brothers' themselves and their friends were received in Constantinople with diplomatic caution by Chrysostom;[81] while others rallied actively to his cause. John Cassian and his companion Germanus joined John's clergy in Constantinople,[82] as did Heraclides, like Palladius a former disciple of Evagrius (and destined, too, for a bishopric).[83] Palladius himself interpreted his own elevation to the see of Helenopolis as 'sharing in the events concerning the blessed John',[84] and he was to have an episcopal career which mirrored closely the political fortunes of his master —from denunciation at the 'Synod of the Oak' in 403 ultimately to imprisonment and exile.[85]

Palladius' evident public involvement with Chrysostom again brought him into contact with a group of people of recognizable loyalties. A number of 'holy women' whom Palladius had met, recorded in *Hist. Laus.* 41, and unfortunately dismissed by Butler as 'not otherwise known to history',[86]

---

[79] Pall. *Dial. passim*; esp. 40ff., when the scene shifts to Constantinople; cf. Socr. *Hist. Eccl.* vi. 9ff., Soz. *Hist. Eccl.* viii. 13ff. For a recent assessment of the value of Palladius' account, see F. van Ommeslaeghe (1977). On the background: Ch. Baur, *John Chrysostom and his time* (Eng. transl. 1960), ii, 192ff., and the modern church histories, e.g. H. Chadwick, *The Early Church* (1967), 184ff.

[80] Cf. J.-M. Leroux (1972).

[81] For John's cautious welcome of the fugitives, see Pall. *Dial.* 40-1, Socr. *Hist. Eccl.* vi. 9.10, Soz. *Hist. Eccl.* viii. 13.13.

[82] Pall. *Dial.* 19; cf. O. Chadwick (1968), 28ff., and A. Guillaumont (1962), 77ff. John and Germanus had withdrawn from Egypt in the turmoil of 399–400. John himself speaks with warm affection of Chrysostom and his congregation in Constantinople: *De Incarn.* vii. 30–1.

[83] Chrysostom made H., a deacon of his, bishop of Ephesus: Socr. *Hist. Eccl.* vi. 11.10, Soz. *Hist. Eccl.* viii. 6.2 ('pupil of Evagrius'), Pall. *Dial.* 92.

[84] *Hist. Laus.* 35 (Butler, 105).

[85] Pall. *Dial.* 126: imprisonment, and exile in upper Egypt. For the synod, cf. above, p. 190.

[86] Butler, 219.

can with some certainty be identified with known supporters of Chrysostom. Adolia, a lady of Antioch, was an old friend of Chrysostom, who received several letters from him in exile: she was urged to make the short journey to visit him, or at least to write more frequently.[87] Also at Antioch Palladius knew the deaconess Sabiniana ('a most renowned woman who kept company with God'), whom he describes as John's 'aunt'—it was surely the same Sabiniana who followed the bishop into exile and vowed that, even if he were banished to Scythia, she would be at his side.[88] Palladius also claims an acquaintance with Vasianilla, wife of the general Candidianus—he emerges, too, as an old and close friend of bishop John.[89] Named in the same context is the wife of a *tribunus*, Theodora, noted for her almsgiving, who retired into a monastery; she may well be the influential lady of Constantinople to whom John wrote to gain support among his powerful friends in the capital, in an effort to change his place of exile.[90] He had evidently been a familiar visitor, for in another letter he pleaded with Theodora on behalf of a servant she had ejected from her household.[91] Nor must we overlook the deaconness Olympias, untiring supporter of John both before and after his exile, and destined to share his fate—she received a whole series of letters from the banished bishop.[92] Palladius' admiration of Olympias is significant in confirming the essential continuity of his association with Chrysostom and his affiliations in the Holy Land and Egypt, for Olympias' mentor was none other than the great Melania, in whose steps she zealously followed.[93] It may be that Olympias, deaconess of the church at Constantinople and widow of a relative of Theodosius,[94] had indeed made a pil-

---

[87] Joh. Chrys. *Epp.* 33, 52, 57, 133, 179 ('τῆς ἀρχαίας ἐκείνης καὶ γνησίας φιλίας), 231.

[88] Id. *Ep.* 6 (13) to Olympias (cf. *SChr* 13*bis*, 130).

[89] *Ep.* 42.   [90] *Ep.* 120.   [91] *Ep.* 117.

[92] On Olympias, see Pall. *Hist. Laus.* 56; id. *Dial.* 98ff., 107–11. The anonymous *Vita* (published in *Anal. Boll.* 15 (1896), 400–23, and reprinted by A.–M. Malingrey in *SChr* 13*bis*) depends upon Palladius.

[93] *Hist. Laus.* l.c.

[94] Jerome's friend the elder Nebridius, *pf. urbi* at Constantinople in 386, cf. above, p. 176. His son's widow, Salvina, was also a deaconness of Chrysostom: Pall. *Dial.* 61. Olympias refused a second marriage to another Spanish kinsman of Theodosius, Helpidius (ibid. 108): see John Matthews (1975), 109–10.

grimage to the Holy Land and come to know Melania in Jerusalem. Sharing with Palladius this association with the Mount of Olives, she left no doubt of her sympathies by offering generous hospitality in the capital to the 'Tall Brothers' and their followers in flight from Theophilus.[95]

After the exile of Chrysostom, Palladius' support for the bishop took him to Italy.[96] Here Melania had returned to prevent her family falling into 'bad teaching, heresy or evil living';[97] she would take care that her grand-daughter, now considering following her into the ascetic life, would not fall victim to the influence of Jerome's friends in Rome.[98] On his diplomatic mission to rouse western consciences against the treatment of Chrysostom, Palladius found himself once again at the very centre of Melania's circle.[99] In Rome he met Turcius Apronianus and his family, a new convert who owed his Christianity to Melania and Rufinus;[100] he had been Rufinus' patron after the latter had returned to Italy, and was the dedicatee of translations of Origen, Basil, and Gregory of Nazianzus;[101] significantly enough (in the light of the previous dissenssion in the Holy Land), the partisan *Apology against Jerome* was also addressed to Apronianus, who, it emerges, was acting as Rufinus' 'scout' in Rome, keeping him informed of the correspondence exchanged between Jerome and Pammachius.[102] Apronianus' wife, Avita, who also received works of Rufinus, was a niece of Melania.[103] The close relations between these people are effectively confirmed by a subscription surviving in two of the manuscripts of a translation of Gregory which Rufinus executed for Apro-

---

[95] Pall. *Dial.* 98ff.

[96] In the winter of 404–5: see *Dial.* 19, *Hist. Laus.* 61 (Butler, 157), with Soz. *Hist. Eccl.* viii. 26.19.

[97] Pall. *Hist. Laus.* 54.

[98] Cf. D. Gorce, *SChr* 90, 38, n. 2.   [99] Cf. P. Brown (1970), 56–62.

[100] *Hist. Laus.* 41. Palladius (ibid. 54) ascribed his conversion to Melania, yet it must have been the influence of Rufinus, on his return to Rome in 397–8, which counted for more; F. X. Murphy (1945), 91–2, 111–12.

[101] See prefaces in *CC* 20, 237, 251, 255.   [102] Rufin. *Apol. c. Hier.* i. 1.

[103] As something less demanding than the Greek fathers Rufinus translated for her the maxims known as the *Sentences of Sextus*: see pref. to Apronianus, in the edition of H. Chadwick (Texts and Studies, n.s. 5, 1959). For her relationship with Melania, see *Hist. Laus.* 54, and Paul. Nol. *Carm.* 21, 72ff.; cf. A. Chastagnol (1962), 159.

nianus: it records that the copy was transcribed from the text held by Melania herself in Rome.[104]

Palladius' reception extended, besides, to other members of Melania's family. With his companions he was hospitably entertained by her grand-daughter and namesake, and her husband, Pinianus, at the villa on the Appian Way to which they had retired from the capital;[105] here we are told they lived out a life of practical virtue which, not least, included the reception of visitors.[106] In meeting the Aproniani and Pinianus and his family, Palladius found himself in the company of precisely those two families who joined with Paulinus at Nola in a great reunion to celebrate the feast of St. Felix in 407.[107]

Meanwhile Rufinus, who had forsaken the Mount of Olives for Italy in 397,[108] was occupied in making some of the literary inheritance of the Greek-speaking church (with which he had become familiar during his years in the East) available to a Latin audience. This included the corpus known as the pseudo-Clementine literature, a collection of legends (of particular interest in the western church) revolving round St. Peter and Clement of Rome.[109] Among these, it was the *Recognitiones* which Rufinus translated for Gaudentius, bishop of the north Italian town of Brescia.[110] He had earlier promised this work, according to his preface, to the virgin Silvia, but her death had intervened before its completion; it was now offered to Gaudentius as the 'heir' to her request.[111] The association here of this Silvia with Rufinus and Gaudentius (himself at one time a pilgrim to the East)

---

[104] See *CSEL* 46, 233 'USQUE HUC CONTULI DE CODICE SCAE MELANIE ROME'.

[105] *Hist. Laus.* 61.

[106] See *V. Mel.* 7, 9 (with Gorce's note on p. 140).

[107] Paul. Nol. *Carm.* 21, 60ff., 210ff. The dating is that of P. Fabre (1948), 39.

[108] For Rufinus' departure from Jerusalem, see Jer. *Apol. c. Ruf.* iii. 24.

[109] See F. X. Murphy (1945), 112ff., and C. P. Hammond (1977), 404ff.

[110] Rufin. *Prolog. ad Gaudentium* (*GCS* 51), 3. Hammond, l.c., dates the translation to 407.

[111] Ibid. '...opus quod olim venerandae memoriae. virgo Silvia iniunxerat, ut Clementem nostrae linguae redderemus, et tu deinceps iure hereditario deposcebas' (cf. the epilogue to his translation of Origen's *Comm. in Rom.*, *CC* 20, 277). For the 'hereditary principle' in such circumstances, cf. the dedication of Jerome's *Comm. in Ioel.* to Pammachius: 'quodque sanctae et venerabili Paulae parenti tuae polliciti sumus, pius haeres suscipe' (*CC* 76, 160).

makes it likely that she is none other than the sister-in-law of the praetorian prefect, whom we have earlier encountered on a pilgrimage to Jerusalem; there she would certainly have met Rufinus, along with the travelling-companions who accompanied her on her way to Egypt, Melania and Palladius.[112] She may well have been dead by the time that Palladius came to Italy in support of John Chrysostom— local tradition at Brescia honours a St. Silvia buried in the basilica founded by Gaudentius[113]—but we connot discount the recent memory of her behind the fact that her bishop Gaudentius was among those Italian bishops who returned with Palladius as envoys to the eastern court on Chrysostom's behalf—and suffered ill-treatment and imprisonment as a consequence.[114]

Palladius' contacts on his visit to the West thus stemmed directly from the world he had entered when he settled, as a young devotee of the faith, on the Mount of Olives some twenty years earlier. Gaudentius' association, through the translation of the *Recognitiones*, with Rufinus and Silvia brought together those who shared common experience of Jerusalem and the holy places; his joining, along with Palladius, in the initiative on behalf of Chrysostom may owe something to the same background. Meanwhile the patronage of the great Melania, which had dominated the course of his career, now introduced Palladius to a new generation of her family, whose pattern of life was to be an echo of the grandmother's. The issue of John Chrysostom had convincingly demonstrated the ramifications which would follow from his first absorption into the politics of the Holy Land: settlement at the holy places and a monastic cell on the Mount of Olives had led eventually to the heart of an influential and close-knit group of the western aristocracy.

It was in 417 that the younger Melania and her family finally arrived to establish themselves in Jerusalem.[115] In the face of Alaric's invasions they had withdrawn, first to Sicily

---

[112] *Hist. Laus.* 55.

[113] For Silvia and Brescia, see E. D. Hunt (1972), 363ff., and P. Devos (1974).

[114] Pall. *Dial.* 22; and for the envoys' bitter experiences on their mission, ibid. 22–4. For Gaudentius' support of John, cf. Joh. Chrys. *Ep.* 184.

[115] *V. Mel.* 34: they had been 'seven years' in Africa after Alaric's devastation of southern Italy. For their settlement in Jerusalem, cf. *V. Pet. Iber.* 33.

(where Rufinus, who was accompanying them, had died[116]),
and thence to north Africa. By the time they reached Jerusalem, Palladius, exile behind him, was settled as bishop of
the Galatian town of Aspuna;[117] from here he observed, and
doubtless involved himself in, the charitable enterprises in
his province.[118] In 420 he presented to the imperial *praepositus*, Lausus, his record of the holy men of the eastern provinces, as a manual of spiritual edification for the imperial
court.[119] Such a work was not the place to dwell on the political implications of his encounters of many years past, and
he allowed himself few allusions to his partisan career; only
in John of Lycopolis' gloomy predictions of his 'eleven
months in a dark cell', and his mention of the anonymous
'exiled bishop' at Antinoe, do we glimpse his fate as an adhe-
rent of John Chrysostom.[120]

It was in any case a time when the old divisions of his years
in the Holy Land and Egypt were breaking down. In one of
his last letters (in 419), Jerome in warm terms conveyed to
Augustine and Alypius the greetings of the new arrivals in
Jerusalem, 'Albina, Pinianus and Melania, the revered children who are ours together';[121] and it would be from Melania
on the Mount of Olives that the young Paula, about whose
upbringing Jerome had written a long letter to her mother
Laeta, would receive her education in the ways of the
Lord.[122]

None the less it would be surprising if the tensions which
had marked the era of the elder Melania's settlement did not
find at least an echo in her grand-daughter's revived establishment on the Mount of Olives.[123] There is more than a
hint of this in the description of the young Paula's education

---

[116] See the prolog. to the translation of Origen's sermons on Numbers (*CC* 20,
285): across the strait Rufinus sees Rhegium in flames. Jerome heard of his death in
Sicily (*Comm. in Hiez.* prolog.): 'Scorpius . . . Trinacriae humo premitur'.

[117] Socr. *Hist. Eccl.* vii. 36.15.   [118] As described in *Hist. Laus.* 66–8.

[119] Ibid. prologue (Butler, 10) ' ὁδηγὸς καὶ σαυτοῦ καὶ τῶν μετὰ σοῦ καὶ τῶν
ὑπὸ σὲ καὶ τῶν εὐσεβεστάτων γινόμενος βασιλέων'.

[120] For the 'dark cell', *Hist. Laus.* 35 (Butler, 105); 'exiled bishop', ibid. 60. It has
been customary to follow Tillemont in supposing that the 'exiled bishop' who received the copy of Clement's work on the prophet Amos is Palladius himself.

[121] Jer. *Ep.* 143.2.

[122] *V. Mel.* 40 (Jerome's letter is *Ep.* 107).

[123] Cf. P. Brown (1970), 62: 'barely expunged palimpsest'.

as a process of leading her into humility 'from arrogance and pride'; this is reminiscent of the elder Melania's return to Rome, presented by Palladius as a mission to rescue the spiritual upbringing of her grand-daughter.[124] More materially, the younger Melania and her husband can be seen to have sustained, through their charity, the connexions established by her grandmother and those around her: thus, for instance, the church of Jerusalem benefited from the liquidation of estates.[125] Significantly, when the author of her biography accompanied her to the court at Constantinople in 436, he encountered many who were full of gratitude for the gifts they had received from Melania and Pinianus. Among these was the presbyter Tigrius, known as a loyal supporter of John Chrysostom, who suffered torture and exile in Mesopotamia on his bishop's downfall.[126] It may be added that it was Proclus, the bishop of Constantinople at the time of this visit of Melania, who, the year after her return to Jerusalem, was responsible for transporting the remains of John Chrysostom back to Constantinople, setting the seal on the process of reconciliation with the 'Johannites'.[127]

It was, appropriately, none other than Palladius' patron Lausus, again at this time *praepositus sacri cubiculi*, who welcomed Melania in the imperial palace on this visit to the court in 436.[128] He received her 'as befitted a man of his virtuous disposition', evidently retaining the same admiration for ascetic devotion which had led him to elicit from Palladius his record of the holy men. Despite his legendary wealth and luxurious possessions, Lausus' prayers had then been sought by Palladius as those of a 'most faithful servant of Christ' who retained his 'fear of the Lord' amid all the worldliness of the court.[129] The imperial chamberlain who

---

[124] *V. Mel.* l.c. (cf. above, p. 197).   [125] Ibid. 37.

[126] Ibid. 19. On Tigrius, see Socr. *Hist. Eccl.* vi. 15.15; Soz. *Hist. Eccl.* viii. 17.7, 24.8–9 (he was summoned to appear with John at the 'Synod of the Oak'). T. was noted for his kindness to the poor and to strangers—was he, like Olympias, involved in the reception of the Egyptian fugitives? For his own exile, see Pall. *Dial.* 127–8.

[127] Socr. *Hist. Eccl.* vii. 45 (27 Jan. 438). On Proclus and Melania, see *V. Mel.* 53.

[128] *V. Mel.* l.c. (with Gorce's note).

[129] *Hist. Laus.* epilog. On the 'palace of Lausus', see R. Janin (1964), 379, and for its statues, Codinus, *De Signis* (ed. Bekker), 37–8.

impressed both Palladius and the grand-daughter of his revered Melania as a man of God may seem a long way from the disagreements over Origen and John Chrysostom. Yet the influential court politician enthusiastically cultivating the ascetic life is surely a reverse image of the aspiring monk at the holy places caught up in ecclesiastical dissension; for Lausus, as for Palladius, pious interests and political involvement became inseparable.

9. Pilgrims and Politics (ii) Pelagius, Orosius, and St. Stephen

THE battle-lines drawn up between the communities in Jerusalem and Bethlehem in the 390s, in which Palladius had found himself a protagonist, turned out only to be the prelude to further dissension. The capacity of the holy places to attract to themselves, in the guise of piety, the central figures of ecclesiastical controversy proved considerable;[1] indeed their unique biblical status in the eyes of the Christian empire might seem to afford a protective authority to any whose theological views were being brought into question. The next issue to divide the holy places concerned the British-born monk, Pelagius, whose controversial views on man's own responsibility for his actions and the consequent reduction in the need for divine grace led ultimately to his condemnation in 418.[2] Yet while Pelagius enjoyed the shelter of the Holy Land, and was absolved by a synod of fourteen local bishops at Diospolis in 415, he might well bask in the confidence that he had been acquitted 'in the land where the Lord revealed the presence of his own incarnation'.[3]

Pelagius had come to the Holy Land in the aftermath of the turmoil of events in the West in the early years of the fifth century. The comparative peace of the holy places was now profoundly disturbed by the influx into Palestine of a new breed of enforced pilgrims—the refugees displaced by the barbarian tribes who were pouring into Italy and the

---

[1] Cf. the 'theological bear-garden' of Peter Brown, *Augustine of Hippo* (1967), 356.

[2] On Pelagius and his views see, among others, R. F. Evans (1968), esp. ch. 6 'The Theology of Pelagius', and P. Brown (1968).

[3] August. *De Gest. Pelag.* 25.

western provinces. Jerome portrays an endless stream of the destitute and dispossessed arriving at the doors of the monastery in Bethlehem—latter-day 'Lazaruses' constantly interrupting his work on his *Commentary on Ezekiel*, and forcing him to struggle with his studies in the night hours while giving up the daytime to attend to their needs.[4]

Most of these refugees must remain unidentified, the anonymous horde who crowded and congested the holy places ('occidentalium fuga et sanctorum locorum constipatio').[5] There are, however, the few who can be isolated from the throng (and who, it must be acknowledged, hardly qualify as 'destitute'). Ladies of noble households, as before, flocked to Jerome.[6] Many, driven from Gaul by the raids of the Vandals, found their way first to north Africa, thence on to Bethlehem: they could bring to Jerome news of some distinguished Roman exiles, the ladies of the Anician family.[7] Another refugee from Gaul, the wife of the landowner Rusticus, prevailed upon Jerome to write to her husband (who had remained behind amid the ruin of his estates) urging him to join her in the Holy Land; while he was surveying the disaster which had befallen his homeland she was pouring out her prayers at the holy places.[8] No such separation, of course, attended the ascetic partnership of Pinianus and the younger Melania; withdrawing before Alaric's onslaught in Italy, they crossed to north Africa where they spent the first seven years of their exile, before establishing themselves on the Mount of Olives in Jerusalem.[9]

The same route was taken by Pelagius, also fleeing from Alaric's invasion of Italy. From Rome, where his theological views had been attracting the attention of devotees among

---

[4] See esp. prefaces to *Comm. in Hiez.* iii, vii, and viii (with allusion to Dives and Lazarus).

[5] Ibid. vii, pref. (*CC* 75, 277).

[6] Jer. *Ep.* 130.4.4 'sanctae et nobiles feminae...'.

[7] Demetrias, accompanied by her prodigious ancestry—her mother (widow of Olybrius *cos.* 395) and grandmother (widow of Sex. Petronius Probus). She was converted to the ascetic life in the shock of the sack of Rome: Jer. l.c.; cf. *Ep.* 130.6.1 'invenisse eam...quod *Romanae urbis cineres mitigaret*'. The glad news of her conversion resounded in Bethlehem, 'penetravit hic rumor orientis litora...' (ibid. 6.4).

[8] Jer. *Ep.* 122.4. For Jerome's contacts with Gaul at this period, see H. Crouzel (1972).

[9] Above, pp. 199–200.

the nobility, he travelled first to Sicily and north Africa—he stayed here long enough to be seen occasionally by Augustine in Carthage (in 411);[10] from there he sailed on to the Holy Land. While in Rome Pelagius had enjoyed the patronage of that same aristocratic circle, dominated by the elder Melania, which had received Palladius on his western mission on behalf of Chrysostom; in this context he is likely, too, to have been in touch with Melania's old associate Rufinus[11] —hence it is hardly surprising that Pelagius the refugee should now find hospitality in Jerusalem and secure the protection of their former ally, bishop John. The latter, we may surmise, would readily welcome to the holy city one who came with the credentials of association with Melania and her friends, and whose arrival would revive memories of his close contacts with the western establishment on the Mount of Olives during the 'Origenist' arguments of the 390s.[12]

But this reawakening of old loyalties may go deeper. For it is likely that Pelagius arrived in the Holy Land not merely as a protégé of Melania—he may also, fittingly, have been an old rival of Jerome. The latter certainly claimed (in 415) an 'old kinship' with Pelagius; and if the two men *had* known each other earlier their relationship must have gone right back to Jerome's stay in Rome in 382–5.[13] It is now widely agreed that Pelagius is in fact the unnamed monk in Rome who in 393 criticized Jerome's teaching on marriage as revealed in the treatise *Against Jovinianus*:[14] resisting the challenge to engage in written controversy with Jerome, this adversary had confined his hostile comments to street •corners and the ladies' quarters of noble households[15]—territory

---

[10] August. *De Gest. Pelag.* 46 'semel vel iterum vidi'. For Pelagius in Sicily, see R. F. Evans, *Four Letters of Pelagius* (1968), 29–30.

[11] See esp. P. Brown (1970). Pelagius and Rufinus: R. F. Evans (1968), 18ff., and C. P. Hammond (1977), 421ff. On Pelagius' connexions, esp. with the *gens Anicia*, see G. de Plinval (1943), 210ff.

[12] For John's closeness to Pelagius, see August. *Ep.* 179 'Pelagium vero...quem audio *quod multum diligis*'.

[13] Jer. *Comm. in Hier.* iv, pref. (*CC* 74, 175) '...cavendum nobis est, ne *veterem* laedere videamur *necessitudinem*'; cf. de Plinval, 64, n. 5.

[14] Jer. *Ep.* 50, *passim*. The identification, presented by de Plinval, 47–55, was systematically defended by R. F. Evans (1968), 31ff.; it is accepted by J. N. D. Kelly (1975), 188, but now questioned by Y.-M. Duval, *Rev. Hist. Eccl.* 75 (1980), 525ff.

[15] Cf. *Ep.* 50.3.2 '...eum libenter virginum et viduarum cellulas circumire', and ibid. 5.1 '...garrire per angulos et medicorum tabernas...'.

familiar to the former habitué of Marcella's Aventine establishment. With this access to aristocratic circles in Rome
Pelagius can hardly have failed to encounter the pervasive
influence of Jerome, exercised no less insistently from his distant retreat in Bethlehem; while Jerome for his part will not
have welcomed news of a rival claimant for the impression-
able audience of pious Roman ladies.[16]

Thus the presence of Pelagius in the Holy Land served to
recall the background of political divisions between Jerusalem and Bethlehem which had existed some twenty years
earlier; and when the controversy over his views flared up at
the holy places much of the argument was in fact a re-
enactment of the earlier debate.[17] On the one hand Pelagius
took up against Jerome some of the accusations which his old
opponents, principally Rufinus, had levelled at him; while
Jerome himself clearly saw the case against Pelagius in the
same light as his previous anti-Origenist onslaught, viewing
his new opponent as a Rufinus *redivivus*, the 'Alpine dog' who
barked to the tune of his now dead adversary (i.e. Rufinus),
whose belief that a man could be sinless was the imagining of
a 'mad old woman' (an allusion to the elder Melania).[18]

What is more (and this is of particular interest to our
theme) those caught in the eye of the Pelagian controversy in
the Holy Land were once again foreign visitors from far
afield, pilgrims and suppliants at the sacred sites—this time
many of them the victims of the unsettled state of the western
empire. With the arrival of the refugees (like Pelagius himself) the holy places were again set to become the theatre of
ecclesiastical dissension. Among the principal contestants
were two deposed Gallic bishops, Heros and Lazarus, exiles
of a different kind in the Holy Land—the casualties of a fallen regime.[19] Heros had been the nominee of the usurper
Constantine to the see of Arles and, in the desperation of the

---

[16] Cf. ibid. 5.3 'postquam Romam mea opuscula pervenerunt, quasi *aemulum* ex-
horruit', with R. F. Evans (1968), 36–7.

[17] On the controversy in Palestine, see Kelly, ch. 26.

[18] Cf. Evans, ch. 2 'Pelagius and the revival of the Origenist controversy'.
Jerome's charges: *Comm. in Hier.* iii, pref. (*CC* 74, 119–20); ibid. iii, 70.4 (162).

[19] On these, compare the favourable testimony of the *Chronicle* of Prosper, s.a. 412
(= *Chron. Min.* i, 466), commending Heros as a disciple of Martin, and the hostile
remarks of pope Zosimus, *Ep.* 2.4 (*PL* 20, 651), and esp. *Ep.* 3.3 (656–7).

final siege in 411, had received his defeated emperor into the priesthood.[20] Driven from his see on the victory of Honorius' *magister militum*, Constantius, Heros fled to the holy places in the company of Lazarus, the deposed bishop of Aix. In the Holy Land this pair were among Pelagius' chief accusers: a hostile dossier from them containing the alleged theological statements of Pelagius was presented to the council of Dios-polis—but, with John and his fellow-bishops rallying to Pela-gius' support, the two prosecutors failed to appear to pursue their case.[21]

Another western refugee at the holy places who became implicated in the Pelagian controversy was Avitus, a presby-ter from Bracara (Braga) in north-western Spain. Early in 416 Avitus wrote to his bishop Balconius and the rest of the congregation, telling of the tears he was shedding in the Holy Land at the thought of the barbarian raids which prevented him from returning home to Spain.[22] He was reluctant, he urged, to leave the holy places at the risk of being unable to complete the journey home, now that Spain was overrun. Avitus had been away from his country for some years, as he appears to have had no actual experience of the incursions across the Pyrenees of Suebi, Vandals and Alani, which had begun in 409[23]—the sufferings of his fellow-parishioners were a matter for his imagination rather than his memory. Mean-while in Jerusalem as a westerner who knew Greek he had come to play a diplomatic role, as translator and interpreter, at the centre of the debate about Pelagius:[24] a Latin view-point was at stake amidst a Greek-speaking church, and the linguistic divide was a sensitive tightrope.[25]

---

[20] For the ordination, Olympiodorus, fr. 16 (*Frag. Hist. Graec.* iv, 60); cf. Ṡoz. *Hist. Eccl.* ix. 15.

[21] For the presentation of the *libellus* to the metropolitan of Caesarea, Eulogius, see August. *De Gest. Pelag.* 9; and their absence, ibid. 2.

[22] For this text, see *PL* 41, 805ff. On the various Aviti, see B. Altaner (1941), and on Balconius (or Palconius), see H. Chadwick (1976), 178.

[23] See Hydatius, *Chron.* s.a. 409.

[24] Orosius, *Apologet.* 6.1, 7.6. His most significant contribution was to be the translation of the *Ep. Luciani* (below, p. 213).

[25] Cf. Oros. *Apologet.* 6.4 '...Latinum esse hereticum, nos Latinos, heresim Lati-nis magis partibus notam Latinis iudicibus disserendam...'; ibid. 7.4 'quomodo Latinum expers Latinitatis Graecus audivit?'.

The opportunity for Avitus to send a letter to his church at home was occasioned by the projected return to Spain of a young fellow-presbyter, Orosius—who had himself originated (most probably) from Bracara.[26] Orosius had first set foot in the Holy Land after being sent on to Jerome by Augustine, to whom he had earlier had recourse as a young and enthusiastic opponent of the heresies, Priscillianism and 'Origenism', which he held to be threatening his own church in Spain.[27] Augustine had briefly answered his points, only to pass him on to Bethlehem, where the case against heresy was always assured of a ready hearing.[28] Orosius presents his own arrival in north Africa as a divine mission, a 'spiriting away' from his homeland: 'with no intention, no compulsion, no consultation I left my fatherland, driven by some hidden force...';[29] while Augustine interpreted his coming as the ardour of a young student of the faith: '... burning with enthusiasm... eager to refute false and dangerous teaching'.[30] Nevertheless, it appears that it was not so much the fight against the heretics which was the immediate cause of Orosius' departure from Spain as, yet again, the pervading havoc of the barbarian raids. In a number of passages in his *History* Orosius betrays his personal experience of the invasions, even at one point suggesting that he evaded capture only by the timely appearance of a protecting cloud;[31] elsewhere he

---

[26] Braulio, *Ep.* 44 (*PL* 80, 698–9), including Orosius among the 'doctissimi viri' of the region around Bracara. The evidence connecting Orosius with this part of Spain has weighed more heavily than the inconclusive 'Tarraconem nostram' of *Hist. adv. pagan.* vii. 22.8, which indicates nothing more than that Orosius was a Spaniard ('nos quoque in Hispania...'); see B. Lacroix (1965), 33–4.

[27] Oros. *Commonit.* 1 (*CSEL* 18, 151ff.); August. *Ep.* 166.2, 169.13. Cf. H. Chadwick (1976), 190ff. Augustine's writings against the Manichees, circulating in Spain, could have inspired Orosius to hope for an onslaught against Priscillianism: August. *Ad Oros.* 1 (*PL* 42, 669). On the influence of Origen in the western churches, see B. Studer (1966).

[28] August. *Ep.* 166.2 '... docui hominem quod potui, quod autem non potui, unde discere possit, admonui, atque *ut ad te iret* hortatus sum'. For Augustine's answer (the *Ad Oros.*), cf. *Ep.* 169.13 '*uno libro non grandi* quanta potui brevitate et perspicuitate respondi'.

[29] *Commonit.* 1.

[30] August. *Ep.* 166.2 '... utile vas in domo domini esse desiderans ad refellendas falsas perniciosasque doctrinas'; cf. *Ep.* 169.13 'solo sanctarum scripturarum ardore flammatus'.

[31] *Hist. adv. pagan.* iii. 20 'repentina nebula circumfusus'. Contrast his charitable attitude to the possibility of escape with the aid of the barbarians, ibid. vii. 41.4–5.

admits a reference to himself as a fugitive on the shores of Africa, though in the context of a resounding confidence in the universal brotherhood of Romans and Christians.[32] Yet, in the Christian optimism of the *History*, Orosius the refugee emerges only at moments of personal candour—just as his arrival in north Africa was that of a protagonist for the faith, not of one in flight from the enemy. Armed with his pamphlet *On the Error of Priscillianists and Origenists*, he came before Augustine proclaiming the danger from these heretics far more serious than the threat of the barbarians.[33]

The move to Bethlehem was likewise charged with heresy-hunting enthusiasm, an appearance in the Holy Land which bears resemblance to the arrivals of bishop Epiphanius and his lieutenant Atarbius in 393 (these had set the simmering 'Origenist' crisis on the boil).[34] Orosius came to the holy places as a partisan, already alerted in north Africa to the questionable views of Pelagius, and ready to force the issue in the Holy Land. He went straight to join 'the blessed' Jerome in Bethlehem, as the natural spearhead of any offensive for the faith, and was soon to acknowledge his eloquence in stamping out heresy.[35] In the light of Augustine's portrayal of the young man of zeal who had first arrived in Africa, it is hardly possible to take seriously the Spaniard's self-depreciating claim that he 'lay hidden' in Bethlehem as a 'poor, unknown stranger', being schooled by Jerome in the 'fear of the Lord'.[36] At least the new arrival travelled to Jerusalem and, like other visitors to the Holy Land, made himself known to the local bishop, John.[37] It was therefore natural, as he was at hand, that Orosius should be summoned by John and his clergy when they gathered to discuss Pelagius in the summer of 415: having recently arrived from

---

[32] Ibid. v. 2, a *locus classicus* for the standpoint of the work: '...ad Christianos et Romanos Romanus et Christianus accedo'. Cf. A. Lippold (1969), and F. Paschoud, *Roma Aeterna* (1967), 276–92.

[33] *Commonit.* 1 'dilacerati gravius a doctoribus pravis, quam a cruentissimis hostibus sumus'. Cf. August. *Ep.* 166.2 '...doctrinas, quae animas Hispanorum multo infelicius quam corpora barbaricus gladius trucidarunt'.

[34] Cf. above, p. 182.

[35] *Apologet.* 4.6 'multi enim iam haeretici cum dogmatibus suis ipso oppugnante supplosi sunt'; cf. the earlier verdict of Postumianus, above, p. 185.

[36] Ibid. 3.2 'ignotus advena pauper' (recalling the boy David).

[37] Ibid. 7.1 '...ad obsequium Iohannis episcopi cucurrissem'.

Africa, he was in a position to give an account of the proceedings there against Pelagius' colleague Caelestius, and
was able to read out a copy of Augustine's letter attacking
the Pelagians in Sicily.[38] Later, however, as bishop John confirmed his support for Pelagius, Orosius (like Heros and
Lazarus) found the political tide running away from him: the
synod which met at Diospolis in December convened without
him, and pronounced Pelagius fully in communion with the
Catholic church.[39]

It must be remembered that this immersion of Orosius in
ecclesiastical politics was taking place against the background of the biblical sites and the pilgrim destinations. Orosius must have made such visits himself. The empty book-
shelves which he observed in the plundered temples of Alexandria could have been seen on his way to Palestine
(although he offers no precise indication of the circumstances
of his visit to the city);[40] while in the course of the same
journey Orosius might seize the opportunity for a detour to
the shores of the Red Sea, where he was confronted by the
remains of the destruction of Pharaoh's army: the tracks of
the chariot-wheels in the sand, which miraculously defied the
efforts of time or over-zealous pilgrims to disturb them.[41]
Orosius' assimilation into the ecclesiastical controversy of the
holy places has tended to exclude from the record other features of his sojourn in the Holy Land: but the young presbyter, arriving from the western edge of the empire, can hardly
have failed to go on pilgrimage to the principal sites, to see
confirmed the truth of the faith in which he was so convinced. In the era of Theodosius I the region of Spain from
which Orosius (and the emperor) originated had, as we have
observed, been prolific of Catholic piety, and in all probability furnished that pilgrim of exemplary devotion, Egeria (she

[38] Ibid. 3.2ff. The letter in question is August. *Ep.* 157, to Hilarius bishop of
Syracuse.

[39] August. *De Gest. Pelag.* 44 '... communionis ecclesiasticae eum esse et catholi-
cae confitemur'. Orosius had by now fallen foul of bishop John, and been accused
of blasphemy: *Apologet.* 7.1.

[40] Oros. *Hist. adv. pagan.* vi. 15.32, with a reference to the destruction of the
Serapeum in 391.

[41] Ibid. i. 10.17.

too had observed the tracks of the Egyptians' chariots).[42]
Orosius belonged to the same tradition of Catholic
orthodoxy,[43] and would take the same confidence from the
sight of the holy places. We can point to other fellow-
countrymen to be found in the Holy Land: the presbyter
Avitus (together with a namesake who had also been on a
pilgrimage to Jerusalem),[44] and the continuator of Jerome's
Chronicle, Hydatius—a native of neighbouring Lemica, who
as a young man ('infantulus') had been on a pilgrimage to
the holy places and had met Jerome, John, and other leading
figures of the eastern church.[45] To set Orosius alongside
these other western visitors, as well as the celebrated official
from Narbonne whom he encountered at Bethlehem (who
talked to him of his friendship with the Gothic leader
Athaulf),[46] is to see something of what underlies the political
involvement which has made his spell in the Holy Land
notorious—pious enterprise is again discovered side by side
with ecclesiastical politics. Behind Orosius the roving diplomat and energetic opponent of Pelagius is still to be found
the continuing tradition of piety at the holy places. Where
Palladius before him had turned to the monasticism engen-
dered in the Holy Land, Orosius on the other hand was implicated in a different, but no less characteristic, product of
Holy Land piety—the movement of relics. For the Orosius
who left Palestine to convey the news of the acquittal of Pelagius at the synod of Diospolis was also to be the man who
gave to the Mediterranean world the remains of the first
Christian martyr, St. Stephen.

In 406 the cult of relics had found a vigorous defence in
Jerome's riposte to Vigilantius: we have seen earlier his port-

---

[42] Cf. above, p. 164. The memory of her observation of the wheel-tracks (she was
impressed by the apparently extraordinary size of the chariots) is preserved by Pet.
Diac. *Liber de locis sanctis*, Y4 (*CC* 175, 100–1).

[43] A 7th cent. hint that he had dabbled in Priscillianism is pronounced 'possible
and doubtful' by H. Chadwick (1976), 191.

[44] The Avitus who, according to Oros. *Commonit.* 3, had brought back from Jerusalem the errors of Origen.

[45] Hydatius, *Chron.* pref. and s.a. 407 (we have now the edition of A. Tranoy, *SChr*
218–9). Cf. E. A. Thompson, *Nott. Mediaeval Studies*, 20 (1976), 4ff.

[46] *Hist. adv. pagan.* vii, 43.4; for an identification see J. F. Matthews, *Latomus*, 30
(1971), 1085ff. (*PLRE* ii, 1232 has another possibility.)

rayal of the enthusiasm which accompanied the revelation of the bones of Samuel.[47] But Samuel was by no means the only biblical figure who made his reappearance in these years. In 385 the tombs of the Old Testament prophets Habakkuk and Micah, revealed in a dream to bishop Zebennos, had come to light not far from Eleutheropolis;[48] and later in the same neighbourhood (at the village of Caphar-zacharia) the resting-place of Zechariah was to emerge, a discovery which Sozomen coupled with that of Stephen as confirming God's favour on the empire of his own day.[49] (This Zechariah discovery in the vicinity of Eleutheropolis, it should be noted, represents a new location for the prophet's tomb—distinct from the rival tradition concentrating on the Cedron valley in Jerusalem and still surviving in the so-called 'Tomb of Zechariah'.)[50]

The crop of relic 'inventions' reached its climax late in 415 with the revelation of the tomb of Stephen, at the village of Caphar-gamala.[51] As the first to 'bear witness' to Christ, echoing the Crucifixion by his death at the hands of the Jewish establishment, Stephen had a place second only to Christ in Christian veneration.[52] A sermon in praise of the protomartyr (attributed to bishop Basil of Seleucia) attests the renown of the discovery, and the rapid distribution of the relics: 'every place is glorified and hallowed by your remains', he exults; 'your protection shines out over all the earth'.[53] As far as the western provinces were concerned, it was Orosius who had a prime role in the distribution of these

[47] Jer. *C. Vigilant.* 5; cf. above, p. 131.

[48] Soz. *Hist. Eccl.* vii. 29; Theophanes, *Chron.* (ed. de Boor), 73. Cf. J. Jeremias (1958), 81–6. By the time that Jerome wrote *Ep.* 108 (404) a church had been built over Micah's tomb at Morasthi: *Ep.* 108.14.

[49] Soz. *Hist. Eccl.* ix. 16.4ff. The prophet Zechariah had become confused in the tradition with other biblical Zechariahs: see Jeremias, 67ff., 73, and J. Wilkinson (1971), 183, n. 9.

[50] Jeremias, 73, n. 3. According to Sozomen, l.c., the discoverers of the remains near Eleutheropolis had to have recourse to an 'ancient Hebrew book' *outside the Scriptures* to explain what they found. The remains of 'Zechariah', and others, had allegedly already been discovered in 351 in the Cedron valley: see above, p. 155, n. 1.

[51] See below, pp. 214–15, for details.

[52] So in the sermons of Asterius of Amasea (ed. Datema, xii.2) and Greg. Nys. (*PG* 46, 704a–b) on St. Stephen.

[53] *PG* 85, 469, recalling the discovery in 415.

remains (and hence of the 'protection' which they afforded): escaping from the mesh of church politics in the Holy Land, he returned to the West much as a pilgrim laden with the rewards of a journey to the land of the Bible.[54]

It was to Avitus, his fellow-presbyter from Bracara, that Orosius owed his possession of a portion of Stephen's remains. In his letter home to his congregation in Spain Avitus tells how he is sending to them, via the hand of Orosius, some dust and bones from the newly-discovered relics, which he has secretly acquired from the local village presbyter who had actually unearthed them;[55] to accompany these he is attaching to his letter his own Latin translation of this presbyter's first-hand account of the discovery, dictated to him in Greek (the *Epistula Luciani*, which survives as the unique contemporary witness of these events).[56] St. Stephen, such is the wish of Avitus, is to stand by the bishop and people of Bracara as their 'help and patron'; his presence and protection is to ensure the safety of the congregation in the difficult times of barbarian occupation.[57]

Bracara was not, however, in the event to receive the benefit of the distinguished guardianship anticipated by Avitus; for Orosius, it appears, never returned to Galicia. From the Holy Land he travelled back (? early in 416), as instructed, to Augustine in Africa, bringing news of the proceedings in favour of Pelagius.[58] Thence he embarked homeward for Spain; but during a halt on the island of Minorca he found it impossible to continue with his journey[59]—because, it must be assumed, the route was cut by the barbarian occupation. It is a mystery why Avitus, doubtful of the possibility of him-

---

[54] Cf. Gennadius, *De Vir. Illust.* 40 '...reliquias beati Stephani...primus intulit Occidenti'.

[55] *PL* 41, 806-7.

[56] For the text, see *PL* 41, 807ff., and for its primacy among the numerous versions (Latin, Greek, Armenian, Georgian, Syriac) of this incident, see P. Peeters (1950), 53-8. For variant versions, cf. S. Vanderlinden (1946), on the Latin recensions, and J. Martin (1958). The *Ep. Luciani* was already known to Augustine: *Hom. in Ioh.* 120.4 (*PL* 35, 1954).

[57] *PL* 41, 808 'auxilio et praesentia tanti patroni...tuti ex hoc quietique vivatis'.

[58] Carrying a letter from Heros and Lazarus (August. *Ep.* 175.1). He may have returned via Rome, for at some stage he delivered to Oceanus there a book of Jerome's: August. *Ep.* 180.5.

[59] *Ep. Severi*, 3 (*PL* 41, 823).

self getting through to his homeland, had expected Orosius to fare any better. The road to Bracara would have taken him right across the breadth of Spain, through the central mountains to the 'shores of Ocean'—a long and difficult journey through areas which would have been in the control of the invaders.[60] Unable to continue his travels Orosius sailed back to Africa, leaving to the Christians of Minorca the relics (or most of them) intended for the congregation at Bracara; they were deposited in the church at Mago, the town at the eastern end of the small island. The patronage which Avitus had hoped would embrace his fellow-Christians at home came to be employed instead by the Christian community in Minorca in their missionary endeavour against the local Jewish population: Stephen's arrival on their island heralded dramatic events, the destruction of the synagogue and a mass conversion.[61]

Orosius' part in the transmission of Stephen's relics from the Holy Land may be taken to be representative of the by now familiar urge to leave the holy places carrying a parcel of their biblical past; he was only echoing what, for instance, Silvia had done with the relics of eastern martyrs, or countless other pilgrims with their pieces of the cross. Yet a discussion of the actual circumstances of the discovery of Stephen's remains may lead us to suggest, once again, that the political context is not irrelevant to Orosius' opportunity to satisfy in this way the *desiderium* of the pilgrim.

It was precisely at the time when, in December 415, bishop John and his colleagues were at Diospolis hearing the evidence of Pelagius, that news came from Lucianus, the presbyter of the village of Caphar-gamala, of the discovery there of the tomb of Stephen, together with those of two converted rabbis of the New Testament, Nicodemus and Gamaliel.[62]

---

[60] Orosius himself had first arrived in Africa 'ab oceani litore': August *Ep.* 166.2, 169.13. On the barbarian settlement of this area, see Hydatius, *Chron.* s.a. 411 'Gallaeciam Vandali occupant et Suevi *sita in extremitate oceani maris occidua*'.

[61] As described in the open letter of the island's bishop, Severus: *PL* 41, 821ff. Some of Stephen's relics also soon reached Africa (though it is not said that it was Orosius who delivered them), see August. *Serm.* 317–8, and the record of miraculous cures in *Civ. Dei*, xxii. 8, and (at Uzalis) *De Mirac. S. Steph.* (*PL* 41, 833ff.).

[62] *Ep. Luciani*, 8 'statim ergo renuntiavi episcopo, cum esset in Lydda, quae est Diospolis, synodum agens'.

John, who had already heard from Lucianus of the succession of dream-visions of rabbi Gamaliel which had led him to the 'invention',[63] hurried to the scene with the bishops of Sebaste and Jericho. When the tombs had been identified from their Hebrew inscriptions, Stephen's was opened, and at that moment the air was filled with such fragrance that, according to Lucianus, 'we thought we were in paradise'. In this heady atmosphere the presbyter claimed that 73 persons were cured of sundry ailments, before the martyr's body was solemnly transferred to the great basilica on Mount Sion in Jerusalem, where he was laid to rest on 26 December. A few fragments of the remains were left for Lucianus, from among which (without bishop John's knowledge?) Avitus acquired those he dispatched in the hands of Orosius.[64]

'Devout men buried Stephen, and made great lamentation over him'; such is all that the author of Acts records on the subject of Stephen's burial.[65] It is, however, the rabbi Gamaliel, teacher of St. Paul, who appears in Lucianus' narrative to urge him to the discovery of the tombs and, more importantly, to explain how Stephen came to the village of Caphar-gamala. As the name of the village proved, claimed the rabbi, it was Gamaliel's own estate, and it was he, as a Christian sympathizer, who had had the body of Stephen brought there, twenty miles from Jerusalem, to lie in his own family mausoleum. Nicodemus, too, another converted rabbi, had fled to the protection of Gamaliel's estate, where he had been laid to rest alongside Stephen.[66] There is, of course, no warrant for any of this in the New Testament, save that the tradition of Gamaliel as a crypto-Christian (which is not confined to the *Epistula Luciani*) clearly derives from his role in the New Testament advising caution on the other Jewish leaders in their condemnation of the new faith.[67] Certainly the prominent part assigned to Gamaliel in

---

[63] The initial vision had occurred on 3 December: ibid. 2.

[64] Ibid. 8–9. Avitus, *PL* 41, 806, says of his portion of the remains '. . . festinato expetitam *secretoque* perceptam'.

[65] Acts, 8.2.

[66] *Ep. Luciani*, 3.

[67] Acts, 5.33–9. For the 'Christian' Gamaliel, cf. Ps.-Clement, *Recognitiones*, i. 65ff. 'qui latenter frater noster erat in fide', and *Doctrina Addai* (ed. G. Phillips, 1876), 3–4 (the envoy of Abgar of Edessa found Christ in the house of Gamaliel).

the discovery points to Jewish-Christian origins for the story. It would be attractive if some element in it could be associated with the like-named Jewish patriarchs of whom we hear around the end of the fourth century—men of wealth and influence who were demoted by Christian emperors; the last of the line was deprived of his honorary prefecture precisely in 415.[68]

But where *is* 'Caphar-gamala'? Lucianus' village was twenty miles from Jerusalem. There have been two rival claimants to the site: Beit-el-jemal, in the district of Eleutheropolis to the south-west of Jerusalem, and Jemmala, north-west of Jerusalem in the direction of Diospolis.[69] Despite the insistence of the Salesian fathers at Beit-el-jemal (where a Byzantine church was discovered earlier this century) that they have the tomb of Stephen,[70] the weight of the evidence favours Jemmala. Caphar-gamala fell within the *territorium* of Jerusalem—Lucianus' bishop was clearly John, bishop of Jerusalem;[71] on this ground alone Beit-el-Jemal, which belongs to the region of Eleutheropolis, would seem to be excluded.[72] Moreover, the crucial figure of Gamaliel, and the Jewish-Christian tradition, points to the northern site:[73] the village of Caphar-selemia, traditional burial-place of Gamaliel's elder son, Selemias, was in the same area;[74] as was Arimathaea, home of the rich Jew, Joseph, in whose tomb the body of Christ was placed.[75] Joseph's association with Nicodemus in the tradition is attested, for example, in the apocryphal *Acta Pilati*.[76] We are thus presented with a concentra-

---

[68] *CTh* xvi. 8.22. Cf. R. Syme, 'Ipse Ille Patriarcha', *Emperors and Biography* (1971), esp. 21–5.

[69] See F. M. Abel (1924), and more recently, S. Mittmann, *ZDPV* 91 (1975), 71–3.

[70] Abel, *Rev. Bibl.* 28 (1919), 244–8; L. H. Vincent, ibid. 35 (1926), 127–32.

[71] Lucianus describes himself as 'presbyter Ecclesiae Dei quae est in villa Caphargamala *in territorio Hierosolymorum*' (*PL* 41, 807). Cf. M. Avi-Yonah (1966), 155, and the comment of Abel (1924), 237 (a region 'en rélation étroite avec Jérusalem').

[72] Cf. G. Beyer, 'Das Stadtgebiet von Eleutheropolis im 4. Jhr. n. Chr.', *ZDPV* 54 (1931), 225–6.

[73] F. M. Abel, ii (1938), 289.　　　　[74] *Ep. Luciani*, 3.

[75] The modern village of Rentis: Abel (1938), 429; Avi-Yonah (1966), 158. Arimathaea was just over the border in the region of Diospolis, see Eus. *Onomastikon*, 32, 144.

[76] See E. Hennecke, *Neutestamentliche Apokryphen* (3rd. edit. Schneemelcher, 1959), i, 341ff.

tion of the traditions involving the leading Christian 'sympathizers' among the Jews of the New Testament, and an area, according to Père Abel, showing considerable evidence of occupation by well-to-do Jews of Gamaliel's stamp.[77] Consequently, it is natural to look for 'Caphar-gamala' in these border regions of Jerusalem and Diospolis;[78] the favoured site of Jemmala is some dozen miles due east of Diospolis, at the extreme limits of the *territorium* of Jerusalem. That the relics should come to light at a spot quite close to the town where the synod was at that moment in session is not without interest to anyone trying to assess the effect of the discovery on the assembled gathering: it was not, after all, every council of the church which was favoured by so evident a token of divine intervention.

But it is the role of bishop John in this episode which is most revealing. Anyone who reads Lucianus' account of the discovery cannot fail to be struck by John's prominence in the proceedings. As his bishop, it is to John that Lucianus must report his encounters with Gamaliel; and the discovery is to be the glory of his episcopate.[79] John immediately lays claim to the relics for the church in Jerusalem; the tomb is not to be opened until his arrival from Diospolis.[80] The resting-place of the body is, not Caphar-gamala, but the church of Sion in Jerusalem. This was the historic focal point of the Jerusalem Christians: the site of the Upper Room which had seen the beginnings of the church, where Stephen himself had been chosen one of the seven deacons, and which had preserved the throne of James, the Lord's brother, and first bishop of Jerusalem.[81] Here John deposited the newly-discovered remains of Christendom's first martyr, an event sufficiently celebrated that it may be the origin of a tradition

---

[77] Abel (1924), 237.

[78] Although it has to be admitted that the Eleutheropolis region had seen a recent cluster of relic 'inventions': cf. above, p. 212.

[79] *Ep. Luciani,* 2 'quia in temporibus tui sacerdotii oportet nos revelari'.

[80] Ibid. 6.

[81] For Stephen's diaconate, see Acts, 6.5—the point was not missed in 415, '... sanctam ecclesiam Sion, ubi et archidiaconus fuerat ordinatus' (*Ep. Luciani,* 8). On the throne, see Pet. Diac. *Liber de locis sanctis* E (*CC* 175, 95), and Eus. *Hist. Eccl.* vii. 19. By the 6th cent. the Sion church had become a treasure-house of relics, including 'many of the stones with which Stephen was stoned': Anton. Placent. *Itin.* 22.

found in a later eastern liturgical calendar that bishop John himself *built* the Sion church.[82]

Nor was it coincidence that the translation of the remains to Jerusalem took place on 26 December. For this was the day on which, certainly for a generation before 415, the feast of St. Stephen had been celebrated in the eastern church. From Asia Minor, for instance, we have sermons of Gregory of Nyssa and of Asterius of Amasea preached on this date in praise of the protomartyr, thus honoured on the day following the newly-introduced feast of Christ's Nativity—and appropriately honoured then, for Stephen's death had been the echo of Christ's own sacrifice.[83] The association with the new festival of 25 December may, however, have been purely fortuitous; for the Jerusalem church, which itself had yet to adopt the western feast of Christ's Nativity, none the less seems already to have had a celebration of Stephen on 26 December in the years before the discovery.[84] Before long, in the course of the fifth century, St. Stephen was to assume a particular prominence in the liturgy of the church in Jerusalem, as is clear from a sermon of the presbyter Hesychius, who, while acknowledging that Stephen was the protomartyr for all Christians, nevertheless claimed him especially as a son of Jerusalem and the holy places, where he had many festivals to his name.[85]

The coincidence of St. Stephen's timely appearance in order to be solemnly introduced into Jerusalem precisely on the day on which the church held him in honour may be left to conjecture. At all events the discovery of the remains in the circumstances of December 415 was a considerable political *coup* for John and the church of Jerusalem. The issue of

---

[82] See G. Garitte (1958), 186–7 (29 March).

[83] E.g. in the sermon of Greg. Nys. (*PG* 46, 701–4), a rhetorical flourish on the parallel between Christ and Stephen: ᾽ἐκεῖνος τὸν ἄνθρωπον ὑπὲρ ἡμῶν ἐνδυσάμενος. οὗτος τὸν ἄνθρωπον ὑπὲρ ἐκείνου ἀποδυσάμενος...᾽.

[84] Cf. A. Renoux in *PO* 35, 176, n. 44. An early piece of evidence is the Syriac *Breviarium* in the British Museum (BM *add.* 12150), a MS. copied at Edessa in 411, which refers to a festival of Stephen on 26 December 'in Jerusalem'.

[85] See P. Devos (1968b), 158 ᾽ἀλλ ἡμεῖς αὐτῷ πλείονας εἰκότως ἑορτὰς ἐποφείλομεν, ἐπειδὴ πολίτης ἐστὶν τοῦ Σταυροῦ, τῆς Βηθλεὲμ οἰκεῖος, τῆς ᾽Αναστάσεως ἔκγονος, τῆς Σιὼν τραπεζοποιός, κῆρυς τῆς ᾽Αναλήψεως᾽. For the 5th cent. festival of Stephen in Jerusalem on 26 (or 27?) December, see *Armen. Lect.* 72. Melania kept the feast in Jerusalem on 26 December 439, see below, p. 232.

Pelagius had been brought to a head by his critics; they had occasioned the synod at Diospolis by their presentation of a *libellus* setting out his alleged views. Yet in the event the opposition crumbled, and the bishops declared themselves satisfied that Pelagius had not put himself outside the communion of the Catholic church. It seems unlikely that the course of the council remained unaffected by the revelation of St. Stephen, possibly only a few miles away; the prestige which already naturally attached to the bishop of Jerusalem can only have been enhanced by this notable acquisition to the holy places under his charge;[86] and so emphatic a confirmation of his patron's position must also have favoured the cause of Pelagius himself.

The situation may be comparable to that which had prevailed in Milan in 386 when the revelation of relics intervened in the confrontation between bishop Ambrose and the Arian-dominated imperial court. The parallel is already suggested by Augustine who, as an eye-witness of the events associated with the discovery of SS. Gervasius and Protasius and (in later years) recalling their impact at the time, endeavoured to secure for the miracles achieved by St. Stephen in Africa the same degree of fame and publicity.[87] The 'invention' of the relics in Milan is, of course, the *locus classicus* from which to observe the potential of martyrs' bones introduced into a highly charged political situation;[88] there is nothing to suggest that the temperature was running so high in the Holy Land in 415, or that John was so practised a political master as Ambrose. None the less the claims that Ambrose made for the *patrocinium* of Gervasius and Protasius do prefigure those we have seen made for Stephen.[89] If Ambrose's rout of the Arians could be effected by a pair of all but unknown local martyrs we should not underestimate

---

[86] On Stephen's identification with the fortunes of the holy places, see the passage of Hesychius quoted in previous note.

[87] For a comparison of the discovery of Stephen with that of Gervasius and Protasius, see August. *Serm.* 318.1 (*PL* 38, 1438). On the publicity, see the classic articles of H. Delehaye (1910) and (1925).

[88] E.g. F. Homes Dudden, *The Life and Times of Saint Ambrose* (1935), i, 298ff.

[89] Ambr. *Ep.* 22.10 'Tales ego ambio defensores, tales milites habeo; hoc est non saeculi milites, sed milites Christi. Nullam talibus invidiam timeo; quorum quo maiora, eo tutiora patrocinia sunt'. Cf. Avitus' letter, above, p. 213.

the potency of the Christian protomartyr. If, indeed, it were possible to read bishop John's version of the church politics of 415, as we have Ambrose's record of the circumstances in Milan, we should better be able to estimate any capital that was made out of the discovery. As it is, neither Augustine nor Jerome alludes to the appearance of the relics at the moment so crucial to the question of Pelagius—a silence which might in itself suggest that St. Stephen had been seen not to be impartial.

Orosius' departure from the Holy Land with relics of St. Stephen may thus reflect the background of current ecclesiastical politics as much as the piety of the holy places—if indeed the two facets can be separated. The miraculous discovery could not be dissociated from surrounding events, any more than Orosius' own partisanship was immune from the reawakening of Christian history peculiar to the Holy Land: as we saw earlier with Palladius, the pious devotee of the holy sites and the committed politician could become one and the same. We cannot say whether bishop John begrudged Orosius, as a political opponent in the Pelagius affair, his possession of a portion of the prize discovery; but in the wider compass of the church at large the relics were to transcend party lines. As Stephen's remains circulated in the empire, the contentious circumstances which had surrounded their origin were forgotten; and, taking pride of place alongside other biblical memorials from the Holy Land, the relics confirmed the faith of the Christian communities to which they came—recalling the preeminence of the first martyr as the model of Christian witness. As Stephen's death was interpreted as an echo of that of Christ himself, so the discovery of his tomb in 415 naturally harked back to the only event with which it invited comparison—the revelation of the Holy Sepulchre. This had been the setting for the first great imperial intervention in the Holy Land; and it was appropriately the veneration of Stephen which was to be the centrepiece of another enterprise emanating directly from the emperor's family: the pilgrimage of the empress Eudocia.

10. Eudocia

WHEN the younger Melania visited Constantinople in the winter of 436–7, and was greeted by the chamberlain Lausus in the imperial palace, the piety of the holy places was brought once again to the heart of the court—but only after Melania at the outskirts of the capital had overcome her anxieties, as her biographer puts it, about entering 'so great a royal city'.[1] Such hesitation is hardly surprising. On the one hand, she was here on an official mission to the court, travelling at public expense, and concerned with an important matter of state—the delicate negotiations preceding the marriage of the western emperor Valentinian III and Theodosius' daughter Eudoxia.[2] The intermediary from the western court, who had summoned her to Constantinople, was Melania's uncle, the celebrated official Rufius Antonius Agrypnius Volusianus, last of a great pagan line.[3] Yet in contrast to such secular standing Melania had behind her twenty years of monastic seclusion on the Mount of Olives; her entry into the court circles of the capital was not that of a public servant, but of the ascetic heroine from the holy places, received by Lausus with the same awe which he had reserved for Palladius' stories of holy men. Her visits to senatorial households were those of a spiritual adviser, giving inspiration in the true faith, while for the emperor and his family she was a fount of edification.[4] Meanwhile, as if in confirmation of this private and religious role, her stay in Constantinople witnessed the death-bed conversion and bap-

---

[1] *V. Mel.* 53.   [2] Ibid. 50; cf. *V. Pet. Iber.* 34.
[3] See A. Chastagnol (1956), and (1962), 276–9.
[4] *V. Mel.* 54, 56.

tism of her uncle.[5] We can only suppose that the impact of
Melania's presence was much enhanced by the news of this
change of heart on the part of Volusianus; and if anything
was needed to convince the notably pious eastern court of the
desirability of the proposed marriage, then this conversion
must surely have swept away any doubts. After the period of
mourning for her uncle, Melania left Constantinople—
having thus achieved, through the reputation of her personal
devotion, the public purpose of her mission, and having reasserted the underlying links between the Christian court and
the Holy Land: she did not depart without urging Theodosius to dispatch his empress on a pilgrimage.[6]

The marriage of the emperor Valentinian III and Theodosius' daughter duly took place in Constantinople on 29 October 437.[7] On their return to the West the couple honoured
the occasion with imperial donations to the newly-built
church of Peter and Paul in Rome (the future S. Pietro in
Vincoli), where Eudoxia fulfilled a vow in the name of her
family.[8] Meanwhile in the East, as a public expression of
thanksgiving for the marriage, the bride's mother, the
empress Eudocia, embarked (in the spring of 438?) on a pilgrimage to the holy places of Palestine. While doubtless in
response to a private longing recently encouraged by the presence of Melania at the court, her journey was no less an
official venture, carried out at the wishes of the emperor
himself.[9]

It is a considerable testimony to the peculiar blend of the
Byzantine court of the day that this learned and cultured
lady, a product of the intellectual environment of the Athe-

---

[5] Ibid. 55; after receiving communion three times from her hands, he died at
Epiphany 437.

[6] Ibid. 56.

[7] See Marcellinus, *Chron.* s.a. 437 (= *Chron. Min.* ii, 79); *Gesta Senatus*, 2 (= *CTh*
ed. Mommsen, 1); Socr. *Hist. Eccl.* vii. 44; *Chron. Pasch.* (ed. Dindorf), i, 582.

[8] See De Rossi, *ICUR* ii, 110 (= *ILCV* 1779) 'Theodosius pater Eudocia cum
coniuge votum/cumque suo supplex Eudoxia nomine solvit.' On the history of this
church, see R. Krautheimer, *Proc. Amer. Phil. Soc.* 84 (1941), 353ff., esp. 396–411;
Eudoxia's association with Peter's chains is later legend.

[9] According to Socr. *Hist. Eccl.* vii. 47 Theodosius 'sent' his wife to the Holy
Land, as is also implied by *V. Mel.* 56. As to the time of her departure, is there any
significance in Eudocia's absence from the procession for the returning remains of
Chrysostom on 28 January 438 (see Theophanes, *Chron.* (ed. de Boor), 93)?

nian 'sophists',[10] will be found kneeling in prayer at the holy
places of Christianity and revering the relics of its martyrs: in
the course of one and the same journey she would both de-
light the citizens of Antioch by her eloquent reminiscence of
Homer and dedicate a church containing the remains of a
foot of St. Stephen in gratitude for the cure of an affliction.[11]
Such a marriage of classical learning and Christian devotion
is illustrated by Eudocia's literary output: verse paraphrases
of books of the Bible, Homeric centos on the life of Christ,
together with three books of hexameters on the martyrs Cyprian and Justina[12] (a topic which might exercise a particular
appeal for her, seeing her own career mirrored in the legend
of Cyprian: born an Athenian, schooled in pagan learning
and the magic arts, and later converted to Christianity).[13] It
may be assumed that it was the religious climate of Theodosius' household and court—already documented by the reception accorded to Melania—which, in grafting its distinctive piety on to Eudocia's intellectual attainments, was responsible for this amalgam of pilgrim and poetess.[14]

The sophist's daughter Athenais became an emperor's wife
on 7 June 421; by this time she was Aelia Eudocia, and had
been baptized by Atticus, the bishop of Constantinople.[15]
She thus came to the centre of a court whose Christian devotion is lauded by the ecclesiastical historians of the day.[16]
The dominating figure at this period was the emperor's older

[10] Her father was the sophist Leontius (Socr. *Hist. Eccl.* vii. 21.8), presumably the same man whom Olympiodorus helped to the chair of rhetoric at Athens (Olympiod. fr. 28 = *Frag. Hist. Graec.* iv, 63). On her career, see Seeck, *RE* vi, 906ff., and H.-G. Beck, *RAC* vi, 844-5.

[11] Below, pp. 229ff.

[12] On the literary Eudocia, see Cohn, *RE* vi, 910-12, and Beck, *RAC* vi, 846-7, with A. Ludwich (1882), and his Teubner edition of her poetry (1897).

[13] See esp. Ch. Diehl, *Byzantine Empresses* (Engl. trans. 1964), ch. ii 'Athenais'. On the Cyprian legend: H. Delehaye, 'Cyprien d'Antioche et Cyprien de Carthage', *Anal. Boll.* 39 (1921), 314-32; A. Amore, *Bibl. Sanct.* iii (1963), 1281-5.

[14] The court of Theodosius II has suffered from scholarly neglect: see A. Momigliano in *Studies in Church History*, 8 (1972), 12ff. On the religious atmosphere of the reign, cf. A. Lippold, *RE* suppl. xiii, 1015ff.

[15] Socr. *Hist. Eccl.* vii. 21.9; Marcellinus, *Chron.* s.a. 421 (= *Chron. Min.* ii, 75); date, *Chron. Pasch.* (ed. Dindorf), 578. She was declared Augusta on 2 January 423 (ibid. 580).

[16] Socr. *Hist. Eccl.* vii. 22, Soz. *Hist. Eccl.* ix. 1-3 (Pulcheria), Theod. *Hist. Eccl.* v. 36.3-5; cf. *V. Pet. Iber.* 24.

sister Pulcheria, by whom Eudocia herself had been advanced. A virgin dedicated to the Christian life, whose example had been followed by her two younger sisters Arcadia
and Marina, Pulcheria is portrayed as Theodosius' adviser
and guide in all matters of state, instructing him in the role
of a Christian emperor.[17] The crucial political influence exercised by the emperor's sister over a long period of years is
outside our sphere;[18] on the religious life of the court, however, her influence was no less pronounced. Imperial patronage
was extended on a grand scale into Christian building: churches, monasteries, and hostels were established as imperial
foundations, and supported from imperial revenues;[19] while
the emperor's treasures came to adorn places of worship.[20]
As a public declaration of her own and her sisters' chosen
path of Christian virginity, and as an act of dedication for
her brother's rule, Pulcheria set up a magnificent altar in the
great church at Constantinople.[21] In the imperial quarters
themselves contemporaries saw less the trappings of state than
the austerity of a monastery: the emperor's sisters leading a
life of pious simplicity, in constant prayer and praise, and
always in attendance on the leading churchmen; Theodosius
himself fasting regularly on two days a week, and disputing
with the bishops on matters of holy Scripture (which he knew
by heart), with the aid of the resources of a vast theological
library.[22] In the Constantinople of Theodosius II the popu-
lace assembled in the hippodrome could be diverted from the
pleasures they awaited into a great act of intercession for the
dispersal of a threatening storm, encouraged by the emperor
himself: dressed as a private citizen, he led the people in a
chorus of hymns—'and the whole city became as one
church'.[23]

All this represents, it may appear, a conducive background
for Eudocia's pilgrimage—but it is, of course, a far from
objective presentation of the court of Theodosius II. We owe

[17] Soz. *Hist. Eccl.* ix. 1.5–6.
[18] Cf. E. Stein, *Histoire du Bas-Empire*, i (1959), 275–6; W. Ensslin, *RE* xxiii,
1954ff.; Lippold, *RE* suppl. xiii, 966ff.
[19] Soz. *Hist. Eccl.* ix. 1.10. On Pulcheria's building, Ensslin, o.c., 1961–2.
[20] Soz. *Hist. Eccl.* ix. 1.8.   [21] Ibid. 4.
[22] Socr. *Hist. Eccl.* vii. 22.3–6; cf. Soz. *Hist. Eccl.* ix. 1.8, 3.1.
[23] Socr. *Hist. Eccl.* vii. 22.15ff.

it to the ecclesiastical historians of the day, who saw the time in which they were compiling their histories in decidedly Christian terms: it was an age (it might seem) of peace and happiness, when the hand of God was demonstrably at work protecting his empire on earth—as had been foreshadowed by Eusebius in his portrayal of Constantine.[24] This was interpreted as a reward for the devotion displayed by Theodosius and his entourage, which guaranteed the well-being of the emperor's subjects.[25] There was thus a temptation to present the worship of the palace as an idealized tableau of Christian holiness, in a form more akin to hagiography than history. Sozomen, it will not be forgotten, dedicated his history to the emperor himself, and wrote a preface of pure panegyric, ascribing to the emperor an incomparable list of virtues.[26]

Setting aside the traditional adulation of the Christian emperor, we may find more persuasive evidence in the court's patronage of monasticism. It is to the reign of this Theodosius that the restoration of monasticism across the Bosphorus belongs; the monastery at Chalcedon, which had been deserted since the departure of the monks whom Flavius Rufinus had brought there from Egypt at the time of Theodosius I, was re-established under the leadership of Hypatius.[27] With a nucleus of monks around him, he reoccupied the derelict site, which lay alongside the palace which Rufinus had built for himself, and which on his downfall had become an imperial possession. When the emperor's sisters resided there they received spiritual visits from Hypatius,[28] while Theodosius himself—apart from seeing him on two occasions—often exchanged letters with the monks' leader, addressing him 'as a father'.[29] Consequently, among the benefits which Hypatius was able to recommend to his fellow-monks was the honour received from rulers: 'princes and kings celebrated in the world pay us respect, revealing that they are Christians'.[30]

---

[24] Cf. Glanville Downey (1965) on their 'apologetic' stance.

[25] Explicitly stated by Soz. *Hist. Eccl.* ix. 3.3.

[26] See esp. pref. 15ff. When writing of Pulcheria Sozomen was concerned to refute the charge of sycophancy: ix. 1.11.

[27] Callinicus, *V. Hypatii*, 66.   [28] Ibid. 112–13.

[29] Ibid. 112.   [30] Ibid. 88.

Such patronage from the court was not, of course, confined to members of the emperor's family. We have already noted the interest in the ascetic life displayed by the *praepositus* Lausus; with him can now be coupled the name of another chamberlain, Urbicius, who served at the court of seven successive emperors, from the reign of Theodosius II through to Anastasius, and, like Lausus, rose to be a figure of immense wealth.[31] Many years later, at the beginning of the next century, Urbicius would undertake a tour of eastern cities, including Jerusalem, bestowing large gifts of money on the inhabitants; in particular, the bishop of Edessa received from him a sum of money to build a church dedicated to the virgin Mary.[32] The visit of this powerful official, 'who crowned the heads of emperors and removed their crowns...', was long remembered in the Holy Land: he had wanted, unsuccessfully, to take back to Constantinople as an altar the stone on which (so tradition affirmed) Mary had rested at the roadside on her way to Bethlehem.[33] In the time of Theodosius II, Urbicius had revered Hypatius as a father, taking to him one of his personal servants to be cured; at his expense the monastery buildings were restored and enlarged.[34] When Hypatius died (446?), it was Urbicius who provided his tomb.[35] In the face of this enthusiastic support of monasticism by imperial officials (which recalled, it will be noted, the days of the first Theodosius), it comes as no surprise that it was monks who played leading roles, and exerted powerful influence, in the ecclesiastical controversies which marked Theodosius II's reign: they naturally found in the eastern court a receptive and sympathetic audience.[36]

The character of Theodosius' entourage is further attested

---

[31] See E. Honigmann (1949), with *RE* ii. 17, 992ff. The man who had charge of Urbicius' personal fortune, the Phrygian Epinicus, was promoted to *comes sacr. largit.*: see Joh. Ant. fr. 211 (*Frag. Hist. Graec.* iv, 618). On Urbicius, cf. now *PLRE* ii, 1188.

[32] See the *Chronicle of Joshua the Stylite* (ed. W. Wright, 1882), 66 (s.a. 504–5), 69 (church at Edessa).

[33] Theodosius, *De situ terrae sanctae*, 28; on this site, cf. below, p. 241.

[34] *V. Hypat.* 73, 74.

[35] Ibid. 138, close to the tomb of the Egyptian Ammonius.

[36] On monastic influence in Constantinople, see H. Bacht (1953); G. Dagron (1970), esp. 261ff.; W. H. C. Frend (1972b), 15ff.

by the honour accorded to the Iberian prince Nabarnugius
—who in fact was to precede Eudocia, by a few months, in
making a journey to the Holy Land; he is better known by
his 'Christian' name, Peter.[37] When twelve years old (429?)
he had arrived at the court in Constantinople as a pledge of
the bond between the empire and the Iberian royal house
against the threat of Persia[38]—a migration which recalls the
career of an earlier Iberian prince, Bacurius, who had served
in the armies of Theodosius I and had been a friend of
Rufinus in Jerusalem.[39] Like Bacurius before him, Peter was
noted for his Christian piety, which blossomed in the congenial surroundings of a quasi-monastic court: the empress
Eudocia, we are told, behaved as a mother to him, while
Melania in visiting the court in 436 was endeared to his evident religious devotion.[40] In this atmosphere he acquired,
despite his youth, a reputation as a leader in sanctity and the
spiritual life; through his influence a number of palace officials became monks.[41] His following was achieved particularly through his unerring attachment to the remains of certain Christian martyrs from Persia, whose cult Peter promoted in the capital as very much his own personal preserve
—to the annoyance, indeed, of some of the attendants who
had accompanied him from his homeland, who looked for
material advancement from their sojourn in Constantinople,
and resented the attentions they were required to pay to the
shrines of martyrs.[42]

Peter still remained in the capital at the time of Melania's
visit there in the winter of 436–7, but shortly afterwards he
left for Jerusalem accompanied by a palace eunuch, John.[43]
Some relics of Peter's martyrs went with them, as well as a

---

[37] On the author of his surviving Syriac *Vita*, see E. Schwartz (1912), and for
further biographical material, D. M. Lang (1951).

[38] *V. Pet. Iber.* 23–4; for revised chronology, P. Devos (1968c). Raabe's German
edition of the *Vita* appeared before the publication of the *V. Mel.*, which provides
crucial information (the date of Melania's visit to the court).

[39] See above, p. 166.   [40] *V. Pet. Iber.* 34, 49.

[41] Ibid. 24–6.

[42] See the complaints of the attendant required to bring oil for the lamps at the
shrine (ibid. 25–6). The martyrs ensured that the lamps burned on water only for
the duration of the Epiphany festival!

[43] Ibid. 27ff. Cf. Devos, 347.

fragment of the cross contained in the Gospel of St. John, guaranteeing them safe passage.[44] As bearers of sacred relics, they were hailed by the faithful in the towns and villages of Asia Minor; on approaching Jerusalem they saw from a distance the holy places and the church of the Ascension on the summit of the Mount of Olives, a view which fired their enthusiasm to enter the holy city in prayer, 'as if they were now with Christ in Heaven'.[45] They were to be welcomed at Melania's monastery on the Mount of Olives, and subsequently received their 'habits' from Gerontius, who had charge of the monks.[46] Peter was soon to establish his own monastery at the so-called 'David's Tower' on Mount Sion, which provided distinguished hospitality for visiting pilgrims[47]—although, now that he had become a monastic recluse, he would have preferred to avoid the embarrassment of receiving an empress in style when Eudocia insisted on seeing him in Jerusalem.[48]

This Iberian prince turned monk was before long (recalling the experience of Palladius) to emerge as a monophysite bishop deeply implicated in the theological divisions which ensued from the council of Chalcedon. But Peter's career at the holy places had originally stemmed from the pious surroundings of Theodosius II's court—and his settlement in Jerusalem (like the visit to Constantinople of the younger Melania) was a reminder of the natural ties between the Christian court and the Holy Land. Even before Eudocia set off on her pilgrimage, the imperial family had already declared its interest in the holy places: not only are Theodosius and Pulcheria recorded as sending money to Jerusalem for distribution to the needy; furthermore, the gilded cross which surmounted the centre of the Christian world, the rock of Golgotha itself, was a gift from the emperor (in return the imperial family received from the bishop of Jerusalem its own relic of Stephen, part of his right hand—which Pulcher-

---

[44] Ibid. 29–30; on the cross as a talisman, see above, p. 134.

[45] Ibid. 32; for the view of the Ascension church on approaching Jerusalem, cf. Jer. *Ep.* 108.12.1.

[46] Ibid. 35. The mention of Gerontius is followed by lavish praise of his activity in Jerusalem; for this man, hero of the monophysites in Jerusalem and author of *V. Mel.*, see D. Gorce, *SChr* 90, 54–62.

[47] *V. Pet. Iber.* 46.   [48] Ibid. 49–50.

ia housed in a new chapel in the palace).[49] Through these donations Theodosius II channelled imperial munificence in the direction of the Holy Land in the manner which had marked the later years of Constantine; and in making her pilgrimage his empress inevitably called to mind its precursor, the now legendary journey of Helena.[50]

Eudocia's venture resembled the earlier imperial pilgrimage in its combination of personal motivation and public style: her journey to and from Palestine was characterized by extravagantly imperial donations to the churches *en route*.[51] Yet the only conspicuous occasion of which mention survives is her halt at Antioch; it was while she was in this city that news of her progress reached Jerusalem.[52] As the empress on a 'state visit', Eudocia contributed to building improvements in Antioch, and her stay there, obviously a famous event in the city's annals, was commemorated in a bronze statue.[53] In a formal speech to the citizens in praise of Antioch she struck a welcome chord by referring to their Greek ancestry, which she proudly shared with them—a theme which was capped by a concluding verse adaptation of Homer.[54] It may be that Eudocia, the 'wandering poet', was here following the contemporary fashion of composing 'πάτρια' — poems in honour of the cities visited by the poet in his travels, and setting out the legends of their foundations.[55] At any rate we may be certain that it was in a literary vein, and hardly as Christian pilgrim, that the empress employed her artistry in entertaining the citizens of Antioch.

Of Eudocia's journeying as a pilgrim most of our knowledge derives from the *Life* of the younger Melania—but this

[49] Theophanes, *Chron.* (ed. de Boor), 86: Pulcheria dreamed of Stephen's approach. Cf. K.'G. Holum, *GRBS* 18 (1977), 163ff., and (with G. Vikan) *Dumb. Oaks Papers*, 33 (1979), 113ff.
[50] For a 7th cent. version of the Helena legend which confused her with Eudocia, see H. A. Drake (1979).
[51] Socr. *Hist. Eccl.* vii. 47.   [52] *V. Mel.* 58.
[53] Evagr. *Hist. Eccl.* i. 20. *Chron. Pasch.* (ed. Dindorf), 585, gives her two commemorative monuments (and misplaces the occasion to her second journey to the East). Cf. G. Downey, *A History of Antioch in Syria* (1961), 450ff.
[54] Evagr. l.c. The line concerned occurs at *Il.* vi. 211, and xx. 241: ‘ὑμετέρης γενεῆς τε καὶ αἵματος εὔχομαι εἶναι’.
[55] See A. Cameron, *Claudian* (1970), 9ff. Ludwich (1882), 207, was tempted by the suggestion that the entire speech may have been a verse cento of Homer.

text is oddly silent about who was in her retinue. We have to look elsewhere to discover that she was being accompanied by no less a dignitary than Cyril, bishop of Alexandria.[56] It is certain from Cyril's own correspondence that he went to Jerusalem about this time, as he later mentions a visit there in a letter (c.440) to his lieutenants in Constantinople; and the fact that he had encountered in Jerusalem an official from the imperial palace might be a hint that the empress was then present in the city.[57] Yet Cyril gives no indication in this letter that the reason for his presence in Jerusalem had been to escort the Augusta on her pilgrimage. That information is to be found in a passage in the seventh century *Chronicle* of John of Nikiu, which records that the emperor Theodosius instructed Cyril to accompany Eudocia in her pilgrimage as her spiritual director.[58] John, although taking full advantage of the romantic legends which came to surround Eudocia in the Byzantine chroniclers from the sixth century onwards, none the less preserves some historical material on her journey to the Holy Land: he is precise, for example, on the circumstances which gave rise to her pilgrimage. We cannot, therefore, neglect entirely his association of Cyril and Eudocia, especially since, as a local source, his testimony carries independent weight when it comes to Egyptian material. Moreover, another source confirms that Cyril was in the empress' company at the culmination of her pilgrimage in Jerusalem.

From the *Life* of Peter the Iberian we learn of Cyril's attendance at Jerusalem, along with a number of Egyptian bishops, for the dedication of a new shrine to house the relics of St. Stephen, erected outside the city's northern gate. This ceremony, presided over by Eudocia, took place on 15 May 439(?).[59] On the following day the same participants

[56] See F. M. Abel (1947), 220ff. The silence of *V. Mel.* can hardly be explained by the political stance of Gerontius (as Abel, 225, n. 50), who was ready to mention 'the most holy bishop Cyril' in *V. Mel.* 34.	[57] Cyril, *Ep.* 70.

[58] Ed. M. H. Zotenberg (*Notices et Extraits*, 24 (1883), i, 125ff.), 470. (The *Chron.* survives in a 1602 Ethiopian version of an Arabic paraphrase of the Greek original. There is an English transl. (1916) by R. H. Charles.)

[59] *V. Pet. Iber.* 37. The year, after Eudocia's arrival and before the death of Melania, must be 438 or 439; May 438 seems too soon after Eudocia's departure from Constantinople. Cf. Devos (1968c), 346.

ascended the Mount of Olives for the deposition of relics in Melania's *martyrium* at the summit. The author of the *Life* makes Cyril appear in Jerusalem at the invitation of the empress, an assumption which at least emphasizes the *official* participation of the bishop of Alexandria at the climax of what had, after all, been a state enterprise. The empress' pilgrimage was a major public event for the eastern empire, the sequel to the wedding celebrations of the previous year. It is to be assumed that it had wide currency in the cities, especially after Eudocia's reception in Antioch; in such circumstances the bishop of Alexandria, having taken upon himself the role of 'court theologian' after the ousting of Nestorius (he had addressed two lengthy treatises on right belief to Eudocia and Pulcheria),[60] may well have felt it appropriate to identify himself with this imperial venture and to join the Augusta at the holy places.

The exclusion of the local bishop, Juvenal, from the record (thus far) of Eudocia's presence in Jerusalem is most likely to be explained in terms of post-Chalcedonian politics: the man whose 'crossing the floor' at Chalcedon was to invite comparisons, in monophysite sources, with the behaviour of Judas, could hardly be expected to take a central role in their accounts of these events.[61] Yet bishop Juvenal, whose dominant purpose was to raise the status of the see of Jerusalem, is unlikely to have overlooked the opportunity offered by the imperial pilgrimage.[62] His recent predecessor, John, had already—it has appeared—made the most of the revelation of Stephen's remains; now, by securing the patronage of Eudocia for a new shrine of the protomartyr at the actual spot where he was believed to have met his death,[63] Juvenal was both inviting a suitable display of imperial munificence

---

[60] Abel, 223; for the treatises, see *Acta Conc. Oec.* i. 1.5, 26ff.

[61] On the hostile tradition, see E. Honigmann (1950), 262ff. For Gerontius' remark, 'I see the face of the traitor Judas', see *V. Pet. Iber.* 36 (although he had referred anonymously to the bishop of Jerusalem as 'the most pious bishop' in attendance on Melania's last hours: *V. Mel.* 67, 68).

[62] On the aims of bishop Juvenal, see Honigmann, o.c.

[63] The traditional site of the stoning used to be disputed: P. Peeters (1908). A northern site is clearly implied by *Ep. Luciani*, 3 'foris portam quae est ad aquilonem ...'; while *V. Pet. Iber.* 37 specifies the northern gate; approaching Jerusalem from the north, the church of Stephen was the first monument reached (ibid. 94).

at the holy places and, at the same time, advancing the prestige of himself and his see. The message registered with at least one contemporary observer: a sermon attributed to Basil of Seleucia commends Juvenal for the new shrine, and praises him as a worthy successor on the throne of James.[64] Thus the ceremony of dedication which took place in the presence of Eudocia (as well as the patriarch of Alexandria) brought lustre as much to the bishop of Jerusalem as to the empress who graced the occasion. Only when in later years Eudocia rebuilt and enlarged the church of Stephen would it be established as *her* monument.

Melania herself, in the very last days of her life, would come to celebrate the feast of Stephen in this newly-dedicated shrine (26 Dec. 439).[65] She had already given evidence of her devotion to Stephen by depositing a portion of the relics in the *martyrium* which she had constructed alongside the church of the Ascension at the summit of the Mount of Olives.[66] This was the shrine which had been dedicated in the presence of Eudocia and the assembled company on the day following the Stephen ceremony; its array of relics included, besides those of Stephen, the Forty Martyrs of Sebaste and those Persian martyrs who had accompanied Peter the Iberian and his companion to Jerusalem.[67] Here, too, the patronage of the empress was evident: according to the author of Peter the Iberian's *Life*, an inscription recorded Eudocia's embellishments to the building; Melania's biographer, none the less, makes clear that the *martyrium* was initially a private sanctuary of her own, and Eudocia's presence simply added distinction to the actual deposition of the relics.[68]

Despite the public ceremony in which Eudocia took part, her role in the foundation of Melania's *martyrium* brings into the foreground the private impetus which had sustained her pilgrimage, revealed in the spiritual relationship existing be-

[64] *PG* 85, 469.   [65] *V. Mel.* 64.
[66] Ibid. 57, 64 (Gorce, 256–8). For the site of Melania's shrine, in relation to the rotunda of Poemenia's church, see V. Corbo, *Liber Annuus*, 10 (1960), 211ff., and J. T. Milik, *Rev. Bibl.* 67 (1960), 558–9.
[67] *V. Pet. Iber.* 37.
[68] E.g. *V. Mel.* 58, the empress asked that the ceremony should take place 'in her presence'.

tween the two women. Before leaving Constantinople, Melania had urged the emperor to encourage his wife in her desire to worship at the holy places; and she had travelled as far as Sidon to meet the approaching pilgrim—just as she would accompany her, too, on her departure.[69] Eudocia, for her part, greeted Melania as her 'spiritual mother', and was as eager to observe the life of her monasteries as she was to pray at the holy places.[70] In such circumstances, the empress would readily believe that it was the prayers of Melania and her sisters before the newly-deposited relics which achieved the cure of an injured foot which troubled her on the occasion of the dedication of the *martyrium*.[71]

A curious piece of evidence corroborates this cure. A copy of an inscription (the stone is lost) from Zapharambolou, in ancient Paphlagonia, records, in Greek iambics, the building of a church to St. Stephen in thanksgiving for the cure of a 'left knee and foot', and the deposition there of the remains of the protomartyr's own foot (a relic of Stephen's right foot was apparently being shown to travellers as late as 1856).[72] On the basis of the abbreviation *ΒΣ ΕΥΔ* appearing in the last line of the inscription the building of this church, and the composition of the poem, may be ascribed to the empress Eudocia—with some plausibility, as she is known to have carried with her on her return to Constantinople relics of the protomartyr, which came to rest in the church of St. Lawrence in the capital.[73] The Augusta thus returned to the court duly provided with a portion of Holy Land relics to be deposited as public confirmation of her presence at the holy places—the conclusion of her 'official' journey; while to Eudocia herself, ascribing to St. Stephen the cure of her ailment, the possession of his remains would give a further dimension to that personal conviction which had been demonstrated by her pilgrimage.

---

[69] Ibid. 58, 59 (she escorted her as far as Caesarea).

[70] Ibid. 58.   [71] Ibid. 59.

[72] Cf. D. Gorce, *ad loc.*; with G. Doublet, *BCH* 13 (1889), 294–9, and F. Halkin, *Anal. Boll.* 71 (1953), 96.

[73] Marcellinus, *Chron.* s.a. 439 (= *Chron. Min.* ii, 80). The relics cannot immediately have been deposited in St. Lawrence, which was not built until *c.* 450 (*Chron. Min.* ii, 85); but the imperial palace already had a church of Stephen, containing remains of his right hand, cf. above, p. 229.

It was probably in the summer of 439 that Eudocia returned to the court, the vow of thanksgiving for her daughter's
wedding fulfilled. About this time, however, intrigues were
developing among the emperor's entourage which were fundamentally to weaken the standing of Eudocia, and to bring
about, within a few years, her second journey to Jerusalem
—a journey which resulted in a permanent exile of nearly
twenty years at the holy places, during which time she
emerged, for a period, in deliberate opposition to the persons
and policies of the court.[74] The circumstances which gave
rise to this withdrawal to the Holy Land remain a dark episode in the history of the relations between the emperors and
the holy places in these years; the fact that the only consistent account to emerge in the sources is a romantic legend of
Eudocia's alleged adultery with the *magister officiorum* suggests
that contemporaries did not really know what had led to her
abandonment of the court, beyond the fact that it was connected with some turmoil in the emperor's immediate
circle.[75]

Eudocia's earlier support for Nestorius had already made
clear that the two Augustae were destined to be rivals at
court.[76] Events proved that Pulcheria was to be disappointed
in any hope she may have had of dominating the wife she
herself had found for her brother; Eudocia's prestige can only
have been heightened by her journey to the Holy Land,
which clearly outclassed the domestic piety of Pulcheria. It is
probable that it is to this period immediately after Eudocia's
return that the emergence of the *eminence grise* of the next decade, the eunuch-chamberlain Chrysaphius, belongs;[77] to his
intrigues, in collusion with Eudocia, tradition ascribes Pulcheria's withdrawal from public life and retirement to the
palace at Hebdomon,[78] leaving the rival Augusta, for the
moment, unchallenged.

[74] On court intrigue in this period, see Ensslin, *RE* xxiii, 1958; E. Stein, *Histoire du Bas-Empire*, i, 296ff.

[75] The legend first appears in John Malalas, *Chron.* (ed. Dindorf), 353ff., followed by *Chron. Pasch.* 584ff. For a full exposition, see F. Gregorovius (1882). It is carefully differentiated from the facts by Seeck, *RE* vi, 909ff., and Beck, *RAC* vi, 845–6.

[76] See Ensslin, *RE* xxiii, 1957.   [77] See P. Goubert (1951), 305–7

[78] So Theophanes, *Chron.* (ed. de Boor), 98–9 (these events are misplaced).

The removal of Pulcheria only set a precedent; having got rid of one empress Chrysaphius might be expected to seize an opportunity of displacing the other. By the last months of 441, it appears, Eudocia was on the point of abandoning the court. The basis for this dating is found in a passage of the *Suda*, deriving from the contemporary historian Priscus, concerned with the fall from favour of Cyrus, praetorian prefect of the East: his demise is associated with the removal to Jerusalem of Eudocia, who, as a lover of poetry (like Cyrus himself), had been his patron.[79] Cyrus of Panopolis is a well-documented figure: already *praefectus urbi* at Constantinople, he had added the praetorian prefecture to this office in December 439; from then on he occupied the two posts simultaneously, at a time which well corresponds to the presumed supremacy of his protectress Eudocia (after her return from her pilgrimage).[80] In 441 he was consul, and still praetorian prefect in August—but had been replaced in that office by February 442; from the highest offices of state he now sank to an obscure Phrygian bishopric.[81] It would appear that it was towards the end of his tenure of office as consul when Cyrus' position came to be undermined—again, almost certainly, through the efforts of Chrysaphius, who was able to induce the emperor into believing that Cyrus was a potential rival in popular support.[82] The withdrawal of Eudocia to the Holy Land, if it rightly belongs in the background of these intrigues,

---

[79] *Suda*, s.v. 'Κῦρος'. For Cyrus as a poet, see A. Cameron (1965), 497–8.

[80] For his career, Seeck, *RE* xii, 188–90, and D. J. Constantelos (1971). For the simultaneous holding of the two offices, see Priscus, fr. 3a (*Frag. Hist. Graec.* iv, 73), and John Lydus, *De Magistr.* ii. 12, iii. 42. On Cyrus, we now have *PLRE* ii, 336ff.

[81] Cotyaeum, where he preached a sermon celebrated for its brevity: Joh. Malal. *Chron.* 362 (*Chron. Pasch.* 588 substitutes 'Smyrna'). Cf. Cameron, o.c., 473, and on the sermon, T. E. Gregory, *GRBS* 16 (1975), 317–24. After Theodosius II's death Cyrus returned to Constantinople, and became a devotee of St. Daniel the Stylite: *V. Dan. Styl.* 31, 36.

[82] It is difficult to reconcile Priscus' 'four years' for his joint tenure of the two offices, at most from the end of 439 to beginning of 442. For attribution of his downfall to Chrysaphius, see *V. Dan. Styl.* 31, and his own epigram blaming the 'drones' in the hive (i.e. eunuchs?): *Anth. Pal.* ix. 136. According to Malalas and *Chron. Pasch.* the people acclaimed Cyrus 'Constantine built the city, Cyrus rebuilt it'.

must then be placed late in 441 or early 442.[83]

Meanwhile, in 440 the *magister officiorum*, Paulinus, had been executed on the emperor's orders at Caesarea in Cappadocia.[84] Around this bare fact subsequent chroniclers wove the story of the emperor's discovery of the supposed adultery of Eudocia and Paulinus, as an explanation both for the sudden manner of his death and for the departure of the empress; at the point of her death some twenty years later in Jerusalem, so the story concludes, Eudocia affirmed her innocence of such charges involving Paulinus.[85] Rumour, romance, and legend became so embroiled in this tradition that we can expect from it little concrete information on the real circumstances of Eudocia's departure. That her move, however, may have been accompanied by attempts to damage her reputation, involving allegations of infidelity, receives confirmation from a distant source: it was long ago observed that Nestorius, in his place of exile deep in Egypt, knew of rumours of the empress' adultery.[86] Such a story is reminiscent of the similar rumours surrounding the domestic scandal which had led to Helena's pilgrimage, or the tradition favoured by pagan sources that the real father of Theodosius II had been Johannes, a confidant of Arcadius.[87] Against the background of the shifting balance of power within the palace, Eudocia's opponents would take any opportunity to bring discredit on her; while observers of her second departure for the holy places might readily believe such an explanation for her journey, coming so soon after the success of her initial pilgrimage. Scandal and disgrace, after all, were as credible a pretext for approaching the Holy Land as had been the official grounds of her first venture.

---

[83] For this date, Seeck, *RE* vi, 908, and Lippold, *RE* suppl. xiii, 992. Other dates have abounded: 440 (Beck), 443 (Stein, Constantelos); this last was favoured by J. B. Bury in his generous coverage of Eudocia, *History of the Later Roman Empire* (2nd edit. 1923), 230.

[84] Marcellinus, *Chron.* s.a. 440 (= *Chron. Min.* ii, 80).

[85] Joh. Malal. *Chron.* 358, *Chron. Pasch.* 585.

[86] See '*Bazaar of Heraclides*', transl. Driver/Hodgson (1925), 379; with E. W. Brooks, *Byz. Zeitschr.* 21 (1912–13), 94–6.

[87] See Zosim. v. 18.8. There is a doublet of this in the genealogy of the Iberian royal house, *V. Pet. Iber.* 15.

But Eudocia was not yet totally divested of her public standing. The final breach with the court did not come until several years later. Under the year 444 the chronicler records the execution of two clergymen, the presbyter Severus and the deacon John, who were in attendance on Eudocia in Jerusalem, by the *comes domesticorum* Saturninus, despatched there by Theodosius. In response Eudocia immediately had Saturninus murdered, and, as a result, was deprived of the imperial entourage which she had hitherto retained— thereafter to be abandoned in Jerusalem until her death.[88] This mission of Saturninus, if not intended to bring about his own death, then at least finally deprived the Augusta of the surviving trappings of her status. Any semblance of the official support which had accompanied her first pilgrimage was thus removed, and her political disgrace complete.

Yet the prestige of Eudocia's presence in the Holy Land ensured that, although an outlaw from the emperor's entourage, she did not withdraw into obscurity; residing in close proximity to the holy places she would be able to sustain from near at hand the tradition of imperial patronage which had marked her pilgrimage a few years earlier. Moreover, with a member of the emperor's family on the spot we may expect to find brought to a head the association of high persons with holy places which we have detected in earlier generations. The advent of Eudocia was not only conspicuous in the continuing development of the Holy Land as a focus of devotion—this was ensured by her patronage of churchbuilding and encouragement of monasticism; but also her direct involvement in the local resistance to the council of Chalcedon once again brought the holy places to the forefront of ecclesiastical politics.

Eudocia's reputation in church-building was not confined to her activities at the holy places; already before withdrawing to the Holy Land she had founded the church of St. Polyeuktos in Constantinople.[89] But it was only after her removal from

---

[88] Marcellinus, *Chron.* s.a. 444 (= *Chron. Min.* ii, 81) 'regiis spoliata ministris'; cf. Priscus, fr. 8 (*Frag. Hist. Graec.* iv, 94).

[89] *Anth. Pal.* i. 10; cf. C. Mango & I. Sevcenko, *Dumb. Oaks Papers.* 15 (1961), 243. Eudocia's building was replaced by a great church built by her great-granddaughter, Anicia Iuliana.

the court that she entered upon the extensive building
schemes which established her fame among visitors to Jerusalem, and which must have done much to transform the
appearance of parts of the city; certainly Jerusalem had seen
nothing to match it since the construction of the Constantinian precinct around the Holy Sepulchre. To this period of
Eudocia's residence belongs, in all probability, the considerable enlargement and expansion of the city to the south,
beyond the bounds of Hadrian's Aelia Capitolina, to
embrace the full extent of the old pre-Roman Jerusalem—
and to include once again Mount Sion within its walls.[90] This
new southern circuit marked the boundary of the Byzantine
development of Jerusalem—revealed, for instance, in the discovery of the remains of a church associated with the name
of Bassa, known from the literature as a lady of notable piety
in Jerusalem, contemporary with Eudocia, who was the su-
perior of a local monastery.[91] Tradition was quick to attribute the building of the new city-wall to Eudocia, under the
influence of a verse from Psalm 51 (v.18): 'Let it be thy plea-
sure ('ἐν τῇ εὐδοκίᾳ σου...') to do good to Sion, to build
anew the walls of Jerusalem'—the coincidence of the
empress' name, the name she had been given at her Christian
baptism, with the words of the Septuagint did not fail to im-
press the pilgrims' biblical imagination.[92] When the news of
Eudocia's building works was spread further afield by returning pilgrims, the aptness of that particular verse was not
overlooked—Cassiodorus, commenting upon the psalm,
appropriately inserted a mention of Eudocia, 'religiosissima
feminarum'.[93]

[90] And the pool of Siloam: Anton. Placent. *Itin.* 25. Cf. the text attributed to
'Eucherius', 3 (*CC* 175, 237)—a ref. which at least gives a *term. post quem* for this
document. On the walls, see K. Kenyon (1974), 267ff., and M. Avi-Yonah (ed.),
Encyclopedia, ii, 621.

[91] See Kenyon, 273–4. For Bassa, see Cyril Scyth. *V. Euthym.* 30, and *Acta Conc.
Oec.* ii. 1.3, 135 (heading of a letter from Pulcheria). The pool of Siloam also reveals
a 5th cent. church, see above, p. 149, n. 104.

[92] For Eudocia as the builder of the walls, see Anton. Placent. l.c. (confusing her
name), Evagr. *Hist. Eccl.* i. 22; cf. *Chron. Pasch.* 585, Joh. Malal. *Chron.* 357–8. J.
Wilkinson (1977), 3, stretches a point in claiming that the walls referred to are 'not
necessarily' the city walls.

[93] *Exp. in Ps. 50* (*CC* 97, 468).

The empress' munificence in the Holy Land manifested itself in what were now the traditional forms: Cyril of Scythopolis attributes to her churches, monasteries, hostels for pilgrims and the sick.[94] The church historian Evagrius mentioned her monasteries, but only as a starting-point for a discussion of local monasticism; he has no precise details of Eudocia's foundations.[95] John of Nikiu found in his source a convent and a pilgrim-hostel.[96] It is only in the history of Nicephorus Callistus, as late as the fourteenth century, that we are confronted with a detailed list: to the narrative of Evagrius, which he (or his source) has been following, he adds the building, among other items, of a bishop's house provided with a revenue of 1000 gold pieces, a hospital for 400 (at 'Phordisii'?), the supply of 10,000 measures of oil for lighting the *Anastasis*, and an annual revenue for the monks of the *Anastasis* of 400 gold pieces.[97] Suspicions of the unreliability of these details are confirmed by the astronomical figure of 20,480 lb. of gold which Nicephorus gives as the total revenue which Eudocia set aside for her foundations; this sum, unrelated to any comparable evidence, quite lacks credibility—and should lead us to disregard this late testimony.[98]

None the less, there is no doubt of the extent of her liberality, which was aided by her possession of a number of properties in the area of Jerusalem, the revenues of which could be used to establish and, what is more, endow her foundations;[99] Eudocia's exclusion from the court does not appear to have deprived her of the estates which will have come to her by her marriage into the imperial family. Thus on the coast, for example, at Jamnia, she founded on an imperial property (where, we are told, she had once resided herself) a charitable 'convalescent home', equipped with a

---

[94] *V. Euthym.* 35 '.... τοσαῦτα ἅπερ τῆς ἐμῆς οὐκ ἔστι δυνάμεως ἀριθμεῖν'. For a particular hostel in Jerusalem, cf. *V. Ioh. Hesych.* 4.

[95] *Hist. Eccl.* i. 21–2.   [96] Ed. Zotenberg, 470.

[97] Nic. Call. *Hist. Eccl.* xiv. 50 (*PG* 146, 1240).

[98] Yet apparently accepted by M. Avi-Yonah (1958), 44, and by Wilkinson (1977), 3. On the unreliability of Nicephorus Callistus, cf. above, on Helena, p. 48.

[99] An aspect appreciated by the sources, cf. *V. Euthym.* 35 '...καὶ ἑκάστῃ ἀρκοῦσαν ἀφορίζουσα πρόσοδον', and John of Nikiu, l.c.

church and an establishment of clergy, and provided for out of her revenues.[100] Peter the Iberian was taken to spend his last days here by an official of Eudocia's entourage, Elias, who himself resided in a village five miles to the north of Jerusalem (Beth Tafsa) which might also have been an imperial preserve.[101] Eudocia's estates, furthermore, provided a ready avenue for the extension of Palestinian monasticism: the village of Ganta, fifteen miles away from the city, was left in her will to the church of Jerusalem, having become the site of a monastery presided over by a local presbyter, Paul.[102] Similarly, the dissident Romanus, a leader of the anti-Chalcedonian monks, returned from exile to establish himself at the head of a monastery in another village of Eudocia's, in the neighbourhood of Eleutheropolis (Kephar Turbn).[103] The 'tower' which the empress built for herself as a vantage-point above the *laura* of Euthymius in the desert east of Jerusalem was also in its turn (when abandoned by Eudocia) to come into the possession of monks;[104] while close by Euthymius' monastery she had founded a church of St. Peter, equipped in its precincts with a huge cistern to serve the needs of the monks.[105]

These details of Eudocia's beneficence, a record of her close association with the monastic community in Palestine, will fall into place beside her involvement with their political role in the years following Chalcedon. They are a telling illustration of the full extent of an empress' patronage in the Holy Land, not exercised from a distance in Constantinople, but utilizing on the spot the properties and revenues at her disposal—in contrast, for example, to the liberality of Melania and Pinianus, who faced the problem of organizing funds from the liquidation of distant estates on the other side of the Mediterranean.

Eudocia's munificence was not confined to the sphere of local villages and desert monks, but was, naturally enough,

---

[100] *V. Pet. Iber.* 114–15.   [101] Ibid. 93.

[102] John Rufus, *Plerophoriae*, 20 (*PO* 8, 39).

[103] *Narr. de obit. Theod. Hieros.* (ed. E. W. Brooks, 1907), 18.

[104] Cyril Scyth. *V. Euthym.* 30; for the history of its monastic occupiers, see id. *V. Sabae*, 38. Description of the site: D. Chitty (1966), 91.

[105] *V. Euthym.* 35.

extended to the principal holy places. In this she was not alone among her contemporaries. Of the foundations in and around Jerusalem itself, we have already noted the monastery of Bassa (she was to receive a letter from the Augusta Pulcheria in an effort to restrain the monks' opposition to Chalcedon).[106] Added to which, there was the monastery and 'church of the martyr Julian' being established on the Mount of Olives by the lady Flavia when the young Cappadocian, Theognius, arrived in Jerusalem in the mid-450s; he found here a haven of orthodoxy at a time when the church establishment in Jerusalem was still dominated by schismatic monks, and remained to take charge of Flavia's monastery.[107] Another new arrival from Cappadocia had an experience similar to that of Theognius: Theodosius, the future colleague of Sabas, found himself recruited to the establishment of a new church of the Virgin being constructed by a certain Icelia at the site known as the 'Kathisma' (Mary's place of rest three miles along the Bethlehem road), where he too was to succeed to the leadership.[108] Of the origins of Flavia and Icelia we know nothing, although their names might suggest a western provenance.[109] Certainly their foundations, on the outskirts of Jerusalem, follow directly in the tradition of previous western visitors; and it might also be observed that, in receiving into their establishments young monastic recruits from Asia Minor, they were repeating a pattern familiar from the last quarter of the fourth century.[110]

Like these contemporaries, Eudocia continued the work of previous well-to-do pilgrims in adding to the buildings of the holy city.[111] She is reported, for instance, to have replaced,

---

[106] Cf. refs. at n. 91, above.

[107] Cyril Scyth. *V. Theogn.* (ed. Schwartz, 241). For the likelihood that 'Julian' was one of the companions in martyrdom of Pamphilus of Caesarea, and much honoured in Jerusalem, see G. Garitte (1958), 234–5, 240–1.

[108] Cyril Scyth. *V. Theod.* (ed. Schwartz, 236). The site belongs to apocryphal tradition: *Protevangelium of James*, 17 (ed. de Strycker, *Subs. Hag.* 33 (1961), 142ff.), with C. Kopp (1959), 30. For possible location: A.M. Schneider, 'Die Kathismakirche', *Journ. Pal. Or. Soc.* 14 (1934), 230ff.

[109] Another *Life* of Theodosius claims Icelia as the widow of an official ('ὕπαρχος'): Theodorus, *V. Theod.* (ed. Usener, 1890), 13.

[110] Cf. Evagrius and Palladius, above, pp. 166ff.

[111] On church building generally in this period, including Eudocia's, see G. T. Armstrong (1969).

after a fire, the cross which surmounted Poemenia's church of the Ascension at the summit of the Mount of Olives—a great landmark of Christian Jerusalem.[112] But it was to be her devotion to St. Stephen, already demonstrated on her earlier pilgrimage, which was to provide the impetus for her most considerable monument in the city. To match her extension of Jerusalem to the south, Eudocia furnished a magnificent new establishment at the site of Stephen's martyrdom at the north gate; the shrine where his relics had been deposited in 439 was now surrounded by a precinct to rival that which the Constantinian builders had constructed around the Holy Sepulchre. An outer wall enclosed a three-aisled basilica 38 m. in length, together with atrium and portico, and an adjoining monastic establishment.[113] Excavated by the Dominicans at the end of the nineteenth century, Eudocia's church of Stephen now lies beneath a modern reconstruction (which dates only from 1900).[114] Her basilica was consecrated on 15 June 460, after the empress had arranged for the maintenance of its revenues, and had placed Gabriel, a disciple of Euthymius, at the head of the establishment.[115] It became one of the principal pilgrim centres in Jerusalem, seen by sixth-century visitors like Theodosius and the pilgrim from Piacenza; while it was to be described by the church historian Evagrius as a 'huge precinct, outstanding in its eminence and beauty'.[116] Eudocia's association with the holy places began and ended with St. Stephen: such was her particular devotion to the first martyr that she chose to have her own tomb here in her newly-built basilica, twenty paces from the remains of Stephen himself.[117] Four months after the consecration, on 20 October 460, she died.[118] In later years there was to be a vivid

[112] John Rufus, *Plerophoriae*, 11 (*PO* 8, 27).

[113] See Vincent/Abel (1914), 766ff.; A. Ovadiah (1970), 77–8.

[114] On the excavations, see M. J. Lagrange (1894), 105ff.

[115] Cyril Scyth. *V. Euthym.* 35.

[116] Evagr. *Hist. Eccl.* i. 22; Theodosius, *De situ terrae sanctae*, 8; Anton. Placent. *Itin.* 25. For its size, cf. the great gathering of 10,000 monks within the precinct in the reign of Anastasius: Cyril Scyth. *V. Sabae*, 56 (ed. Schwartz, 151).

[117] Anton. Placent. l.c. paced it out. For her tomb, cf. Joh. Malal. *Chron.* 358, and *Chron. Pasch.* 585.

[118] Cyril Scyth. *V. Euthym.* 35.

recollection of her presence in the Holy Land, when her grand-daughter and namesake, the child of that marriage of 437 which had been the reason for Eudocia's first pilgrimage, fled to Jerusalem from her Vandal husband, Hunneric—to worship at the holy places and venerate her grandmother's tomb; and ultimately to end her days in the same spot.[119]

Eudocia's burial in her own church of St. Stephen set the seal on her years of pious liberality at the holy places. There was nothing about the occasion to recall the other prominent aspect of her activities after withdrawing to Palestine, her patronage and active support (for a time) of the monophysite monks' opposition to Chalcedon and of a usurping bishop of Jerusalem.[120] It is hardly surprising to find her acting in resistence to an orthodoxy issuing from a court from which she was an exile; whatever was being imposed from Constantinople by her now dominant sister-in-law and her new imperial consort would naturally be viewed with hostility by Eudocia, herself a victim (it has appeared) of court intrigue. Even after her restoration to orthodoxy, Eudocia still managed to remain astride the doctrinal divisions which persisted in the Holy Land, with a foot in both camps—continuing her patronage of monks who were unreconciled to Chalcedon, including her old protégé, Peter the Iberian.[121] Tradition recounts that what persuaded her to cease her active support of the rebellious leaders was, characteristically, the prompting of a monk—the revered Euthymius, who had never wavered from the path of orthodoxy. Letters from her relatives, including the western emperor Valentinian III (her son-in-law), and from Leo bishop of Rome had failed to change Eudocia's allegiance;[122] but with the news of the disasters suffered by her family in Rome in 455, the assassination of the emperor and the seizure by the Vandals of her daughter

[119] Theophanes, *Chron.* (ed. de Boor), 118.

[120] For the political background of what follows, see A. Couret (1869), 117ff.; E. Honigmann (1950), 247ff.; D. Chitty (1966), 89ff.; W. H. C. Frend (1972a), 148–54.

[121] Honigmann, 256, and above, p. 240 (Romanus).

[122] Cyril Scyth. *V. Euthym.* 30 speaks of letters from her brother Valerius and from her grand-daughter's husband Olybrius (destined to be emperor, briefly, in 472); for letters from Valentinian III and Leo, see *Acta Conc. Oec.* ii. 4, 69.

and grandchildren, her conviction was shaken.[123] She turned
first for advice to Symeon Stylites, and it was he who recom-
mended the authority of Euthymius; this holy man, coming
to meet her in her 'tower' in the desert, there exhorted her to
end her support of the schismatics and return to the true
faith of the church as enunciated by four general councils.
Consequently Eudocia returned to communion with bishop
Juvenal in Jerusalem, bringing over with her many monks
and laymen eager to follow her example.

The aftermath of Chalcedon was obviously not the first
occasion which had seen the holy places at odds over a major
issue of church politics: the dissension between Jerusalem
and Bethlehem, first over Origenism, then over Pelagius, was
recent history. These earlier disputes had focused on two
particular immigrant settlements which had confronted each
other, drawing into the conflict the network of influential
contacts which each of them could command—contacts
established and fostered by the pattern of movements to and
from the holy places. By 451, however, it was no longer true
that the protagonists were a relatively confined group of foreign visitors to the holy places; the first half of the fifth century witnessed a concentration of monks in Jerusalem and
the surrounding desert which far outnumbered the first western settlements, and whose origins represented, by their diversity, the 'international' appeal of the Holy Land.[124]
Among Euthymius' early recruits to his monastery, to take a
well-documented example, there were, besides some from
Palestine itself, three brothers from his own home-town of
Melitene in Armenia, three more brothers from Cappadocia, as well as the Antiochene Domnus (the future
bishop of his city);[125] the most illustrious of his disciples,
Sabas, would come to Jerusalem from his village on the
outskirts of Cappadocian Caesarea.[126] These monks did not
remain aloof in their desert retreats, but rose to high office in
the local church. Of the brothers from Melitene, one

---

[123] Cyril Scyth. l.c.; cf. E. Stein, *Histoire du Bas-Empire*, 365ff.

[124] Cf. the summary of evidence in E. Schwartz's edition of Cyril of Scythopolis,
359.

[125] *V. Euthym.* 16; on this list, cf. Chitty, 85.

[126] *V. Sabae*, 1 (his origins), 6 (removal to Jerusalem).

(Stephen) joined the clergy of the church of the *Anastasis*, and subsequently became bishop of Jamnia, while another (Andrew) was placed in charge of Bassa's monastery in Jerusalem.[127] The Cappadocians all came to hold office in the Jerusalem church: Cosmas in the important position of 'guardian of the cross' (he became bishop of Scythopolis), and his brothers Gabriel and Chrysippus, through the patronage of Eudocia, as presbyters of the *Anastasis*;[128] it was Gabriel whom Eudocia placed in charge of the new church of St. Stephen.[129] The monks of Palestine, their diversity represented by this group of Euthymius' followers, thus came to be intimately connected with the public life and worship of the church in the Holy Land; by their proximity to, and involvement with, the affairs of the Jerusalem church they brought to the holy places themselves the controversies in which they were participants. The contrast with the situation in the 390s is marked. Before, the arguments and their repercussions had been limited to a select company of foreigners settled in and around Jerusalem, mostly asectic devotees or well-born refugees, who developed and exploited their own particular far-flung spheres of influence. By now the growth of pilgrimage and the status of the holy places in the Christian empire meant that their 'internationalism' was no longer something sustained at the more remote level of the alliances of Jerome or Melania, but was very evidently represented on the spot—not only in the varied personnel of the ecclesiastical establishment, but in the presence of so distinguished and influential a patron as Eudocia, actually resident in the Holy Land (and not 1200 miles away at the court in Constantinople). Still, however, this widespread focus on the holy places was no guarantee of unanimity. The visitor might observe that they spoke (as in previous controversies) with a divided voice: on the Mount of Olives, for example, the monasteries of Melania now presided over by Gerontius remained unre-

---

[127] Stephen: *V. Euthym.* 20. Andrew: ibid. 30. The third brother became a bishop, of Madaba (ibid. 34).

[128] Cosmas: *V. Euthym.* 20. Gabriel and Chrysippus: ibid. 30. Chrysippus replaced Cosmas as 'guardian of the cross' when the latter was promoted to Scythopolis (ibid. 37).

[129] *V. Euthym.* 30, 35.

conciled to bishop Juvenal and maintained the anti-
Chalcedonian view, while the nearby foundation of Flavia
championed the official orthodoxy.[130]

Nor could the argument be confined to the Holy Land.
The thread running through previous chapters has been the
transformation of the holy places from their local status
among the congregation of Jerusalem and its surroundings
into a pivot of devotion for Christians all over the empire.
This universal veneration in which the biblical sites were
held, as the visible nucleus of the faith, was potentially a
uniquely influential weapon in ecclesiastical politics. Just as
at the time of the discovery of the Tomb the holy places had
been triumphantly held up by Eusebius as proclaiming to a
non-Christian world the truth of the claims of Christianity,
so their 'evidence' might now be cited against opposition
within the church itself; and especially so where the doctrinal
disagreement centred on the status of Christ's earthly existence, of which there might be no more manifest statement
than the physical remains of the Gospel record. In this way
the holy places entered the argument in firm support of
orthodoxy. Pope Leo made full use of them in his appeals to
the opponents of Chalcedon: he complained that bishop
Juvenal's dissent 'from the truth of the Lord's incarnation'
had been in the face of the witness of the holy places, 'by
which the whole world is taught';[131] writing to Juvenal himself, Leo listed the separate witnesses to the life of Christ
represented by the holy places, the 'unassailable proofs of the
Catholic faith'—Bethlehem, the cross, the Tomb, the Mount
of Olives: surrounded as he was by this evidence of his own
eyes, Juvenal did not have the option of disbelief.[132] It was in
the same vein that Leo, at the behest of the eastern court,
wrote to Eudocia herself; her decision to reside in Jerusalem,
he argued, confronted her with the truths of the faith which
she could not ignore:

---

[130] For Gerontius' persistence in opposition, ibid. 30; on Flavia and orthodoxy,
above, p. 241.

[131] Leo, *Ep.* 113 (11 March 453) to Julian bishop of Cos (*Acta Conc. Oec.* ii. 4, 66);
cf. *Ep.* 109 (ibid. 138) 'ipsa sanctorum locorum circa quae habitant testificatione'.

[132] *Ep.* 139 (4 Sept. 454: *Acta Conc. Oec.* ii. 4, 91ff.) 'quod alibi non licet non credi,
ibi non potest non videri. quid laborat intellectus, ubi est magister aspectus?'.

...where the signs of his miracles and the proofs of his sufferings proclaim that Jesus Christ is true God and true man in one person.[133]

That the holy places might thus be appealed to by a bishop of Rome writing to an eastern empress is some indication of the central place which the Holy Land had now come to occupy across the geographical and ecclesiastical divisions of the later Roman empire. The place which to a Roman magistrate in 310 had been known only as part of the incomprehensible fantasy of a would-be martyr had now been openly transformed into the acknowledged heart of a Christian empire, its holy places seen as visible, present confirmation of the faith and testifying to the fact of the biblical narrative. The presence of Eudocia in Jerusalem, and the evidence of her buildings—echoing the role of Helena at an earlier time—were reminders that it was the interest of the imperial court and its patronage and beneficence which since the time of Constantine had been the stimulus for the new recognition of the Holy Land. This was the goal which had drawn pilgrims from east and west, whose satisfaction was to see the biblical sites and participate in their worship, even to take a portion of them away to their homelands. It was also the goal which in attracting the attention of leading churchmen attracted also the political controversies which they waged. The holy places had become too important to be left out.

A modern writer has spoken of 'the power of the holy places in keeping their devotees to a sober, historical faith'.[134] There will be many who have found in the early development of the holy places neither history nor sobriety, preferring instead to see the experience of the late Roman pilgrims (to say nothing of their successors over the centuries) as heady credulity—even contemporaries, like Jerome or Gregory of Nyssa, could at times be sceptical of the Holy Land pilgrimage. Yet much of the evidence recounted in this book has reflected a reality too substantial to be brushed

[133] *Ep.* 123 (15 June 453, ibid. 77). Similar arguments were used by the monks at the holy places in a letter to the emperor Anastasius: Cyril Scyth. *V. Sabae*, 57.
[134] D. Chitty (1966), 114.

aside: emperors and their courts, and men and women of the
nobility, lavishing their fortunes on the Holy Land; bishops
and church politicians laying claim to the holy places to bol-
ster their points of view; pilgrims from far afield determinedly
in search of the biblical past. We have seen the holy places,
and the solid piety which surrounded them, very evidently
answering to the newly confident Christianity of the later Roman empire. Bishop Leo of Rome, indeed, in seeking to win
over his counterpart in Jerusalem to orthodoxy, was able to
take for granted the conclusive contribution which the holy
places had given to the faith: 'why need the mind toil, when
sight is the master?'

Bibliography

(I) PRINCIPAL ANCIENT SOURCES

AMBROSE, *De Obitu Theodosii*, ed. O. Faller (*CSEL* 73, 1955).

ANTONINUS PLACENTINUS, *Itinerarium*, ed. P. Geyer (*CC* 175 (1965), 127–53).

Armenian Lectionary, ed. A. Renoux, *Le Codex Arménien Jérusalem 121* (*PO* 35–6, 1969–71).

AUGUSTINE, *De Gestis Pelagii*, ed. C.F. Urba & J. Zycha (*CSEL* 42, 1902).

——, *Epistulae*, ed. A. Goldbacher (*CSEL*, 1895–1923).

Breviarius de Hierosolyma, ed. R. Weber (*CC* 175 (1965), 107–12).

CALLINICUS, *Vita Hypatii*, ed. G.J.M. Bartelink, *Vie d'Hypatios* (*SChr* 177, 1971).

Chronicon Paschale, ed. L. Dindorf (Bonn, 1832).

CYRIL OF JERUSALEM, *Catecheses* and *Epistula ad Constantium*, ed. G.C. Reischl & J. Rupp (Munich, 1848–60).

CYRIL OF SCYTHOPOLIS, *Vita Euthymii, Vita Sabae,* and other saints' lives, ed. E. Schwartz, *Kyrillos von Skythopolis* (*TU* 49, 1939).

EUSEBIUS, *Demonstratio Evangelica*, ed. I. A. Heikel (*GCS*, 1913).

——, *Historia Ecclesiastica*, ed. G. Bardy (*SChr*, 1952–60).

——, *Onomastikon*, ed. E. Klostermann (*GCS*, 1904 repr. 1966). This volume includes the translation by Jerome.

——, *Tricennial Oration*, ed. I. A. Heikel (*GCS*, 1902).

——, *Vita Constantini*, ed. F. Winkelmann (*GCS*, 1975).

EVAGRIUS, *Historia Ecclesiastica*, ed. J. Bidez & L. Parmentier (London, 1898).

GREGORY OF NYSSA, *Epistulae*, ed. G. Pasquali (Leiden, 1959).

——, *Vita Moysi*, ed. J. Daniélou (*SChr* 1, 3rd edn., 1968).

Historia Monachorum in Aegypto, ed. A.–J. Festugière (*Subs. Hag.* 53, 1971).

Itinerarium Burdigalense, ed. P. Geyer & O. Cuntz (*CC* 175 (1965), 1–26).

Itinerarium Egeriae, ed. A. Franceschini & R. Weber (*CC* 175, 29–90).

JEROME, *Apologia contra Rufinum, Contra Ioannem Hierosolymitanum* and *Contra Vigilantium*, ed. J.-P. Migne (*PL* 23).

——, *Chronicon*, ed. R. Helm (*GCS*, 1956).

——, *De Viris Illustribus*, ed. E. C. Richardson (*TU* 14, 1896).

——, *Epistulae*, ed. I. A. Hilberg (*CSEL* 54–6, 1910–18). The biblical commentaries of Jerome, when referred to in the footnotes, are cited from *CC* where available, otherwise from *PL*.

JOHN MALALAS, *Chronographia*, ed. L. Dindorf (Bonn, 1831).

MARCUS DIACONUS, *Vita Porphyrii*, ed. H. Grégoire & M.-A. Kugener (Budé *Coll. Byz.* 1930).

ORIGEN, *Commentary on St. John*, ed. E. Preuschen (*GCS*, 1903).

——, *Commentary on St. Matthew*, ed. E. Klostermann and others (*GCS*, 1933–68).

——, *Contra Celsum*, ed. M. Borret (*SChr*, 1967–76).

——, *De Principiis*, ed. P. Koetschau (*GCS*, 1913).

OROSIUS, *Commonitorium de errore Priscillianistarum et Origenistarum*, ed. G. Schepss (*CSEL* 18, 1889).

——, *Historiae adversum Paganos* and *Liber Apologeticus*, ed. C. Zangemeister (*CSEL* 5, 1882).

PALLADIUS, *Dialogus de vita S. Joannis Chrysostomi*, ed. P.R. Coleman-Norton (Cambridge, 1928).

——, *Historia Lausiaca*, ed. C. Butler (Texts and Studies 6, Cambridge, 1898–1904).

PAULINUS OF NOLA, *Carmina* and *Epistulae*, ed. G. de Hartel (*CSEL* 29–30, 1894).

PETRUS DIACONUS, *Liber de locis sanctis*, ed. R. Weber (*CC* 175 (1965), 91–103). This text contains passages deriving from Egeria.

PRUDENTIUS, *Peristephanon* and *Tituli Historiarum*, ed. M.P. Cunningham (*CC* 126, 1966).

RUFINUS OF AQUILEIA, *Apologia ad Anastasium* and *Apologia contra Hieronymum*, ed. M. Simonetti (*CC* 20, 1961).

——, *Historia Ecclesiastica*, ed. T. Mommsen (*GCS*, 1908).

SOCRATES, *Historia Ecclesiastica*, ed. R. Hussey (Oxford, 1853).

SOZOMEN, *Historia Ecclesiastica*, ed. J. Bidez & G.C. Hansen (*GCS*, 1960).

SULPICIUS SEVERUS, *Chronica* and *Dialogus*, ed. C. Halm (*CSEL* 1, 1866).

THEODORET, *Historia Ecclesiastica*, ed. L. Parmentier & F. Scheidweiler (*GCS*, 1954).

THEODOSIUS, *De situ terrae sanctae*, ed. P. Geyer (*CC* 175 (1965), 113–25).

THEOPHANES, *Chronographia*, ed. C. de Boor (Leipzig, 1883).

Vita Melaniae, ed. D. Gorce, *Vie de Sainte Mélanie* (*SChr* 90, 1962).

Vita Petri Iberi, ed. R. Raabe, *Petrus der Iberer* (Leipzig, 1895).

(II) SECONDARY WORKS

ABEL, F. M., 'La sépulture de Saint Jacques le Mineur', *Rev. Bibl.* n.s. 16 (1919), 480–99.

——, 'St. Jérôme et Jérusalem', *Miscellanea Geronimiana* (Rome, 1920), 131–55.

——, 'Ou en est la question de Caphargamala?', *Rev. Bibl.* 33 (1924), 235–45.

——, *Géographie de la Palestine* (2 vols., Paris, 1933–8).

——, 'St. Cyrille d'Alexandrie dans ses rapports avec la Palestine', *Kyrilliana* (Cairo, 1947), 203–30.

ALEXANDER, S.S., 'Studies in Constantinian Church Architecture', *Rivista di Archeologia Cristiana*, 47 (1971), 281–330; ibid. 49 (1973), 33–44.

ALTANER, B., 'Avitus von Braga', *ZKG* 60 (1941), 456–68 (= *Kleine patristische Schriften* (Berlin, 1967), 450–66).

ANTIN, P., 'La ville chez Saint Jérôme', *Latomus*, 20 (1961), 298–311.

ARMSTRONG, G.T., 'Fifth and Sixth Century Church Buildings in the Holy Land', *Greek Orthodox Theological Review*, 14 (1969), 17–30.

ARNHEIM, M.T.W., *The Senatorial Aristocracy in the Later Roman Empire* (Oxford, 1972).

AVI-YONAH, M., *Map of Roman Palestine* (Jerusalem, 1940).

——, *The Madaba Mosaic Map* (Jerusalem, 1954).

——, 'The Economics of Byzantine Palestine', *IEJ* 8 (1958), 39–51.

——, *The Holy Land from the Persian to the Arab Conquests (536 BC—AD 640), a historical geography* (Grand Rapids, 1966).

—— (ed.), *Encyclopedia of Archaeological Investigations in the Holy Land* (Engl. edn., London, 1975–8).

——, *The Jews of Palestine: a political history from the Bar Kokhba War to the Arab Conquest* (Oxford, 1976).

BACHT, H., 'Die Rolle der orientalischen Mönchtums in den kirchenpolitischen Auseinandersetzungen um Chalkedon', in *Das Konzil von Chalkedon*, ii (Würzburg, 1953), 193–314.

BAGATTI, B. 'Eulogie Palestinesi', *Or. Christ. Period.* 15 (1949), 126–66.

——, *Gli antichi edifici sacri di Betlemme* (Jerusalem, 1952).

——, *L'Eglise de la Gentilité en Palestine* (Jerusalem, 1968a).

——, 'Recenti scavi a Betlemme', *Liber Annuus*, 18 (1968b), 181–237.

BARDY, G., 'Pèlerinages à Rome vers la fin du ive siècle', *Anal. Boll.* 67 (1949), 224–35.

BARNES, T.D., 'The Composition of Eusebius' Onomasticon', *JTS* n.s. 26 (1975), 412–15.

——, 'Two Speeches by Eusebius', *GRBS* 18 (1977), 341–5.

BASTIAENSEN, A.A.R., *Observations sur le vocabulaire liturgique dans l' Itinéraire d'Egérie* (Latinitas Christianorum Primaeva 17, Nijmegen, 1962)

BAUMSTARK, A., 'Frühchristlich-palästinesische Bildkompositionen in abendländischer Spiegelung', *Byz. Zeitschr.* 20 (1911), 177ff.

——, *Comparative Liturgy* (ed. F.L. Cross, London, 1958).

BEAUVERY, R., 'La route romaine de Jérusalem à Jericho', *Rev. Bibl.* 64 (1957), 72–101.

BECKER, E., 'Konstantin der Grosse, der "neue Moses" ', *ZKG* 31 (1910), 161–71.

BERKHOF, H., *Die Theologie des Eusebius von Caesarea* (Amsterdam, 1939).

BLACK, M., 'The Festival of Encaenia Ecclesiae', *JEH* 5 (1954), 78–85.

BLUDAU, A., *Die Pilgerreise der Aetheria* (Paderborn, 1927).

BOTTE, B., *Les origines de la Noël et de l'Epiphanie* (Louvain, 1932).

BROCK, S.P., 'The rebuilding of the Temple under Julian, a new source', *PEQ* 108 (1976), 103–7.

BROWN, P., 'Pelagius and his supporters: aims and environment', *JTS* n.s. 19 (1968), 93–114 (= *Religion and Society in the Age of St. Augustine* (London, 1972), 183–207).

——, 'The Patrons of Pelagius: the Roman Aristocracy between East and West', *JTS* n.s.21 (1970), 56–72 (= *Religion and Society*, 208–26).

BUCK, D.F., 'The Structure of the *Lausiac History*', *Byzantion*, 46 (1976), 292–307.

BUTLER, C., 'Palladiana', *JTS* 22 (1920–1), 21–35, 138–55.

CABIÉ, R., *La Pentecôte: L'évolution de la cinquantaine pascale au cours des cinq premiers siècles* (Tournai, 1965).

CABROL, F., *Les Eglises de Jérusalem. La Discipline et la Liturgie au ive siècle* (Paris, 1895).

CAMERON, A., 'Wandering Poets: a literary movement in Byzantine Egypt', *Historia*, 14 (1965), 470–509.

CASSON, L., *Ships and Seamanship in the Ancient World* (Princeton, 1971).

——, *Travel in the Ancient World* (London, 1974).

CAVALLERA, F., *Saint Jérôme, sa vie et son oeuvre* (Louvain, 1922).

CHADWICK, H., 'The Fall of Eustathius of Antioch', *JTS* 49 (1948), 27–35.

——, *The Circle and the Ellipse: Rival Concepts of Authority in the Early Church* (Inaug. Lect. Oxford, 1959).

——, 'Faith and Order at the Council of Nicaea', *Harvard Theological Review*, 53 (1960), 171–95.

——, *Priscillian of Avila* (Oxford, 1976).

CHADWICK, O., *John Cassian, a study in primitive monasticism* (2nd. edn. Cambridge, 1968).

CHARLESWORTH, M.P., *Trade Routes and Commerce of the Roman Empire* (Cambridge, 1924).

CHASTAGNOL, A., 'Le sénateur Volusien et la conversion d'une famille de l'aristocratie romaine au Bas-Empire', *Rev. Et. Anc.* 58 (1956), 241–53.

——, *Les Fastes de la Préfecture de Rome au Bas-Empire* (Paris, 1962).

CHITTY, D.J., *The Desert a City* (Oxford, 1966).

CONANT, J., 'The Original Buildings at the Holy Sepulchre in Jerusalem', *Speculum*, 31 (1956), 1–48.

CONSTANTELOS, D.J., 'Kyros Panapolites, Rebuilder of Constantinople', *GRBS* 12 (1971), 451–64.

COÜASNON, C., *The Church of the Holy Sepulchre in Jerusalem* (British Academy Schweich Lecture, London, 1974).

COURCELLE, P., 'Paulin de Nole et Saint Jérôme', *Rev. Et. Lat.* 25 (1947), 250–80.

COURET, A., *La Palestine sous les empereurs grecs* (Paris, 1869).

CROWFOOT, J.W., *Early Churches in Palestine* (British Academy Schweich Lecture, London, 1941).

CROUZEL, H., *Origène et la 'connaissance mystique'* (Paris, 1961).

——, 'Saint Jérôme et ses amis toulousains', *Bull. Lit. Eccl.* 73 (1972), 125–46.

DAGRON, G., 'Le monachisme à Constantinople jusqu'au concile de Chalcédoine', *Travaux et Mémoires*, 4 (1970), 229–76.

DAUPHIN, C., 'Symbolic or Decorative? The inhabited scroll as a means of studying some early Byzantine mentalities', *Byzantion*, 48 (1978), 10–34.

DAVIES, J.G., 'The *Peregrinatio Egeriae* and the Ascension', *Vig. Christ.* 8 (1954), 93–100.

——, 'Eusebius' Description of the Martyrium at Jerusalem', *Amer. Journ. Arch.* 61 (1957), 171–3.

DEICHMANN, F.W., & TSCHIRA, A., 'Das Mausoleum der Kaiserin Helena', *Jahrb. des deutschen archäol. Inst.* 72 (1957), 44ff.

DE LANGE, N.R.M., *Origen and the Jews, studies in Jewish-Christian rela-*

tions in third century Palestine (Cambridge, 1976).

DELEHAYE, H., 'Les premiers "libelli miraculorum" ', *Anal. Boll.* 29 (1910), 427–34.

——, 'Les recueils antiques de miracles des saints', *Anal. Boll.* 43 (1925), 74–85.

——, *Les origines du culte des martyrs* (2nd edn. Brussels, 1933).

DELVOYE, Ch., 'Etudes d'architecture paléochrétienne et byzantine', *Byzantion*, 32 (1962), 261ff.

DEVOS, P., 'La date du voyage d'Egérie', *Anal. Boll.* 85 (1967a), 165–94.

——, 'Egérie à Edesse', *Anal. Boll.* 85 (1967b), 381–400.

——, 'Egérie à Bethléem', *Anal. Boll.* 86 (1968a), 87–108.

——, 'Le Panégyrique de Saint Etienne par Hésychius de Jérusalem', *Anal. Boll.* 86 (1968b), 151–72.

——, 'Quand Pierre l'Ibère vint-il à Jérusalem?', *Anal. Boll.* 86 (1968c), 337–50.

——, 'La "Servante de Dieu" Poemenia', *Anal. Boll.* 87 (1969), 189–212.

——, 'Silvie la sainte pèlerine', *Anal Boll.* 91 (1973), 105–20.

——, 'Silvie la sainte pèlerine II', *Anal. Boll.* 92 (1974), 321–43.

DIX, G., *The Shape of the Liturgy* (Westminster, 1945).

DÖLGER, F.J., 'Das Anhängekreuzchen der hl. Makrina und ihr Ring mit der Kreuzpartikel', *Antike und Christentum*, 3 (1932), 81–116.

DOWNEY, G., 'The Perspective of the Early Church Historians', *GRBS* 6 (1965), 57–70.

DRAGUET, R., 'L'Histoire Lausiaque, une oeuvre écrite dans l'esprit d'Evagre', *Revue d'histoire ecclésiastique*, 41 (1946), 321–64; ibid. 42 (1947), 5–49.

DRAKE, H.A., *In Praise of Constantine* (Univ. of California Publications: Classical Studies 15, Berkeley, 1976).

——, 'A Coptic version of the discovery of the Holy Sepulchre', *GRBS* 20 (1979), 381–92.

DUCHESNE, L., *Christian Worship: its origin and evolution* (5th edn. London, 1919).

EVANS, R.F., *Pelagius: Inquiries and Reappraisals* (London, 1968).

FABRE, P., *Essai sur la chronologie de l'oeuvre de Saint Paulin de Nole* (Paris, 1948).

FAVALE, A., *Teofilo d'Alessandria, scritti, vita e dottrina* (Turin, 1958).

FAVEZ, Ch., 'L'épisode de l'invention de la croix dans l'Oraison Funèbre de Théodose', *Rev. Et. Lat.* 10 (1932), 423–9.

FÉROTIN, M., 'Le veritable auteur de la "Peregrinatio Silviae", la vierge espagnole Ethéria', *Revue des questions historiques*, 74 (1903), 367–97.

FRANKENBERG, W., *Evagrius Ponticus (Abhandlungen Göttingen,* phil.-hist. Klasse, n.f. 13, 2; Berlin, 1912).

FREND, W.H.C., 'Paulinus of Nola and the last century of the western empire', *JRS* 59 (1969), 1–11.

——, *The Rise of the Monophysite Movement* (Cambridge, 1972a).

——, 'The monks and the survival of the east Roman empire in the fifth century', *Past and Present,* 54 (1972b), 1–24.

FROLOW, A., *La Relique de la Vraie Croix* (Paris, 1961).

GARITTE, G., *Le Calendrier Palestino-géorgien du Sinaiticus 34 (xᵉ siècle)* (*Subs. Hag.* 30, Brussels, 1958).

GAUDEMET, J., *L'Eglise dans l'Empire Romain* (Paris, 1958).

GIET, S., *Les Idées et L'Action Sociales de Saint Basile* (Paris, 1941).

GILLMAN, I., 'Some reflections on Constantine's "apostolic" consciousness', *TU* 79 (1961), 422–8.

GOLDSCHMIDT, R., *Paulinus' Churches at Nola* (Amsterdam, 1940).

GORCE, D., *La Lectio Divina* (Diss. Poitiers, 1925a).

——, *Les voyages, l'hospitalité et le port des lettres dans le monde chrétien des ivᵉ et vᵉ siècles* (Diss. Poitiers, 1925b).

——, Die Gastfreundlichkeit der altchristlichen Einsiedler und Mönche', *JbAC* 15 (1972), 66–91.

GORDINI, G.D., 'Il monachesimo romano in Palestina nel iv secolo', in *Saint Martin et son temps* (= *Studia Anselmiana,* 46 (1961), 85–107).

GOUBERT, P., 'Le rôle de Sainte Pulchérie et de l'eunuque Chrysaphios', in *Das Konzil von Chalkedon,* i (Würzburg, 1951), 303–21.

GRABAR, A., *Martyrium, recherches sur le culte de reliques et l'art chrétien antique* (Paris, 1946).

——, *Ampoules de Terre Sainte* (Paris, 1958).

GREGOROVIUS, F., *Athenais. Geschichte einer byzantinischen Kaiserin* (Leipzig, 1882).

GRIBOMONT, J., 'L'influence du monachisme oriental sur Sulpice Sévère', in *Saint Martin et son temps* (= *Studia Anselmiana,* 46 (1961), 135–49).

GUILLAUMONT, A., *Les 'Kephaleia Gnostica' d'Evagre le Pontique* (Patristica Sorbonensia 5, Paris, 1962).

GUTHRIE, P., 'The execution of Crispus', *Phoenix,* 20 (1966), 325–31.

HAMILTON, R.W., 'The Churches at Gaza, as described by Choricius of Gaza', *PEFQS* 62 (1930), 178–91.

——, *The Church of the Nativity at Bethlehem: a Guide* (Jerusalem, 1947).

HAMMOND, C.P., 'The last ten years of Rufinus' life and the date of his move south from Aquileia', *JTS* n.s. 28 (1977), 372–429.

HARVEY, A.E., 'Melito and Jerusalem', *JTS* n.s. 17 (1966), 401–4.

HEISENBERG, A., *Grabeskirche und Apostelkirche, zwei Basiliken Konstantins* (Leipzig, 1908).

HOHLWEIN, N., 'Déplacements et Tourisme dans l'Egypte romaine', *Chronique d'Egypte*, 15 (1940), 253–78.

HONIGMANN, E., 'Le cubiculaire Urbicius', *Rev. Et. Byz.* 7 (1949), 47–50.

——, 'Juvenal of Jerusalem', *Dumbarton Oaks Papers*, 5 (1950), 209–79.

HUNT, E.D., 'St. Silvia of Aquitaine: the role of a Theodosian pilgrim in the society of East and West', *JTS* n.s. 23 (1972), 351–73.

——, 'Palladius of Helenopolis: a party and its supporters in the church·of the late fourth century', *JTS* n.s. 24 (1973), 456–80.

JANIN, R., *Constantinople Byzantine* (2nd edn. Paris, 1964).

JEREMIAS, J., *Golgotha* (Leipzig, 1926).

——, *Heiligengräber in Jesu Umwelt* (Göttingen, 1958).

——, *Jerusalem in the Time of Jesus* (transl. F.H. & C.H. Cave, London, 1969).

KELLY, J.N.D., *Jerome, his life, writings, and controversies* (London, 1975).

KENYON, K.M., *Digging up Jerusalem* (London, 1974).

KLEBERG, T., *Hôtels, Restaurants et Cabarets dans l'antiquité romain* (Uppsala, 1957).

KLOSTERMANN, E., 'Eusebius Schrift περὶ τῶν τοπικῶν ὀνομάτων', (*TU* 23, Leipzig, 1902).

KÖTTING, B.J., *Peregrinatio Religosa* (Münster, 1950).

——, 'Gregor von Nyssa's Wallfahrtskritik', *Studia Patristica*, 5 (= *TU* 80, 1959), 360–7.

KOPP, C., *Die heiligen Stätten der Evangelien* (Regensburg, 1959).

——, *The Holy Places of the Gospels* (transl. R. Walls, Freiburg, 1963).

KRAUTHEIMER, R., 'Mensa—Coemeterium—Martyrium', *Cahiers Archéologiques*, 11 (1960), 15–40.

——, *Early Christian and Byzantine Architecture* (Harmondsworth, 1965).

——, 'The Constantinian Basilica', *Dumbarton Oaks Papers*, 21 (1967), 117–40.

KRETSCHMAR, G., 'Himmelfahrt und Pfingsten', *ZKG* 66 (1954–5), 209–53.

——, 'Die frühe Geschichte der Jerusalemer Liturgie', *Jahrb. für Liturgik und Hymnologie*, 2 (1956), 22–46.

——, 'Festkalender und Memorialstätten Jerusalems in

altkirchlicher Zeit', *ZDPV* 87 (1971), 167–205.

——, 'Mambre: von der "Basilika" zum "Martyrium"', *Mélanges liturgiques offerts au r. p. dom B. Botte* (Louvain, 1972), 272–93.

LACROIX, B., *Orose et ses idées* (Montreal, 1965).

LAGRANGE, M.J., *Saint Etienne et son sanctuaire à Jérusalem* (Paris, 1894).

LANG, D.M., 'Peter the Iberian and his biographers', *JEH* 2 (1951), 158–68.

LASSUS, J., 'Images de Stylites', *Bulletin d'Etudes Orientales*, 2 (1932), 67–82.

——, 'L'Empereur Constantin, Eusèbe et les Lieux Saints', *Revue de l'Histoire des Religions*, 171 (1967), 135–44.

LEROUX, J.-M., 'Jean Chrysostome et la querelle origéniste', *Epektasis. Mélanges patristiques offerts au card. J. Daniélou* (Paris, 1972), 335–41.

LIEBESCHUETZ, J.H.W.G., *Antioch: City and Imperial Administration in the Later Roman Empire* (Oxford, 1972).

——, 'Epigraphic Evidence on the Christianisation of Syria', *Akten des xi internationalen Limeskongresses* (Budapest, 1978), 485–505.

——, 'Problems arising from the conversion of Syria', *The Church in Town and Countryside* (= *Studies in Church History* 16, 1979), 17–24.

LIPPOLD, A., 'Orosius, christlicher Apologet und römischer Bürger', *Philologus*, 113 (1969), 92–105.

LOUIS, R., 'La Visite des Saintes Femmes au Tombeau', *Mémoires de la Société Nationale des Antiquaires de France*, 9e série, t. 3 (1954), 109–22.

LUDWICH, A., 'Eudokia, die Gattin des Kaisers Theodosius II, als Dichterin', *Rhein. Mus.* 37 (1882), 206–25.

MACCORMACK, S., 'Change and Continuity in Late Antiquity: the Ceremony of *Adventus*', *Historia*, 21 (1972), 721–52.

MACMULLEN, R., *Constantine* (London, 1970).

MADER, E., *Mambre* (Freiburg im Breisgau, 1957).

MAGIE, D., *Roman Rule in Asia Minor (to the end of the third century after Christ)* (Princeton, 1950).

MARTIN, J., 'Die Revelatio S. Stephani und Verwandtes', *Historisches Jahrbuch*, 77 (1958), 419–33.

MATEOS, J., 'La vigile cathédrale chez Egérie', *Or. Christ. Period.* 27 (1961), 281–312.

MATTHEWS, J.F., 'A Pious Supporter of Theodosius I: Maternus Cynegius and his family', *JTS* n.s. 18 (1967), 438–46.

——, *Western Aristocracies and Imperial Court AD 353–425* (Oxford, 1975).

MILLAR, Fergus, *The Emperor in the Roman World, 31BC-AD337* (London, 1977).

MOMIGLIANO, A. (ed.), *The Conflict between Paganism and Christianity in the Fourth Century* (Oxford, 1963).

MONTGOMERY, H., 'Konstantin, Paulus und das Lichtkreuz', *Symbolae Osloenses*, 43 (1968), 84–109.

MOSSAY, J., *Les Fêtes de Noël et d'Epiphanie d'après les sources littéraires cappadociennes du iv* siècle (Louvain, 1965).

MURPHY, F.X., *Rufinus of Aquileia (345-411), His Life and Works* (Diss. Washington, 1945).

——, 'Melania the Elder, a biographical note', *Traditio*, 5 (1947), 59–78.

——, 'Rufinus of Aquileia and Paulinus of Nola', *Rev. Et. August.* 2 (1956), 79–91.

NAUTIN, P., 'L'excommunication de Saint Jérôme', *Ecole Pratique des hautes études (v* section), *Annuaire*, 80–81 (1971–2, 1972–3), fasc. 2, 7–37.

——, 'Etudes de chronologie hieronymienne (393–397)', *Rev. Et. August.* 18 (1972), 209–18; ibid. 19 (1973), 69–86, 213–39; ibid. 20 (1974), 251–84.

——, *Origène, sa vie et son oeuvre* (Paris, 1977).

OAKESHOTT, W.F., *The Mosaics of Rome* (London, 1967).

OMMESLAEGHE, F. van, 'Que vaut le témoinage de Pallade sur le procès de saint Jean Chrysostome?', *Anal. Boll.* 95 (1977), 389–413.

OVADIAH, A., *Corpus of the Byzantine Churches in the Holy Land* (transl. R. Kirson, Bonn, 1970).

PARROT, A., *Golgotha and the Church of the Holy Sepulchre* (transl. E. Hudson, London, 1957).

PASCHOUD, F., 'Zosime 2, 29 et la version paienne de la conversion de Constantin', *Historia*, 20 (1971), 334–53 (= *Cinq Etudes sur Zosime* (Paris, 1975), ch. 2).

PAULIN, A., *Saint Cyrille de Jérusalem Cathéchète* (Paris, 1959).

PEETERS, P., 'Le sanctuaire de la lapidation de S. Etienne', *Anal. Boll.* 27 (1908), 359–68.

——, *Le Tréfonds Oriental de l'Hagiographie Byzantine* (*Subs. Hag.* 26, Brussels, 1950).

PFLAUM, H., *Essai sur le cursus publicus sous le haut-empire romain* (Acad. Inscr. et Belles Lettres, *Mémoires présentés par divers savants*, 14, 1940).

PIETRI, Ch., *Roma Christiana* (Rome, 1976).

PIGANIOL, A., *L'Empire Chrétien* (2nd edn. Paris, 1972).

PLINVAL, G. de, *Pélage: ses écrits, sa vie et sa réforme* (Lausanne, 1943).

RAMSAY, W.M., *The Historical Geography of Asia Minor* (London, 1890).

——, 'Roads and Travel in the New Testament', in *Dictionary of the Bible* (ed. J. Hastings, extra vol. 1904), 375–402.

REEKMANS, L., 'Siedlungsbildung bei spätantiken Wallfahrtsstätten', *Pietas* (Festschrift B. Kötting, Münster, 1980), 325–55.

REES, B.R., 'Theophanes of Hermopolis Magna', *Bull. John Rylands Library*, 51 (1968), 164–83.

ROBERTS, C.H., 'The Archive of Theophanes', *Catalogue of the Greek and Latin Papyri in the John Rylands Library*, 4 (1952), 104ff.

ROUGÉ, J., 'Voyages officielles en Méditerranée orientale', *Rev. Et. Anc.* 55 (1953), 294–300.

——, *Recherches sur l'organisation du commerce maritime en Méditerranée* (Paris, 1966).

SALLER, S.J., *The Memorial of Moses on Mount Nebo* (Jerusalem, 1941).

SCHÜRER, E., *The History of the Jewish People in the Age of Jesus Christ, 175BC-AD135* (Engl. edn. F. Millar & G. Vermes, Edinburgh, 1973-).

SCHWARTZ, E., 'Johannes Rufus, ein monophysitischer Schriftsteller', *Heidelberg Sitzungsberichte*, phil.-hist. Klasse, 3 (1912).

——, 'Palladiana', *ZNTW* 36 (1937), 161–204.

SEECK, O., 'Die Verwandtenmorde Constantins des Grossen', *Zeitschr. für wissenschaftliche Theologie*, 33 (1890), 63–77.

——, *Regesten der Kaiser und Päpste für die Jahre 311 bis 476 n. Chr.* (Stuttgart, 1919).

SEGAL, J.B., *Edessa, 'The Blessed City'* (Oxford, 1970).

SHEPHERD, M.H., 'Liturgical Expressions of the Constantinian Triumph', *Dumbarton Oaks Papers*, 21 (1967), 57–78.

SMITH, James, *The Voyage and Shipwreck of St. Paul* (4th edn. London, 1880).

STEIDLE, W., 'Die Leichenrede des Ambrosius für Kaiser Theodosius und die Helena-legende', *Vig. Christ.* 32 (1978), 94–112.

STRAUBINGER, J., *Die Kreuzauffindungslegende* (Paderborn, 1912).

STUDER, B., 'Zur Frage des westlichen Origenismus', *Studia Patristica*, 9 (= *TU* 94, 1966), 270–87.

TELFER, W., 'Constantine's Holy Land Plan', *Studia Patristica*, 1 (= *TU* 63, 1957), 696–70.

THIBAUT, J.-B., *Ordre des Offices de la Semaine Sainte à Jérusalem* (Paris, 1926).

THOMSEN, P., 'Palästina nach dem Onomastikon des Eusebius', *ZDPV* 26 (1903), 97–141, 145–88.

THÜMMEL, H.G., 'Zur Deutung der Mosaikkarte von Madeba', *ZDPV* 89 (1973), 66–79.

TURNER, C.H., 'The Lausiac History of Palladius', *JTS* 6 (1904–5), 321–55.

VANDERLINDEN, S., 'Revelatio Sancti Stephani', *Rev. Et. Byz.* 4 (1946), 178–217.

VERMEER, G.F.M., *Observations sur le vocabulaire du pèlerinage chez Egérie et chez Antonin de Plaisance* (Latinitas Christianorum Primaeva 19, Nijmegen, 1965).

VILLETTE, J., *La Résurrection du Christ dans l'art chrétien du iie au viie siècle* (Paris, 1957).

VINCENT, L.H., & ABEL, F.M., *Jérusalem. Recherches de topographie, d'archéologie et d'histoire*, ii, 'Jérusalem Nouvelle' (Paris, 1914).

——, 'L'Eléona, Sanctuaire Primitif de l'Ascension', *Rev. Bibl.* 64 (1957), 48–71.

VITESTAM, G., *Seconde partie du traité qui passe sous le nom de 'la grande lettre d'Evagre le Pontique à Mélanie l'ancienne'* (Scripta Minora Regiae Societatis Humaniorum Litterarum Lundensis, 1963–4).

VOGT, J., 'Berichte über Kreuzeserscheinungen aus dem 4. Jahrhundert n. Chr.', *Annuaire de l'Institut de philologie et d'histoire orientales et slaves*, 9 (1949), 593–606.

——, 'Helena Augusta, das Kreuz und die Juden', *Saeculum*, 27 (1976), 211–22.

WALLACE-HADRILL, D.S., *Eusebius of Caesarea* (London, 1960).

WARD-PERKINS, J.B., 'Constantine and the Origins of the Christian Basilica', *PBSR* 22 (1954), 69–90.

WARMINGTON, E.H., *The Commerce between the Roman Empire and India* (2nd edn. London, 1974).

WEITZMANN, K., '*Loca Sancta* and the arts of Palestine', *Dumbarton Oaks Papers*, 28 (1974), 31–55.

WIESEN, D.S., *St. Jerome as a Satirist* (Ithaca, 1964).

WIGHTMAN, E.M., *Roman Trier and the Treveri* (London, 1970).

WILKINSON, J., *Egeria's Travels* (London, 1971).

——, 'The Tomb of Christ', *Levant*, 4 (1972), 83–97.

——, 'L'apport de Saint Jérôme à la topographie', *Rev. Bibl.* 81 (1974), 245–57.

——, 'Christian Pilgrims in Jerusalem during the Byzantine Period', *PEQ* 108 (1976), 75–101.

——, *Jerusalem Pilgrims before the Crusades* (Warminster, 1977).

——, 'Jewish influences on the early Christian rite of Jerusalem', *Le Muséon*, 92 (1979), 347–59.

WINDISCH, H., 'Die ältesten christlichen Palästinapilger', *ZDPV* 48 (1925), 145–58.

WISTRAND, E., *Konstantins Kirche am heiligen Grab in Jerusalem nach den älltesten literarischen Zeugnissen* (Göteborg, 1952).

ZERFASS, R., 'Die Rolle der Lesung im Stundengebet', *Liturgisches Jahrbuch*, 13 (1963), 159–67.

——, *Die Schriftlesung in Kathedraloffizium Jerusalems* (Münster, 1968).

ZIEGLER, J., 'Die Peregrinatio Aetheriae und das Onomastikon des Eusebius', *Biblica*, 12 (1931a), 70–84.

——, 'Die Peregrinatio Aetheriae und die hl. Schrift', *Biblica*, 12 (1931b), 162–98.

Index

Printed in the United States
859800002B